AF539599

MEMORY REMAINS

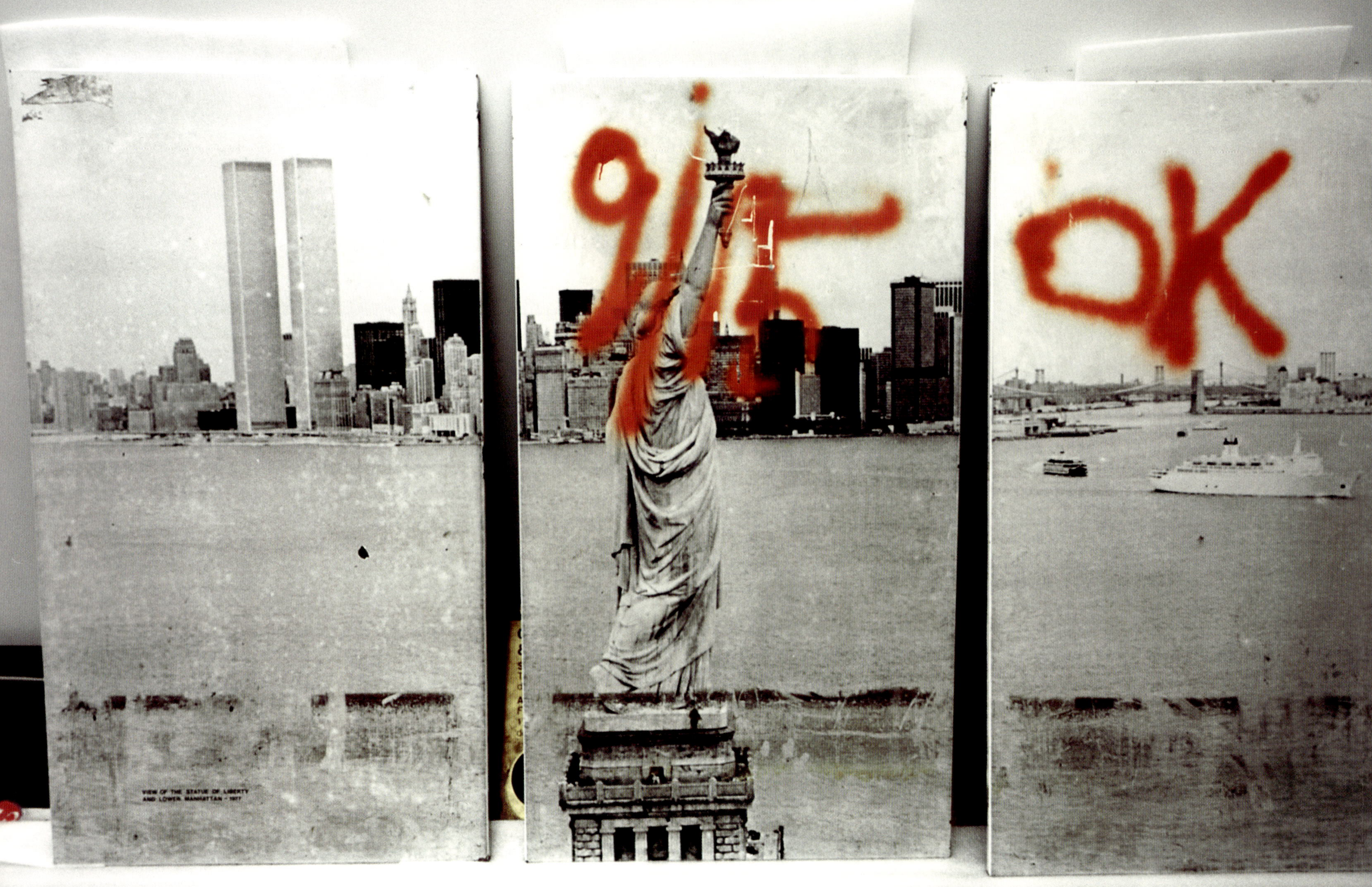
9/15
OK

FRANCESC TORRES

MEMORY REMAINS

9/11 ARTIFACTS AT HANGAR 17

EDITED BY CLIFFORD CHANIN

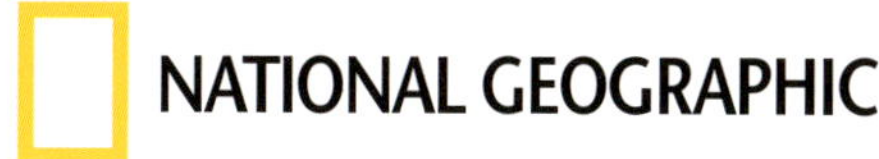

Washington, D.C.

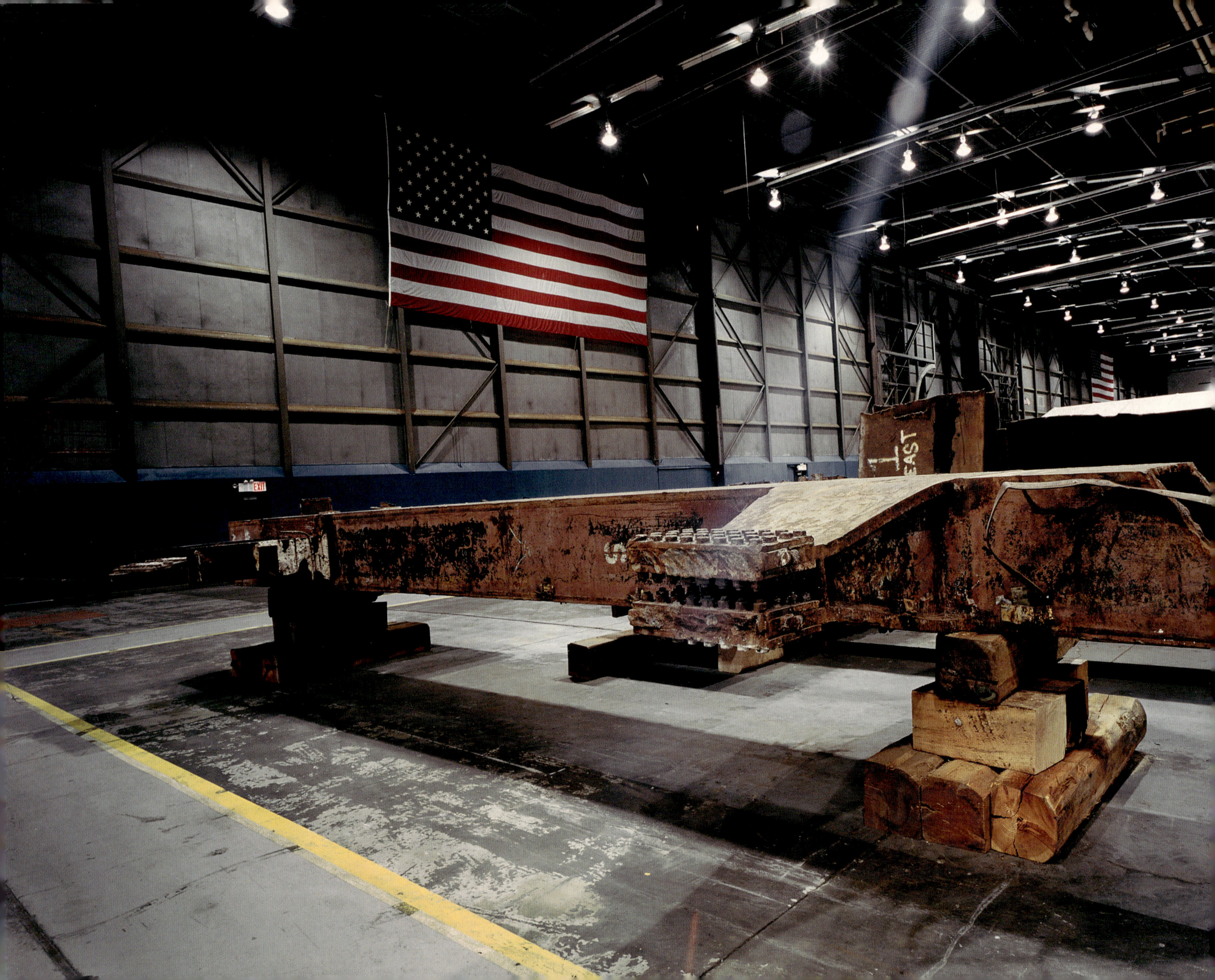
EXIT
EAST

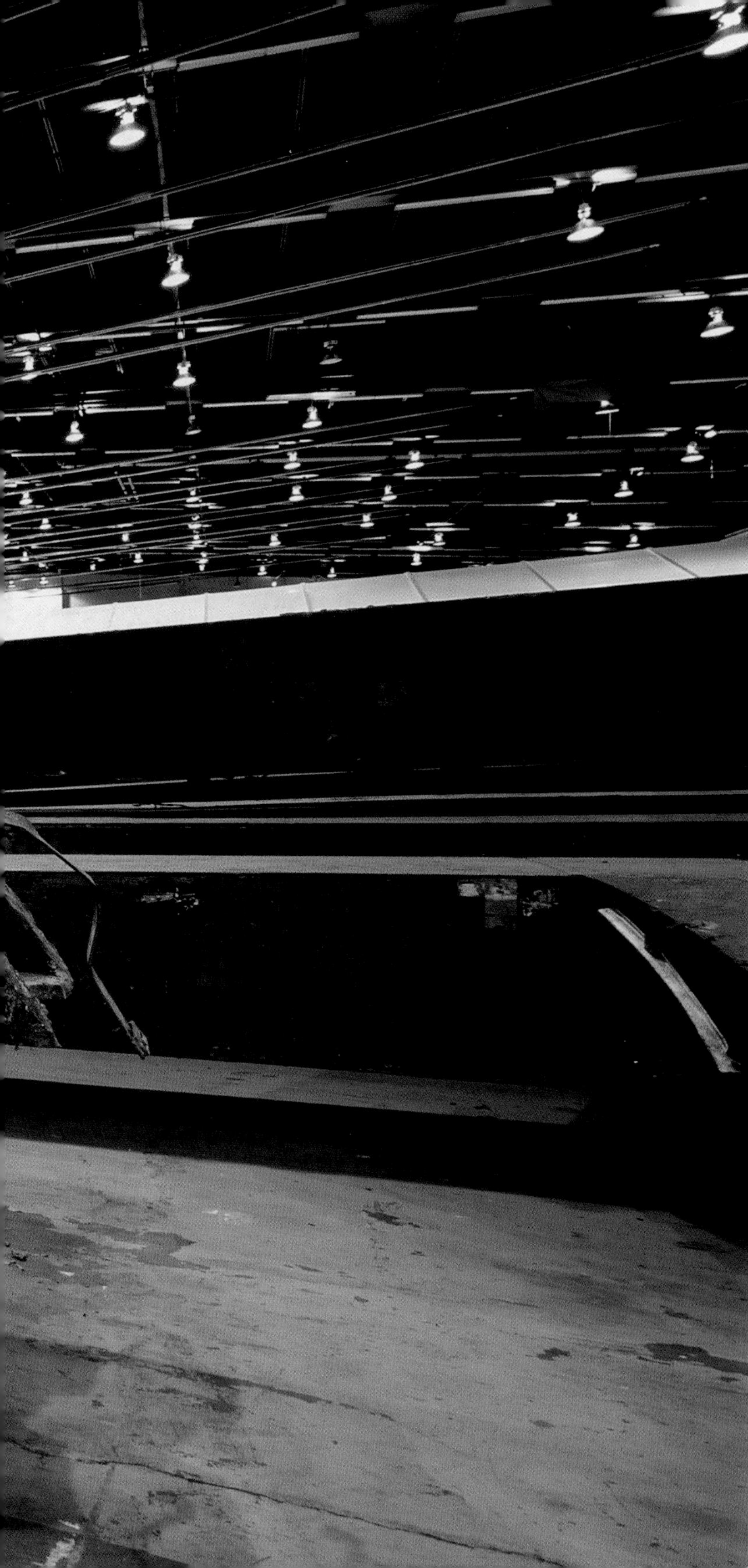

This volume is dedicated to the victims of the terrorist attacks on the World Trade Center—specially recognizing the employees of the Port Authority of New York and New Jersey killed on February 26, 1993, and September 11, 2001—and to all those killed at the Pentagon and aboard Flight 93 on 9/11.

CONTENTS

Page 2: These three panels, offering a view of the Statue of Liberty from 1977, were salvaged from the Cortlandt Street subway station under the World Trade Center. The spray-painted markings indicate that the area nearby had been searched by rescue workers for survivors or victims. Pages 4-5: Steel beams taken from ground zero for storage at John F. Kennedy International Airport's Hangar 17.

FOREWORD

All those who have been there remember their first visit to Hangar 17. The memory is indelible.

Entering the former Tower Air hangar at John F. Kennedy International Airport, one was not prepared for the experience that would follow. This 80,000-square-foot space was filled with remnants of the World Trade Center salvaged in the aftermath of the terrorist attacks of 9/11. Everywhere lay monumental pieces of steel columns that were twisted and curved, or folded like an accordion, or shredded and curled like pieces of ribbon. There were vehicles, human scale and achingly familiar—fire trucks, an ambulance, a K-9 jeep, cars that had been parked on neighborhood streets or in the World Trade Center garage, a yellow taxi—each bearing the scars of unfathomable destruction. Entire PATH train cars were there, as were pieces of the 360-foot-high communications antenna that once stood atop 1 World Trade Center, the north twin of the twin towers. There were enormous elevator motors, concrete portions of parking garage floors, and hundreds of sections of aluminum cladding that had once comprised the exterior skin of the towers. Bent fragments of a once clean-lined sculpture by Alexander Calder were set onto tables in a separate room, and the detritus of merchandise that once filled store shelves in the bustling concourse level now filled its own space: fragments of clothing, an optician's display of eyeglass frames, even a nine-foot, three-dimensional figure of Bugs Bunny from the Warner Bros. Studio Store, completely surreal in this setting, and even more so in juxtaposition to nearby fragments of a sign whose painted letters, when put back together, read chillingly: "That's All Folks!"

In the wake of the 9/11 attacks, some 1.8 million tons of debris were removed from the World Trade Center site during a nine-month cleanup and recovery operation ending in May 2002. What was housed at Hangar 17 represented less than two-tenths of one percent of what had been there. This is what remained.

The hangar was a space of awe and a place of stunned silence. The remains of the architectural elements that once supported the 110-story twin towers were a tribute to human ingenuity. Those same remains, once recognized, displayed the human capacity for destruction and acts of evil, as evidenced by the sheer devastation wrought upon these same wounded columns.

In 2001, the Port Authority of New York and New Jersey, the agency that built the World Trade Center, endeavored to preserve these remnants as documentation of what had been at the World Trade Center and as a testament to what happened there on 9/11. In 2008, the National September 11 Memorial & Museum understood the urgency of documenting the hangar itself, and its extraordinary contents, as comprising a fundamental chapter in the story of the aftermath of 9/11. Over the next few years, many of these relics were transferred to the 9/11 Memorial for presentation in the museum. Others became centerpieces of 9/11 memorials in communities, firehouses, and town halls around the nation and abroad. The hangar would not always be there. The time had come to ensure that it became a part of the historic record in its own right.

Francesc Torres was engaged to create this documentary record. An internationally renowned photographer and artist, Torres has split his time between his native Barcelona and New York City, where he lived for 28 years. As it happens, Torres was in lower Manhattan on September 11, 2001, just blocks from the World Trade Center. His personal relationship to this story was just one factor in selecting him for this challenging assignment. Another was his unique perspective on questions of historical accountability and memory. Torres's haunting photographic chronicle of the reclamation of civilian victims of the Spanish Civil War from anonymous gravesites, *Dark Is the Room Where We Sleep,* had been presented at the International Center of Photography in New York City in the fall of 2007. The work—visually compelling, intellectually challenging, and emotionally troubling—revealed a sensibility attuned to questions of unusual complexity and sensitivity. Torres spent five weeks at Hangar 17 in the spring of 2009, daily confronting the legacy of terror and the ghosts of ground zero. Through his eyes, we also see the potential for resilience and the triumph of the human spirit over adversity.

This body of work invites all of us inside Hangar 17. Once you see these photographs, you will never forget them. They are indelible.

Joe Daniels
CEO/President
National September 11
Memorial & Museum

Alice M. Greenwald
Director, Memorial Museum
National September 11
Memorial & Museum

Chris Ward
Executive Director
Port Authority of
New York and New Jersey

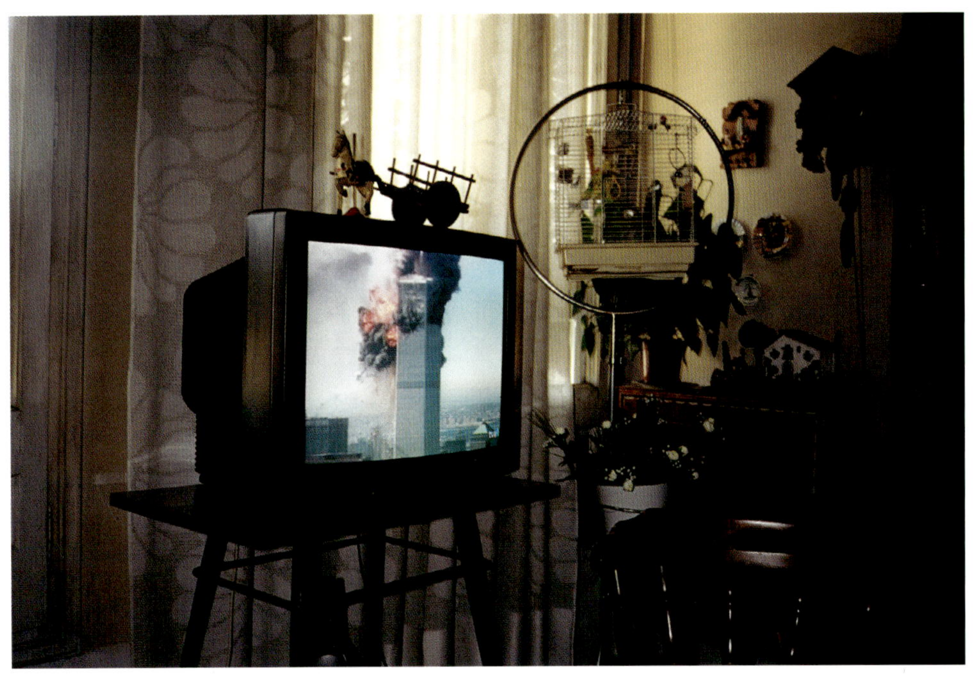

9/11, as seen live on television in Barcelona, Spain. Photographed at roughly 3 p.m. local time by Maria Iturrioz de Torres, Francesc Torres's mother, while they spoke by phone.

THE MUSEUM OF UNNATURAL HISTORY

HANGAR 17 AND THE PHYSICAL SEDIMENT OF 9/11 BY FRANCESC TORRES

On the morning of September 11, 2001, I was on the phone, standing by the window of an apartment at 11 Cortlandt Street, two blocks from the World Trade Center, when, suddenly, the 20th century came to an end.

I didn't know it at that very moment. I didn't even see the cause of that strange noise that sounded like crumpling aluminum foil mixed with a cascade of crashing porcelain, and the screams that followed it. I was facing in the wrong direction. I hung up. When I turned around, I saw the top of the north tower belching out black smoke like a chimney. No visible fire, not yet. There was also a lot of white paper floating around the crown of the tower, clearly visible against the background smoke, although I cannot be sure now if I really saw it or if it became a virtual image imprinted in my visual memory after the fact.

I took a few black-and-white pictures perched on the windowsill. I realized that, due to the time difference with Europe, my mother would be watching the early afternoon news in Barcelona and, no doubt, she would find out about what I still thought was an aviation accident. I called her to let her know I was okay. Then, as I was telling her not to worry while keeping a distracted eye on the towers, the second plane hit its target. I told her I had to go. I grabbed the camera and went to the street. My mother, in Spain, took her camera and shot the TV screen in her living room, showing the burning towers in real time thousands of miles away from New York. I found those pictures in her home several years later.

I kept taking pictures until I ran out of film. People were abandoning the area, out of fear or following the orders of the police. I heard an officer say, "Just get the hell out of here, these things always come in threes." I ended up on the rooftop of my studio on North Moore Street, watching with my neighbors as innocent people trapped in the towers chose to jump into the void rather than be consumed by fire. Finally the towers gave in, first one, then the other, and there was silence, or maybe I went numb.

This book is part of a project that makes reference to historical memory, national remembrance, social and individual mourning, and the ongoing process of managing deep trauma to attain healing. It centers on a substantial amount of the physical sediment that is tied to the beginning of this healing process: the clearing of the monumental accumulation of debris at ground zero, which was preserved, in a sort of suspended animation, inside Hangar 17 at Kennedy International Airport in New York City. Though there will be a National September 11 Memorial & Museum, the temporary quality of Hangar 17 gave it an evocative singularity of unmatched power. The physical residue of the 9/11 attack was preserved in an aviation hangar, a space built to keep the blameless machines that were turned into deadly weapons that fateful morning ten years ago.

This project attempts to capture Hangar 17 as a narrative artifact in its own right, as well as its significance as one of the most extraordinary experiments in the preservation of contemporary history since World War II. The basis of this work rests on a thorough but selective photographing of the holdings. On the one hand, I captured general images of the uniqueness of the environment: the hangar, its location, areas not in use, remains of its time as an airline terminal. These images are revealing in terms of how, in specific circumstances, a museum can spontaneously emerge as an organic entity in the most unlikely places.

On the other hand, I attempted to capture what could be, perhaps, blurred by a conventional museum setting. In seeing, choosing, and editing through the camera lens, photographers can steer visitors to an exhibition, or readers to a procession of images. Consequently, as a methodology, I proceeded by going from macroenvironment to micro-detail, from the general to the particular, from the atmosphere of the site to the texture of the surfaces, such as the burned-out steel of the vehicles, the rough surfaces of the beams, and the volcanic quality of the scorched material that resulted from the collapse of the towers.

An unresolved issue accompanied me throughout the photographic sessions: The nature of the subject demanded a very precise balance between straight visual documentation and the goal of obtaining a good, powerful picture. It doesn't make much sense to raise a camera with the deliberate intention of taking a nondescript picture to avoid the perception of a possible indulgence in aesthetics. The problem, however, is compounded by the fact that over the last century we have developed in the retinal and conceptual arts a visual vocabulary that didn't exist before modernism. We have grown accustomed to perceiving bent steel (Richard Serra) and crushed cars as sculpture (John Chamberlain), and charred and eroded surfaces as painting (Jasper Johns, Antoni Tàpies, Anselm Kiefer). All these and more—discarded clothes, personal belongings, papers, and documents—are now fully assimilated into the history and tradition of modern Western art, making very difficult a strict distinction between documentary and aesthetic qualities.

Ultimately, I felt that there was a tradition for facing this challenge that reached back into the history of art: The visual potency and technical skill of a 17th-century baroque painter didn't betray or diminish the tragedy of martyrdom depicted in his canvas. A memorable picture bridges the gap between subject, emotional charge, meaning, and visual merit. War photography is perhaps the best example of what I am saying.

After several one-day visits that started in early 2006, I spent April 2009 going to Hangar 17 every day, slowly photographing its contents. Most of the time I was on my own, except when I talked to Steven Weintraub and Peter Gat, conservators of the sediment, or Peter Miller from the Port Authority of New York and New Jersey. They also volunteered to take me back and forth from Manhattan, not a small favor. The shooting itself, however, was done for the most part in complete solitude, under the constant roar of planes landing and taking off next to the hangar. The stillness of the contents seemed to embody, in an inverted sequence, the calm that precedes an earthquake. Here the earthquake came first. As I concentrated on an object, the emotional tension between that landscape of quiet, mutilated artifacts and the chaotic memory of the day of the attack was sometimes overpowering. Everything down to the smallest residue was of the utmost importance, I felt: the objects, their textures, and the dust that in some cases still covered them; that dust, a mixture of pulverized debris, ash, and perhaps the microscopic traces of human beings.

Past the entrance to the hangar with its great concentration of beams, powerful as they were because of their scale, and eloquent as the product of the unbelievable destructive energy recorded in their twisted shapes, past all that, one would find humidity and temperature-controlled enclosures holding objects with a closer connection to human presence and aura. The vehicle enclosure was dramatic in a particular way because so many of the vehicles were from the fire department, police and medical services, carrying people who went rushing to the scene of the tragedy, many of them never to come back. Some of the vehicles still have gear inside, right where it belonged; others are half-scorched, yet their other halves are almost untouched, as if a blade had cut though them with robotic precision; the interior of the single ambulance in the tent is badly charred, but is otherwise easily identifiable. Amid all those service vehicles, there was an exception: a New York City taxicab, the generic Ford sedan that all of us have waved at hundreds of times in our daily chores. All of us were in that cab.

Each enclosure held a specific cluster of objects from what had been distinct areas of the towers. In one, I found the surviving contents of stores from the WTC shopping mall. Oversize cartoon characters like Bugs Bunny from the Warner Bros. Studio Store, including a sign with the famous "That's All Folks" that appeared at the end of the animated films we watched on TV when we were kids; clothing still folded for display; a standing case full of glasses; a charred single pair of glasses in its carbonized carrying case; a red-haired doll on its back on a shelf, as if in a morgue; a dress on a mannequin showing a water line in mid-skirt, a reminder of the water level in that flooded mall.

Another enclosure held the remnants of an Alexander Calder sculpture that once stood on the WTC plaza but was now barely recognizable. This was the counterpoint to the charge of the mundane building elements that had been transformed far beyond their intended purposes by violence. Here, the Calder was barely distinguishable from scrap metal.

In all, I thought, if there is a way to illustrate the fragility of culture in a head-on collision with history at its most destructive, these mangled chunks of steel couldn't be more eloquent.

In another enclosure were two adjacent spaces of enormous power. In the first, there were—and I am speaking in past tense because I don't know if some of these objects are still there as I write these lines—blocks of what appeared to be volcanic rock, commonly referred to as composites. In one of the two large blocks, the one facing the entrance, four horizontal layers of slightly different coloration are clearly discernible. This block, roughly ten feet by six feet, is actually four compressed floors from one of the towers.

Looking at the composites at close range, it becomes evident that the energy necessary for such compression might have been close to a nuclear reaction. However, in a way that defies comprehension, one can see clusters of black carbon on the surface of one of the composites. These are, in fact, compressed sheets of office paper, or rather the tangible shadows of office documents from somewhere in the towers. Although they are pure ash, one can still read the words imprinted on them. They cannot be touched because they would disintegrate instantly. How printed words could convey a sense of permanence in the midst of such cataclysm stands as a metaphor for the resilience of constructive culture over its opposite.

Next to the composites, by itself, was the Last Column, the very last structural beam removed from ground zero. Lying horizontally as if in state, a contrast with the position for which it was designed, the column is covered with words, pictures, and mementos attached or inscribed by the workers who salvaged it. The challenges of conserving such material—to describe it as nonarchival would be an understatement—and how that has been achieved are a credit to the conservators at Hangar 17. This significant piece has already left the hangar and now stands inside a protected encasement, with the new 9/11 museum being built around it. Once built, the museum won't have a door large enough for the beam to be brought in.

The largest enclosure at the hangar held large parts of the north tower antenna. One could see a literal metaphor in those mangled structures, originally constructed as a tool of communication now rendered useless but still speaking to us of that fateful, late summer day.

There were also objects of a different nature, such as beams with multiple cutouts of Stars of David and Christian crosses, carved out by recovery workers with blowtorches and given as mementos to relatives of the victims. After so many cuts, the negative contours of the symbols turned the beams into astounding relics of spiritual affirmation.

Other objects included rows of two-by-fours used as fencing on the viewing platform overlooking the recovery work at the site, covered with messages to the victims from their close relatives; signage from the towers and the stores below; turnstiles and so on.

Finally, in one corner were clothes, not from stores, but from some, very few, of those who were there that day, presumably both victims and survivors. Cataclysmic destruction tends to homogenize human bodies and their external identities; what we use to protect ourselves from both meteorological and social exposure, the outward signage that defines each of us as cultural, professional, social, and even, political beings. Although individual victims are by no means interchangeable, once massive violence has been inflicted, there is very little qualitative difference between what was left of human physicality in Dresden, Rotterdam, Nanking, Leningrad, Beirut, Sarajevo, or New York City: broken and quartered bodies, shredded clothing, and someplace, in the middle of that field of chaotic devastation, a miraculously intact, fragile object such as, for example, an American Airlines courtesy slipper. The dialogue established between the remnant clothing and the handwritten two-by-fours was, for me, a really hard one to bear.

By the time this book sees the light of day, most of the contents of Hangar 17 will have been dispersed. At one point in the near future, the hangar will be empty again or used for much different purposes. Many of the most significant objects will be displayed to the general public at the National 9/11 Memorial & Museum at ground zero, the echo of an event that changed the world.

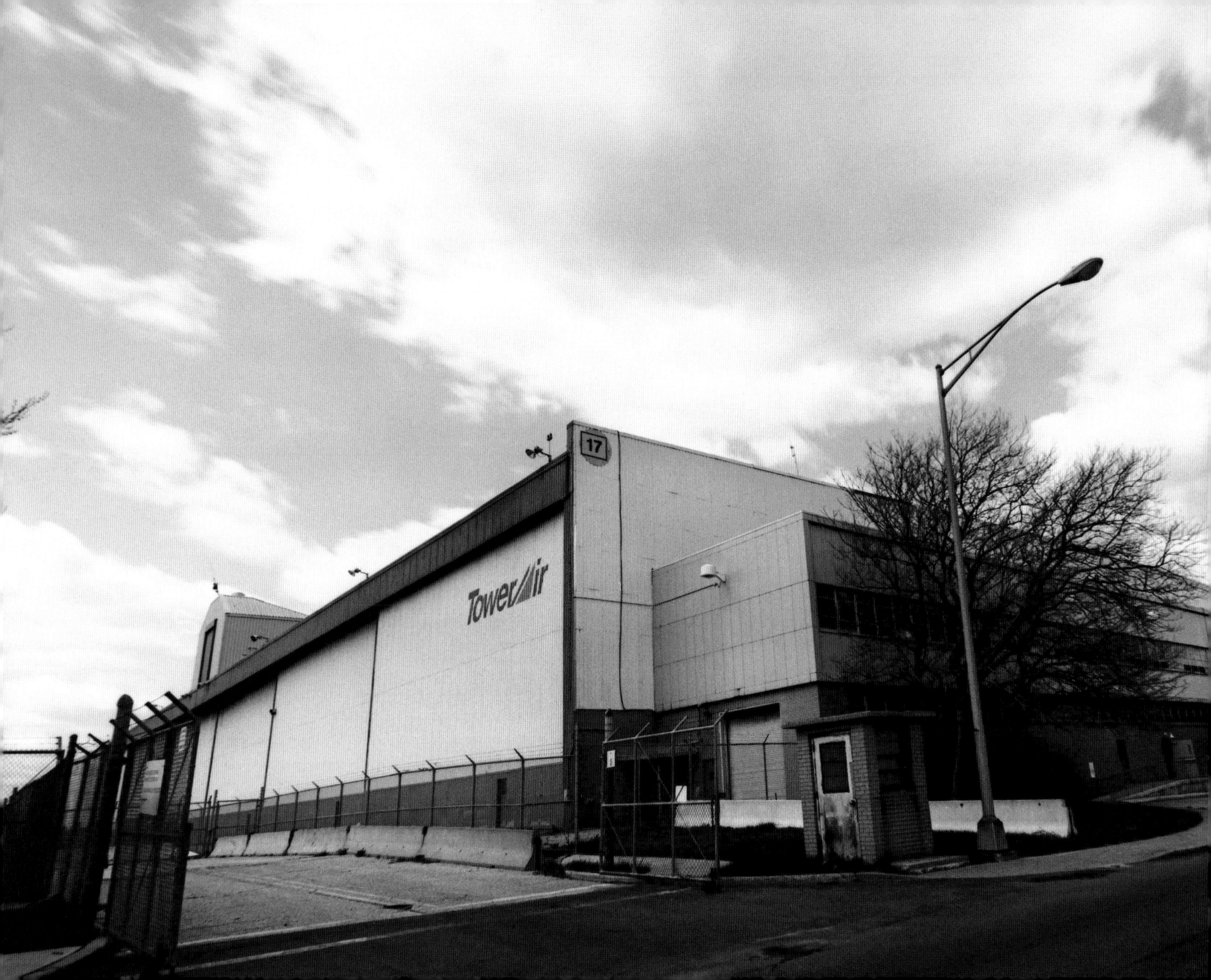
17
Tower Air

RECOVERING HISTORY

THE STORY OF HANGAR 17 BY JERRY ADLER

Disregarding air resistance, a one-ton beam dropped from a height of 1,312 feet (400 meters) will fall for nine seconds and hit the ground at around 200 miles an hour. It will expend—as noise, vibration, heat, and deformation of the beam itself and whatever it happens to land on—nearly twice the energy of a stick of dynamite. Laid out on the floor of an airplane hangar at Kennedy International Airport that Tower Airlines had abandoned in 2000 are many such beams, comprising most of what remains of the twin towers and the other buildings of the World Trade Center. They are scabbed over with rust, broken off or cut into pieces that could fit on a truck, and often bent or twisted into fantastic shapes—giant S-curves, fish hooks, and hairpins—testifying to the awful force of their impact and the heat of the fire into which they fell. Some of them show curious cutouts, in the shapes of crosses, Stars of David, police shields, and cityscape skylines—the voids left by ironworkers who used the steel to make keepsakes.

The beams were brought there in the months after 9/11, either directly from ground zero, from the debris sorting and collection site on Staten Island, or from the scrap yards of New Jersey through which they were passing on their way to the smelter. They were joined by many objects that people thought were worth saving, including wrecked vehicles, compressed masses (of concrete, shards of the buildings' aluminum cladding, segments of the antenna mast, and scraps of outdoor sculpture). But almost as interesting is what's missing. How many chairs did the 35,000 people who worked in the twin towers occupy? How many desks, computers, and conference tables filled those ten million square feet of office space? Whatever the number, almost none of them survived in pieces large enough to recognize. What there is, overwhelmingly, is structural steel, engineered to hold the building up against the gravitational pull of the entire Earth, to stand upright in a 50-year wind, but which met its match on September 11, 2001.

The effort to collect artifacts from the World Trade Center got underway in the very first days after the attacks, when ground zero was still a six-story-high pile of burning rubble, a crime scene, and a rescue site. It began with a phone call from Bob Davidson, the chief architect of the Port Authority of New York and New Jersey, which owned the Trade Center site, to Bartholomew Voorsanger, an architect who had worked closely with the Port Authority on projects, including a new terminal at Newark Liberty International Airport and the LaGuardia Airport control tower. Davidson asked Voorsanger to be part of a small group to help select objects worth preserving from the wreckage—a group that would also include Marilyn Taylor, a principal in the New York office of Skidmore, Owings, and Merrill (who served only briefly) and Saul Wenegrat, the former director of the art program for the Port Authority. Wenegrat had overseen the acquisition of many of the objects, including a large outdoor sculpture by Alexander Calder, that were now presumed buried in the rubble. The next day, Voorsanger and a young associate in his office, Mark Wagner, took a taxi to the corner of West and Canal Streets and began walking south. Although he had been there many times, Wagner found as he approached ground zero he couldn't recognize any of the buildings around him. Eventually, he realized this was because he was seeing them from the second floor, walking on a carpet of debris one story high.

For the next several months, Wagner was at the site every day. Starting at the northwest corner, he would make a slow counterclockwise circuit, arduously clambering over rubble, ducking out of the way of heavy machinery, passing among ironworkers, cops, firemen, officials in suits and hardhats, and knots of family members grimly watching and consoling one another. Among those he passed was his brother David, an NYPD officer from a precinct in Brooklyn, who had been spending 24 hours a day at the site since right after the attack; David Wagner had called their mother on the night of 9/11 to tell her he was alive, but for days after the family had no word from him.

As Mark Wagner walked through the site, he would see objects worth saving, and point them out to workers or mark them with spray paint. He knew he was in a race against the imperative to clear the site as quickly as possible. A complete circuit took up to four hours, and by the time he returned to his starting point, the topography of the rubble might have changed enough to be almost unrecognizable from when he had set out.

Voorsanger's mandate was vague, essentially to save whatever seemed interesting or significant to him. As an architect, he was naturally interested in preserving a record of the design and structure of the twin towers. Like many architects of his generation, Voorsanger, who began practicing in the 1960s, had softened in his view of Minoru Yamasaki's epoch-making design. The two huge square towers, dominating a vast raised plaza, represented an apotheosis of modernism, an architectural idea that began to go out of fashion soon after the buildings were completed in the early 1970s. For three decades, they stood in defiance of the fashion for preserving architectural context and for maintaining at all costs the pedestrian-friendly street wall of existing buildings. The twin towers made their own context, and pedestrians approached them across the plaza in a state of appropriate awe, able to look straight up at the stacks of acre-sized floors and appreciate their immensity.

Though the collecting effort at ground zero began shortly after the attacks, the use of Hangar 17 for storage and conservation was not finalized until the middle of 2002. Until then, artifacts were held in a wide range of locations in the New York area: the Fresh Kills Landfill on Staten Island, scrap yards, and dispersed Port Authority facilities, including Kennedy International Airport. Once the hangar was made available for the collection, a floor plan was devised that placed like objects together. Steel was not stacked more than four or five pieces high, and smaller objects were placed in front of larger ones—all to maximize access for forklifts and the other pieces of heavy equipment that would be needed to move them. Though some pieces like the Last Column were covered in plastic sheeting and brought into the hangar almost immediately upon arrival, others were brought inside gradually, as the floor plan took shape.

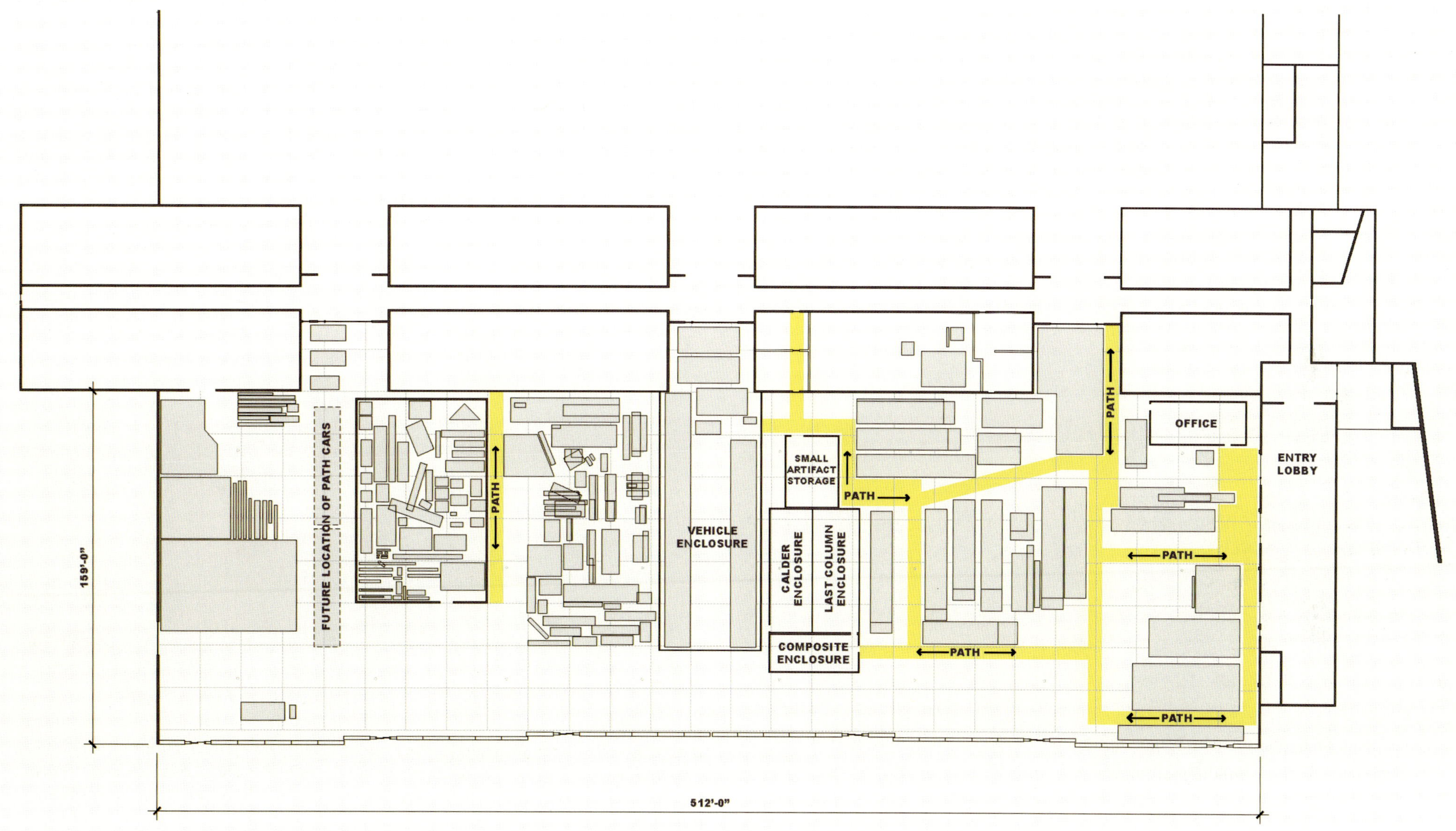

ARTIFACTS LAYOUT

HANGAR 17 COLLECTION LAYOUT

0 16' 32' 64' 128'

By the turn of the 21st century, the towers had become an iconic and even beloved feature of the New York skyline, and a touchstone for architects and engineers who had come to appreciate the efficiency and simplicity of their design. In their very destruction, Voorsanger could see evidence of the immense strength concealed behind their seemingly delicate curtain walls. So he began collecting the evidence: hollow box columns with walls six inches thick; Medusa-like nests of rebar embedded in clumps of concrete; wide-flange I beams in a variety of lengths and weights, bristling with connection plates and bolts. He saved many hundreds of tons of steel, although this was just a tiny fraction of the 200,000 tons that went into the WTC in the first place. Each piece was measured, examined, photographed, and painstakingly cross-checked against the files of the towers' structural engineer, Leslie Robertson, to identify its original location. (Amory Houghton, a Port Authority executive who helped coordinate the artifacts program, estimates that they achieved definitive locations for about half the beams and columns based on markings; most of the rest could be assigned approximate locations on the basis of measurements.) One 20-foot-long segment, whose weight was estimated by Wagner at as much as 400 pounds per running foot, was bent by the collapse into an almost perfect horseshoe shape so cleanly and symmetrically—with barely any telltale cracks of compression or tension along the edges of the curve—that the ironworkers who found it insisted it must have been forged in that shape. But there was no such piece in the buildings when they stood.

Others shared the impulse to memorialize the event by preserving structural and architectural features of the towers, including Philippe de Montebello, then director of the Metropolitan Museum of Art. In an op-ed column in the *New York Times,* de Montebello urged saving, as a permanent memorial, the hollowed-out curtain-wall shard left standing in one corner of the site, with its iconic trident columns open to the sky. Those who shared this sentiment may have fallen victim to a trick of perspective that led to seriously underestimating the size and weight of the tridents (or triads or tuning forks, as they were also sometimes called): They could reach as high as 100 feet and weighed dozens of tons. That the corner shard remained standing, propped up at the base by a

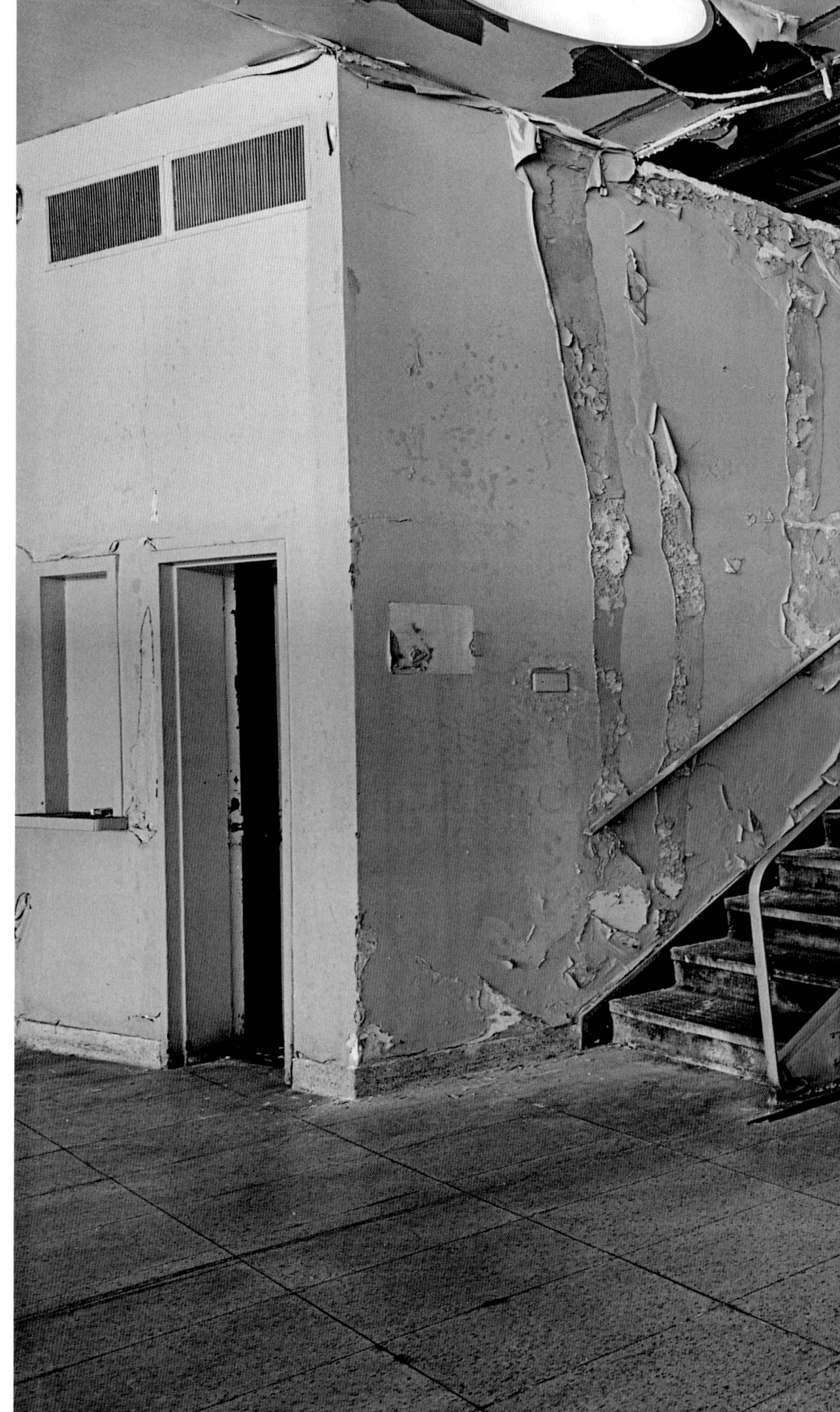

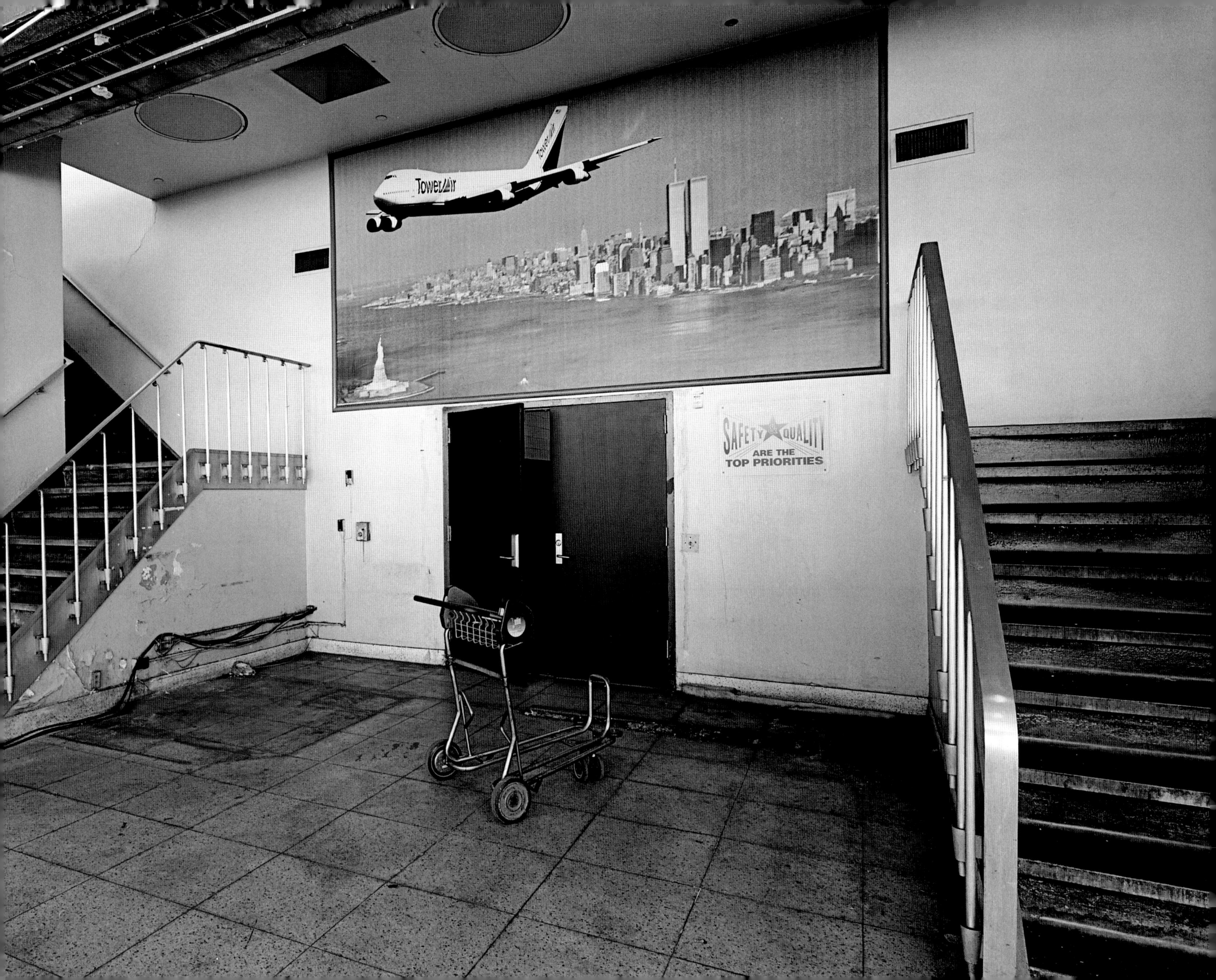
Tower Air
SAFETY QUALITY
ARE THE
TOP PRIORITIES

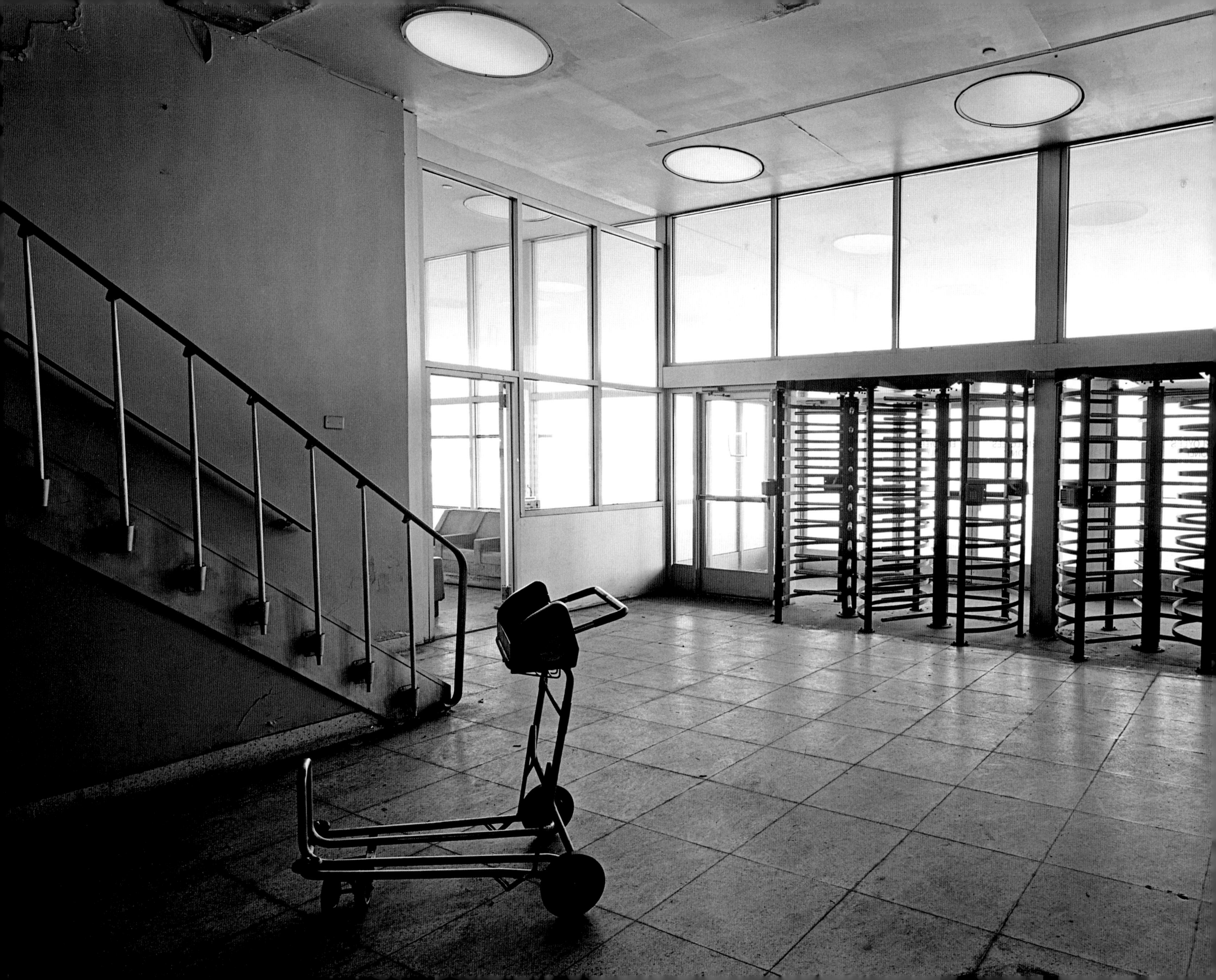

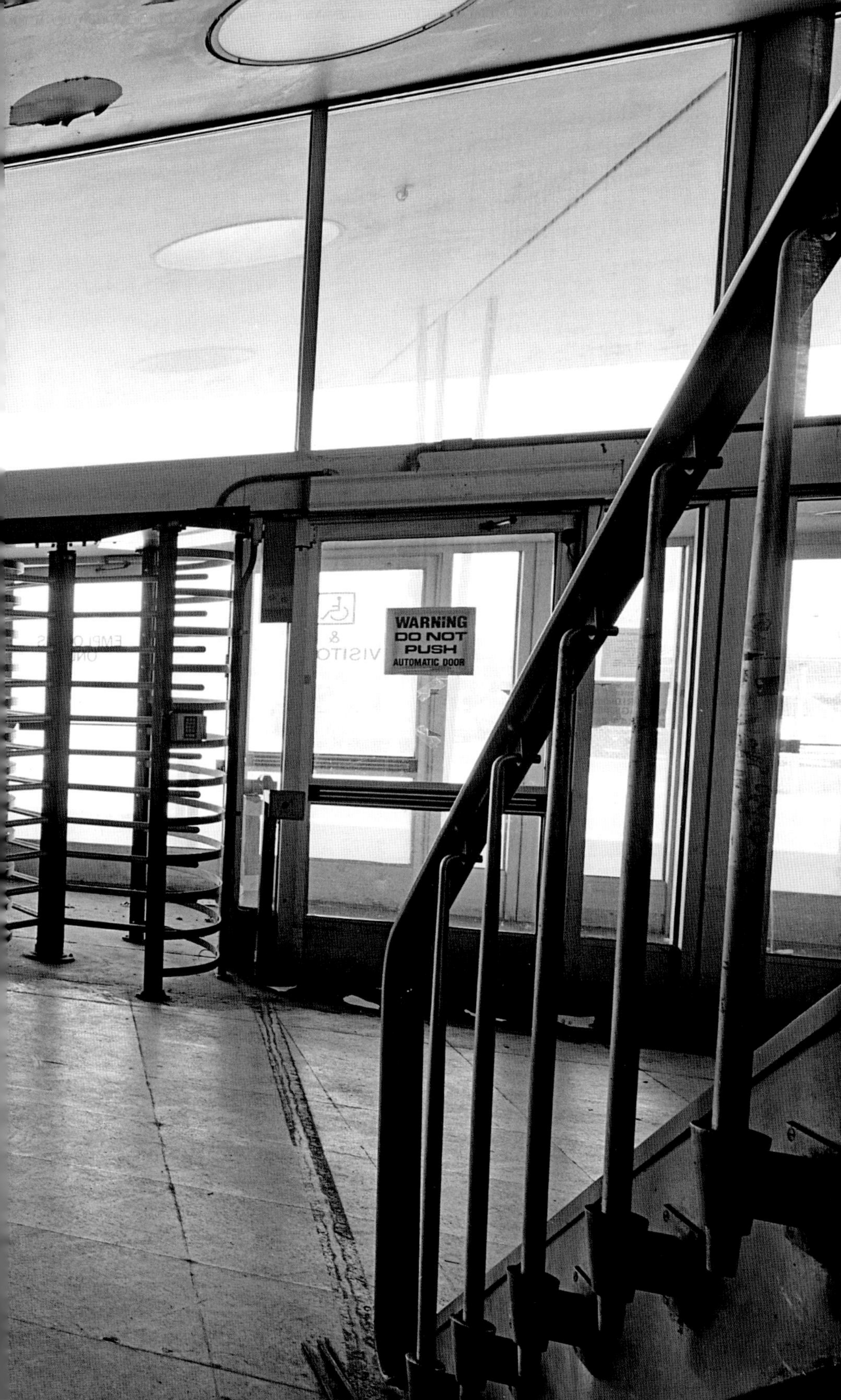

small mountain of rubble, was a minor miracle, but not one that most engineers thought could be duplicated intentionally—at least not so they'd want their families walking underneath it someday.

Almost all of the concrete—approximately 425,000 cubic yards—that went into the World Trade Center complex was reduced to dust in the collapse. But in a few instances, the dust—along with steel rebar or decking, pulverized drywall, carpeting, and furniture—was forged by heat and pressure into more or less cohesive chunks that were dubbed composites or meteorites, from their blackened, pitted surfaces and irregular contours. At least two were recovered, roughly five to eight feet on a side and weighing an estimated 25,000 to 30,000 pounds. In one of them, the striations of at least four floors are faintly visible, compressed to a couple of feet in height. Which floors? Why these and no others? What might be buried inside them? Whatever secrets they conceal are sealed forever.

Voorsanger's team was not the only one collecting artifacts from the site. Five miles north of the attacks, on the morning of September 11, Jan Seidler Ramirez, the museum director and vice president at the New-York Historical Society, was absorbed in preparing a collecting plan for the 200-year-old institution. Sometime around 11 a.m., she went outside, only to realize the city was eerily silent, except for the distant wail of sirens. Then she began seeing people walking north on Central Park West. They were covered in dust.

The Historical Society closed its doors that day and stayed shut most of the rest of the week. On Friday, the society's new president, Kenneth T. Jackson, gave a speech to the staff pointing out that, as custodians of the city's history, they were in the unusual position of living through a critical moment in it. He asked for volunteers for a task force to document the towers, the attacks, and the aftermath. An obvious approach was to begin collecting materials addressing the mood of the city and nation, and to brainstorm about artifacts from the site that might be secured for posterity. The Historical Society was in a good position to undertake this effort, partly owing to Jackson himself, who was recognized by the workers at ground zero from his appearances on their favorite television network, the History Channel. (Wagner had the opposite experience, early on:

Circling the site with a camera and notebook, he was sometimes mistaken for a reporter, or a simple gawker, and would draw jeers from the cops and firefighters still searching for the remains of their colleagues.) Other museums—including the Museum of the City of New York, the New York State Museum, the Smithsonian National Museum of American History, and the New York Police and Fire Museums—were already expressing interest in preserving artifacts from the site in their collections. "We knew about the Voorsanger team," says Ramirez, who went on to become chief curator of the National September 11 Memorial & Museum, "but they were looking at it with an engineering and architectural mindset, and we were interested in documenting the life of the World Trade Center, as a neighborhood, a tourist destination, a workplace, and a human hub."

In preparation, Ramirez and her colleagues compiled a list of everyday objects to look for, items such as computer keyboards, office furniture, coffee mugs, and telephones. But after arriving at ground zero that October, she realized it was a futile exercise; almost nothing of that sort was recovered, except months later from the smaller buildings in the complex, which had been damaged by fire and falling debris but left standing. The force of the towers' collapse had pulverized virtually everything inside them. Some personal belongings were recovered from the surrounding area and returned to their owners when they could be located. The objects with the best odds of survival were those small enough to have lodged safely in a crevice: keys, coins, and rings. As a lesson in which artifacts of civilization are most likely to survive a collision with an asteroid, the list is instructive. It includes sneakers—most likely ones that were kept by women to change into at work—and an impressive number of golf balls, which are small, round, and designed to withstand enormous compressive force. When Ramirez toured the Fresh Kills site with a team of curators, she saw buckets full of ID badges, wallets, key rings, eyeglasses, and wigs (some of which were ultimately returned to survivors or next of kin). Parts of the underground shopping and transit concourse survived more or less intact, although badly damaged by smoke, fire, and water. Fate chose to spare the large statues of Bugs Bunny and Foghorn Leghorn in the Warner Bros. Studio Store, along with a selection of branded

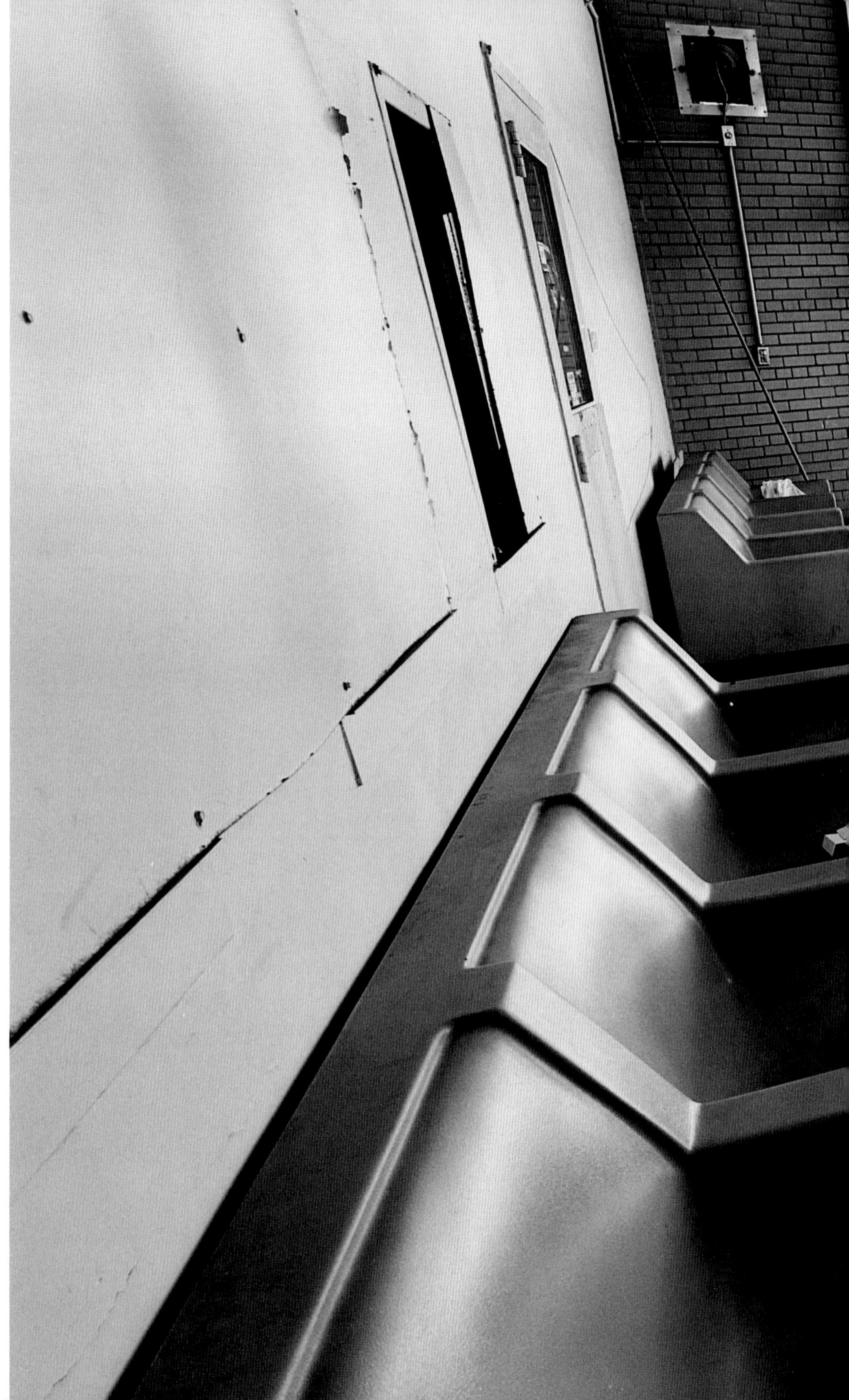

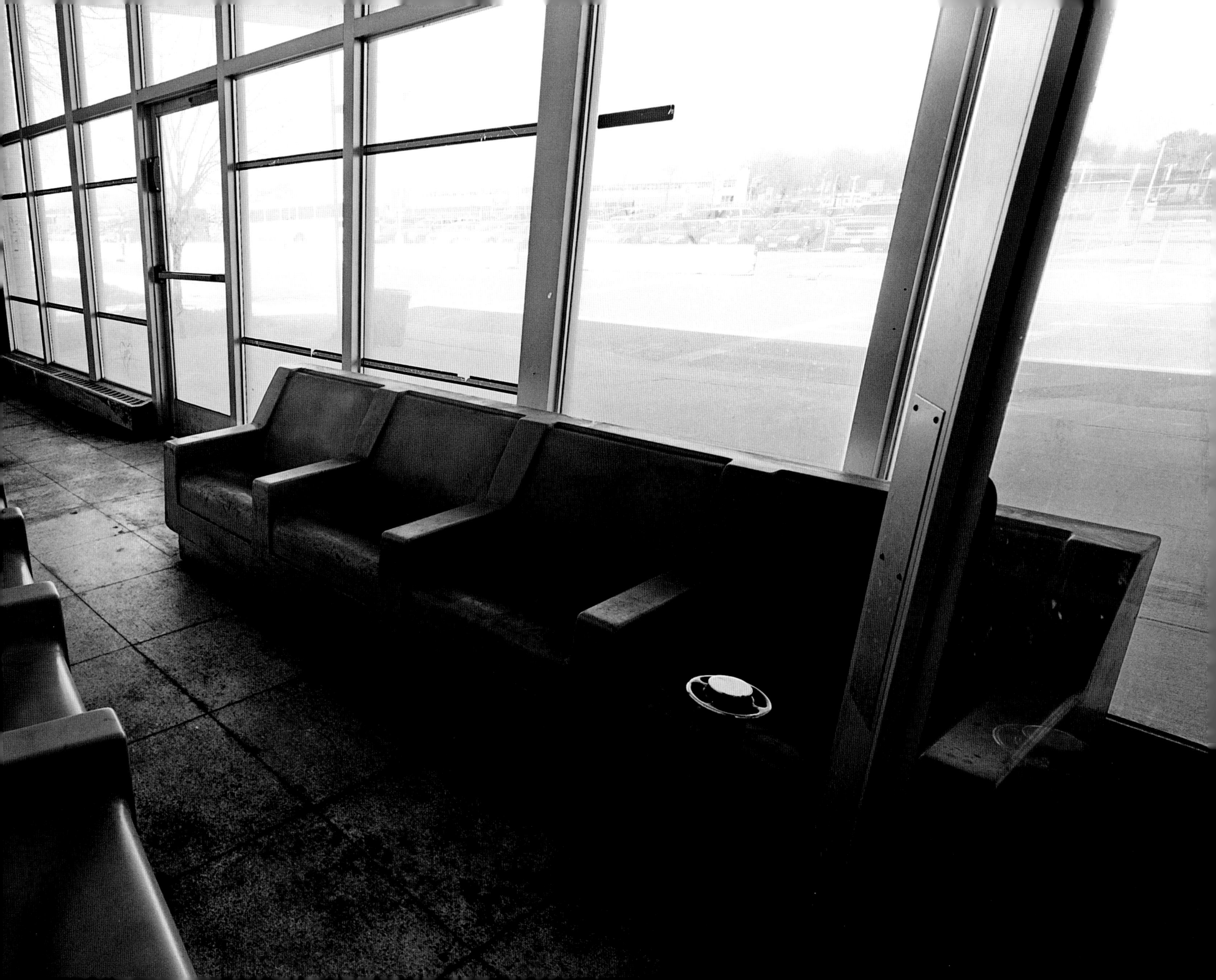

T-shirts, hats, and toys, all listed, photographed, and assigned catalog numbers in the Port Authority's two-volume inventory of more than 1,500 artifacts ultimately taken to the hangar. Among the other miscellaneous objects recorded are "brown paper bag," a "group of 7 shirts," "mannequin body with leopard print bathing suit," a room-service tray from the Marriott hotel that might have been used to cover the head of a fleeing guest or worker, and a wall clock, stopped at 9:47.

A few articles rode out the collapse inside one of the towers' hollow columns, evidently left there by workers during the original construction. They included (empty) cans of Schaefer and Rheingold beer, iconic New York brands of the period, and a copy of the *New York Times*, dated June 23, 1969, carrying the news of Judy Garland's death and the retirement of Chief Justice Earl Warren. One morning Ramirez turned the corner onto Vesey Street and spotted a bicycle rack near the shell of 5 WTC. Locked to it were seven dust-coated bicycles, their wheel rims bent but otherwise surprisingly intact. "There it was," she thought, "the legacy of absence, mournful and ambiguous. Whose bikes were these? Messengers making deliveries? Workers who rode them to their jobs that morning?" In at least one case, the question was answered after the rack was mentioned in a newspaper story, and a bicycle messenger arrived with a key, asking for the return, not of his bike, but the expensive lock that was still attached to it. "It was the right key," remembered Mark Wagner with a shrug, "so we gave it to him."

The artworks at the World Trade Center fared much worse than the bicycle rack. In early 2002, the International Foundation for Art Research held what amounted to a postmortem on an estimated $100 million in artwork destroyed in the attacks, including the substantial collections in the offices of Cantor Fitzgerald, Citigroup, and other tenants, and the works in progress at an artist-in-residency program that occupied two floors of the north tower.

But the most dramatic losses involved the large pieces of public art from the plaza and lobbies of the towers. Saul Wenegrat knew, of course, there was no hope of recovering the two signature pieces from the lobby walls: a 700-square-foot abstract tapestry by Joan Miró and Louise Nevelson's "Sky Gate, New York," a wooden bas-relief inspired by the view of the New York skyline from an airplane window. Of the outdoor art, one major piece—Masayuki Nagare's low, brooding arrangement of black granite pyramids—apparently survived the attacks but blocked access to the plaza for emergency vehicles and was intentionally demolished the same day. Most of the others were buried under debris and recovered, if at all, in fragments. A single piece was recovered from the low granite fountain by Elyn Zimmerman that marked the spot on the plaza directly above where a bomb exploded underground in 1993, killing six and injuring more than 1,000.

Found in shards was Alexander Calder's large, playful, bright-red stabile, nicknamed "Bent Propeller" or "Three Wings." The Calder Foundation passed out flyers to the workers on the site with photographs of the piece, asking for their help in recovering it. This presumably helped, although Wagner recalls trying to describe it to an ironworker as "this big piece of twisted red steel" and being met with a derisive snort. "Look around, buddy," the hard hat said, "everything you see here is twisted red steel." The one major piece that survived in recognizable shape was Fritz Koenig's "Sphere for Plaza Fountain," a deconstructed bronze globe that stood 25 feet high between the towers. Battered and partly crushed, it was pulled from the rubble, brought to Hangar 17 at JFK for quick rehabilitation, and then brought back downtown to Battery Park as the centerpiece of a temporary memorial in March 2002.

A week or so after 9/11, Peter Rinaldi, a senior engineer for the Port Authority, entered a manhole on West Street and descended a set of emergency stairs to the PATH tracks, a commuter line to New Jersey whose New York terminal was beneath the World Trade Center. The water was waist-deep in the tunnel, and Rinaldi and his colleagues inflated a raft in which they paddled for some 400 feet, in complete darkness, to reach the station. Rinaldi inspected the station and concourse area. He tried, but failed, to remove a turnstile mechanism, which the PATH maintenance department wanted for spare parts (one would later be salvaged for the collection) and he noted the locations of two intact PATH rail cars. They had been stopped in the tunnel after the attacks and evacuated before the towers' collapse.

Much later, when the site had been cleared down to the station level, Rinaldi would supervise the removal of the cars, which first required straightening and repairing 100 feet of damaged track. Eventually, powerful backhoes hauled the cars into the open, where they were lifted by crane onto flatbed trucks for the journey to JFK. There they joined about two dozen other vehicles from among the 1,400 or so that had been found at ground zero. The hangar collection included crushed fire engines and ladder trucks, staved-in Port Authority police cars, a burned-out taxicab, and a splay-wheeled motorcycle. A careful inspection would reveal the absence of vehicles from the New York Police Department, which reclaimed all its damaged vehicles.

Early on, the question arose of where to store the artifacts until their ultimate disposition. In terms of size and proximity to ground zero, an unused pier in downtown Brooklyn was one obvious choice. But engineers warned that it might not support the weight of all that steel. It also raised another question that would begin to take on increasing urgency over time, that of conservation. If the artifacts were to be part of a memorial someday, they would have to be preserved, and keeping them away from salt water would be a good start.

Tom Amoia, a Port Authority engineer who was pulled from his job supervising construction at JFK on September 13 and spent the next three years working in and around ground zero, knew where there was plenty of flat, empty land in the remote reaches of the airport. Soon flatbed trucks bearing huge pieces of rusting steel were pulling up to the tarmac outside Hangar 17, a cavernous building far from the bustle of the airport's terminals that had been empty for years.

However, even after the artifacts were moved indoors, they weren't completely protected. The hangar's roof leaked, and birds, mostly pigeons and starlings, flew about freely. Steven Weintraub, a consultant on environmental controls for museums, was hired to oversee the preservation efforts, and he brought along Peter Gat, a Hungarian-born conservator whose specialty in Roman and Egyptian antiquities gave him ample experience in dealing with corrosion. Weintraub's first efforts involved just getting the steel up off the damp floor of the hangar and removing the accumulated bird droppings with what he calls a "water-based solvent," or spit.

Soon it became clear that certain items needed more elaborate protection, which emerged in the form of plastic-walled interior tents, equipped to control temperature and, crucially, humidity. Obviously, most large pieces of structural steel didn't need to be treated like a first-century bronze breastplate. But at least one did: the Last Column, 37 feet long and huge in cross-section that had been buttressing the dirt ramp leading to the bottom of the Trade Center's concrete-walled foundation, and was thus left standing until the very end. By the time it was removed in a special ceremony on May 30, 2002, it had become a kind of totem for the workers at ground zero, who had covered it with memorials to the dead: "FDNY 343," "PAPD 37," "NYPD 23"—the numbers of victims from the fire department, Port Authority police, and New York police department, respectively.

There were photographs, fliers, decals, and inscriptions: "My brothers," one officer wrote, "you ran into hell. Now you walk with angels." But all of that precious memorabilia was inscribed or taped to a fragile coating of mill scale, the thin layer of oxidation that forms naturally on hot-rolled steel. The steel beneath it was rusting; the rust was expanding and so the scale was flaking off in irregular pieces, ranging from a fraction of an inch to the size of a man's palm. Weintraub, heading a team that at times numbered as many as nine, began a laborious and almost unimaginably delicate job of restoring the surface of the column: capturing the flakes as they fell and gluing them back in place, locating loose spots and injecting adhesive behind them with medical syringes. They built a steel cradle for the column, supporting it off the ground so that—reclining on beach chairs to reach the underside—they could work on all four faces. Weintraub and Gat brought to the job an art-preservation sensibility in which not just a photograph but the duct tape holding it in place—even the wrinkles on the duct tape—were deemed precious and worthy of saving. Again using syringes, Gat injected a solvent to remove the glue from the back of the tape, while preserving the fabric and wrinkles. Then he would carefully attach the photograph or flier to a thin sheet magnet that would hold it in place on the steel but could be easily removed if some curator in the future wanted to study it or make a copy.

The Last Column's final destination is the 9/11 Memorial Museum at ground zero. Certain other artifacts will join it there, but far more was collected than could be displayed in even a large exhibition. As word of the collection spread, museums and memorials all over the world began seeking relics of the towers. Almost no town in the United States is too small to have a firefighters' memorial, and by the hundreds they wrote to say how honored they would be to include some of the steel that had once held up the World Trade Center. All seventeen of the recovered tridents were spoken for, including two that were installed to stand post at the entrance to the 9/11 Memorial Museum. Gradually, as the tenth anniversary of 9/11 approached, the hangar began to empty out.

It had to happen, of course, but there was a certain reluctance on the part of the men and women who had assembled and guarded the collection to see it disperse. The number of visitors to the hangar can be counted in the hundreds, including military and police officials and family members of the victims; the security and logistical problems involved in opening it to the public were insoluble. But those who did visit were profoundly moved by the experience, the mute, horrible evidence of the unimaginable violence of that day. Chris Ward, who had been a high-ranking Port Authority official in 2001, returned in 2008 as executive director and made a visit to the hangar one of his first orders of business. He wandered among the rust-covered beams, laid out side by side like disaster victims in a morgue, the remains of the tridents, immense even after their partial dismemberment. Their power as icons was enhanced by viewing them this way, arbitrarily arranged on the concrete floor beneath the flat industrial lighting, with only the viewer's own memory and imagination to provide the context. They belong in a museum, Ward mused, and yet at the same time, "they're not sculptures. You don't want them to be beautiful." Beautiful they are not: brutally functional artifacts of heavy industry, battered and fire-scarred, rescued from the junkyard to which they would otherwise have been consigned. They are something more than beautiful: They are sacred.

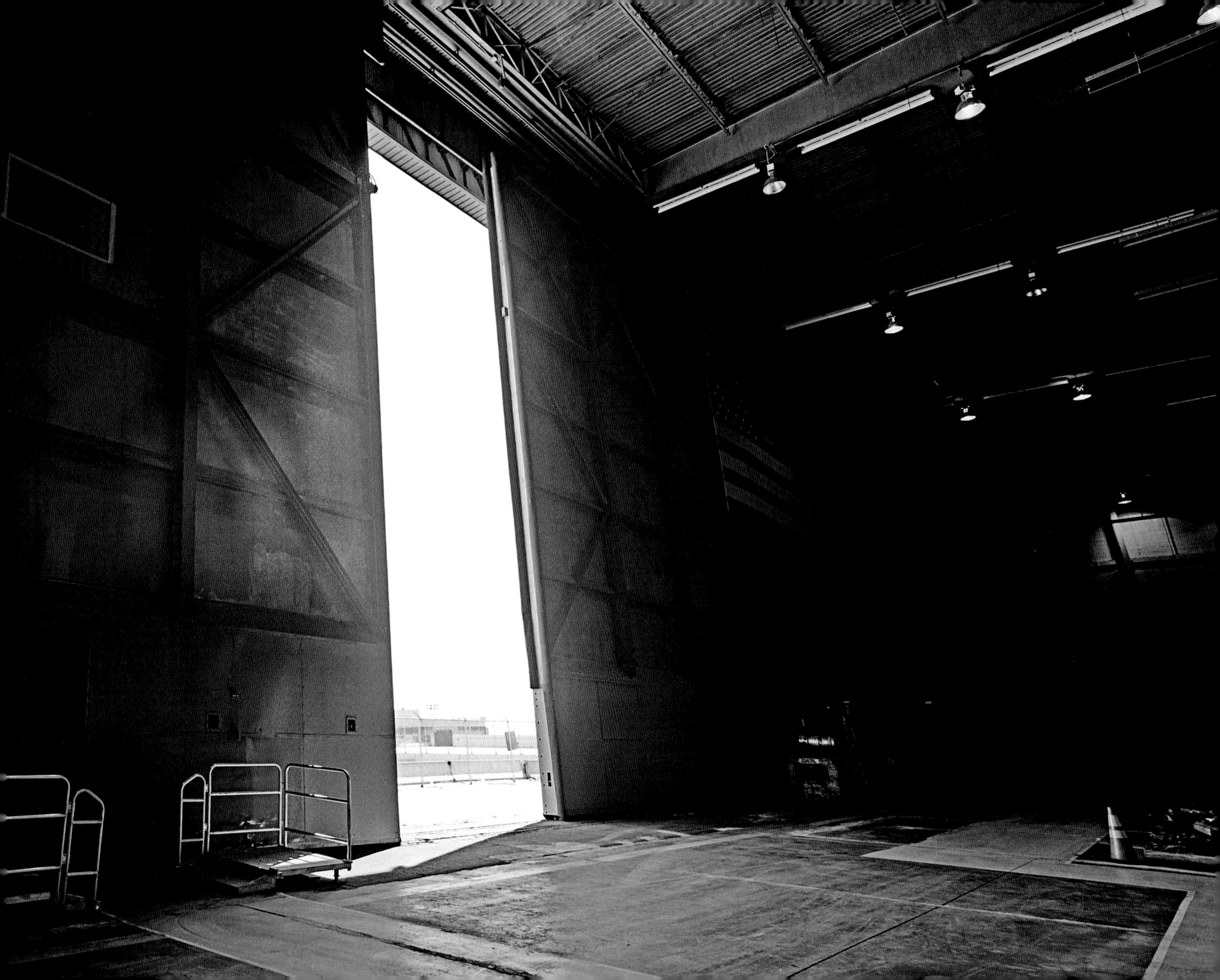

WTC STEEL

It took nine months to clear the World Trade Center site of 1.8 million tons of rubble and debris. A tiny fraction of that material was selected for possible use in a future museum and kept at Hangar 17 at John F. Kennedy International Airport, which had been empty since the bankruptcy of Tower Airlines in 2000. Eventually, more than 1,200 pieces of steel, as well as other objects, filled the 80,000 square feet of Hangar 17.

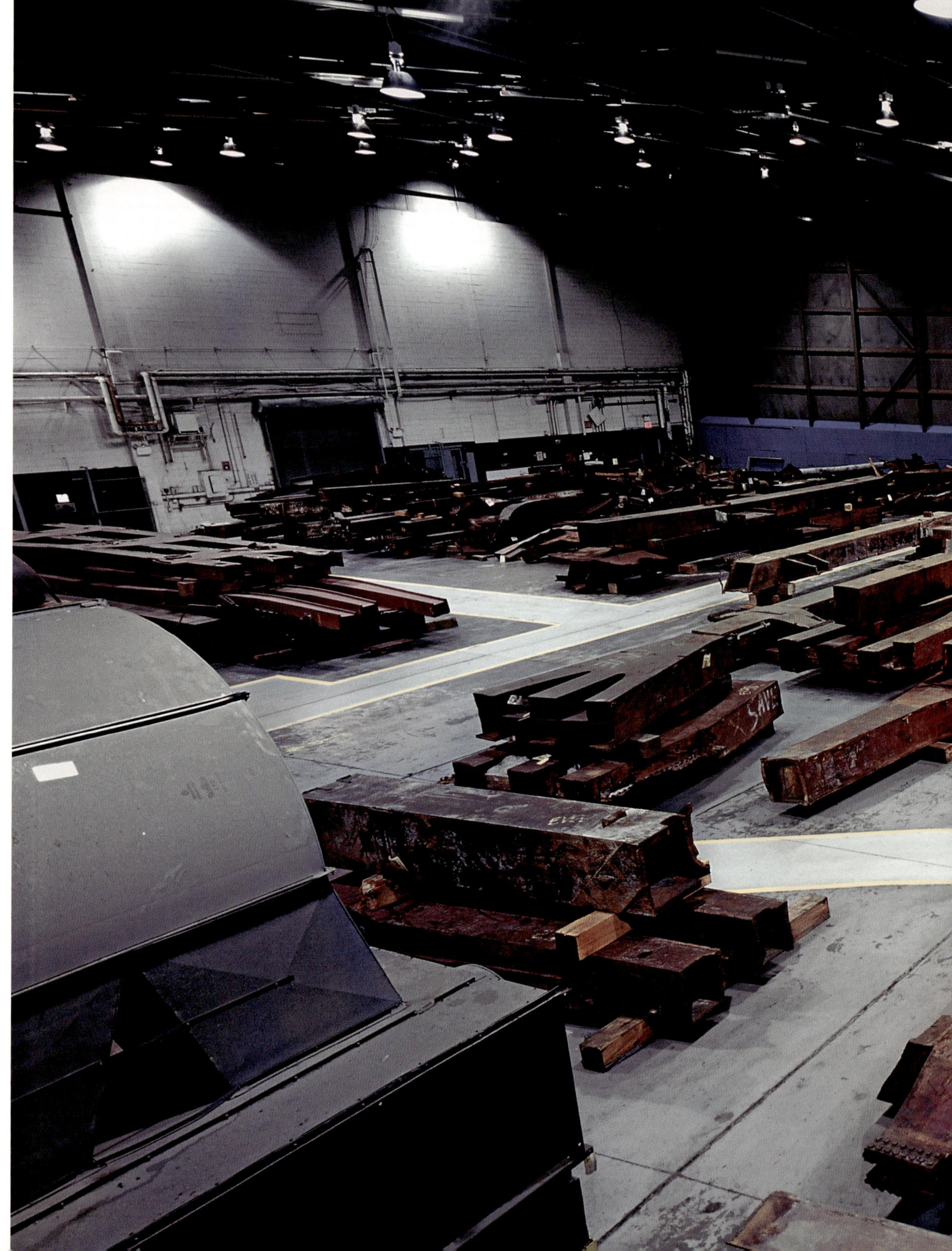

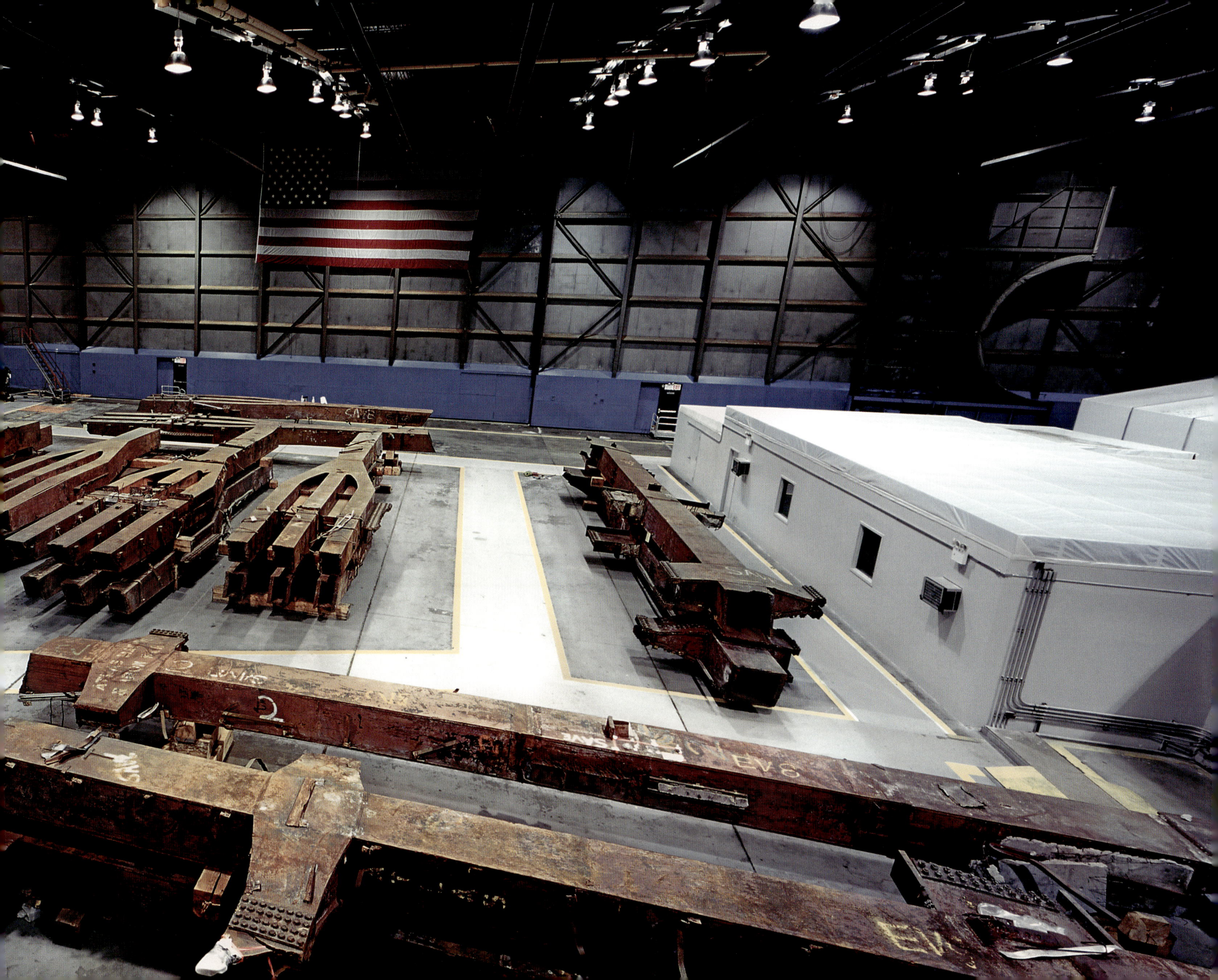
SAVE
EV8

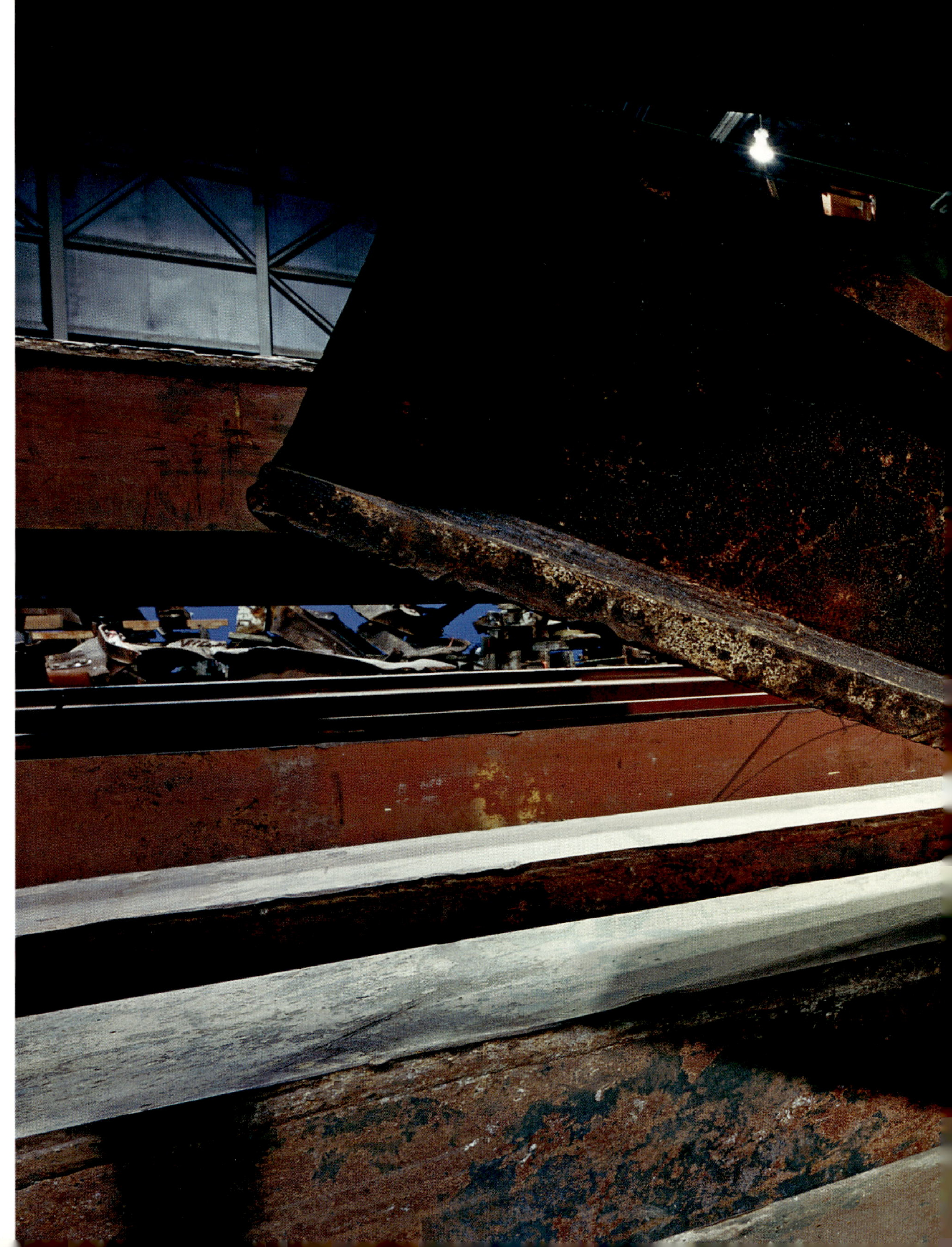

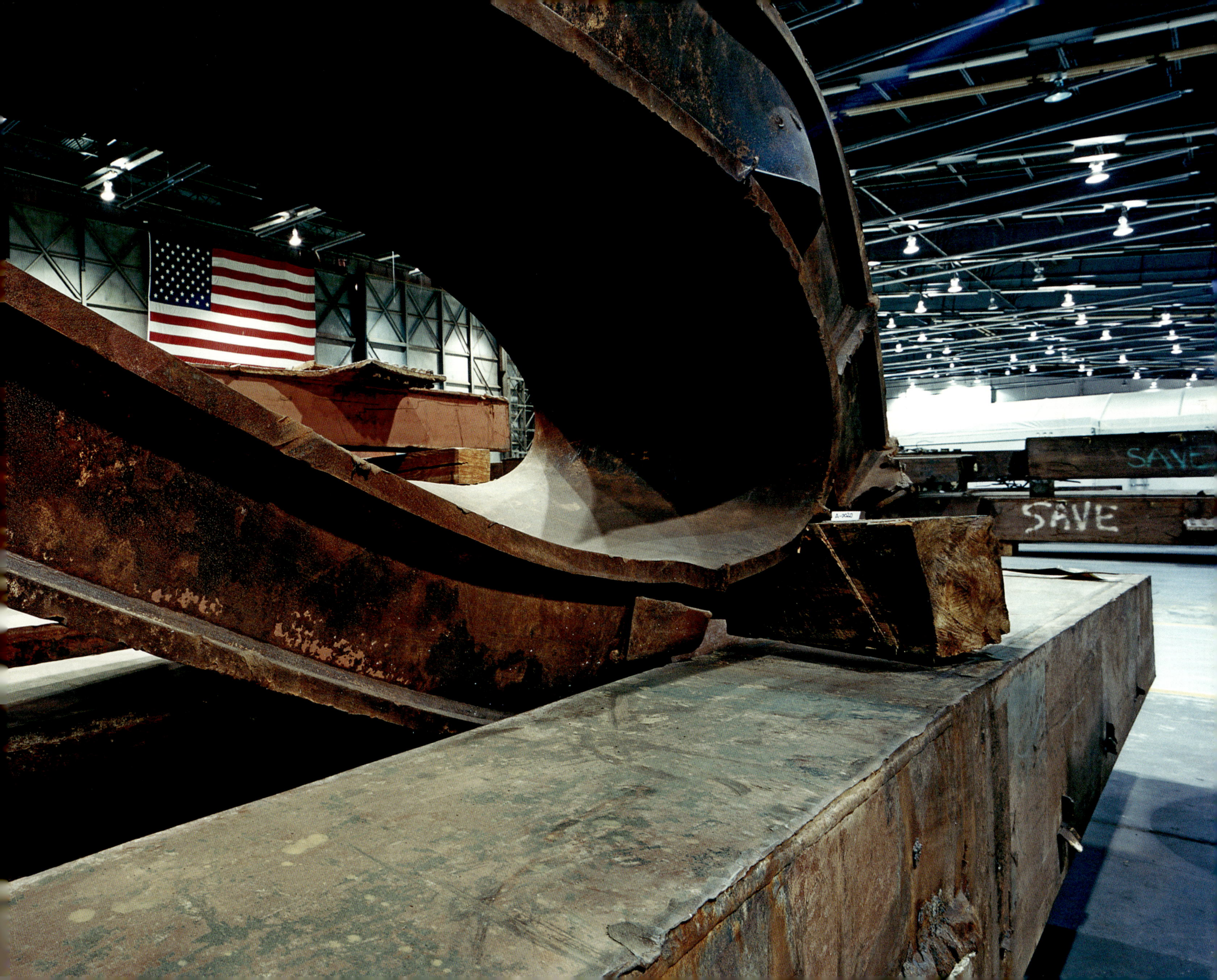
SAVE
SAVE

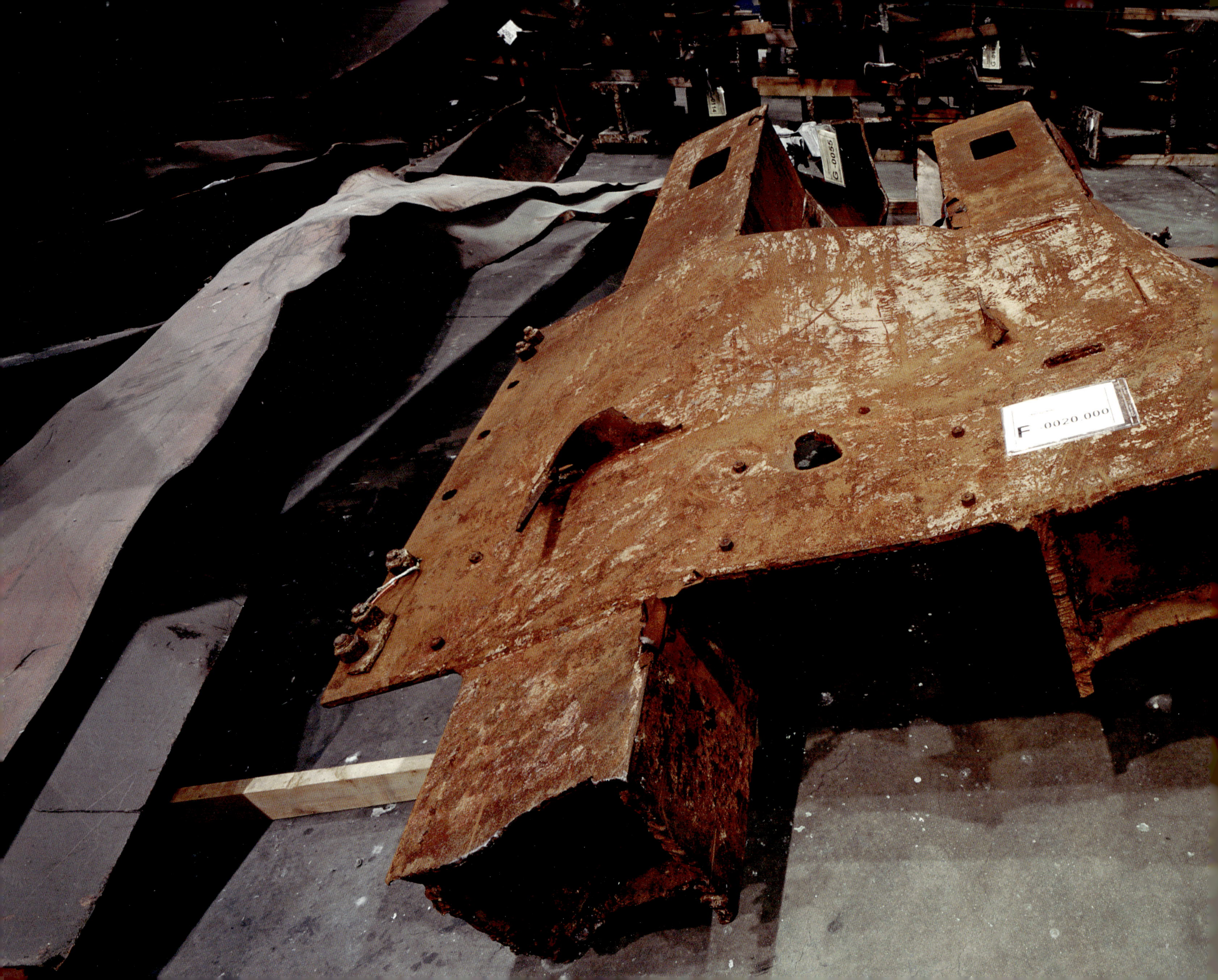
F 0020.000
G-0055

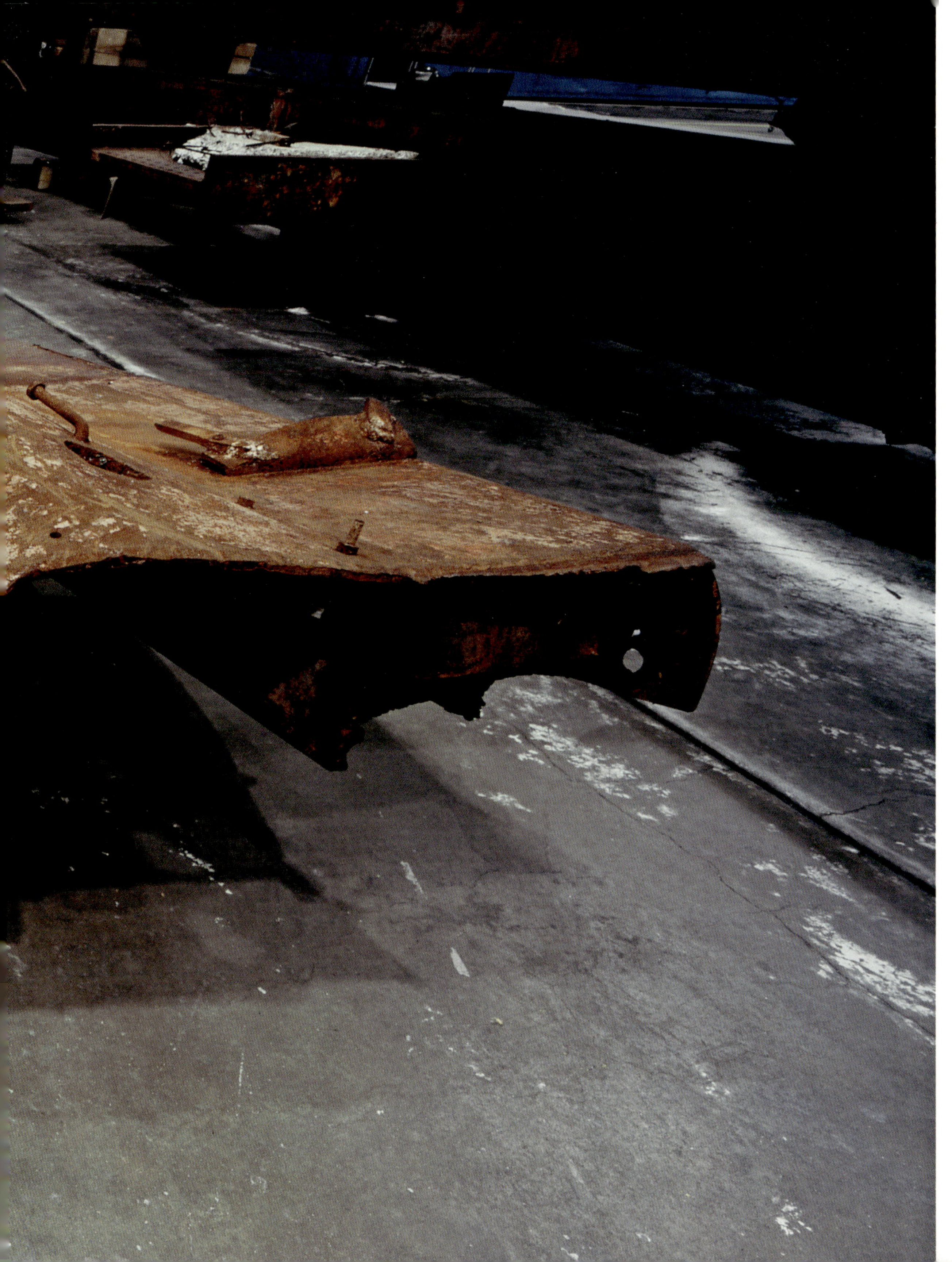

Objects brought into the Hangar 17 collection were tagged and cataloged. The majority of these objects were structural elements of the buildings, which often showed extreme damage from pressure or heat. Much of the large steel had to be cut down into smaller sizes for transport to the hangar.

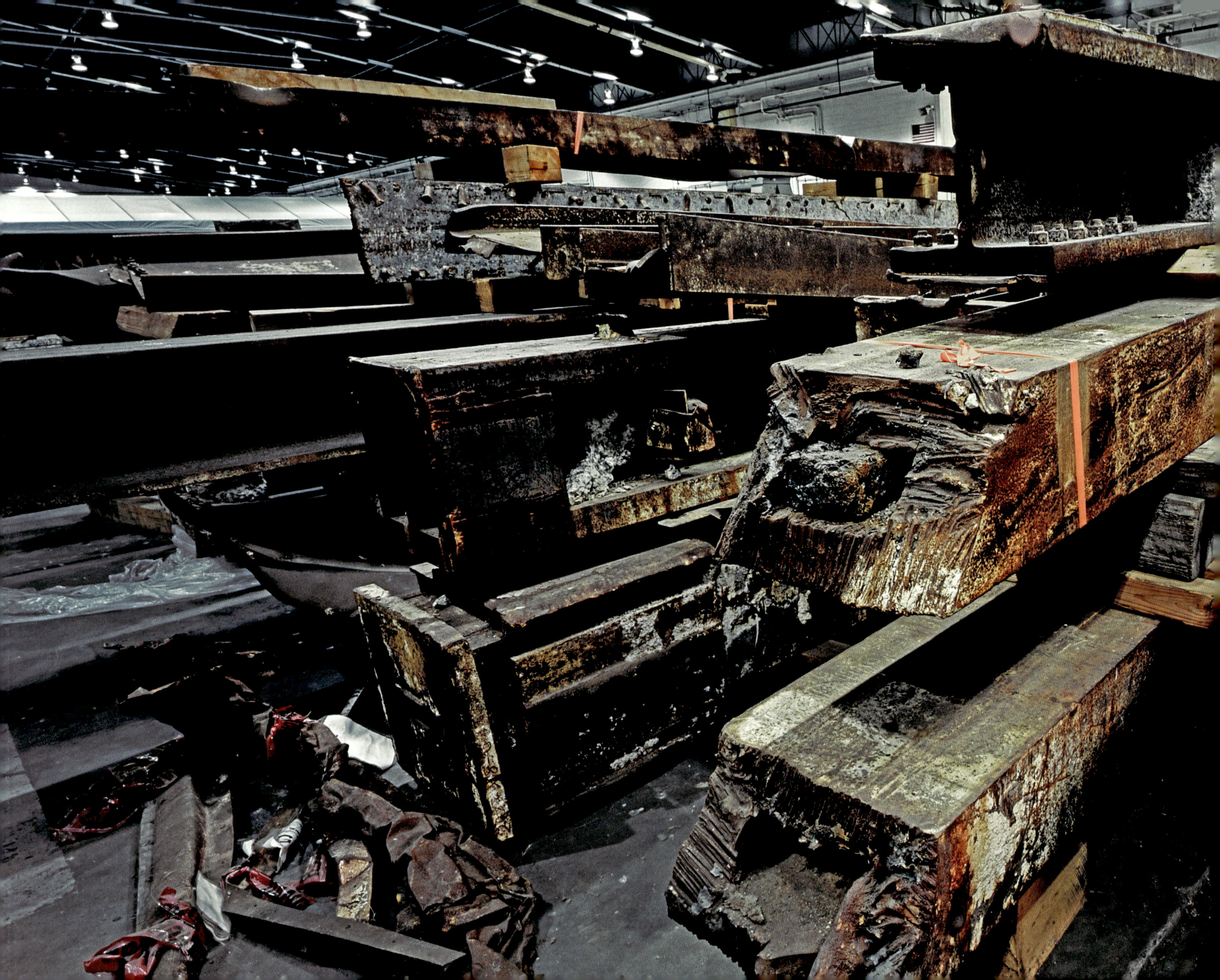

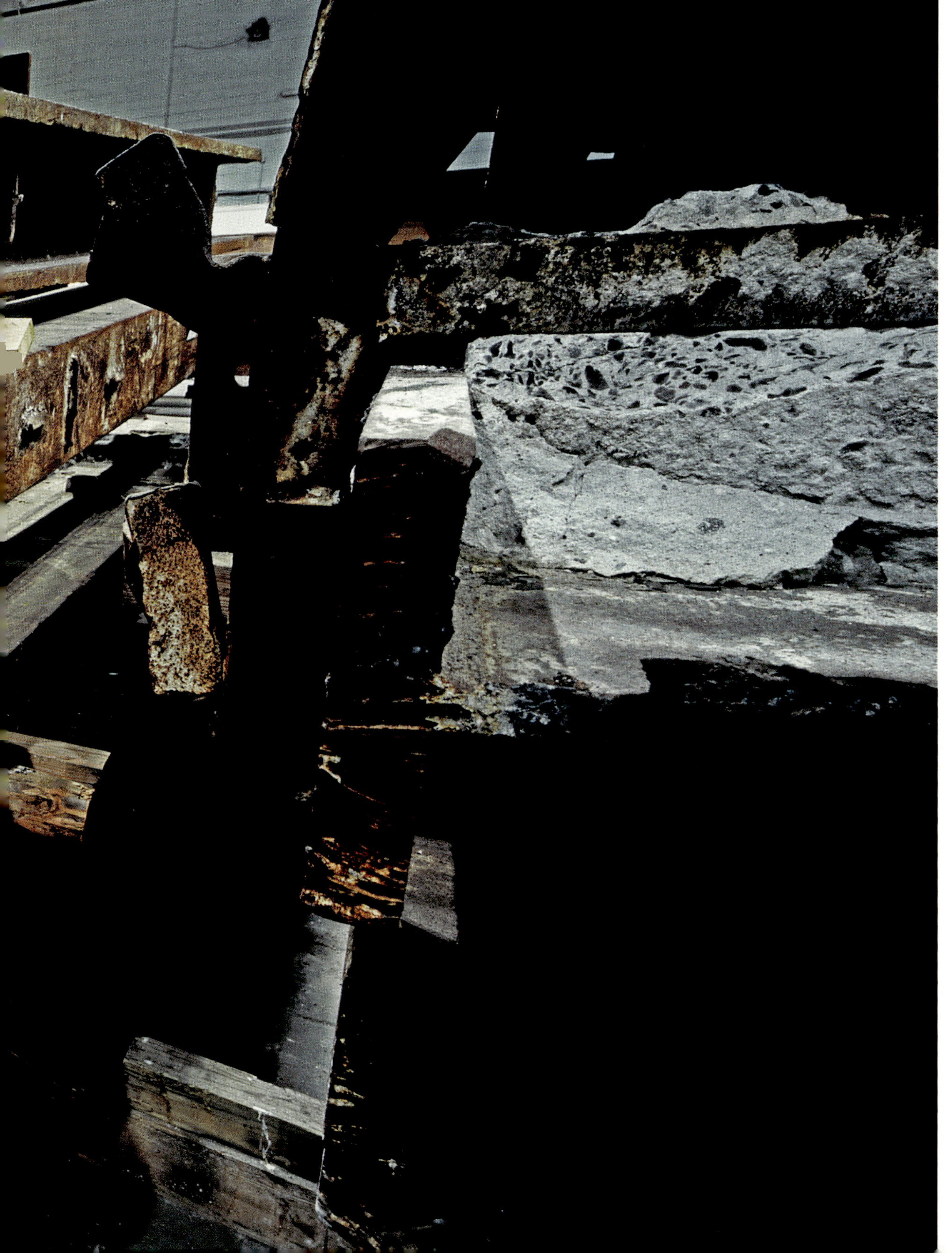

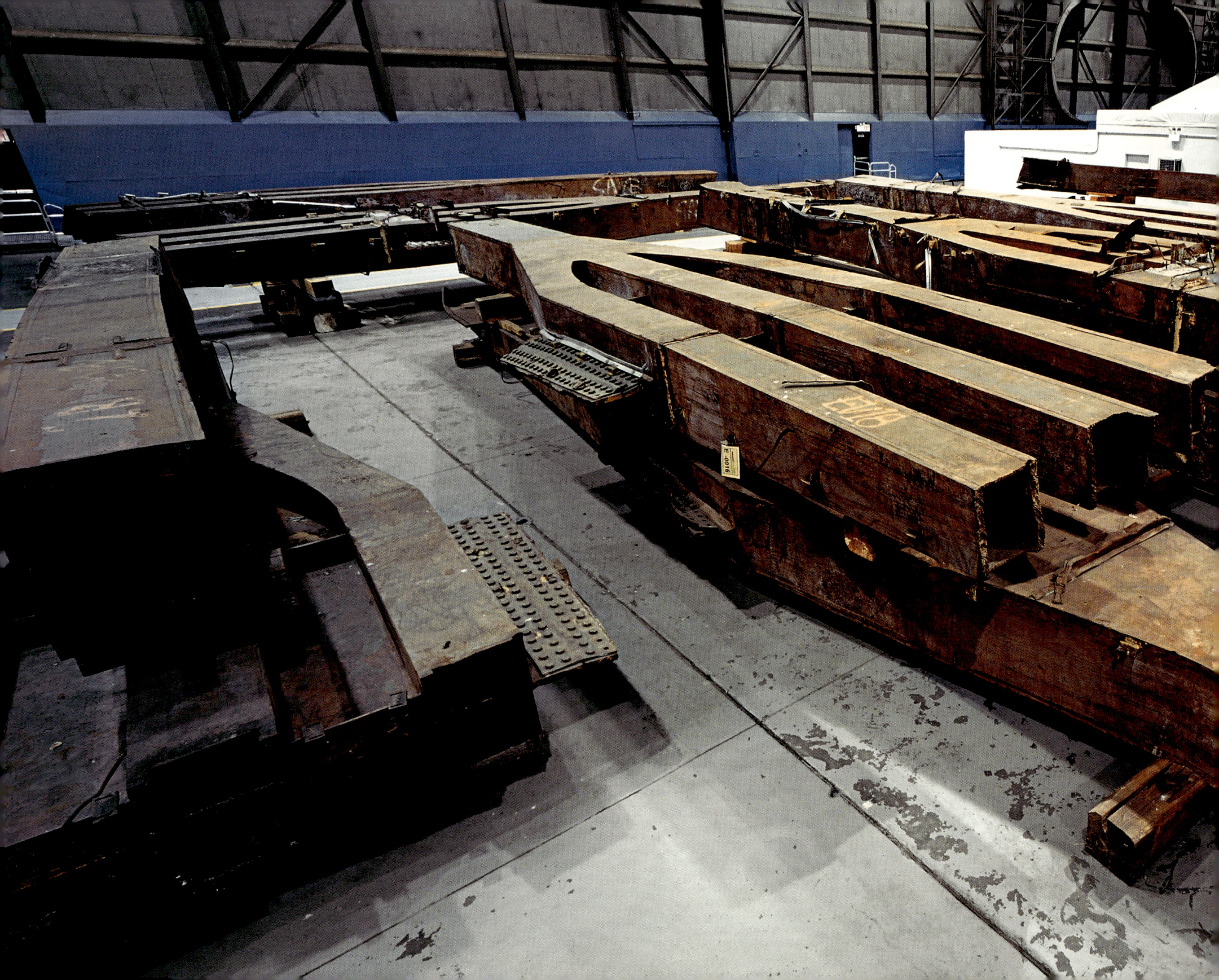
E-0016

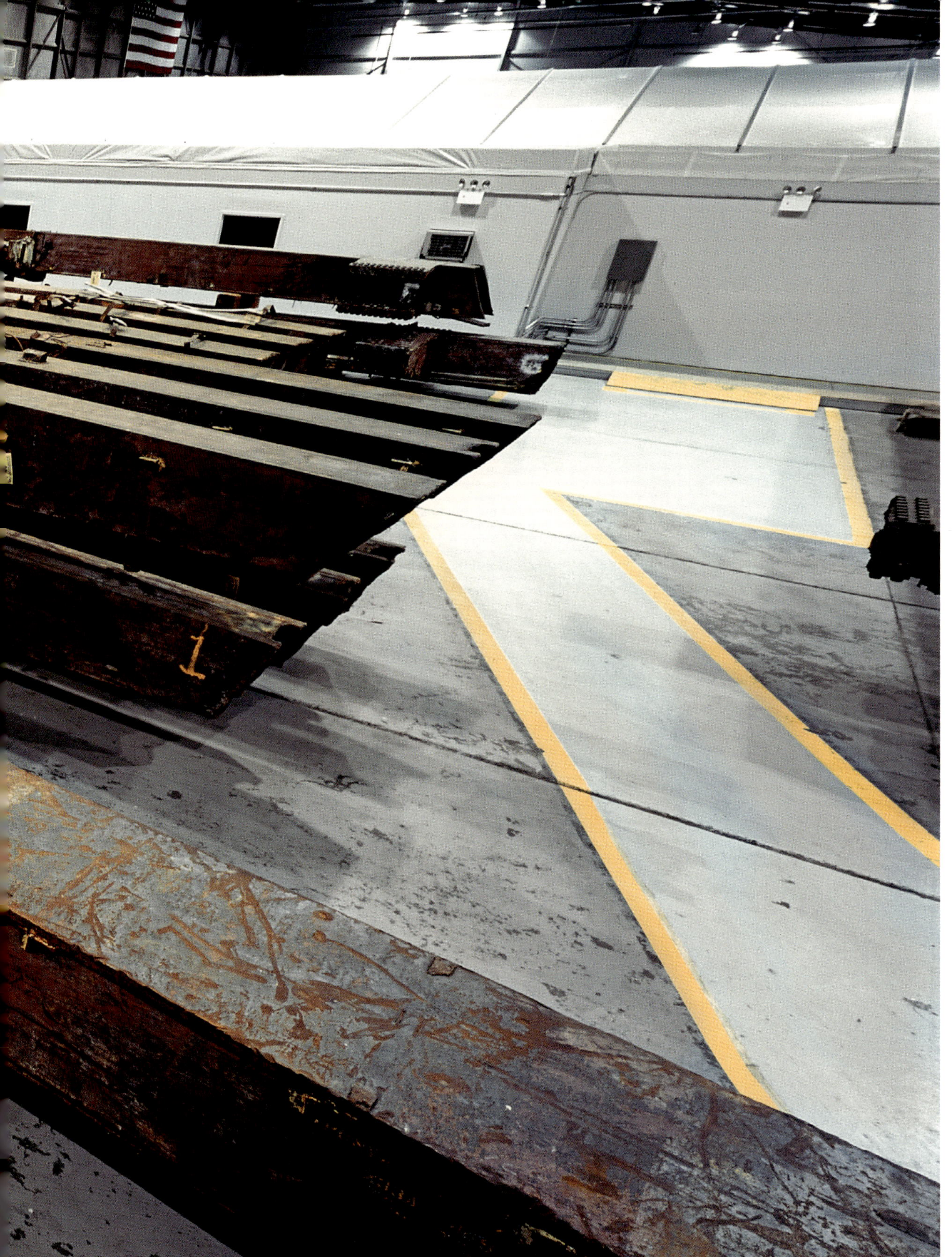

Among the most distinctive architectural features of the twin towers were the Gothic-style arches at the base of the buildings created by the side-by-side placement of three-pronged structural elements, which have come to be known as tridents. More than 80 feet tall and weighing more than 50 tons, the tridents were too large to be brought to the hangar intact and were cut in pieces for removal. Two of the tridents have been returned to the World Trade Center site and installed behind a glass wall in the entrance to the Memorial Museum, where they are visible from the Memorial Plaza.

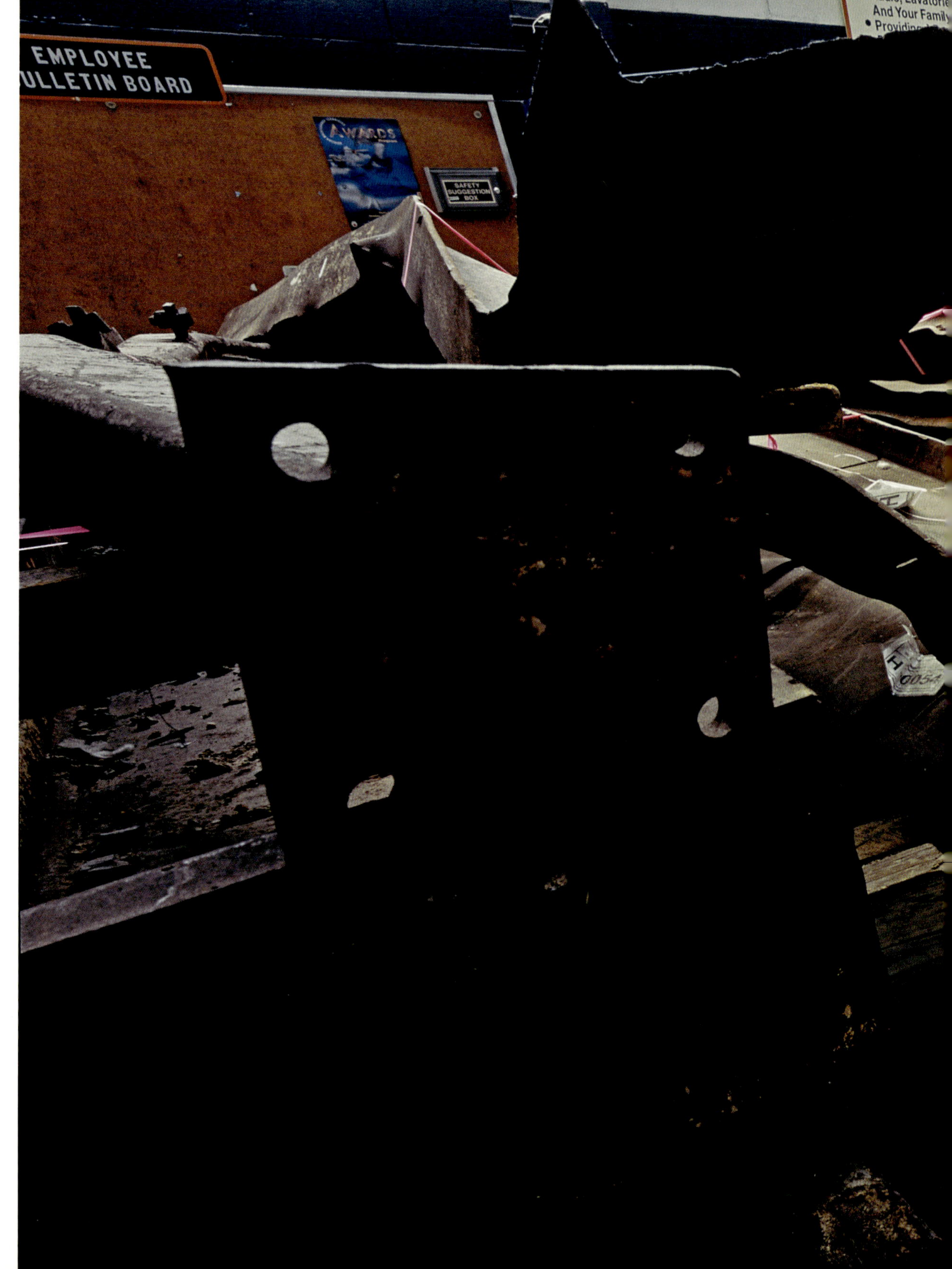

The fall of the twin towers created unimaginable amounts of pressure. Indestructible under normal circumstances, the buildings' steel testifies to the physics of the collapse. Thick beams were left bent and torn, their rivets popping. Engineers studying the collapse examined different structural elements of the towers to understand what had happened.

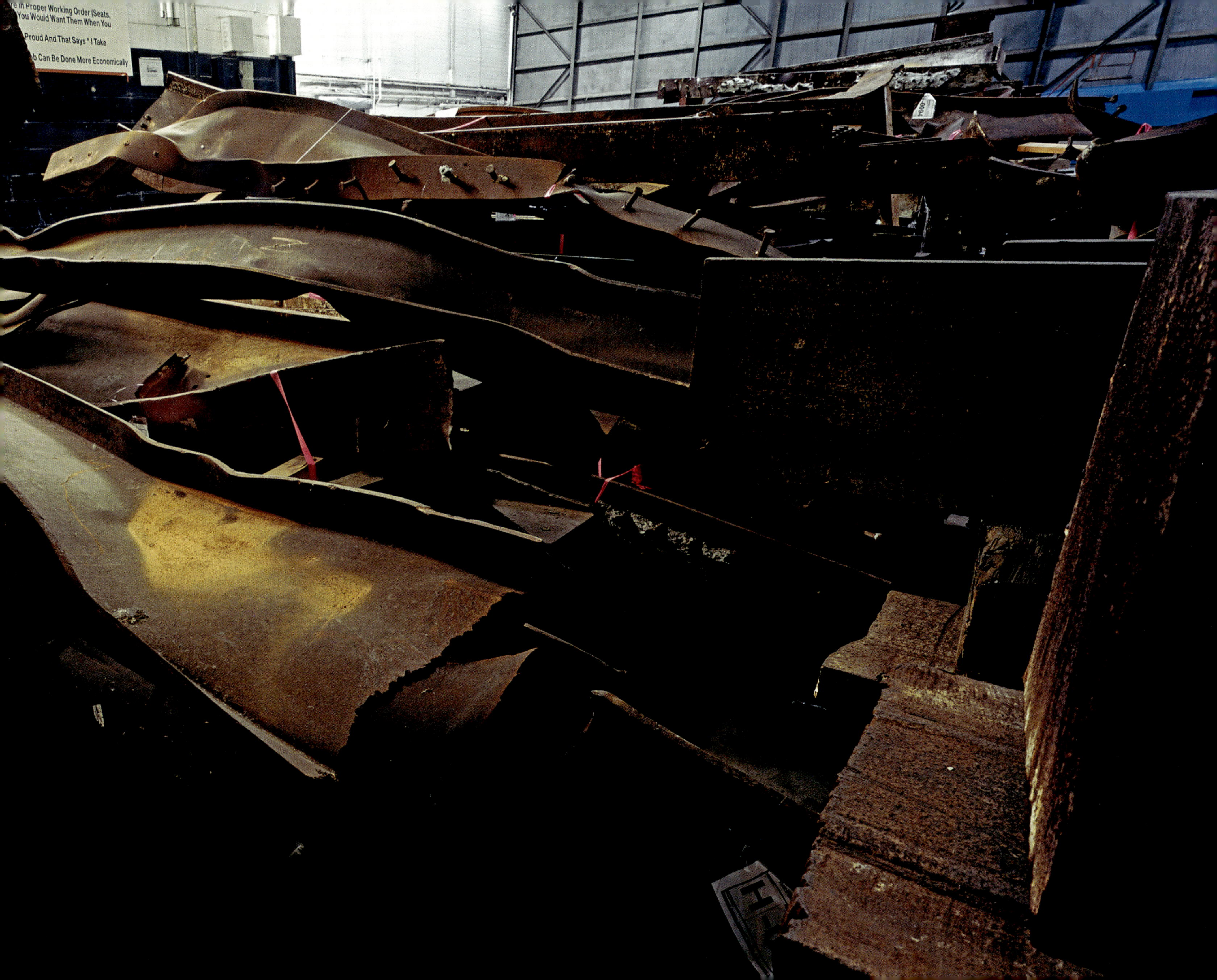
in Proper Working Order (Seats,
You Would Want Them When You
Proud And That Says " I Take
Can Be Done More Economically

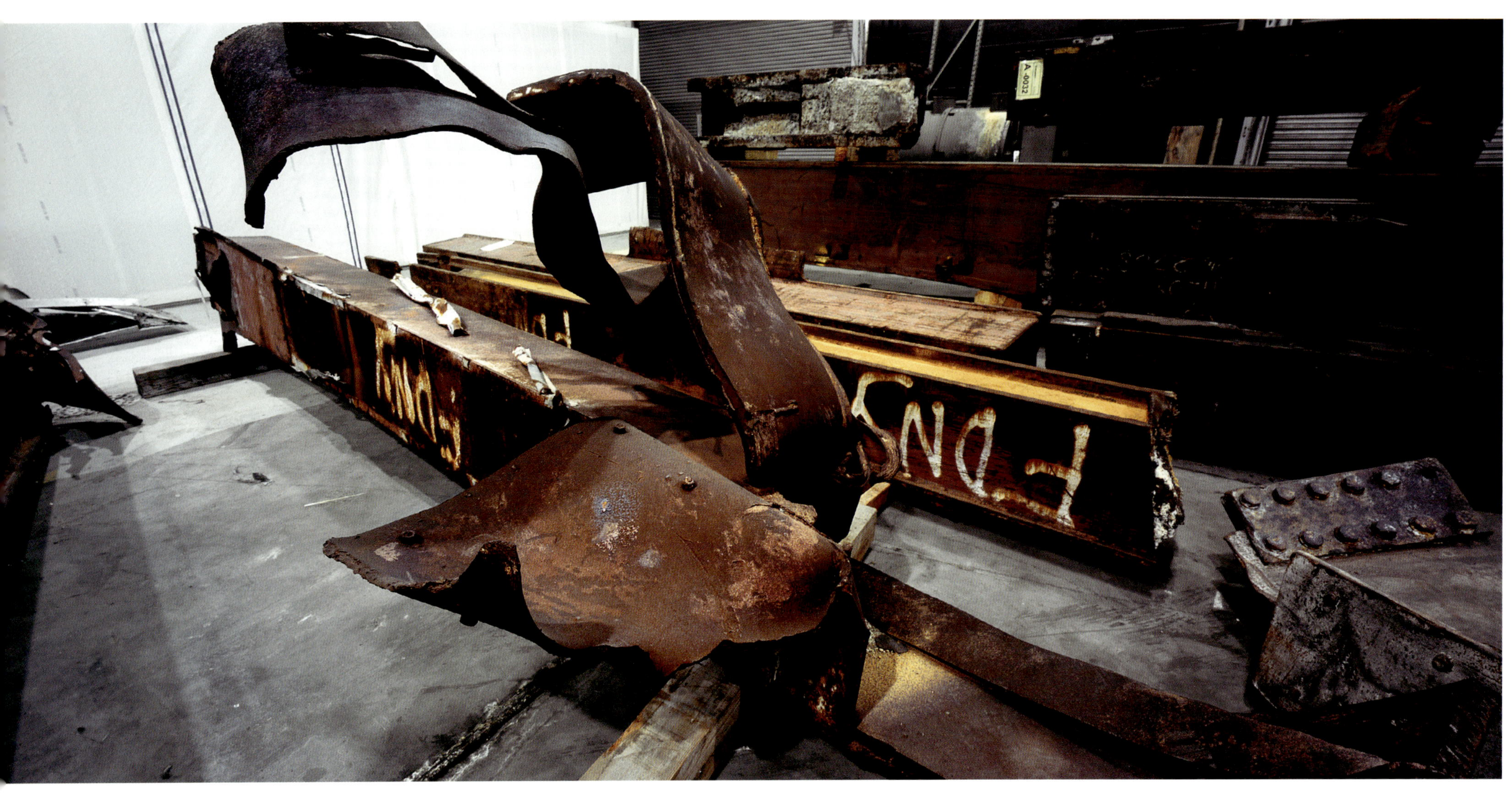

From the Port Authority's inventory report: "As a result of extreme overloading along the column's vertical axis, the welds holding the box together have failed, causing the steel to buckle and roll or fold downward."

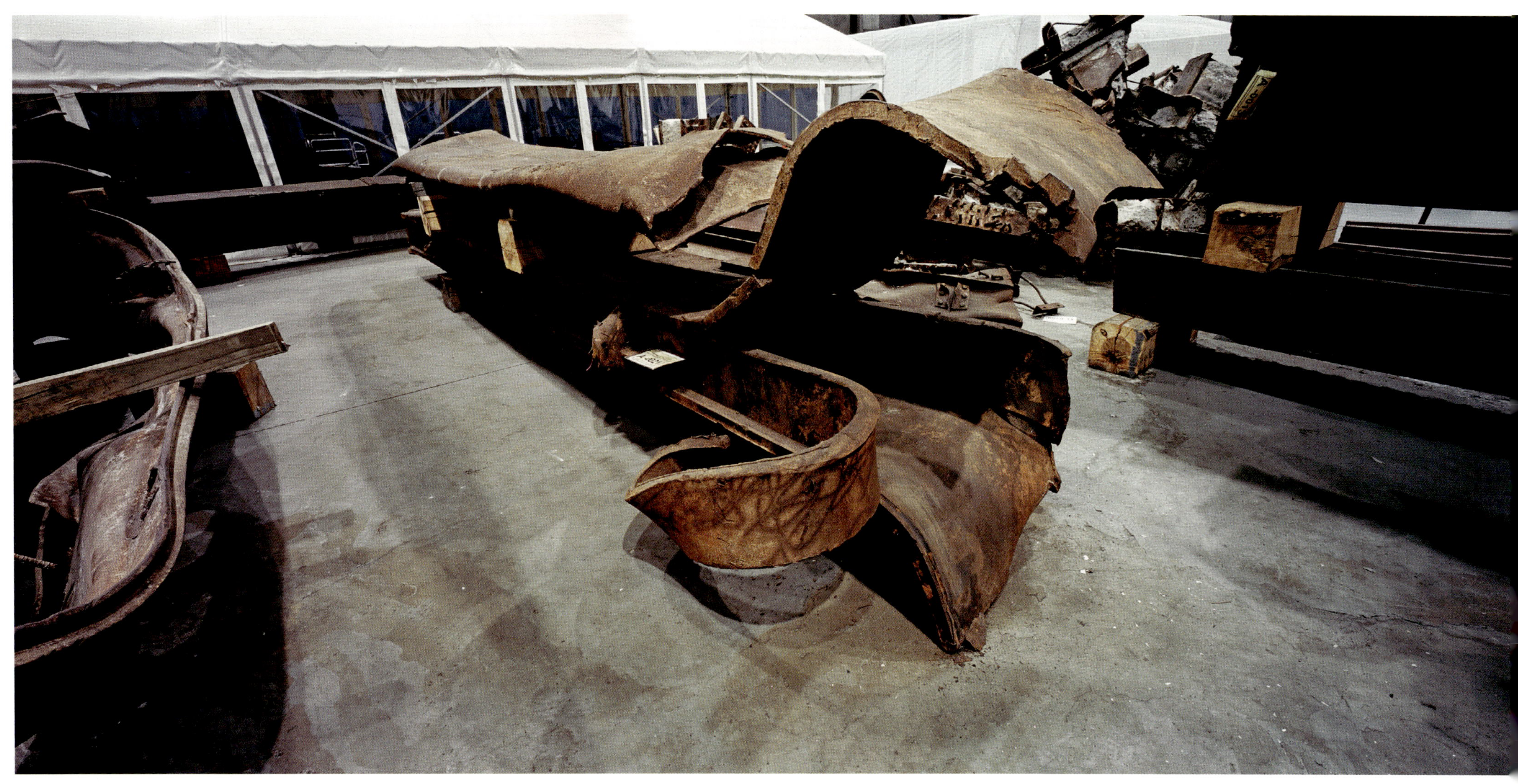

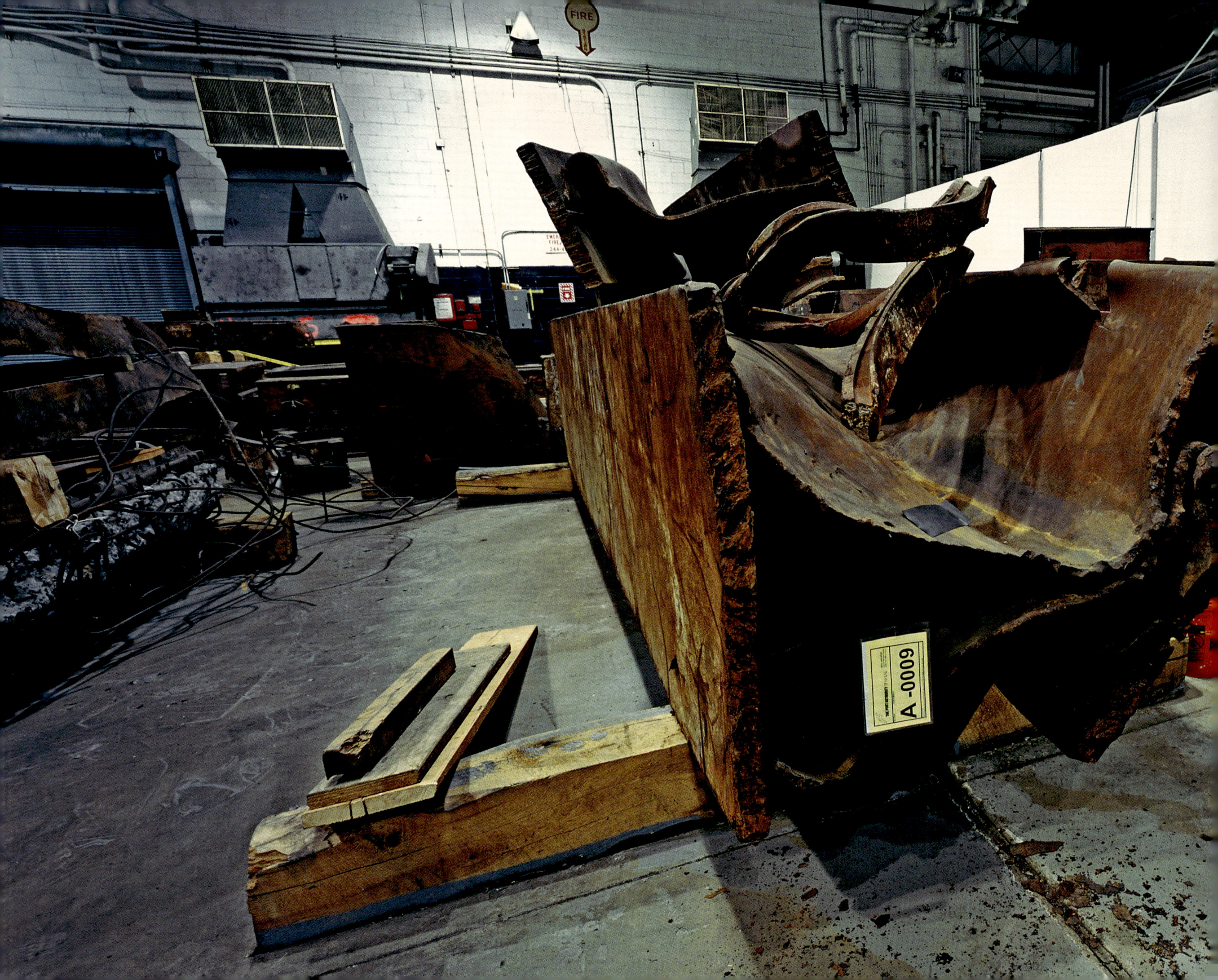
FIRE
A -0009

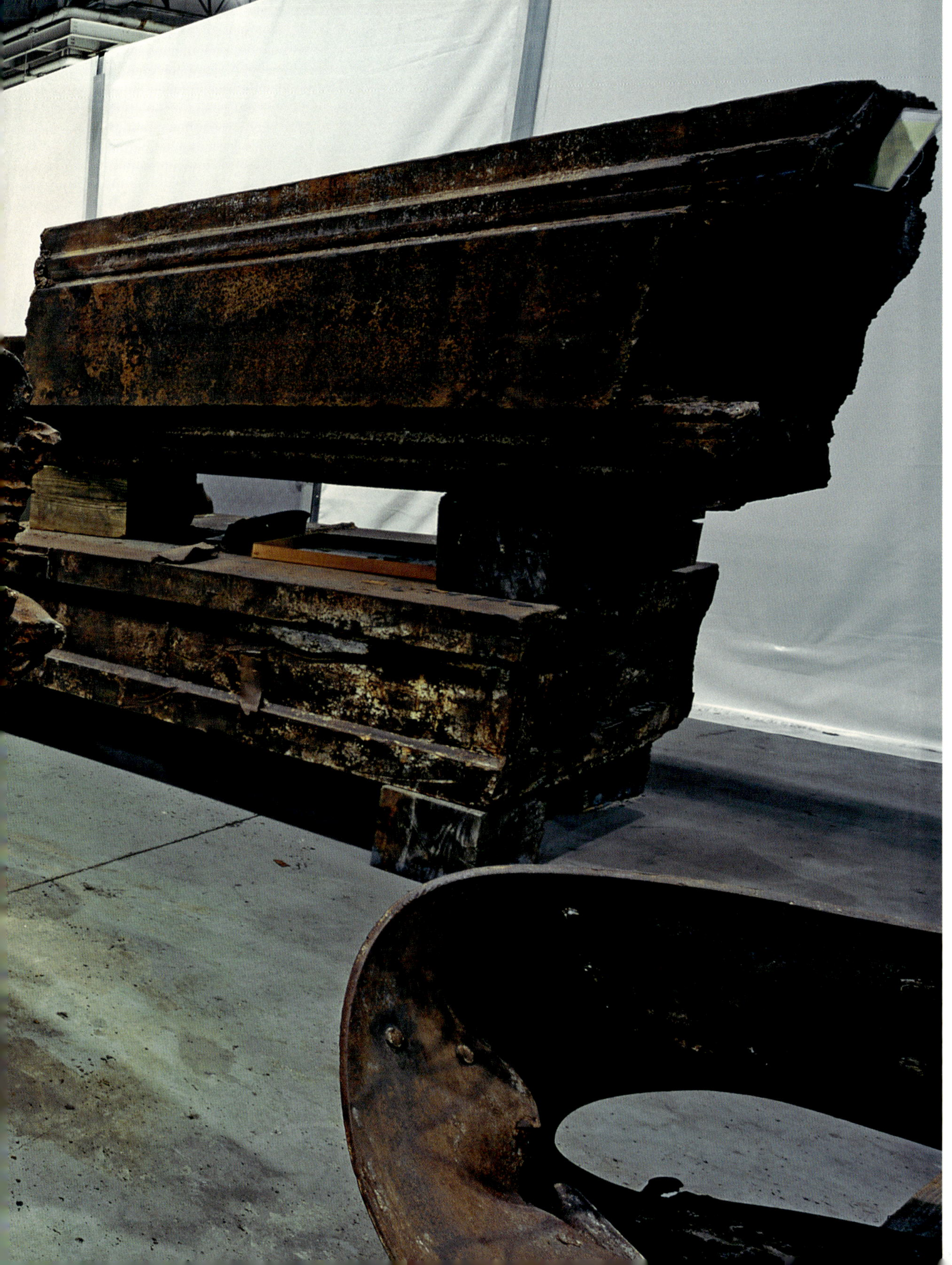

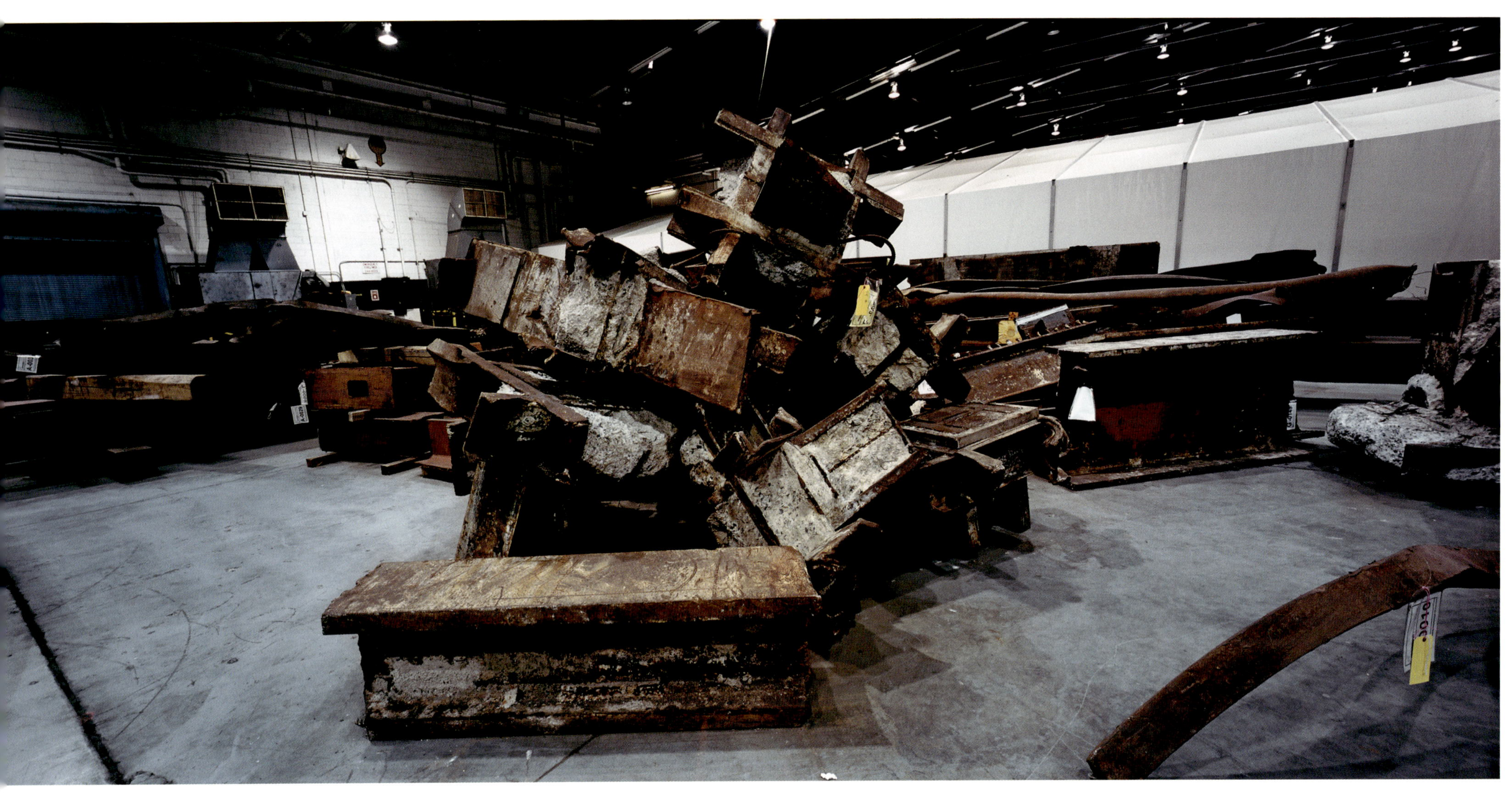

Stacks of cut beams with shear heads, which connected the concrete foundation slabs to structural columns that made up the base of the World Trade Center. These pieces were retrieved from a salvage yard, where they had been brought for recycling.

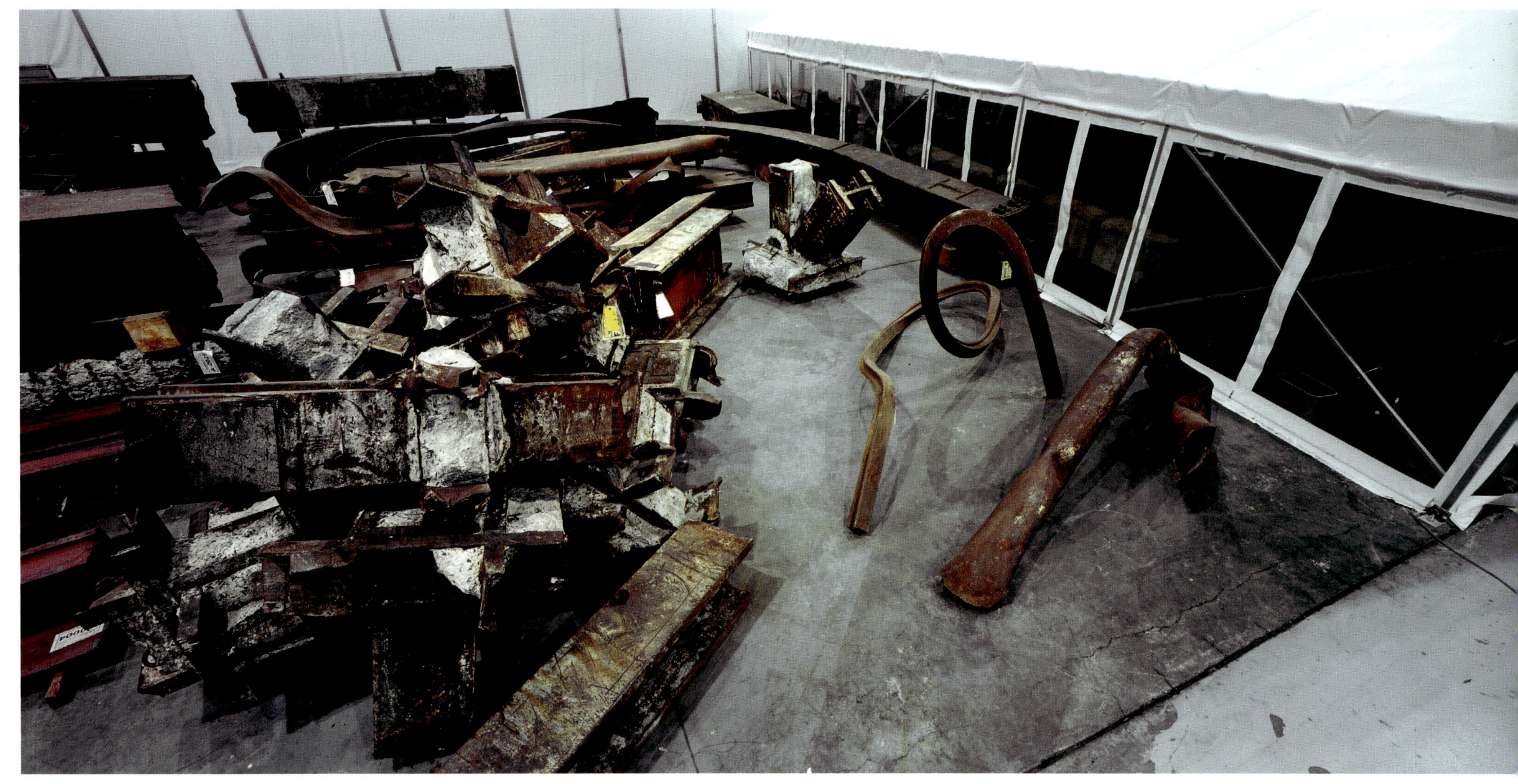

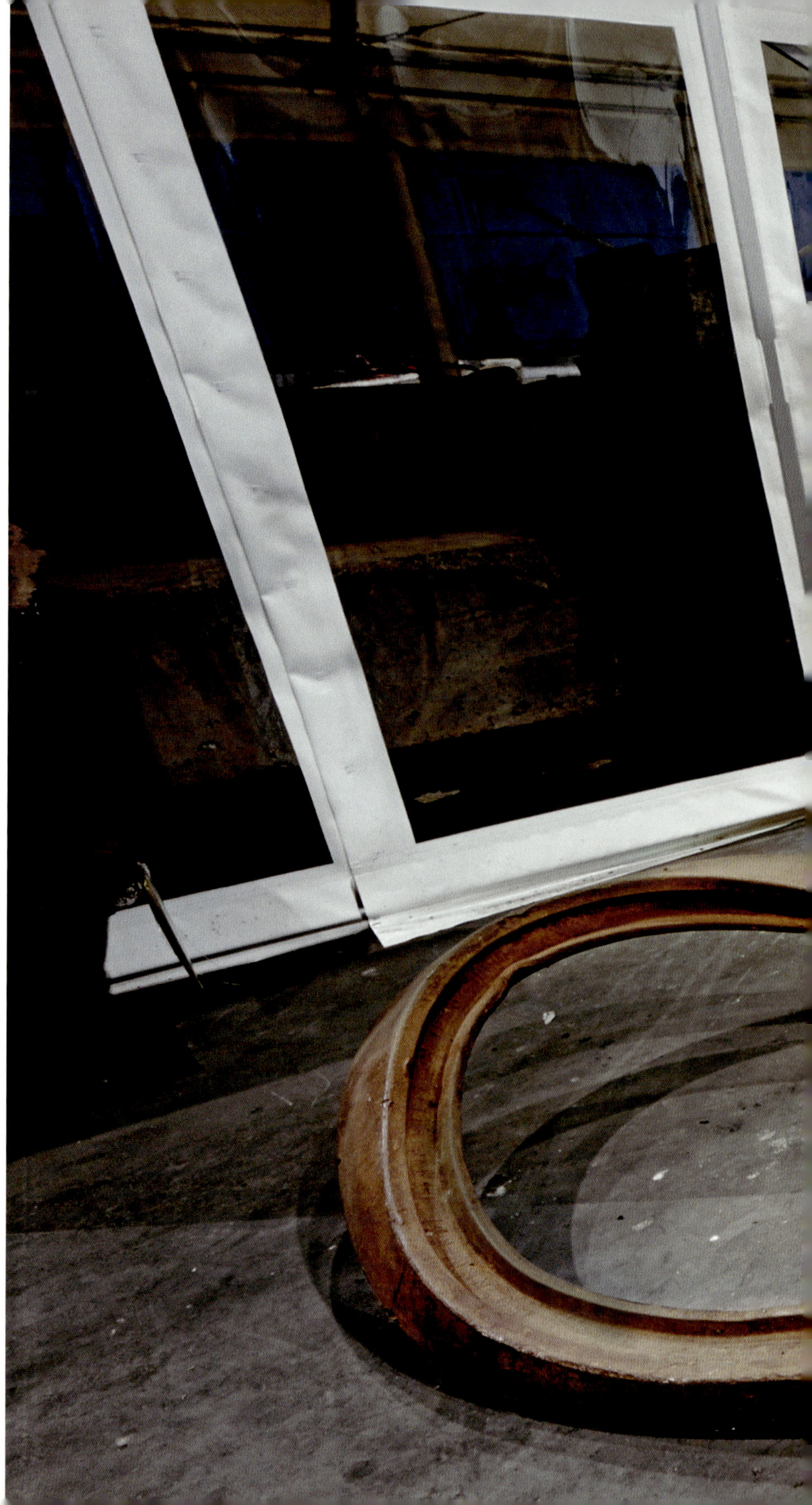

The passage of time has not resolved all the mysteries associated with objects at Hangar 17. The Port Authority inventory calls this twisted object a "steel train rail," but no rails were found to be missing from any of the train lines around the WTC. Speculation that it might be an elevator car railing has not been confirmed. More recently, a story emerged that old train tracks had been used to fortify the roof of one of the buildings in the WTC complex.

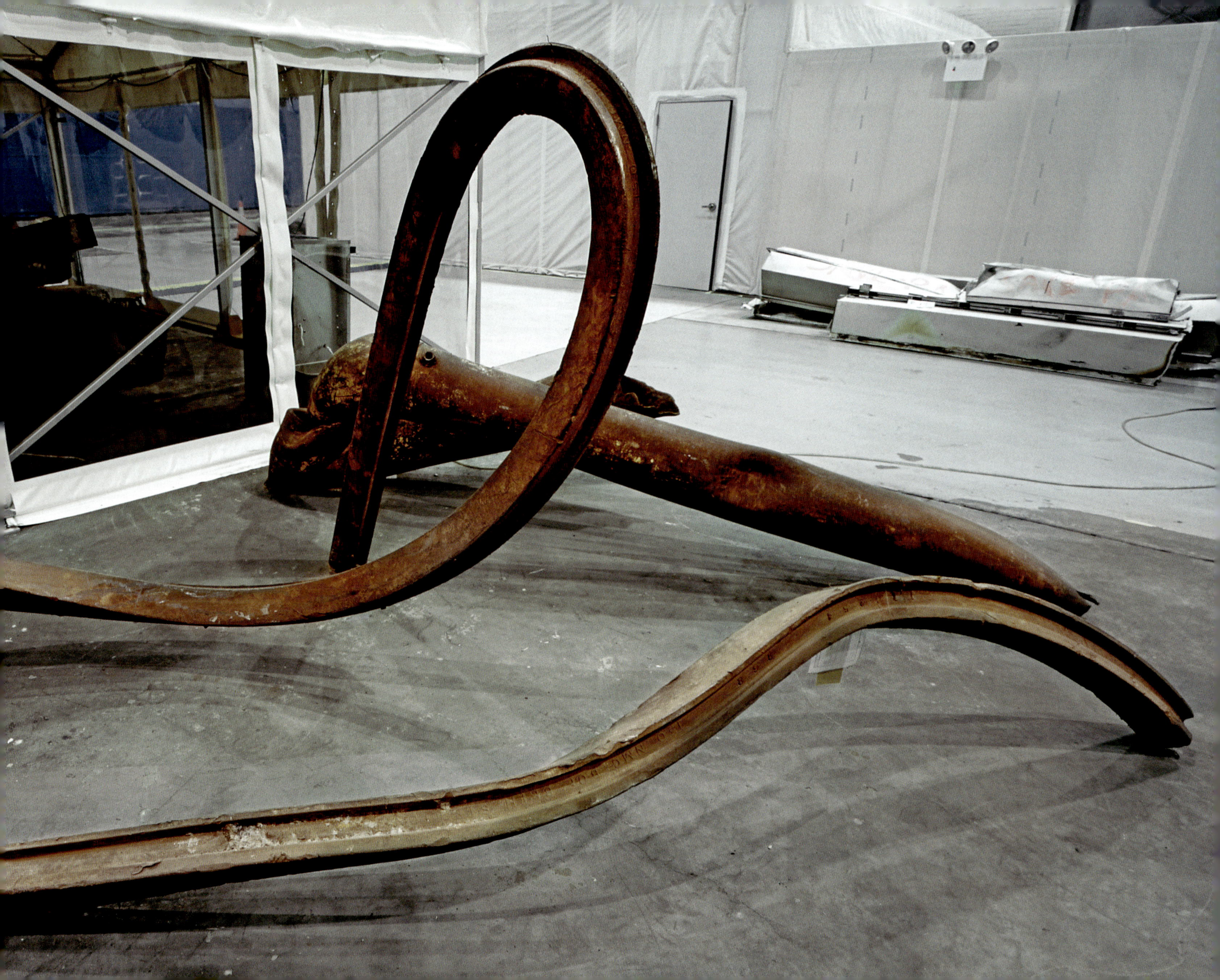

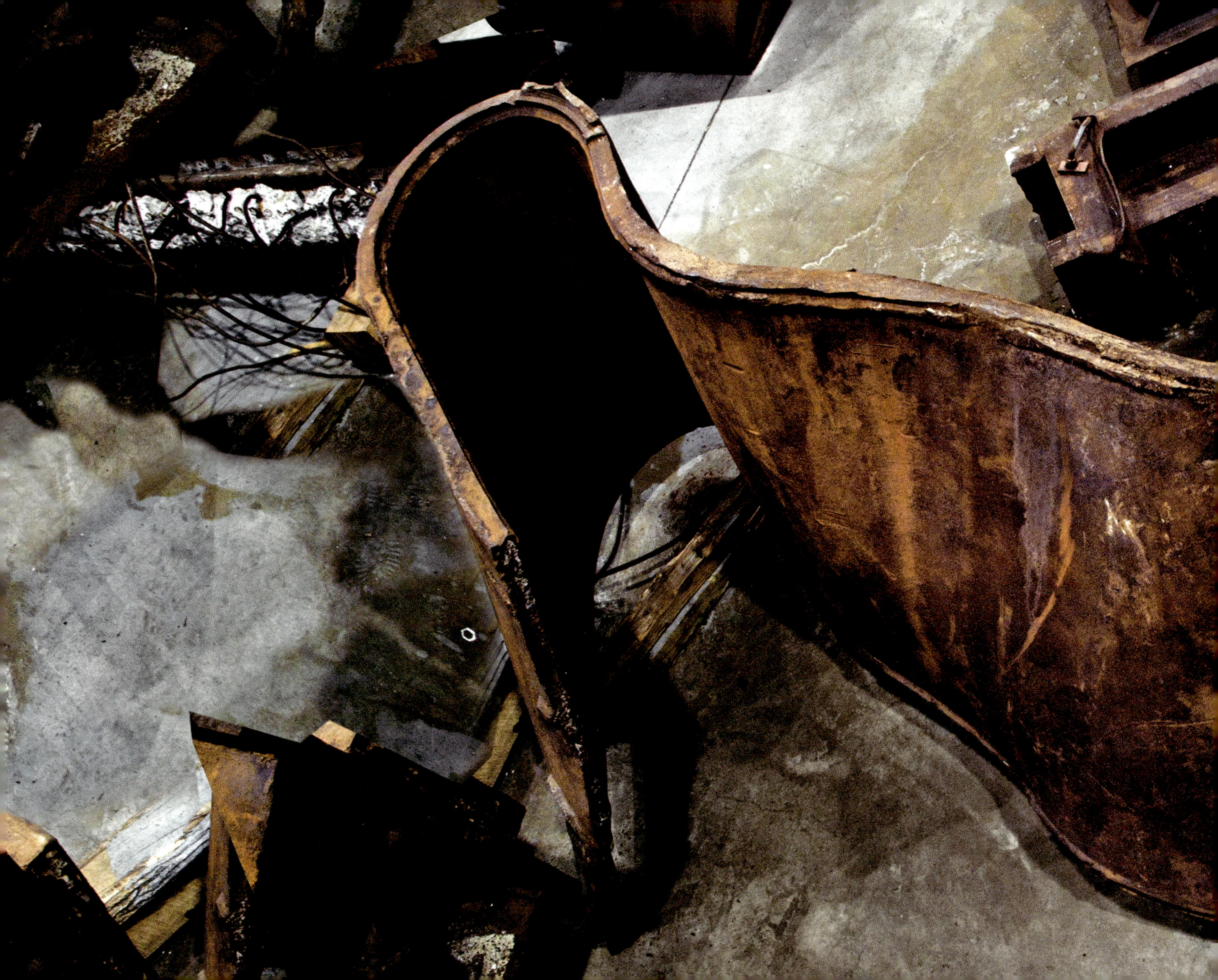

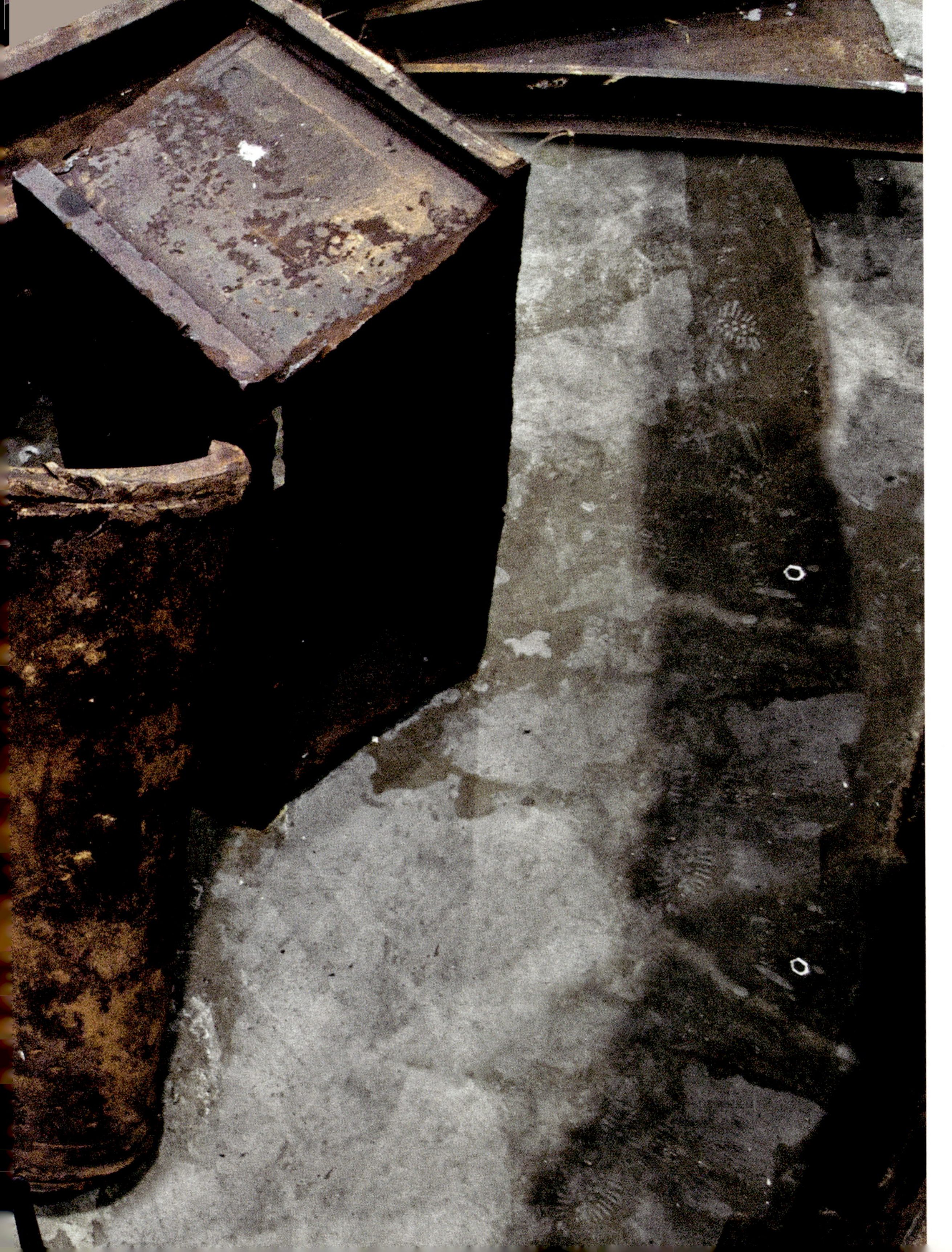

The likely origins of these steel plates are revealed by the welded seams along their edges, which indicate that they were attached to similar plates to make up structural, box beam columns.

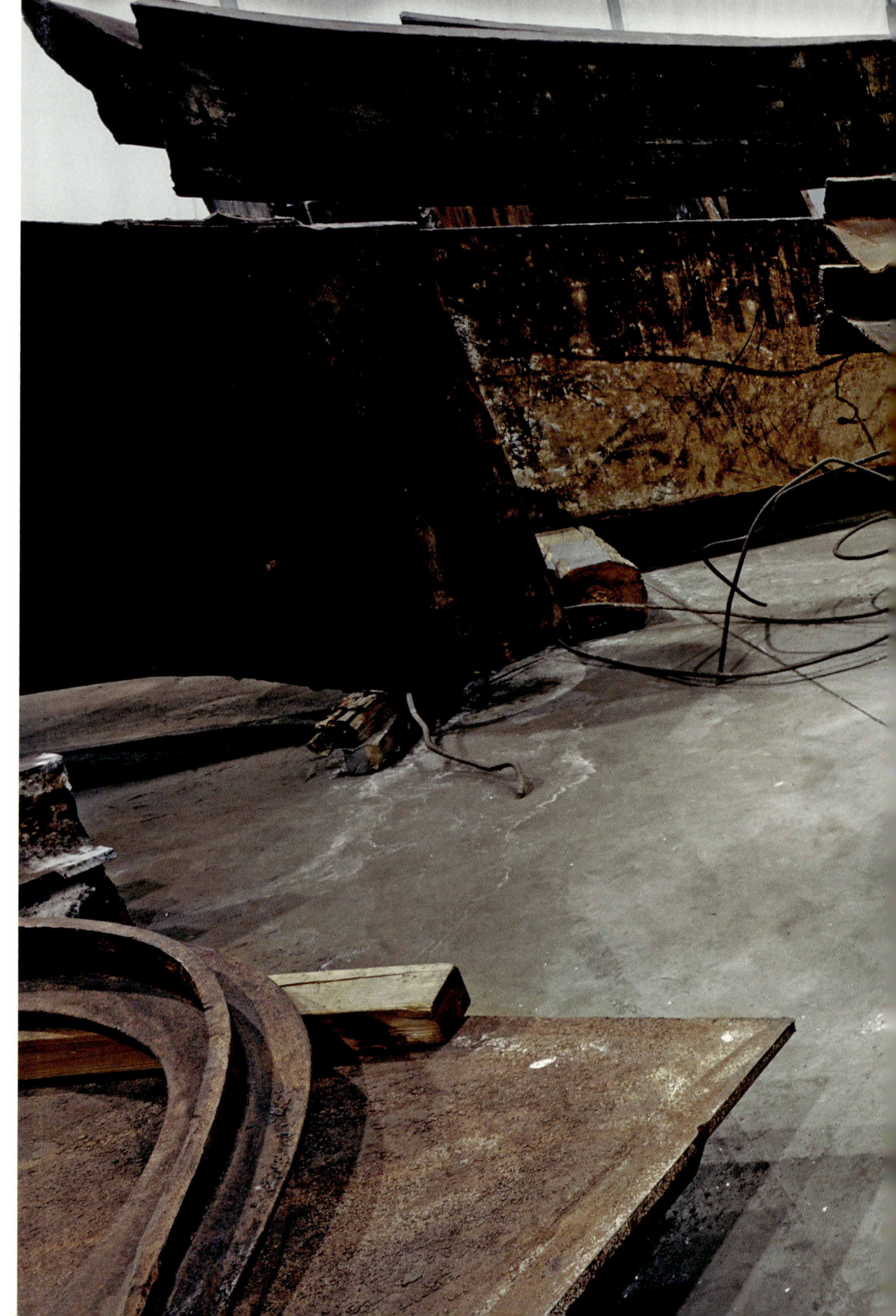

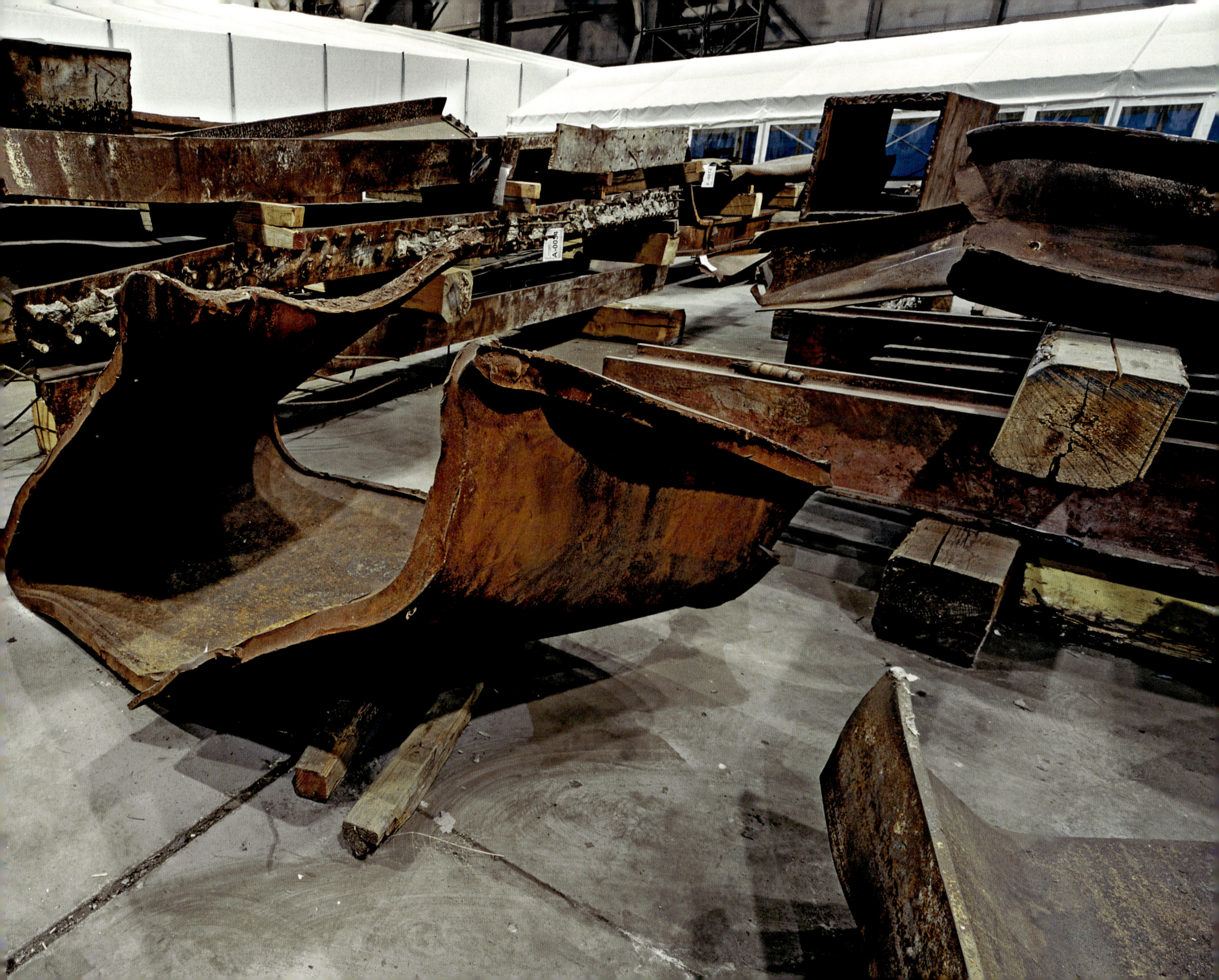

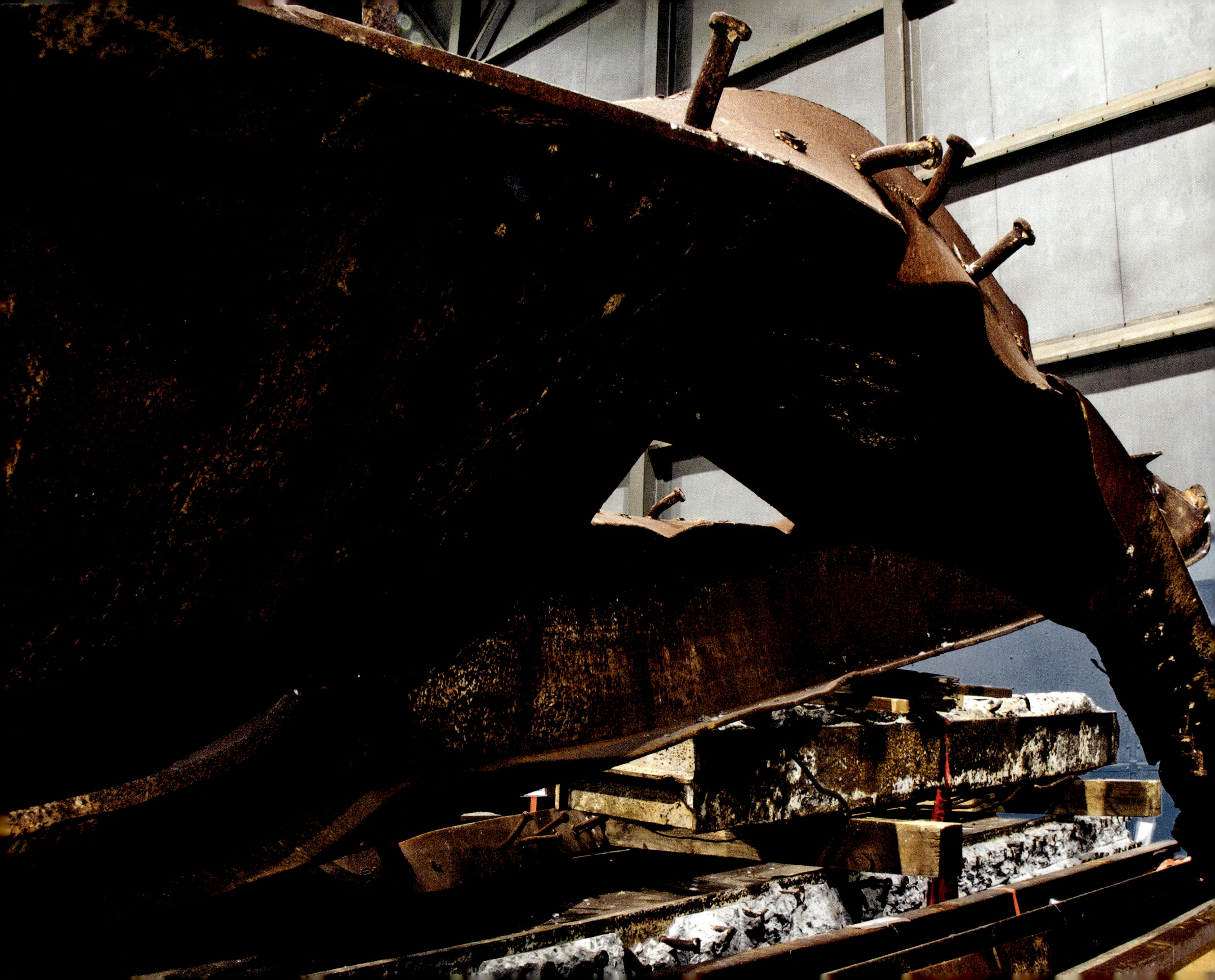

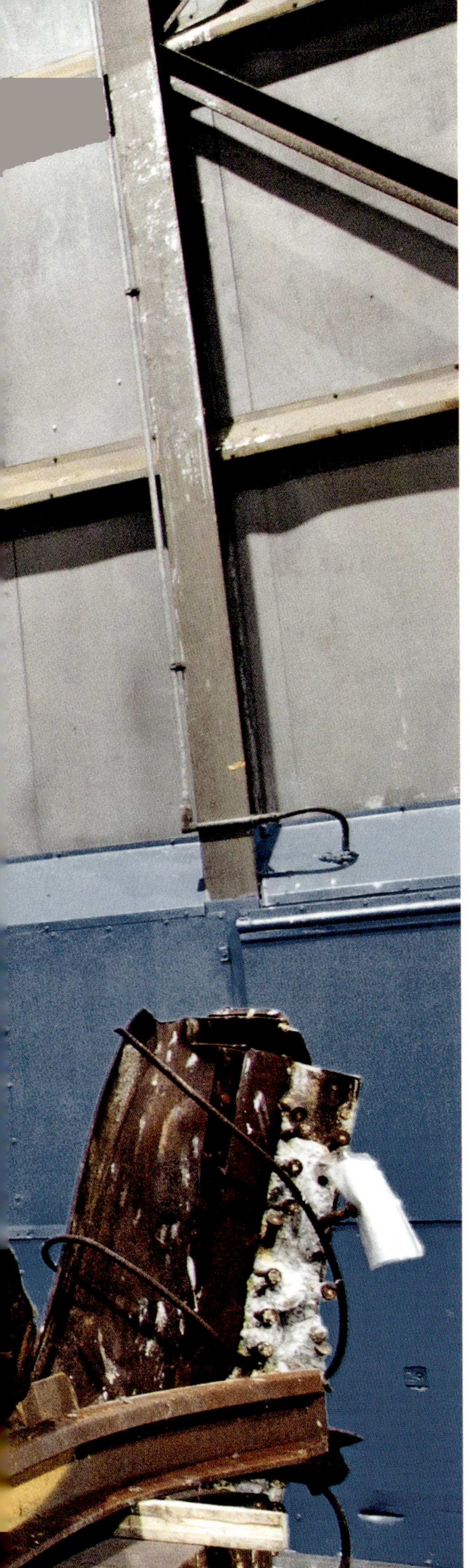

BENT PROPELLER BY ALEXANDER CALDER

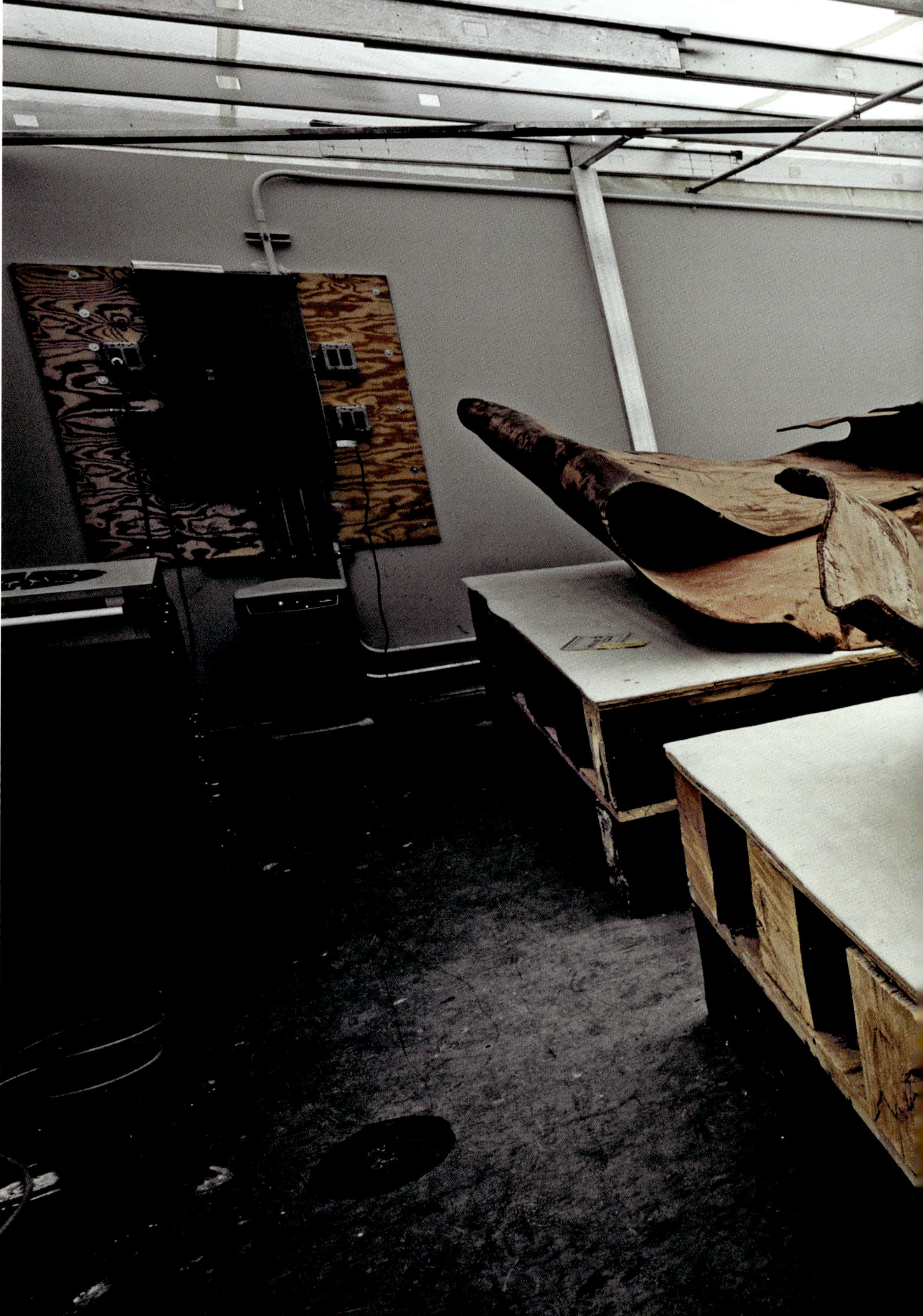

Remnants of a sculpture made by Alexander Calder, which was installed at the World Trade Center complex in 1971. Known as "Bent Propeller," the work was bright red and stood 25 feet tall. The recovery of these pieces raised hopes that the sculpture might be restored, but no other pieces were found.

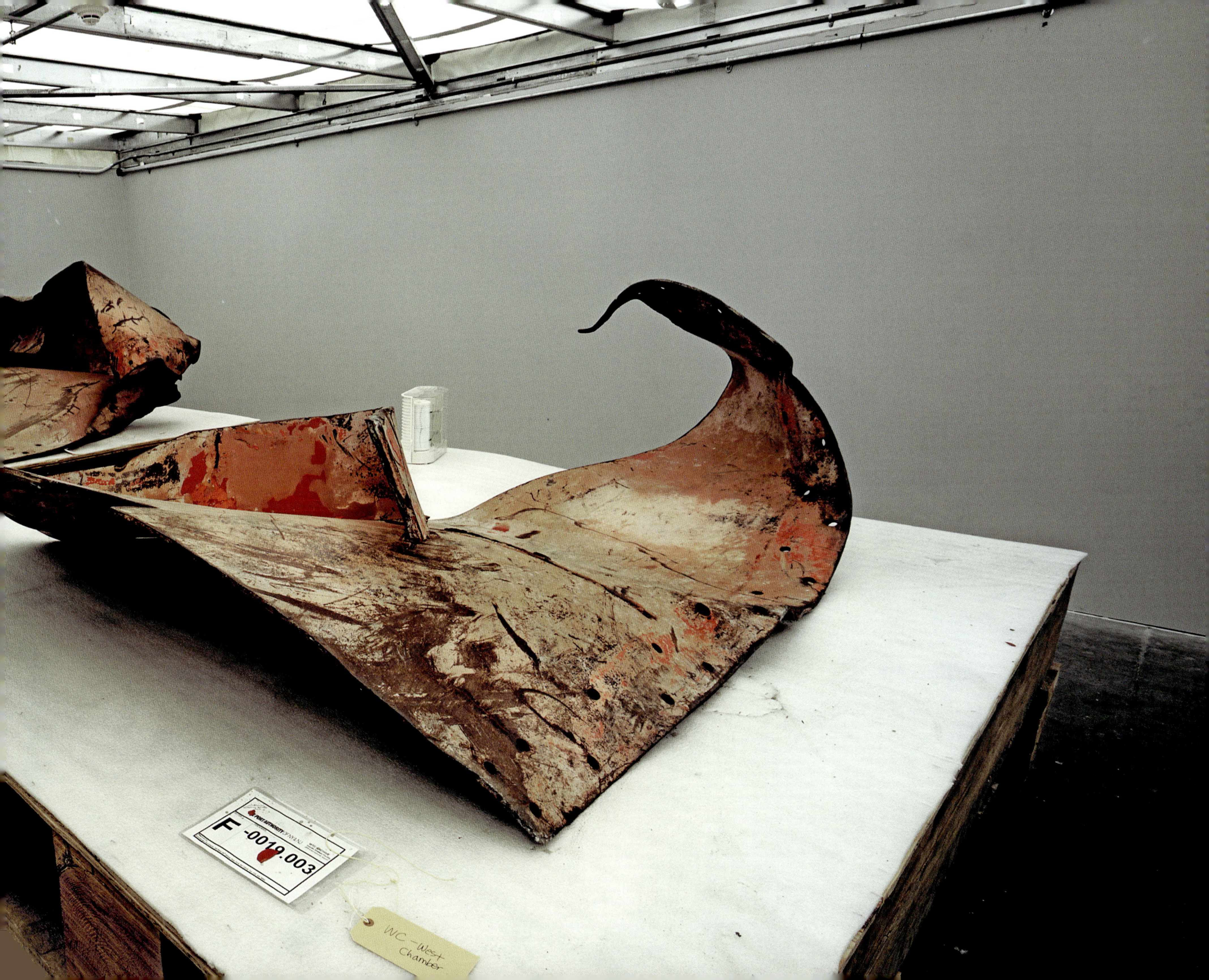
PORT AUTHORITY OF NY&NJ
F -0019.003
WC - West Chamber

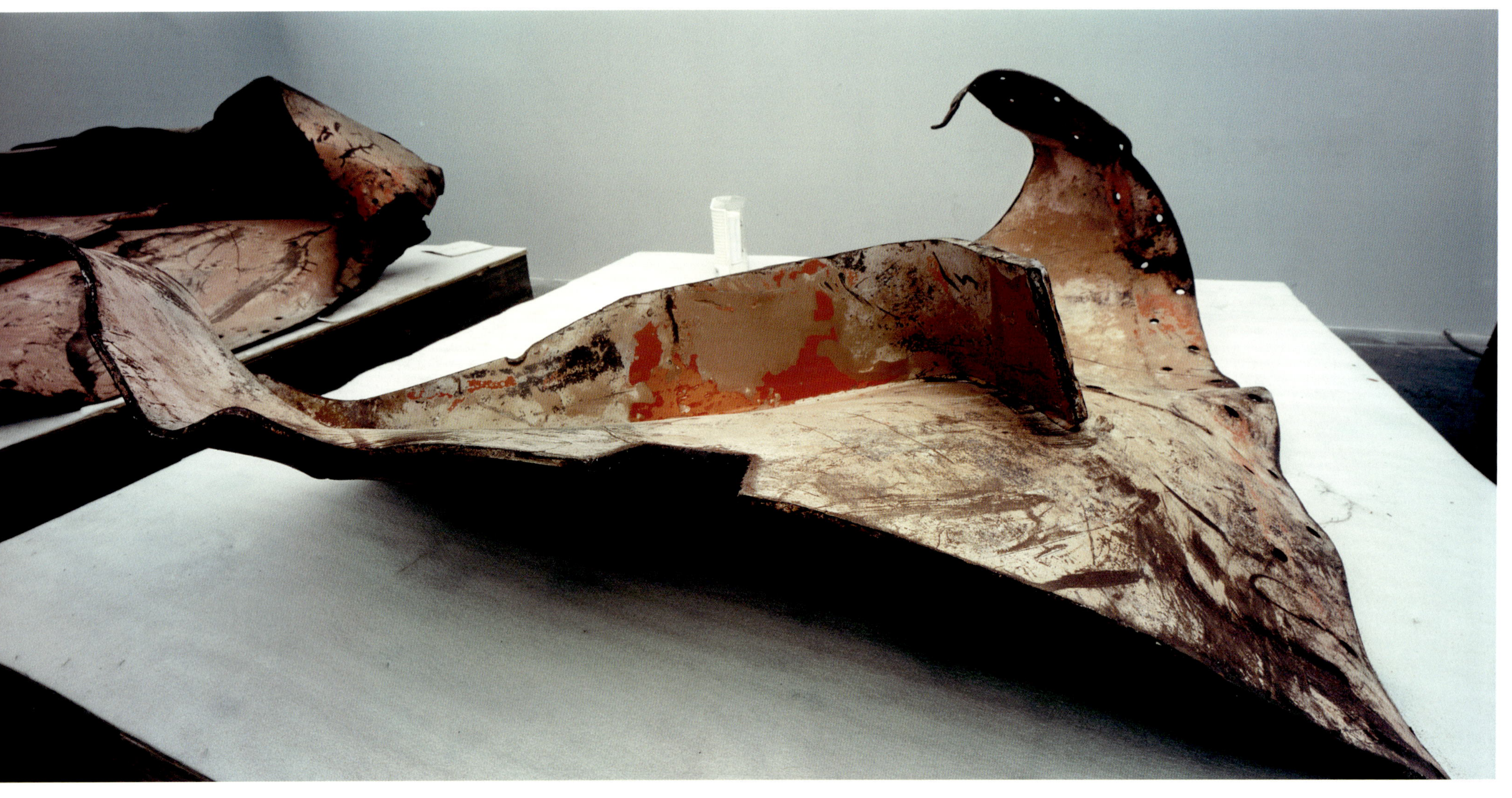

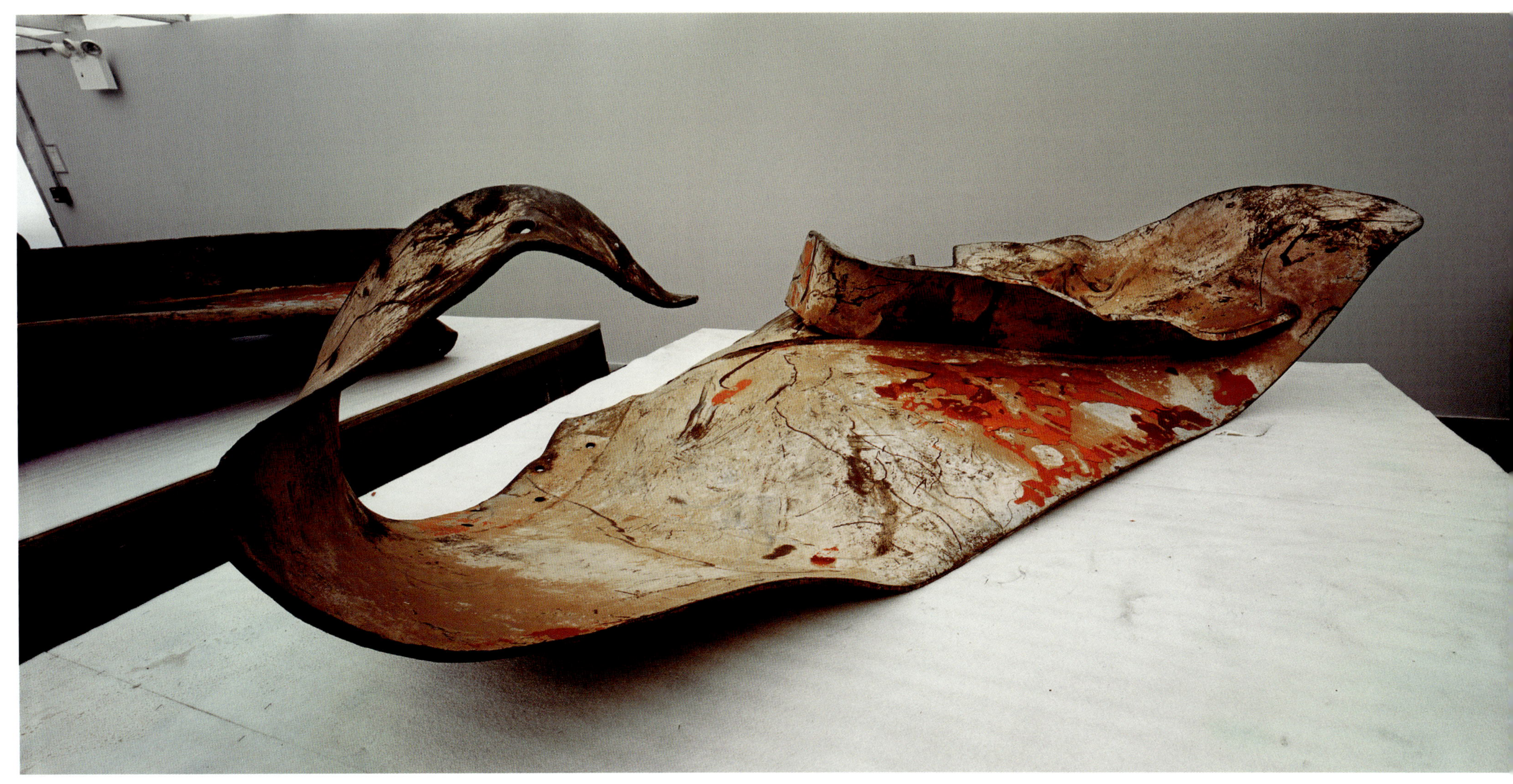

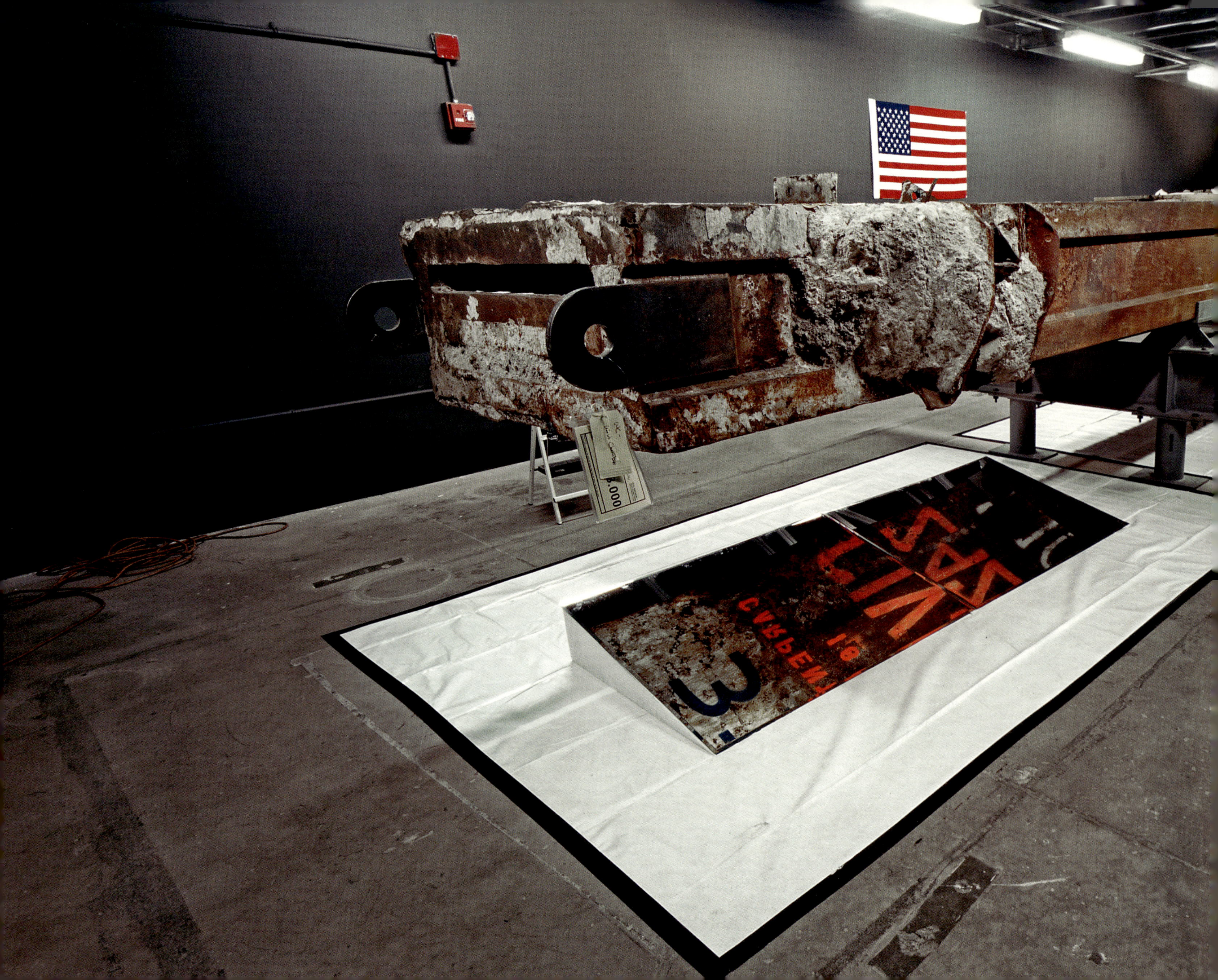

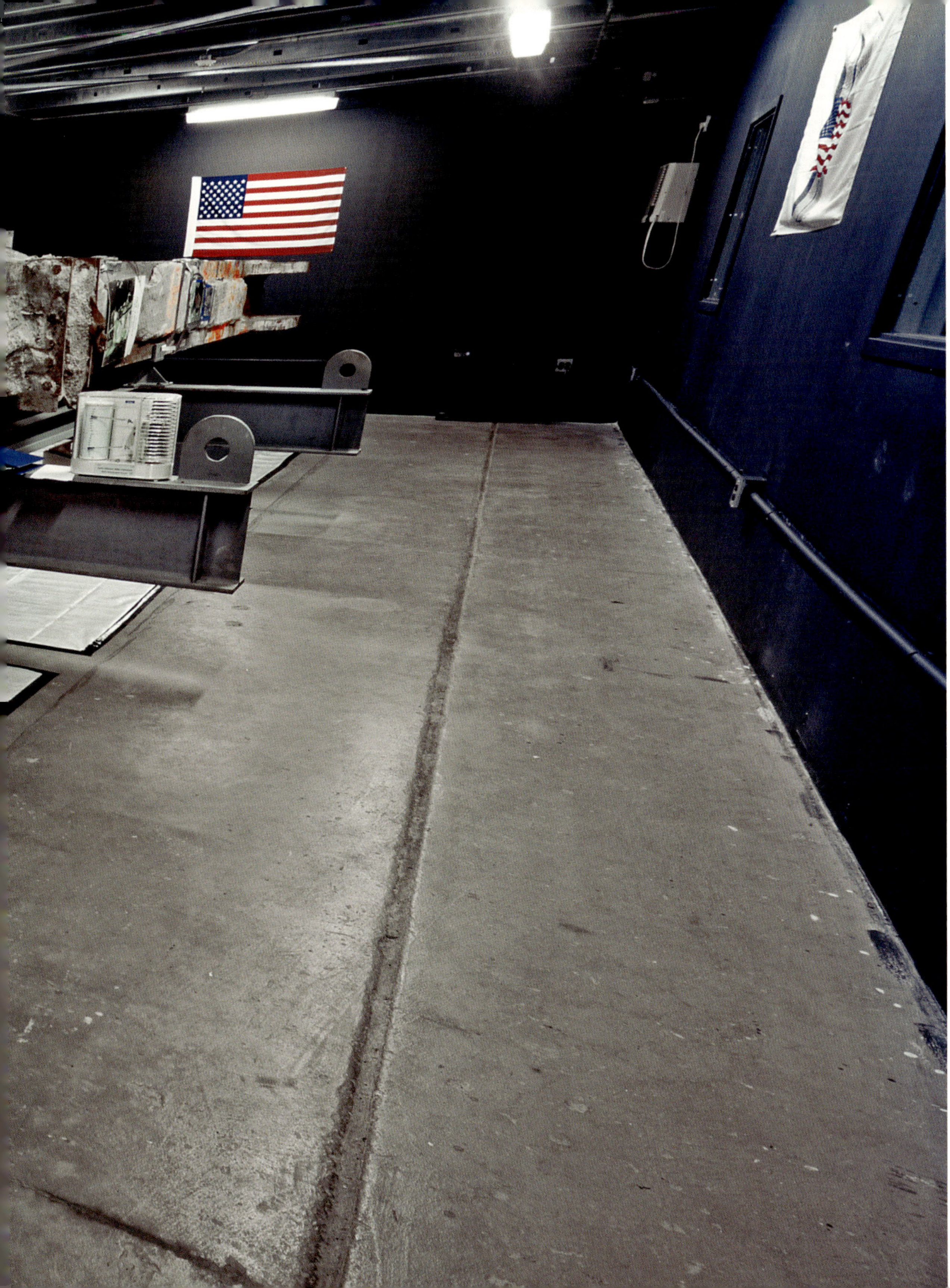

THE LAST COLUMN

The Last Column was the final piece of structural steel to be removed from the twin towers site, on May 30, 2002. Weighing 58 tons and measuring 37 feet long, the Last Column was a section of one of the 47 interior structural columns that spanned the south tower, from six stories below ground to 110 stories in the air. After the remains of three of their colleagues were found near the column in March 2002, members of Fire Department, City of New York (FDNY) Squad 41 spray-painted "SQ 41" on the beam, as a marker to continue the search for the remains of three other colleagues. Eventually, the remains of all six firefighters were found: Lieutenant Michael K. Healey, 42; and Firefighters Thomas Patrick Cullen III, 31; Robert W. Hamilton, 43; Michael J. Lyons, 32; Gregory Sikorsky, 34; and R. Bruce Van Hine, 48.

That first marking on the Last Column attracted many others, as workers and family members covered the column with individual memorial markers and personalized messages. By the time excavation reached the Last Column's base, it had become a memorial icon. The last structural piece of the towers standing, it was cut down and lowered onto a flatbed truck, shrouded in black, and covered with an American flag. As it was slowly driven up the ramp, the Last Column was accompanied by a uniformed honor guard, and bagpipers played "America the Beautiful."

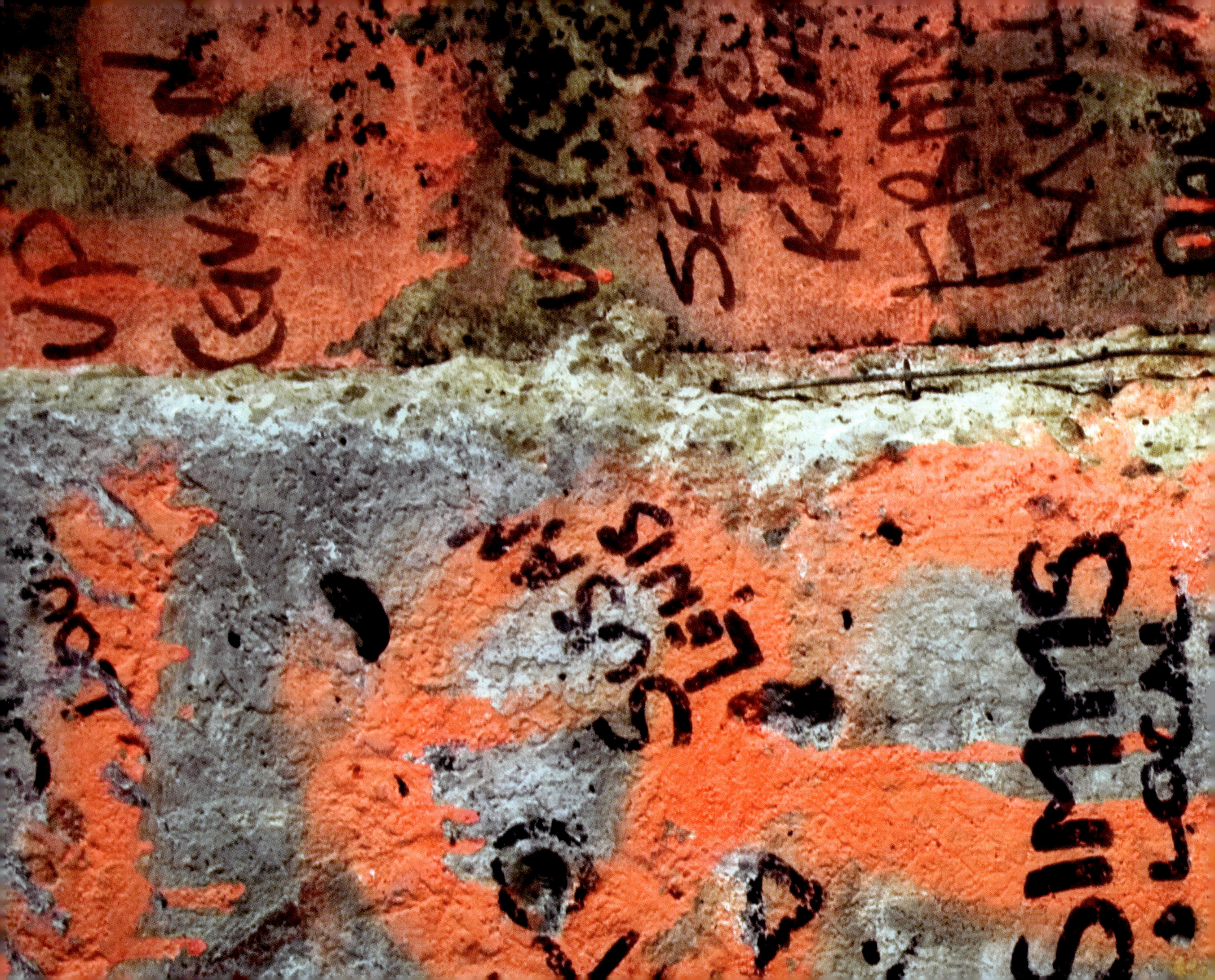

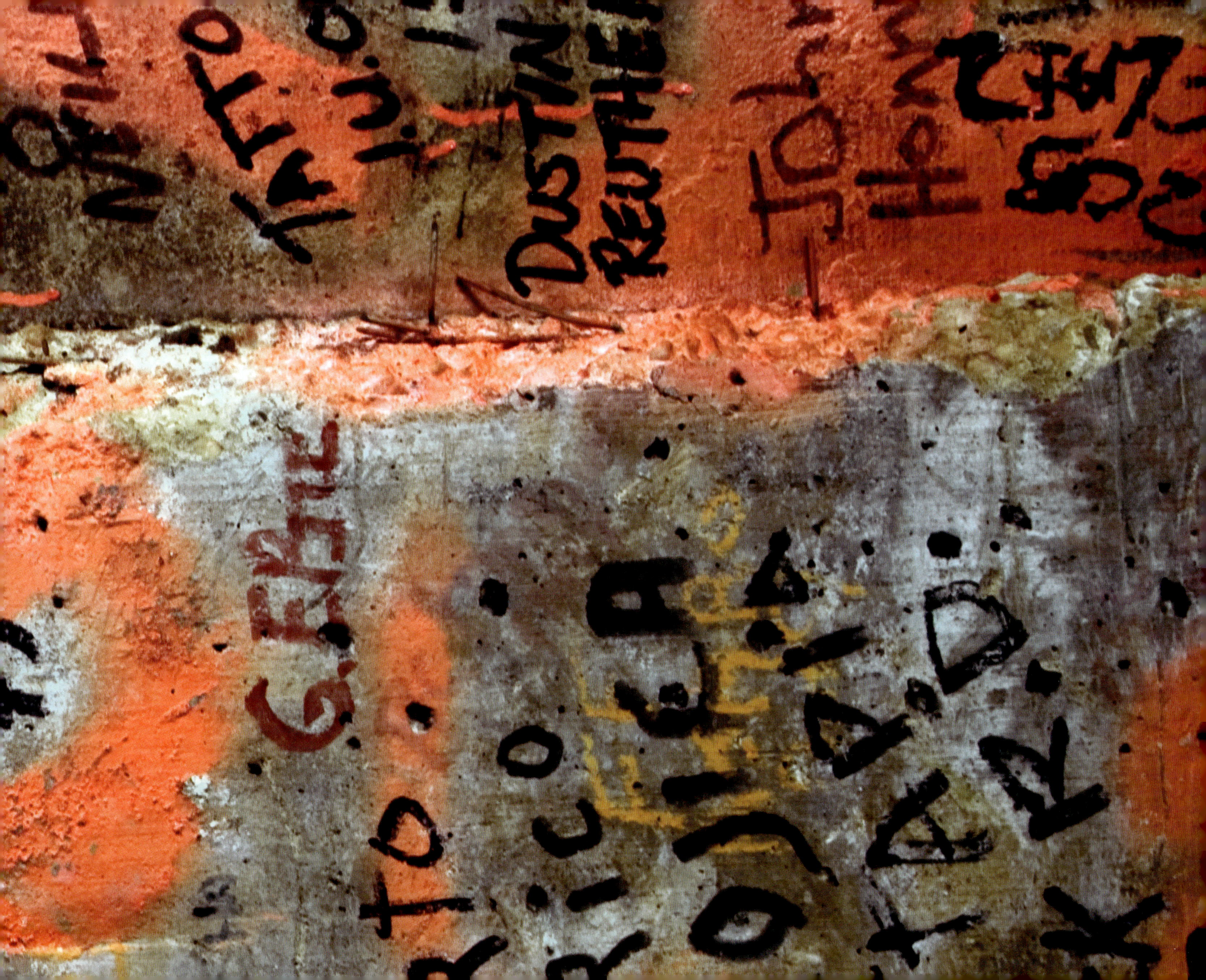

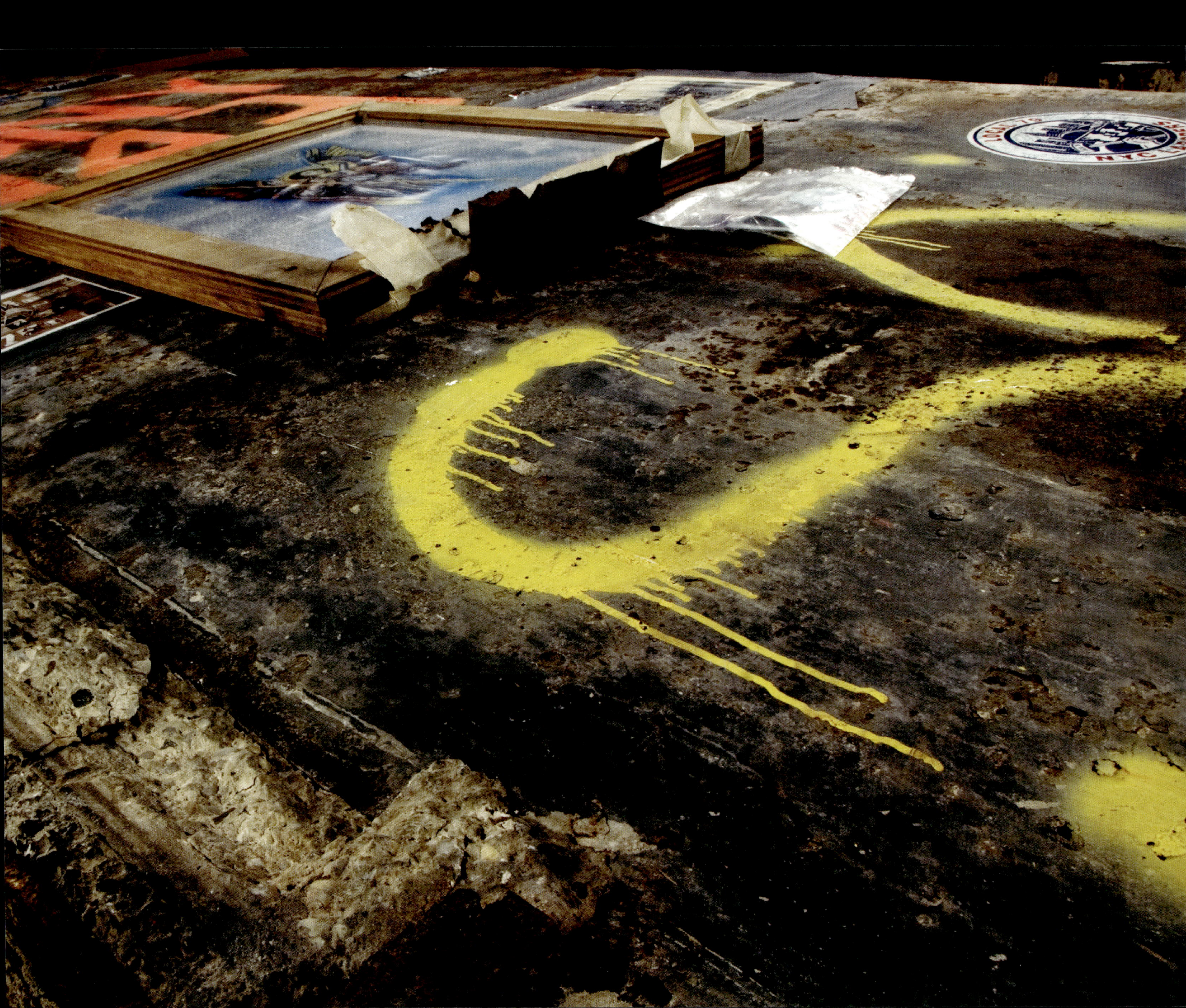

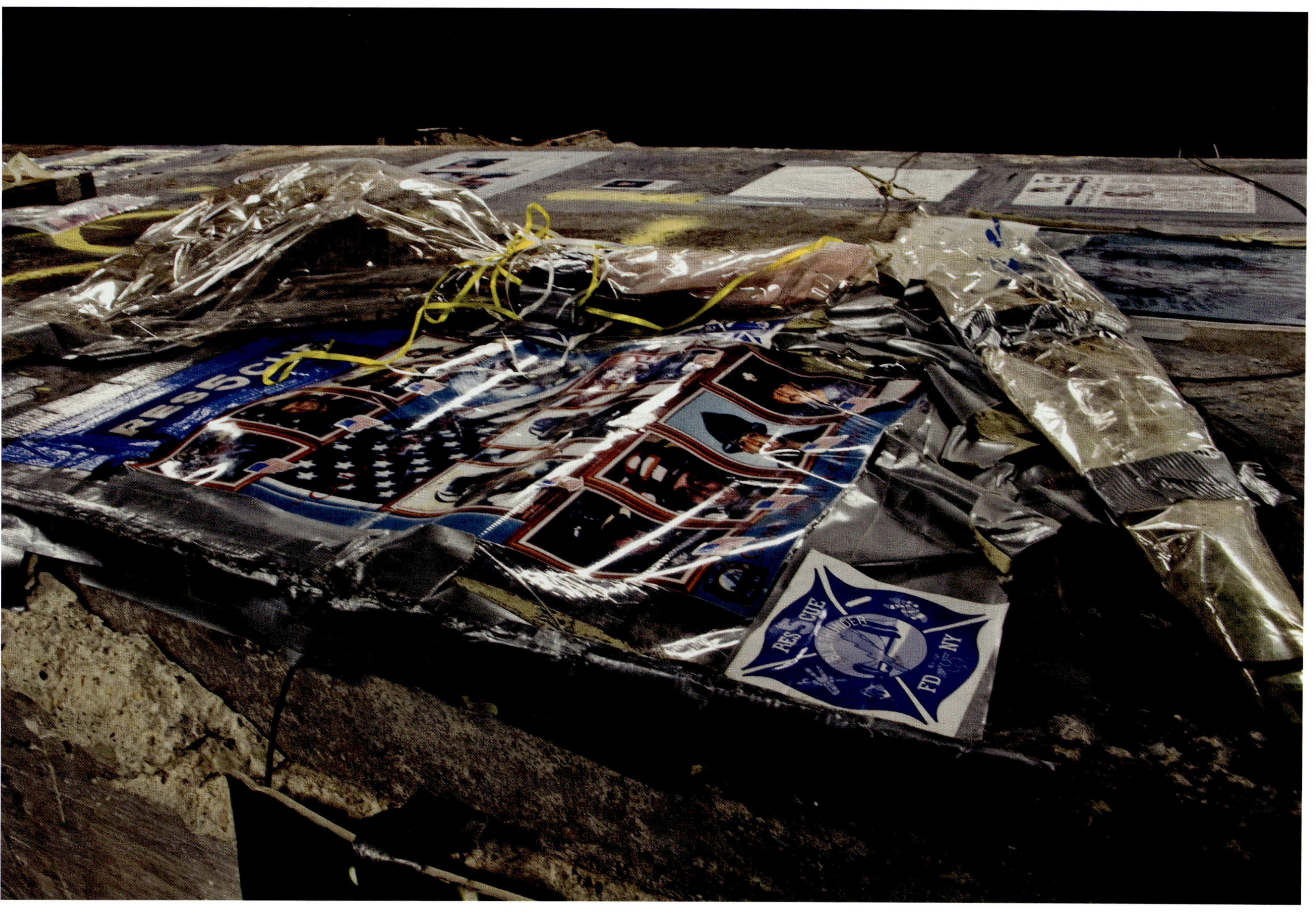

Air and water damaged the surface of the Last Column, which was originally an inner-core beam and not factory-finished for external exposure. Fortunately, extensive conservation efforts stabilized the beam and allowed for the preservation of the writings and memorial items attached to it.

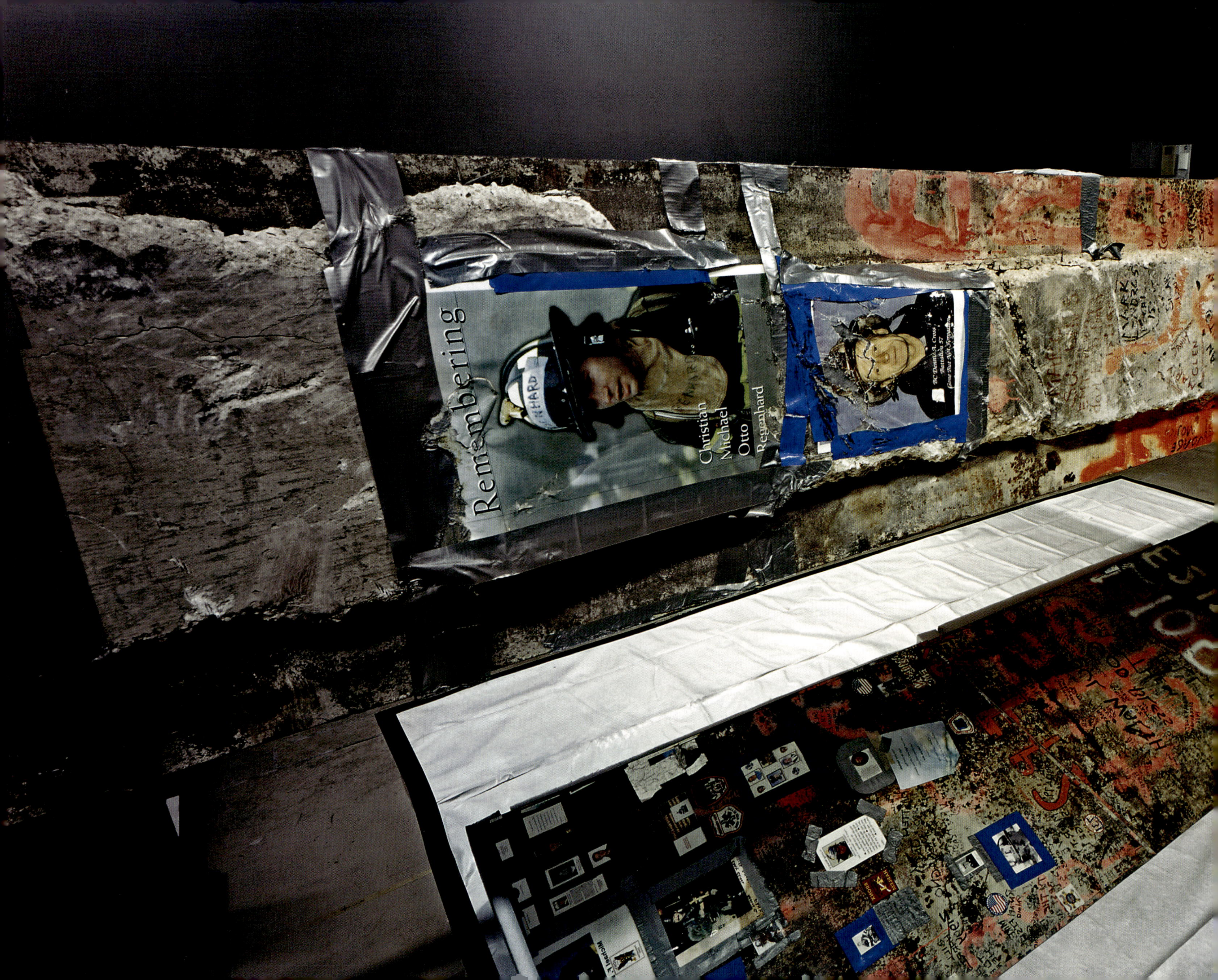
Remembering
Christian
Michael
Otto
Regenhard

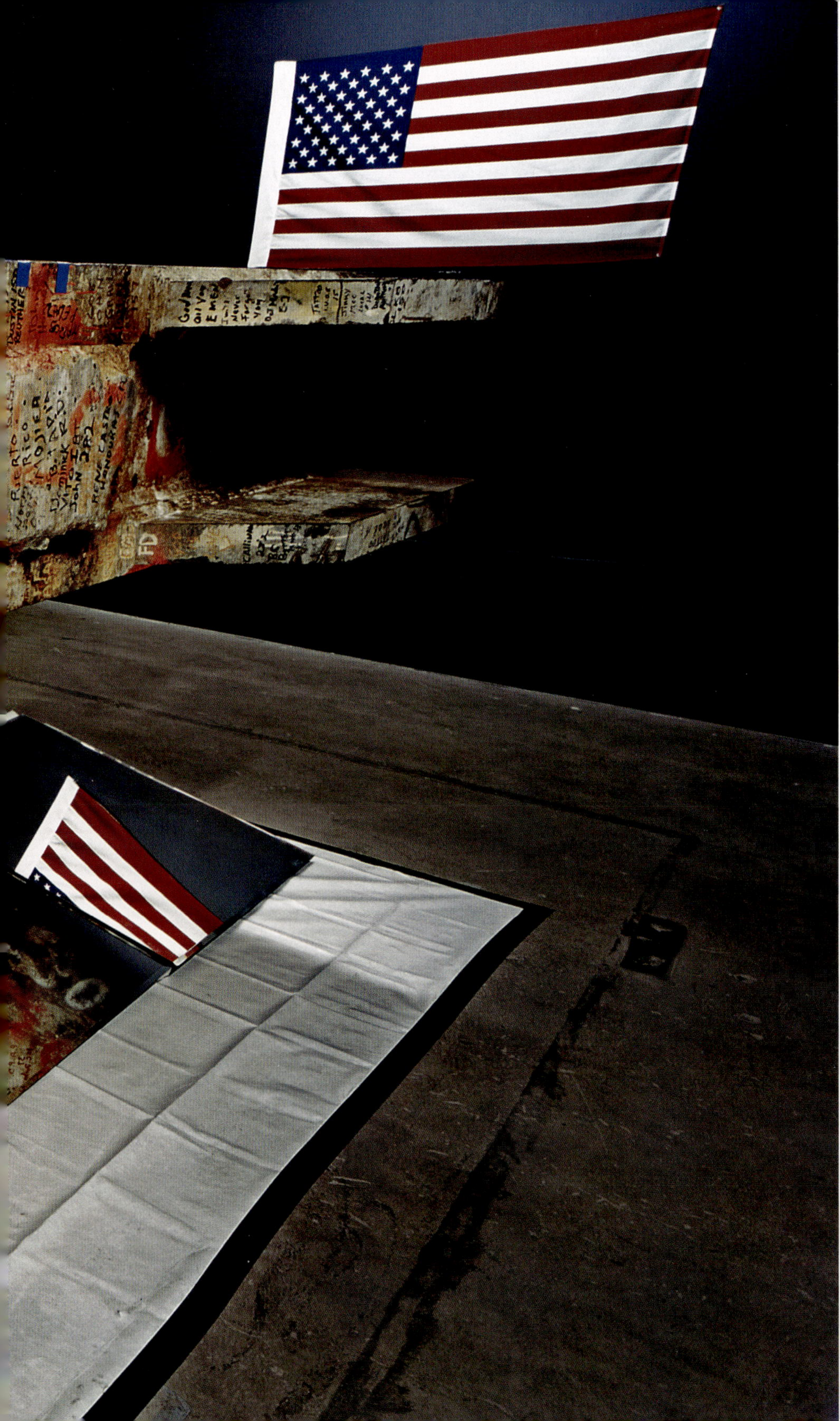

Because the Last Column had inscriptions and attachments on all sides, it was raised onto a specially constructed steel cradle at Hangar 17 so conservators had enough clearance to work. A mirror provides a glimpse of tributes on the underside of the column. Visible on the facing side are the taped-on memorials for Firefighter Christian Regenhard, 28, and Deputy Battalion Chief Dennis Cross, 60.

VEHICLES

The collapse of the twin towers created a series of iconic objects, transformed by force and fire from their daily uses into artifacts that tell a story. At Hangar 17, tented enclosures were built for artifacts of various kinds that, in the view of curators and conservators, needed the added protection of humidity control and stillness. Perhaps the most dramatic example of this transformation could be found inside the vehicle tent, where trucks and cars, normally left outside in all conditions, were given shelter.

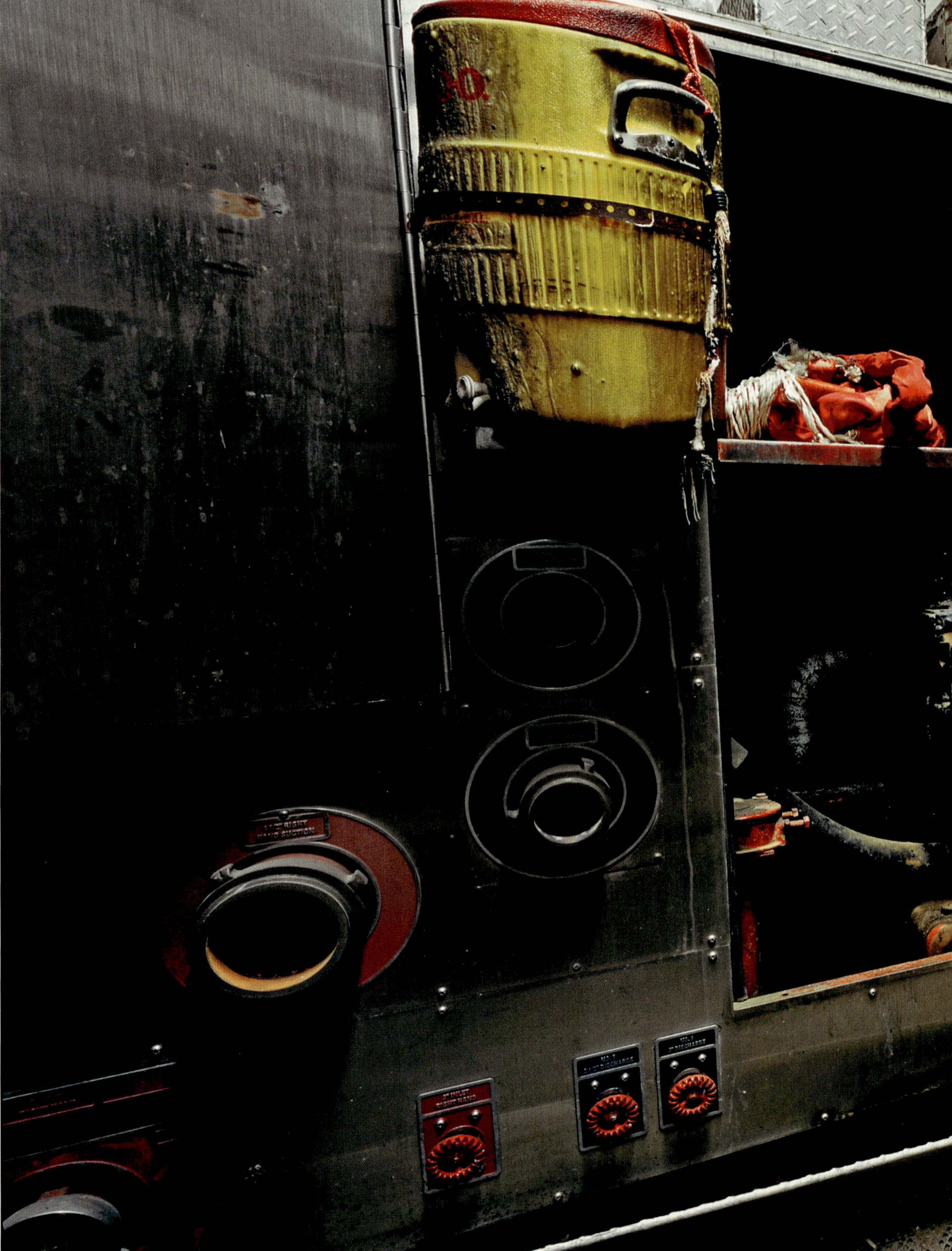

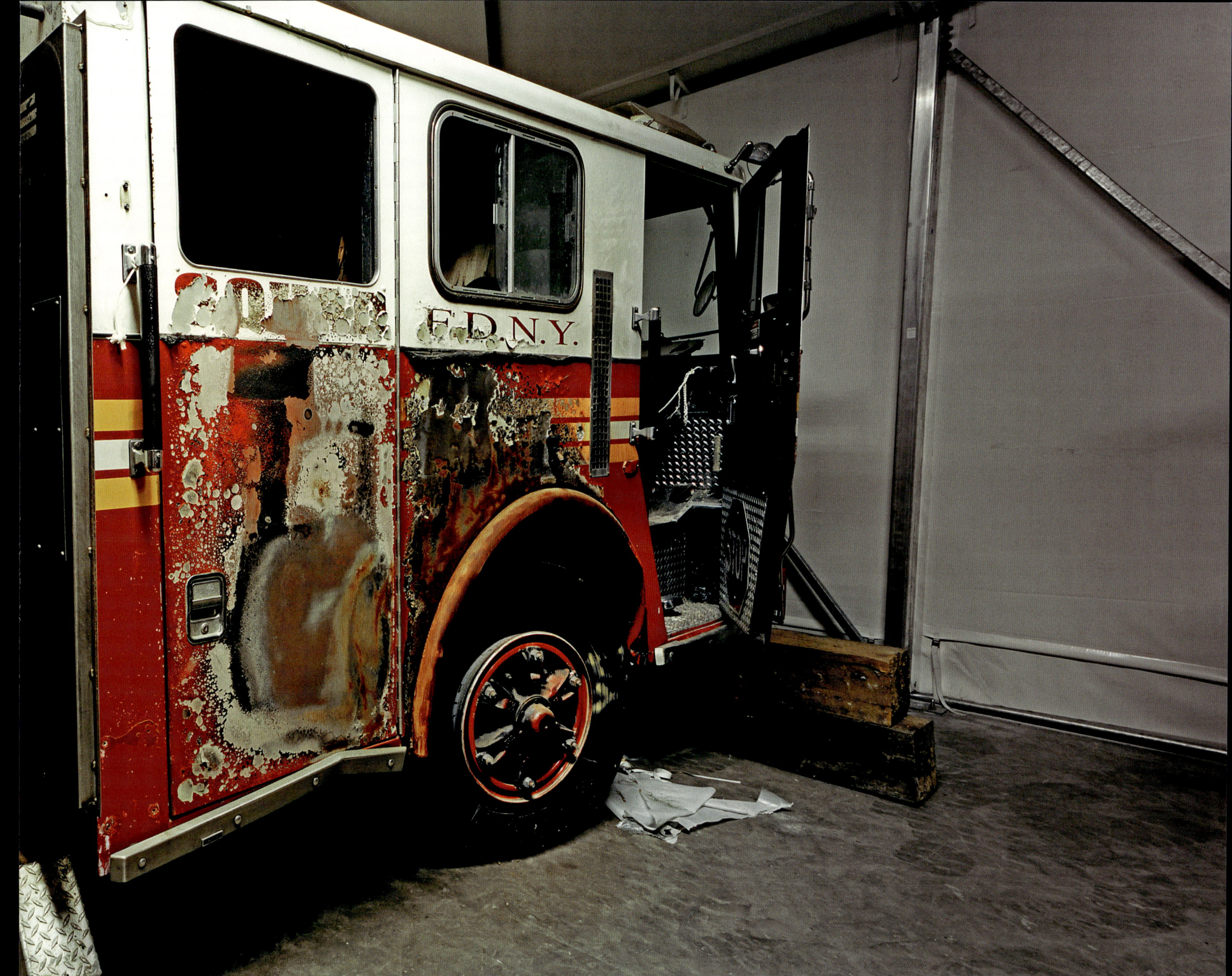
F.D.N.Y.

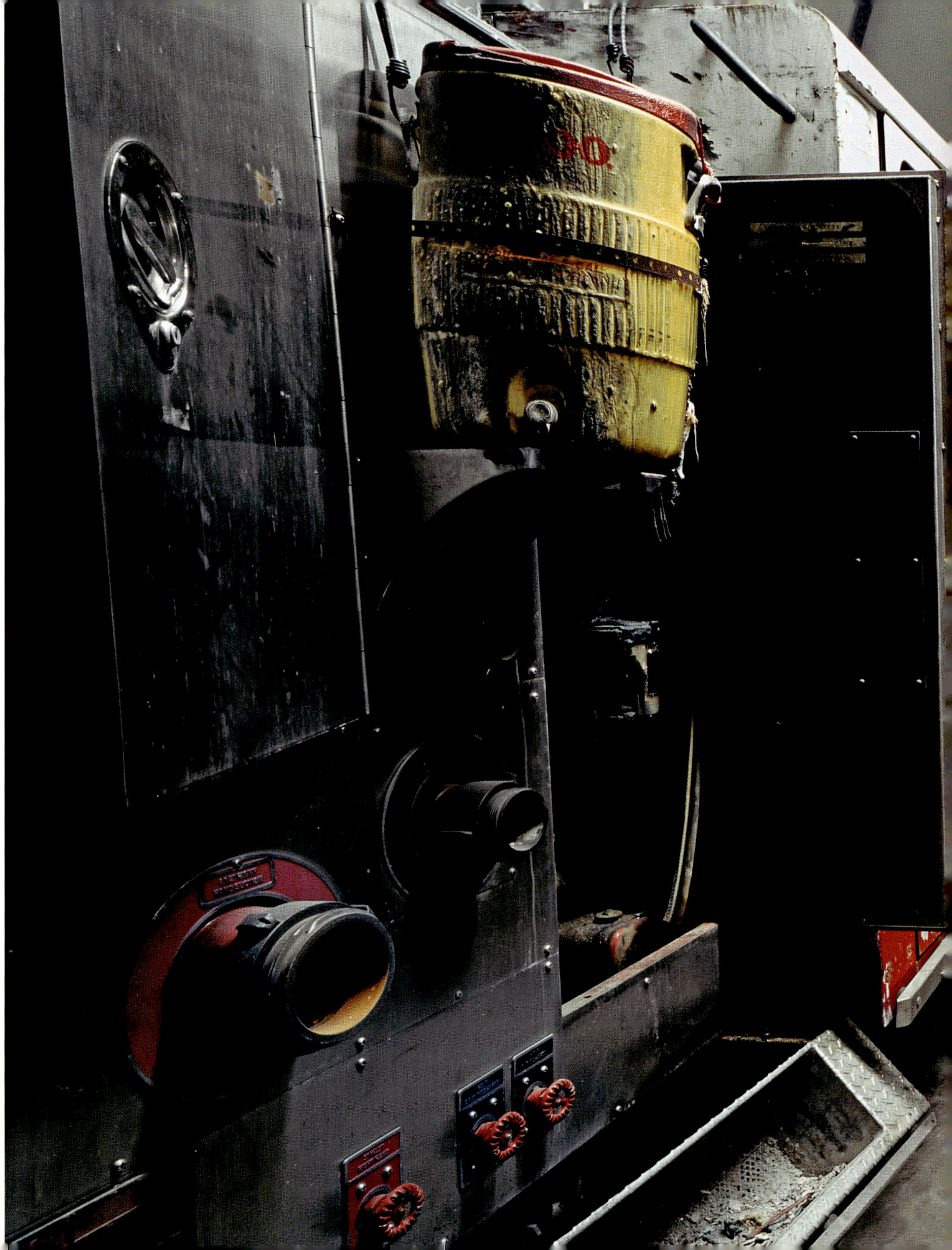

Truck on the left: The truck belonging to FDNY Squad 270. No members of this company died on 9/11.

Truck on the right: Engine Company 21 responded to the WTC attacks from its house on Manhattan's East Side. Captain William F. (Billy) Burke, Jr., 46, was on the 27th floor of the north tower, clearing the building, when he learned of the south tower's collapse. He ordered his fellow firefighters to evacuate the building, telling them he would meet them back at their truck. Burke stayed behind to assist Ed Beyea, 42, a wheelchair-bound computer programmer for Empire BlueCross BlueShield. Beyea, Abe Zelmanowitz, 55, his friend and co-worker, and Captain Burke had reached the 21st floor when the building collapsed. Burke would be the only member of Engine 21 killed on 9/11.

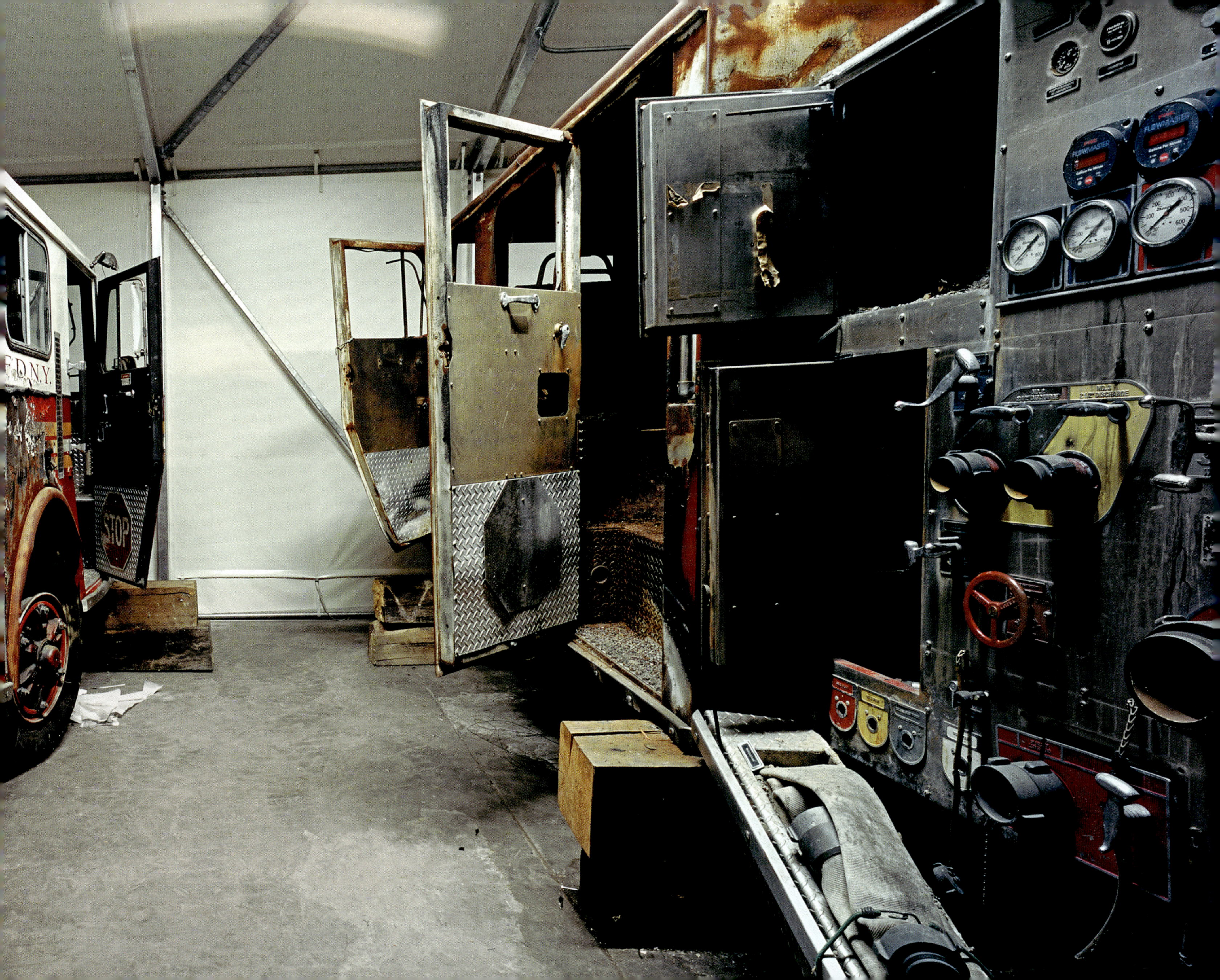
F.D.N.Y.
STOP

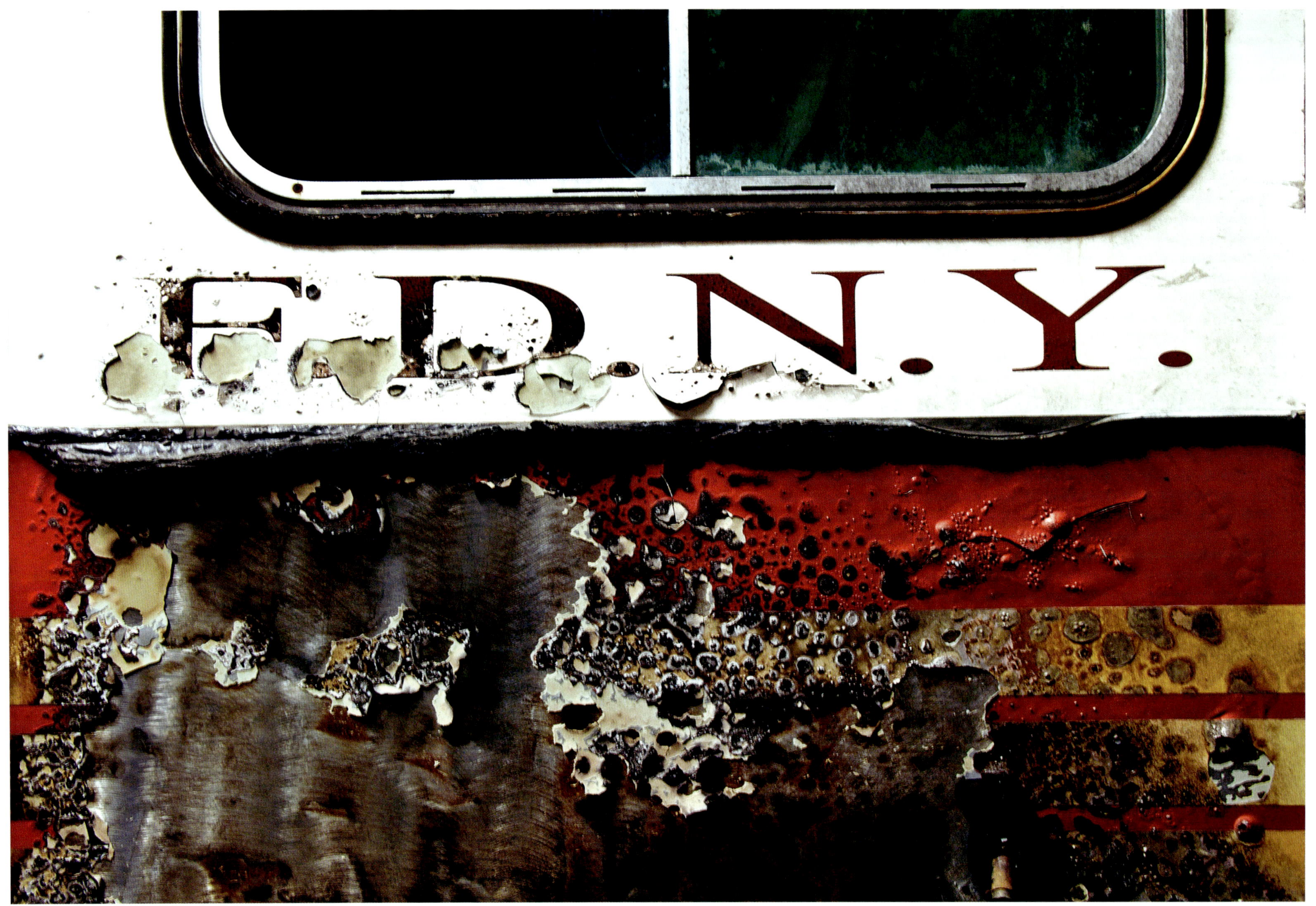
F.D.N.Y.

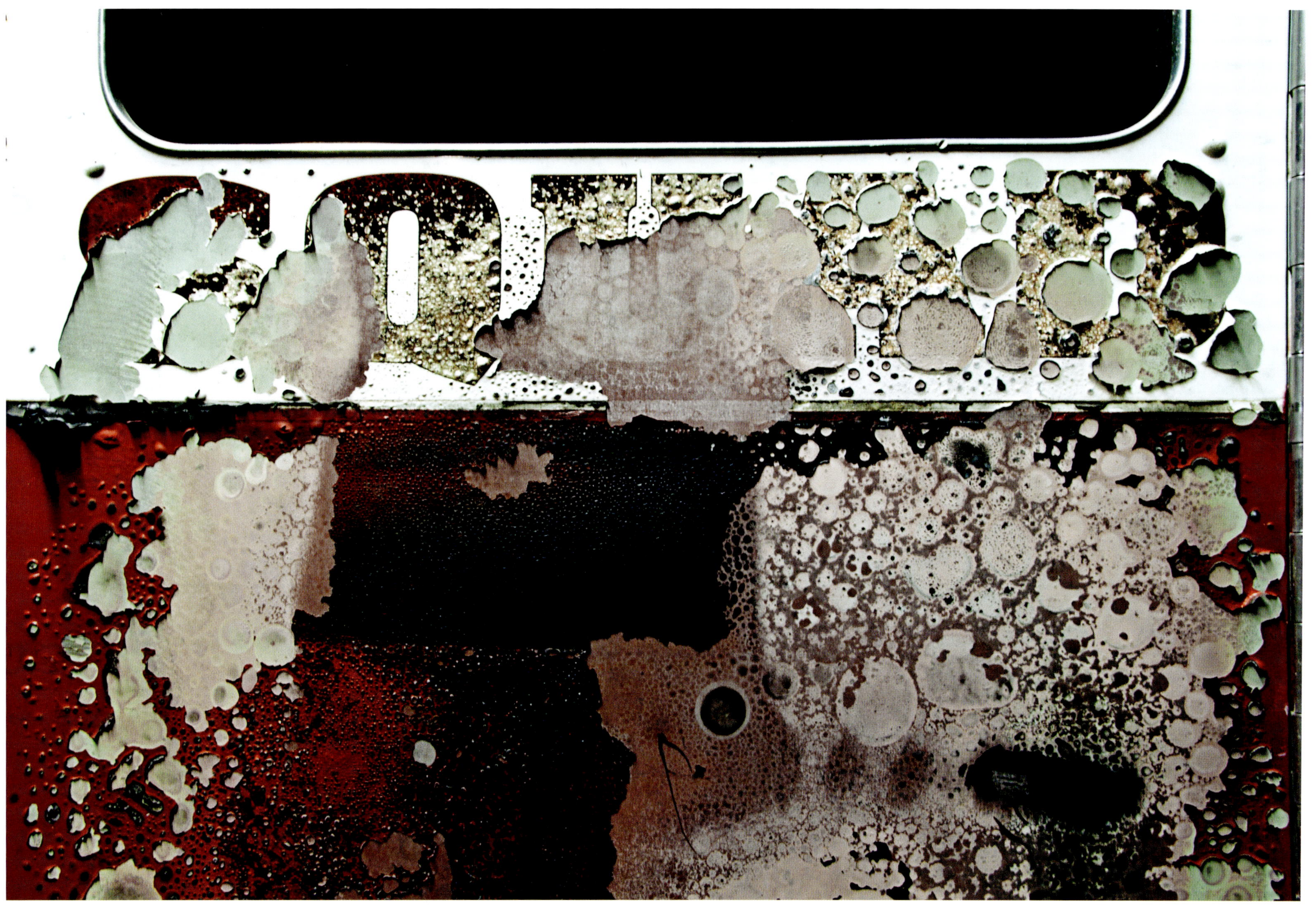

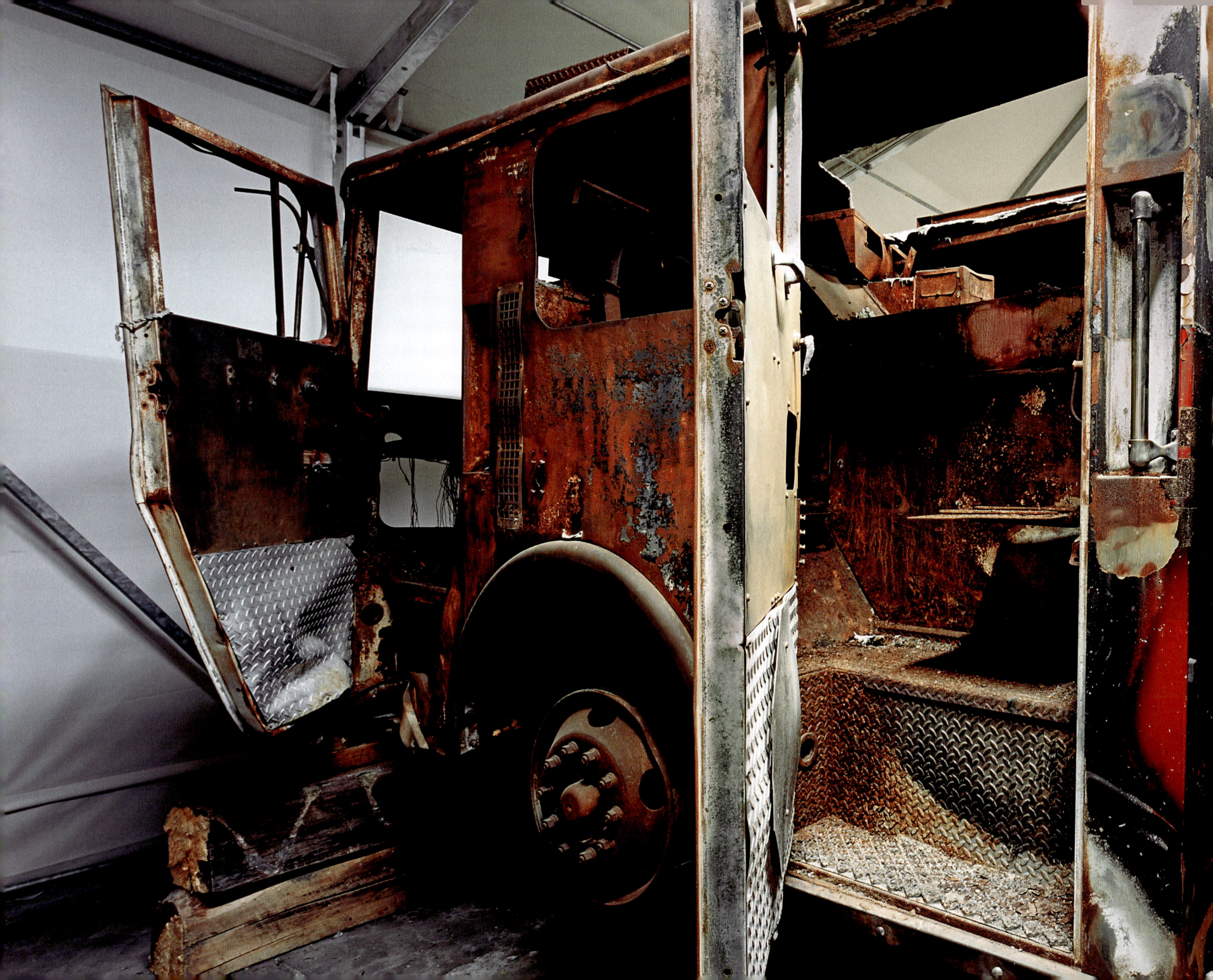

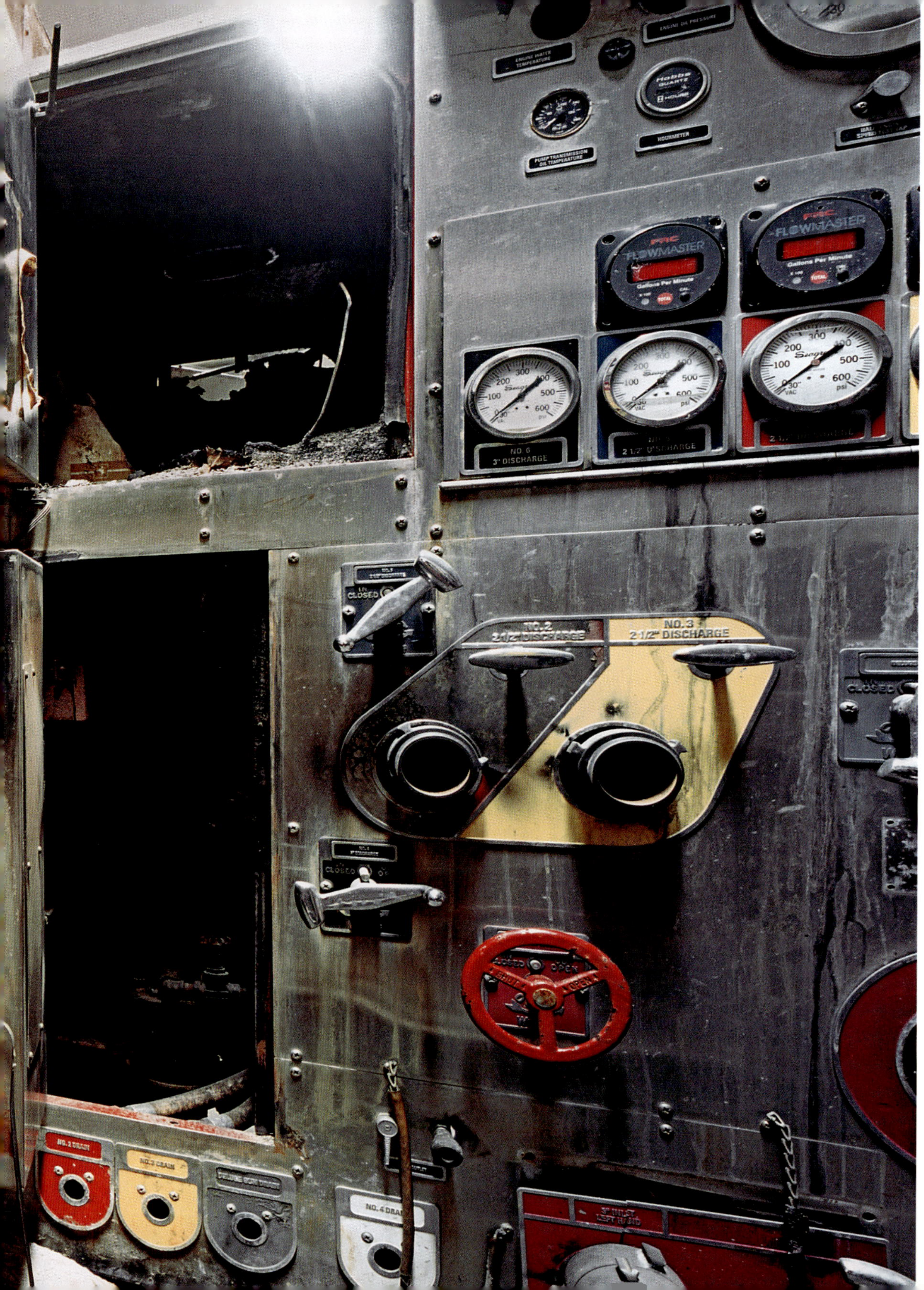

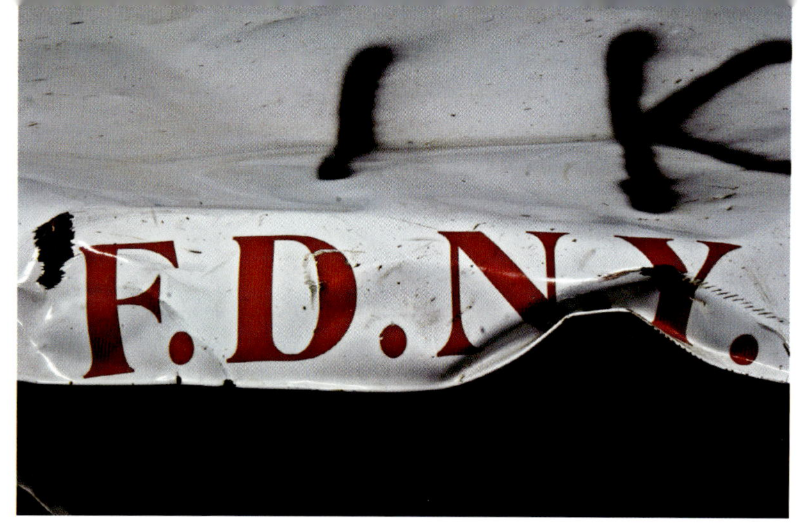
F.D.N.Y.

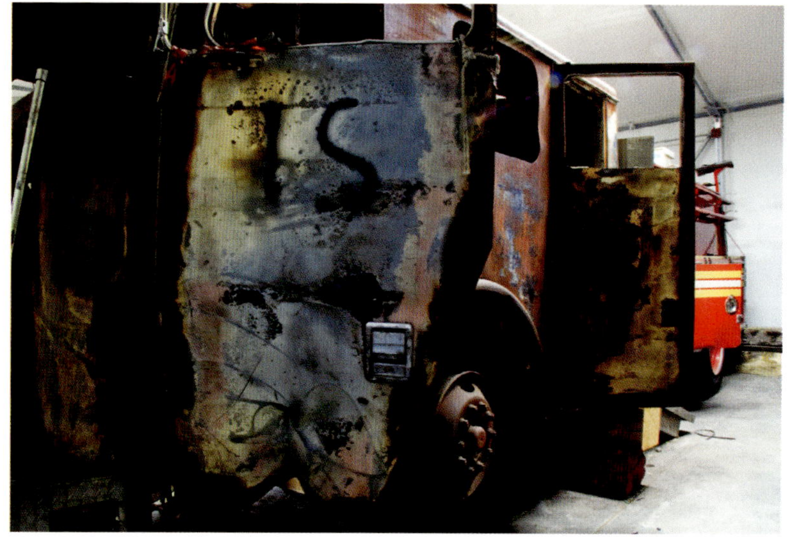

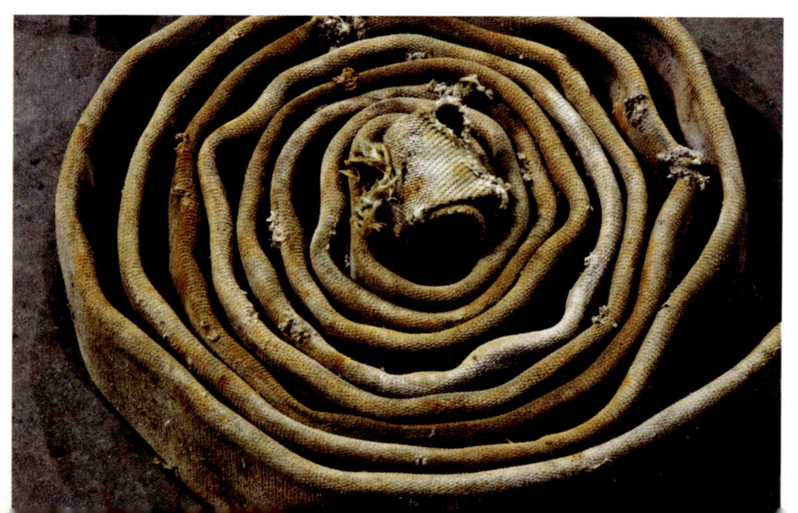

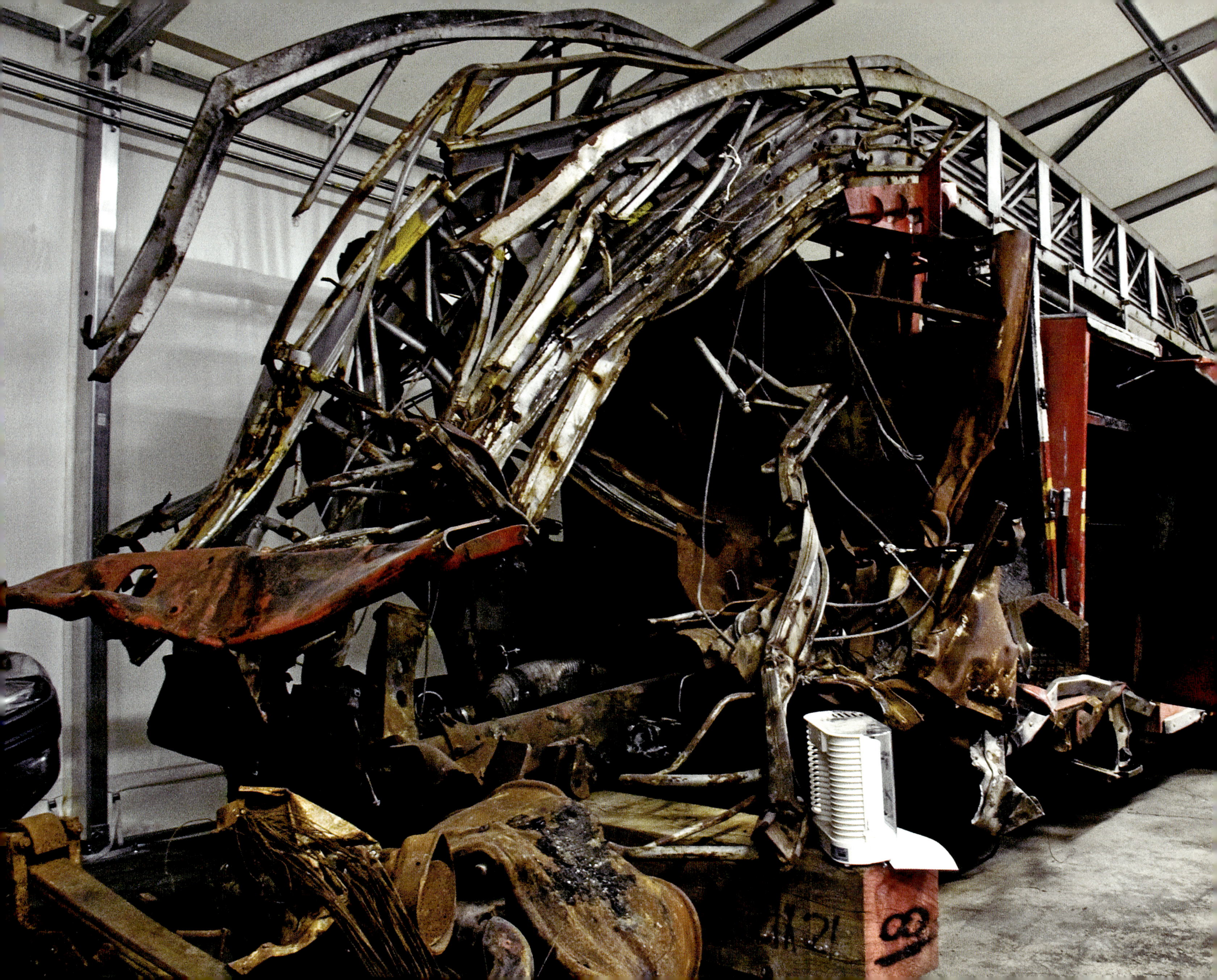

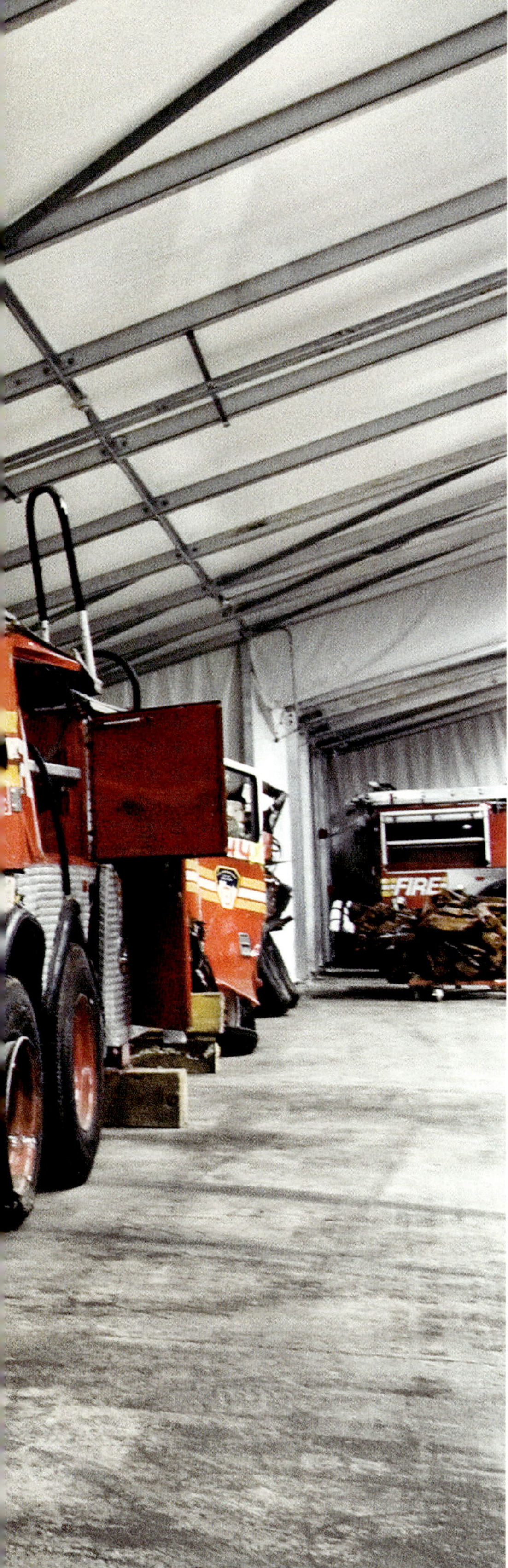

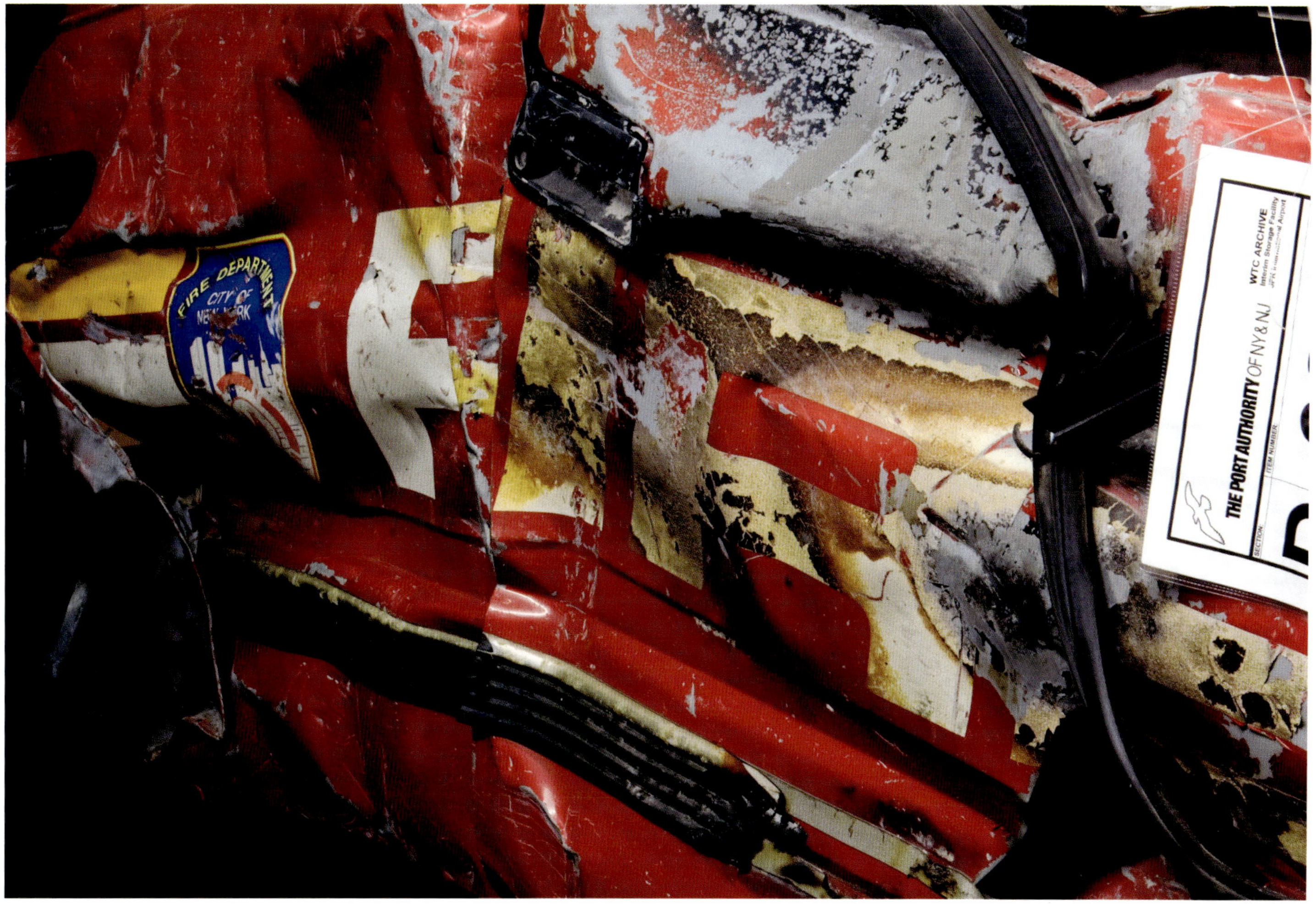

September 11, 2001, had a playful start for the firefighters of Ladder Company 3, located in New York's East Village neighborhood. A local television station was in the firehouse early, taping a cooking demonstration. Because the shift change was scheduled for 9 a.m., crews from both shifts responded when a call came in from a dormitory at New York University. The second alarm from the World Trade Center brought the firefighters from Ladder 3 to the scene. From radio transmissions inside the north tower stairwell, it is thought that they reached somewhere above the 35th floor when the building collapsed. All were killed: Battalion Chief John P. Williamson, 43; Captain Patrick "Paddy" J. Brown, 48; Lieutenant Kevin W. Donnelly, 43; Firefighters Michael T. Carroll, 39; James Raymond Coyle, 26; Gerard P. Dewan, 35; Jeffrey John Giordano, 45; Joseph E. Maloney, 45; John Kevin McAvoy, 47; Timothy Patrick McSweeney, 37; Joseph J. Ogren, 30; and Steven John Olson, 38.

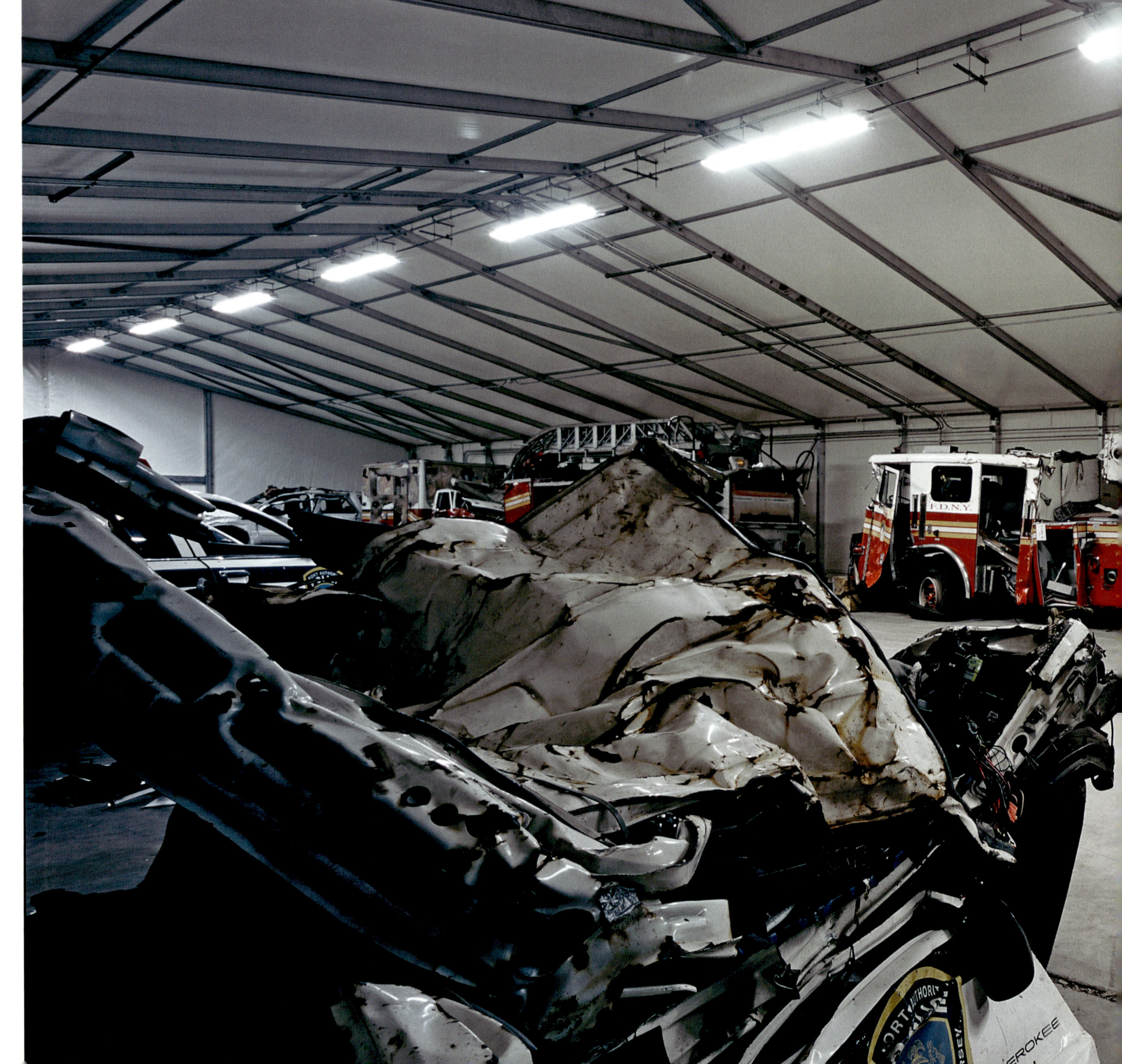
F.D.N.Y.

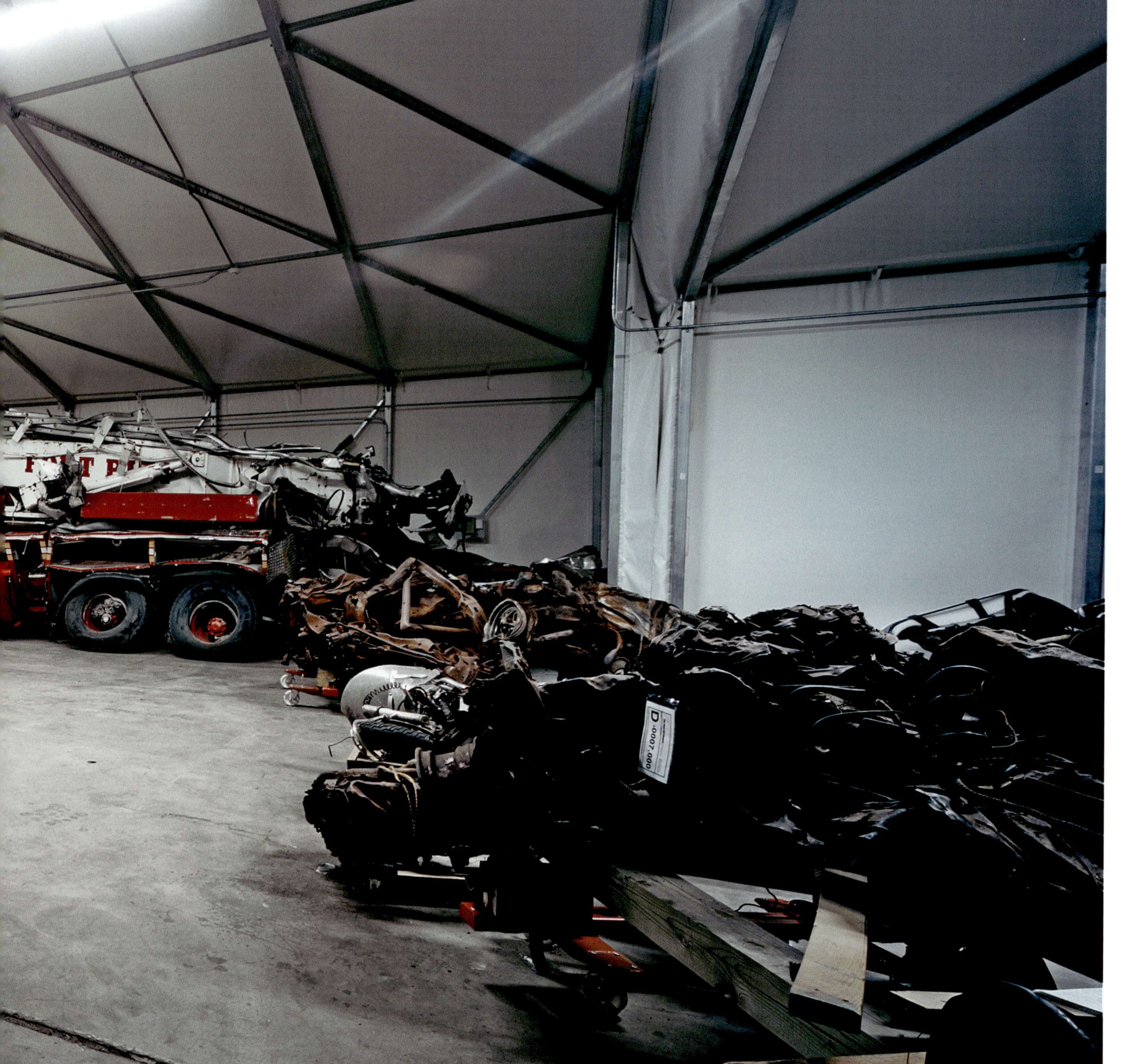

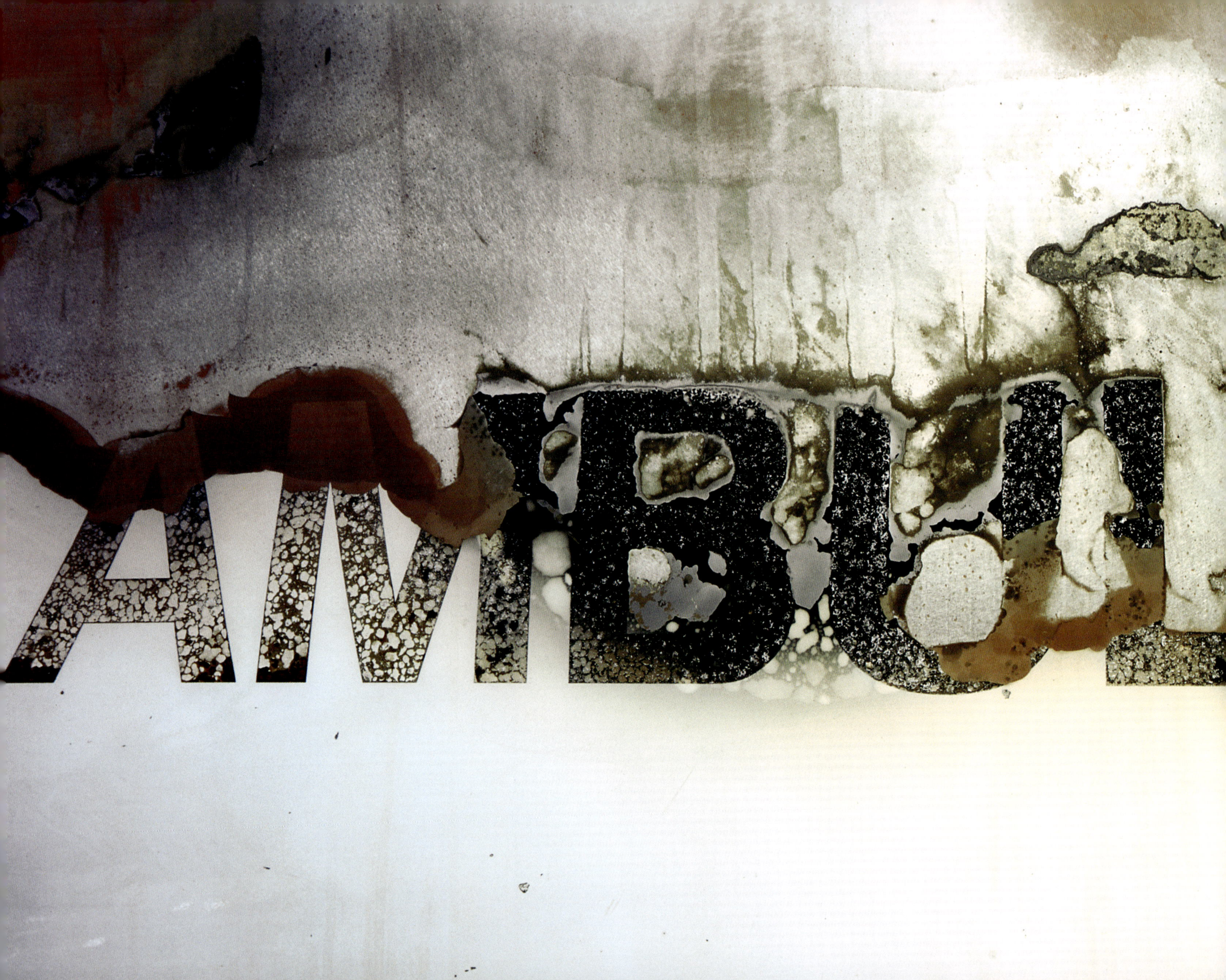
AMBU

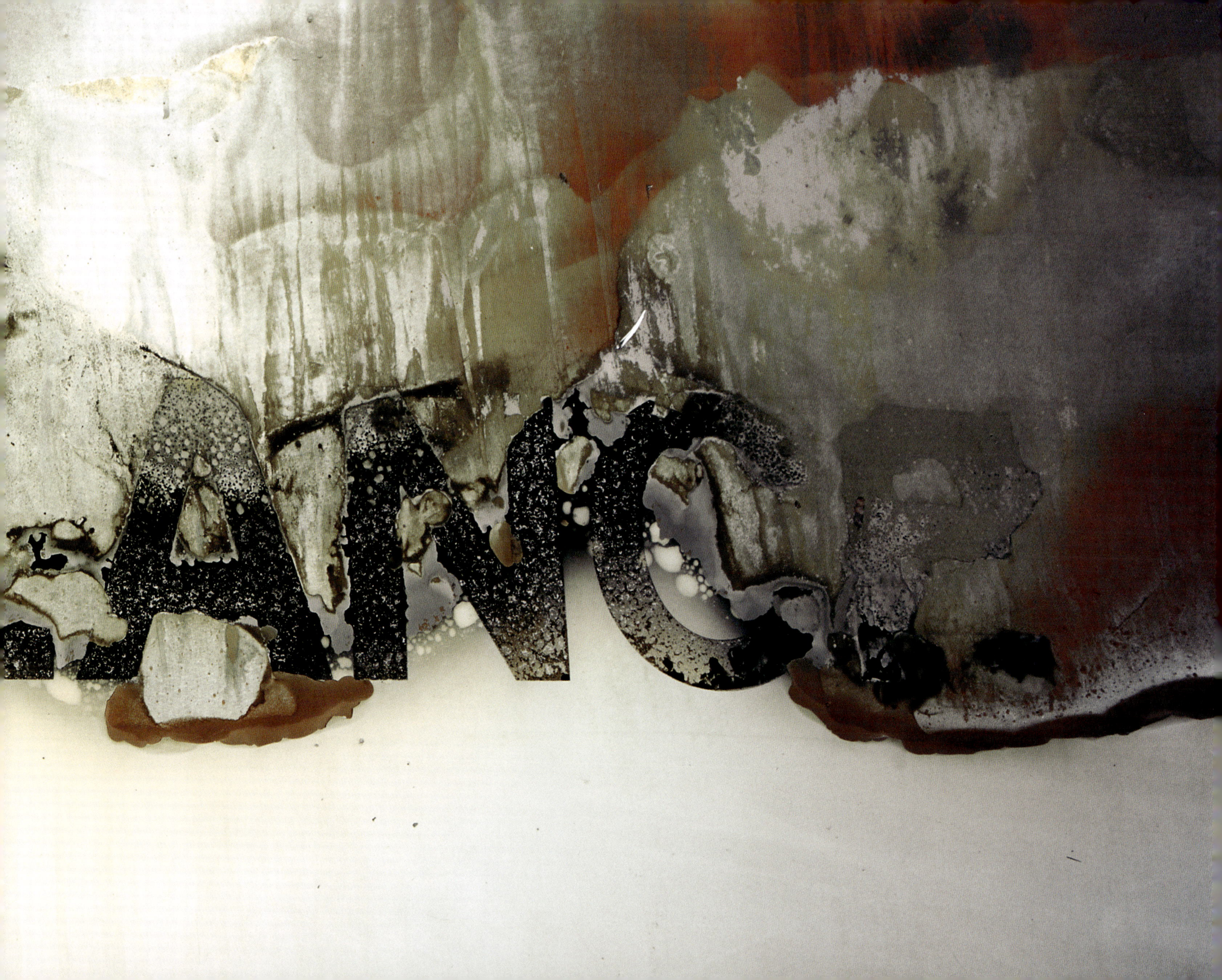
ANC

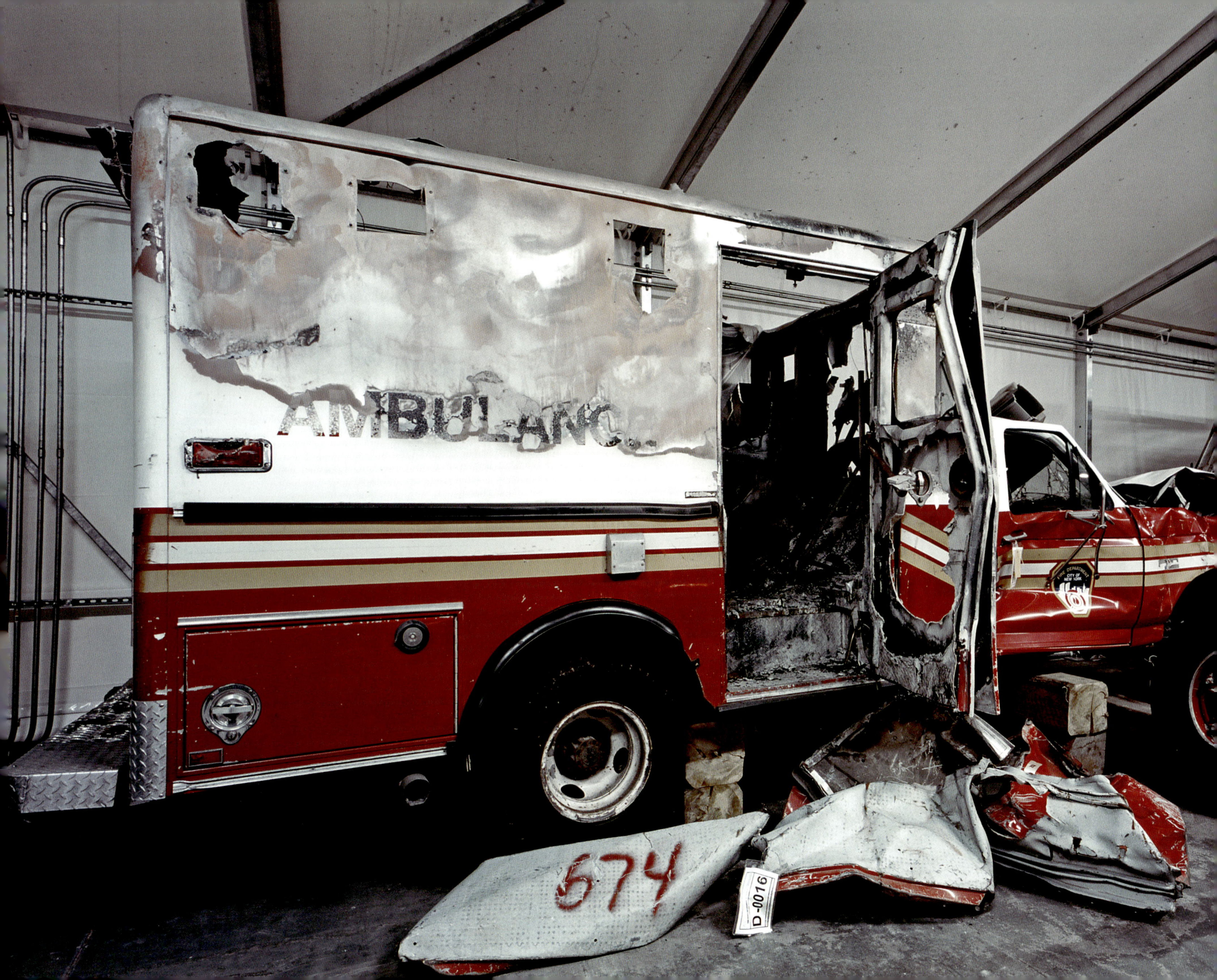
AMBULANC
674
D-0016

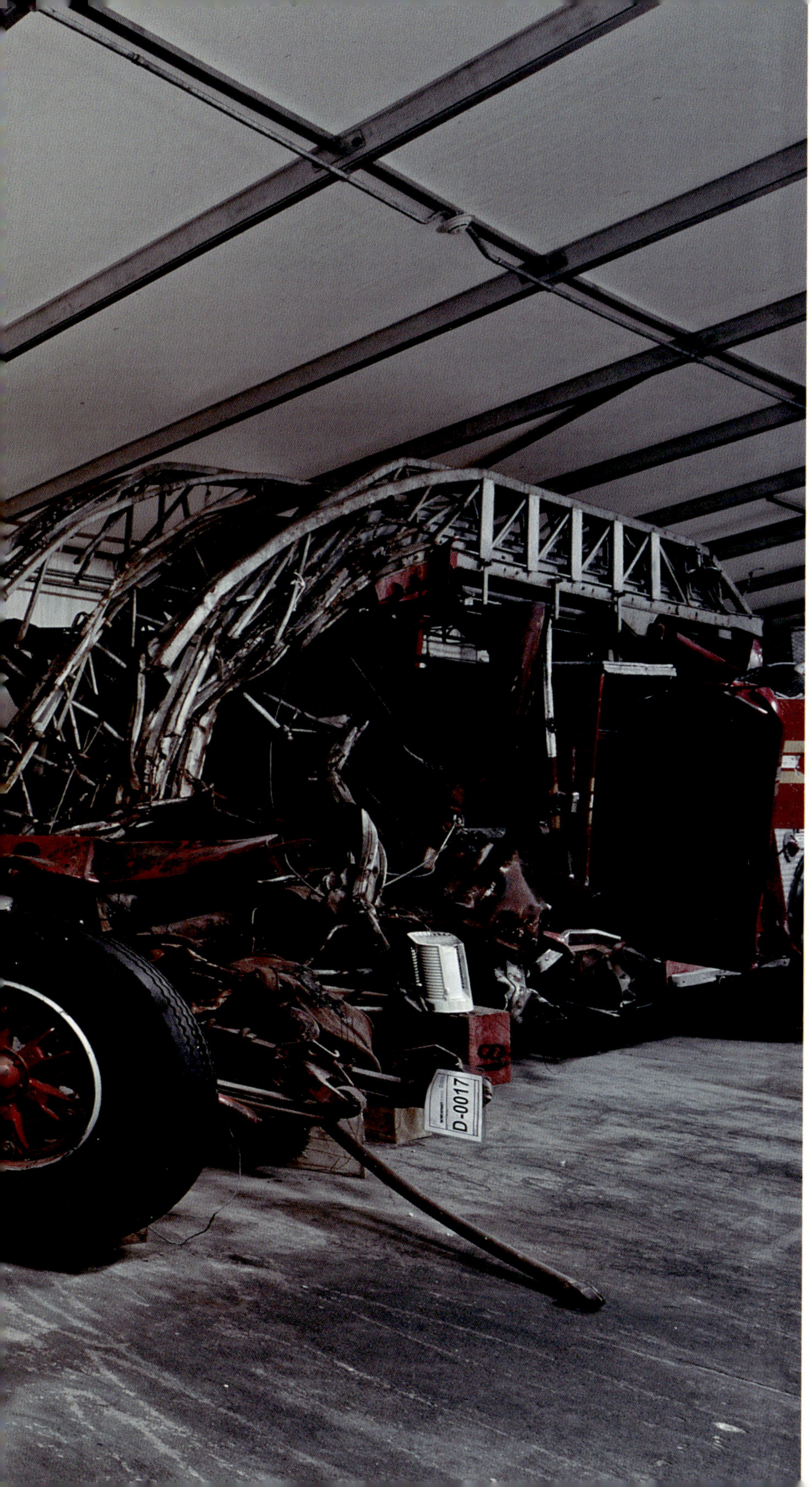

D-0017

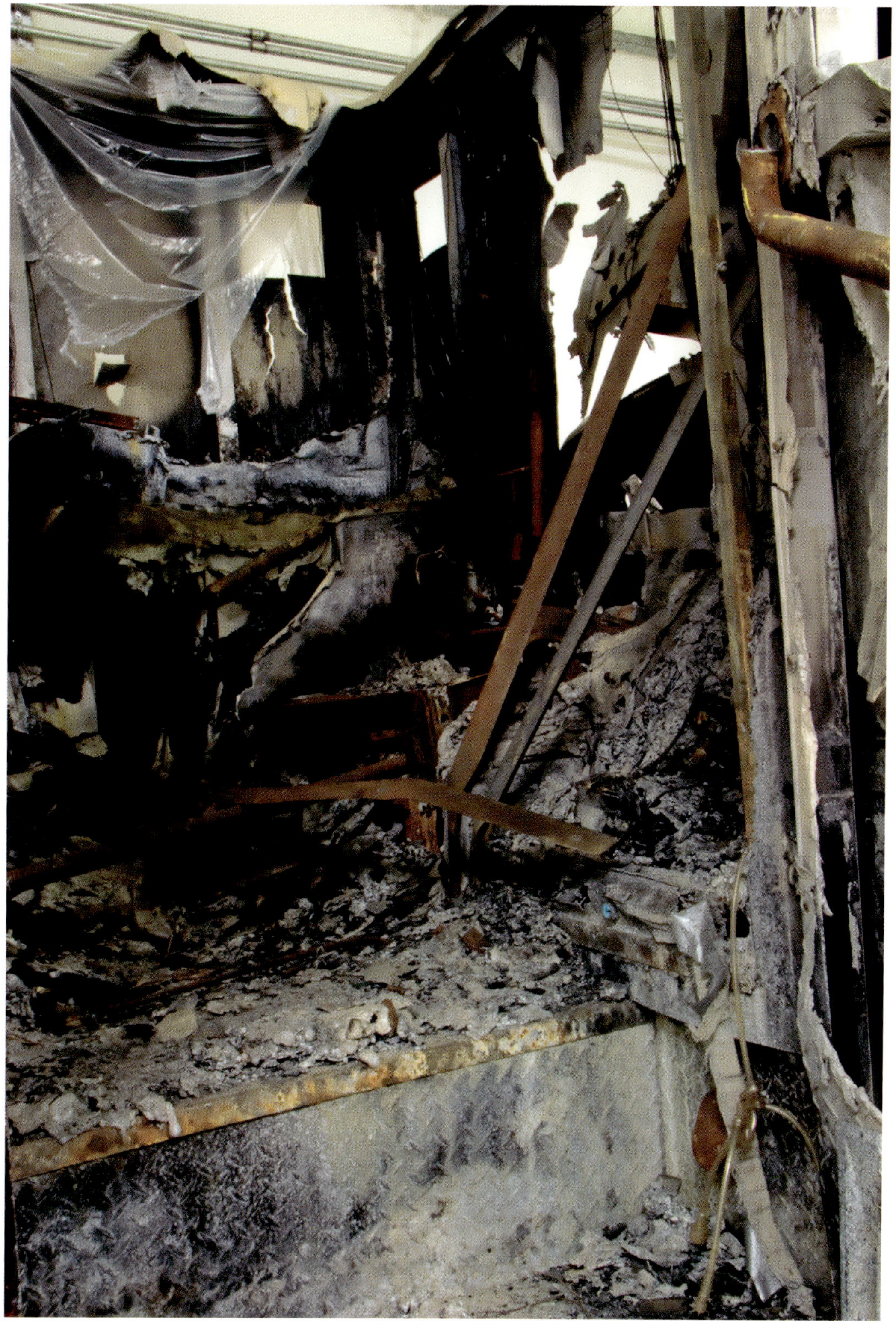

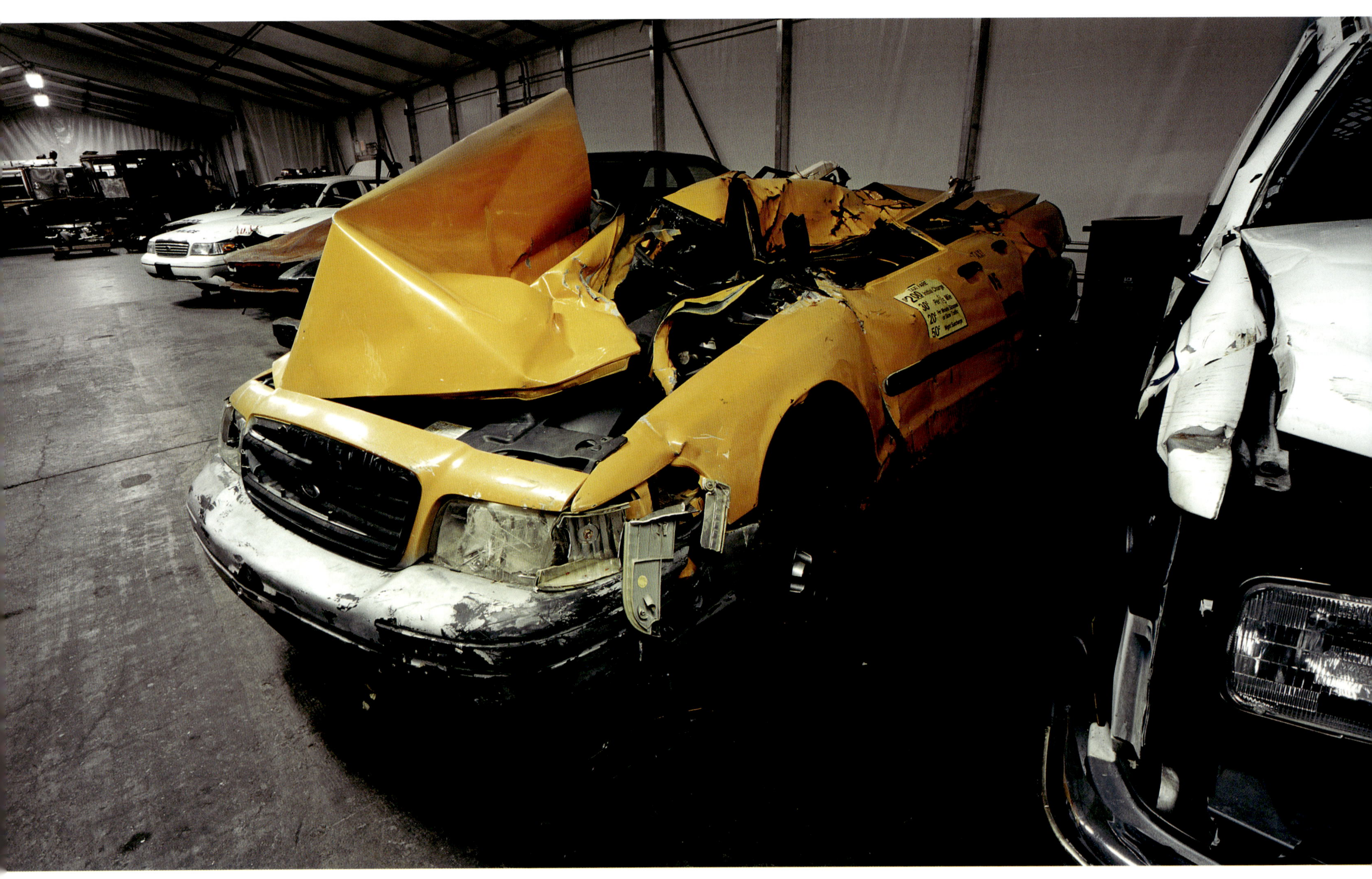

Though most of the vehicles at Hangar 17 came from first responders, this taxi, an emblem of daily life in New York, was also preserved. At right, the tags hanging from the frame indicate its Port Authority inventory number (white) and mark its selection for inclusion in the permanent collection of the Memorial Museum (yellow).

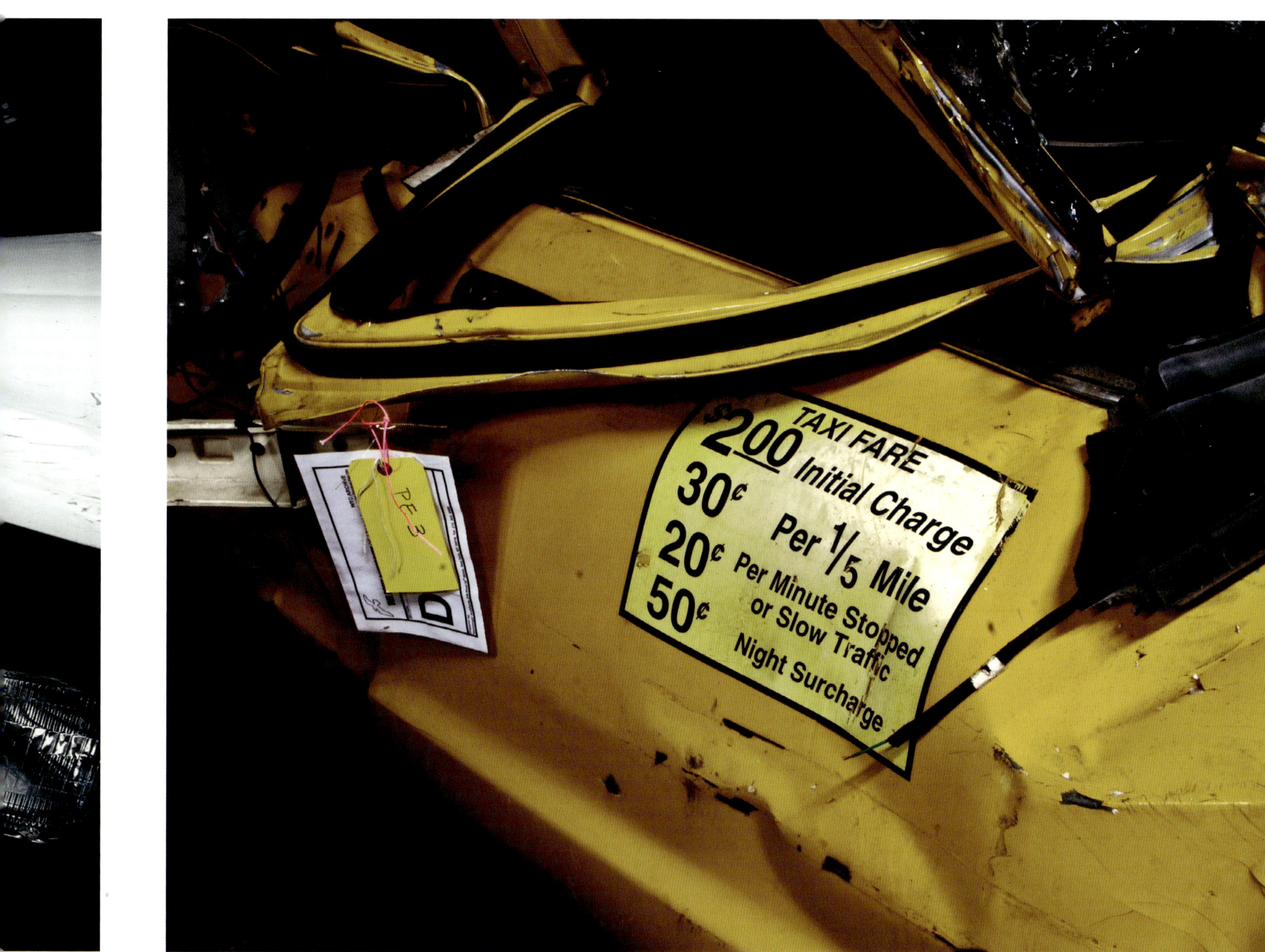
TAXI FARE
$200 Initial Charge
30¢ Per 1/5 Mile
20¢ Per Minute Stopped or Slow Traffic
50¢ Night Surcharge
PE 3
D

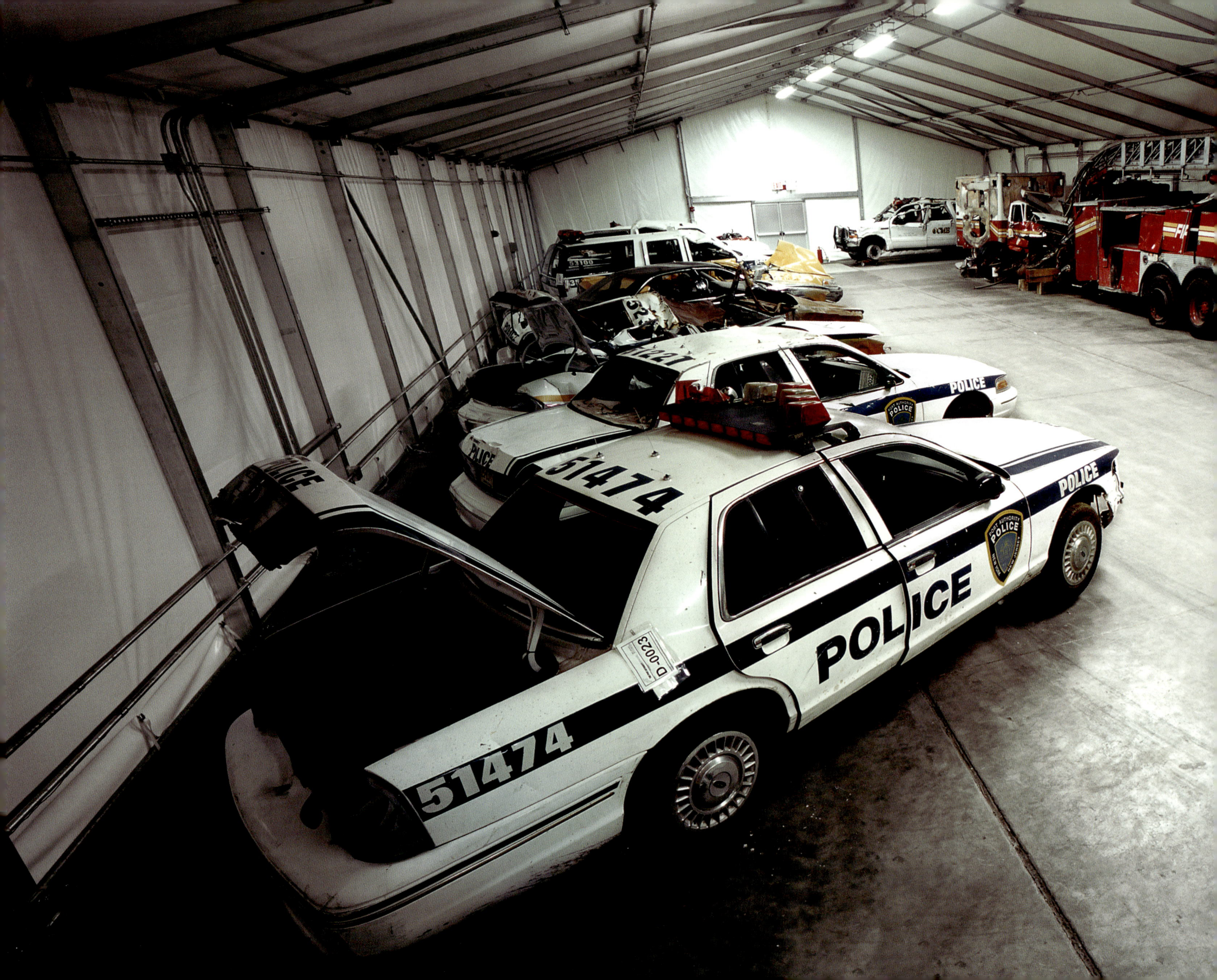

POLICE
51474
D-0023

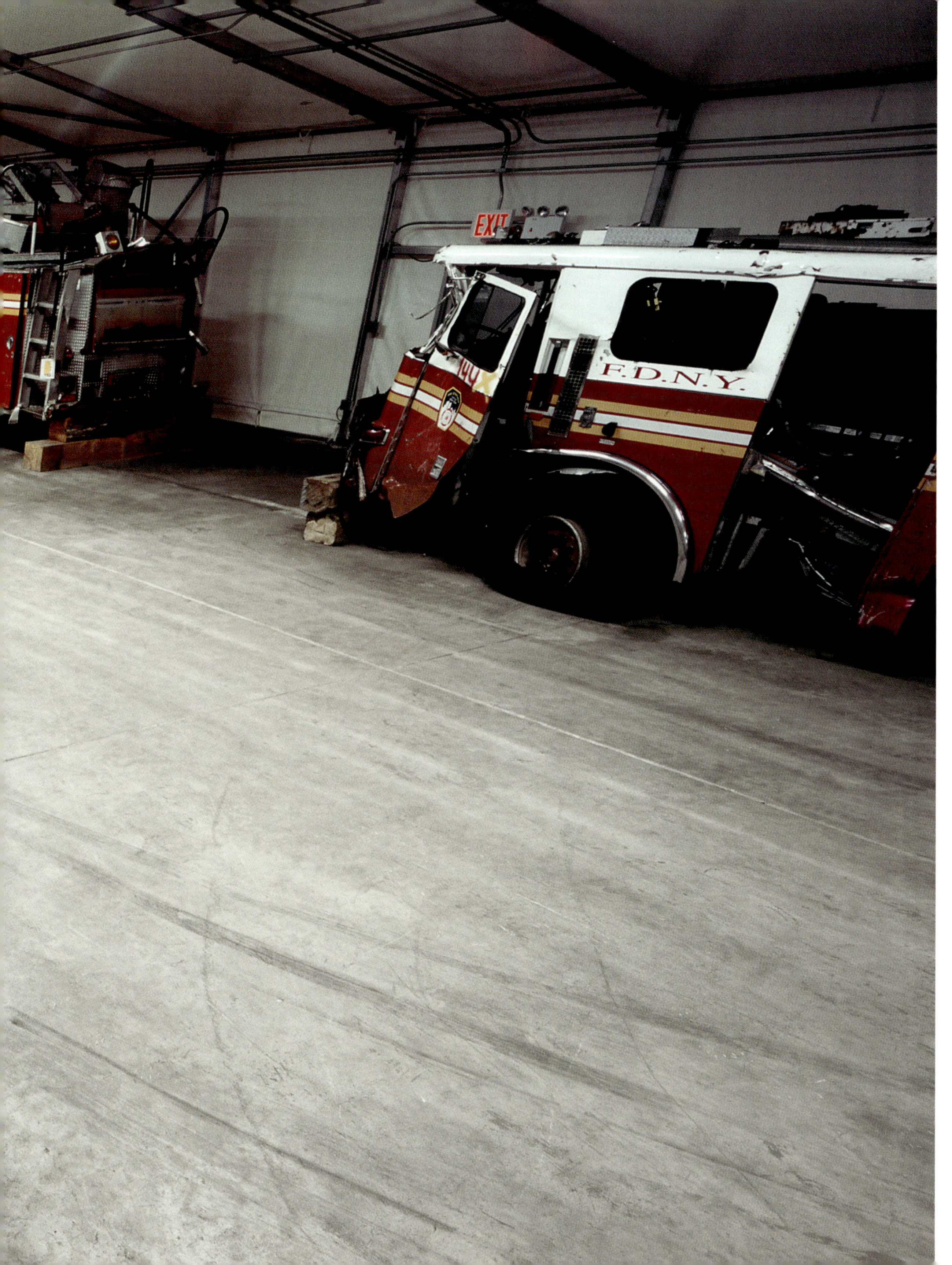

Responsible for airports, train lines, the World Trade Center, and numerous bridges and tunnels, the Port Authority of New York and New Jersey had its own police force of 1,331 officers on 9/11. The Port Authority Police Department (PAPD) officers based at the WTC command post were active in organizing the evacuation of the towers and in searching the buildings.

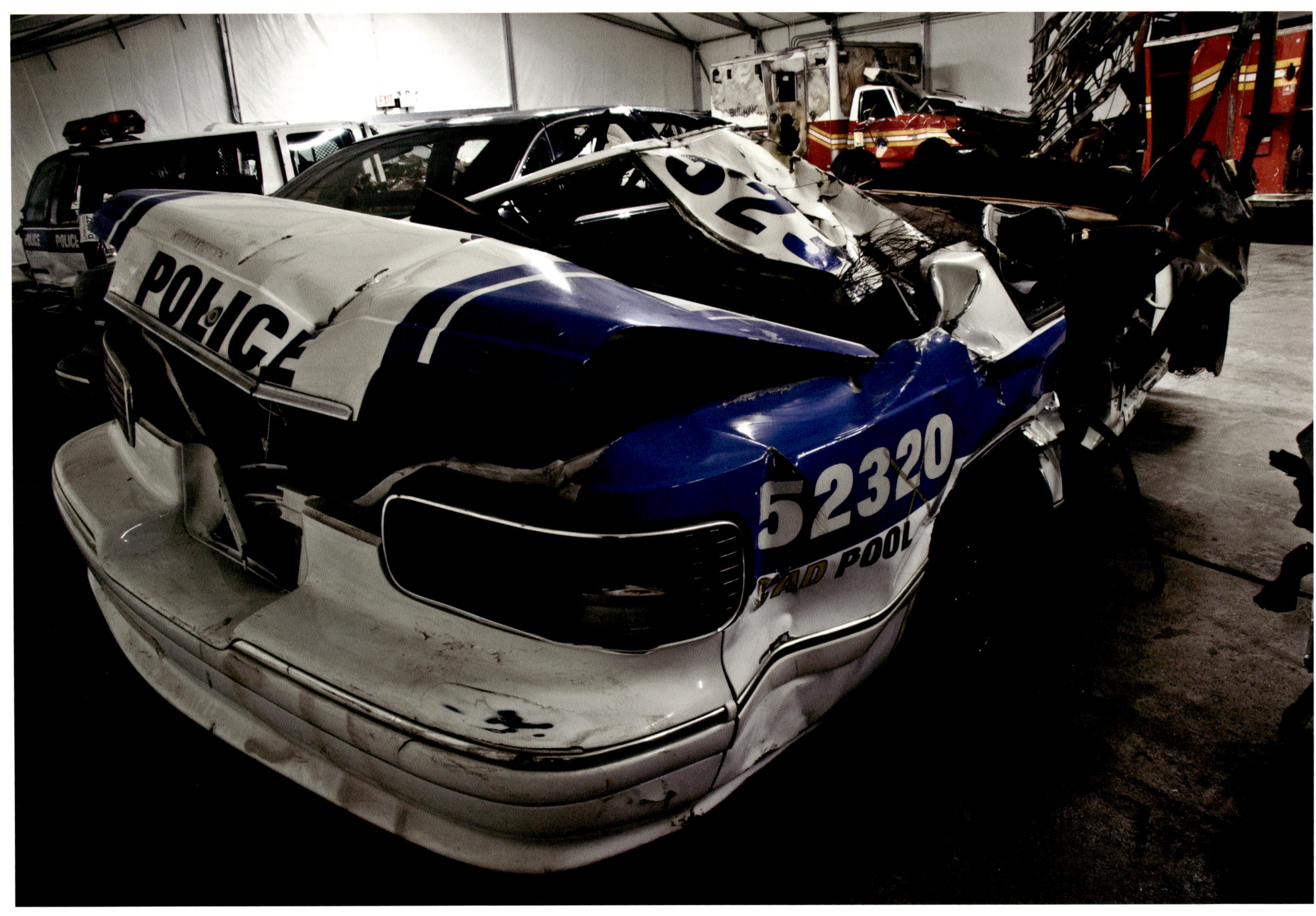

The Port Authority, which had its executive offices in the north tower of the WTC, lost 84 employees on 9/11, including 37 members of the PAPD.

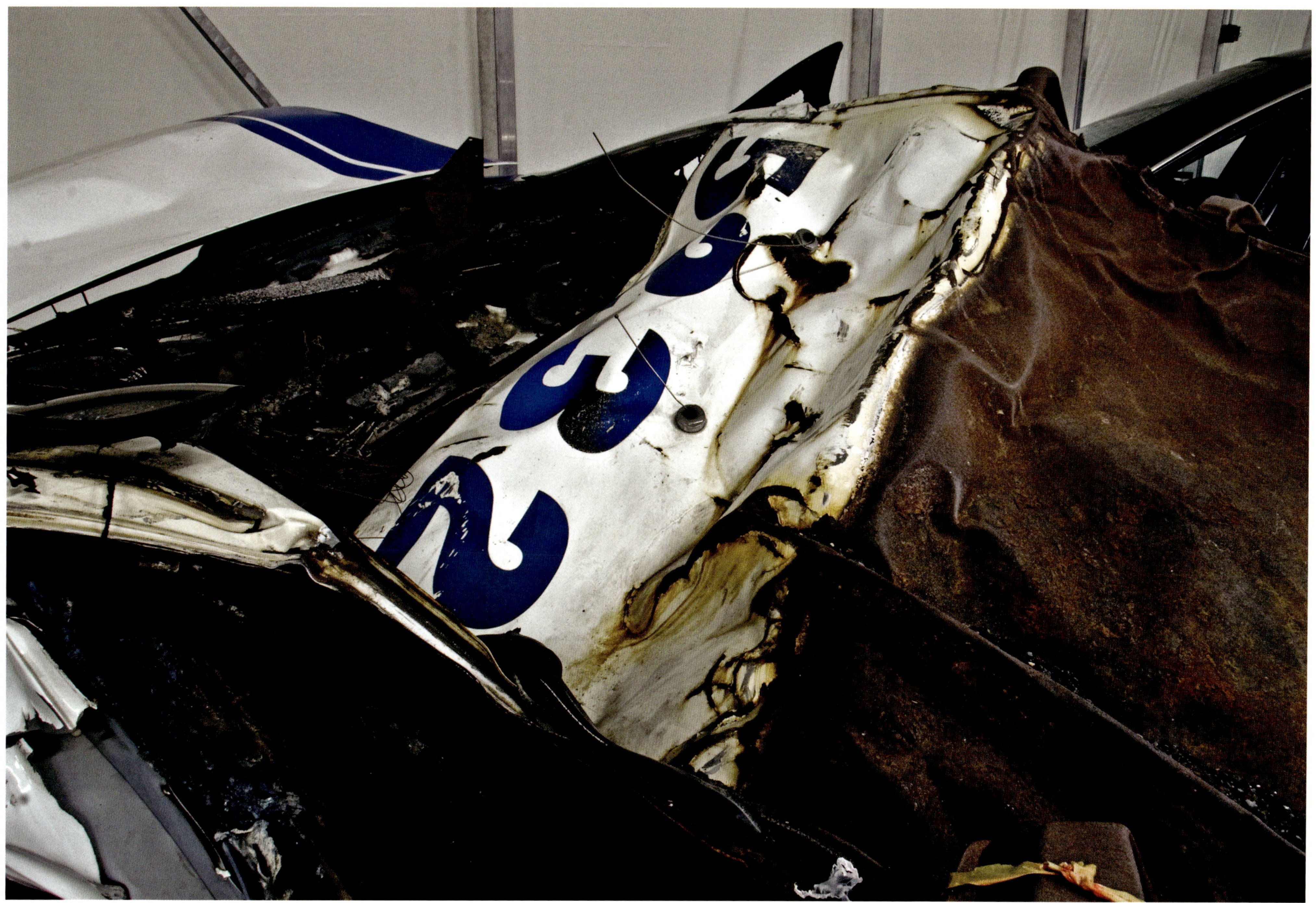

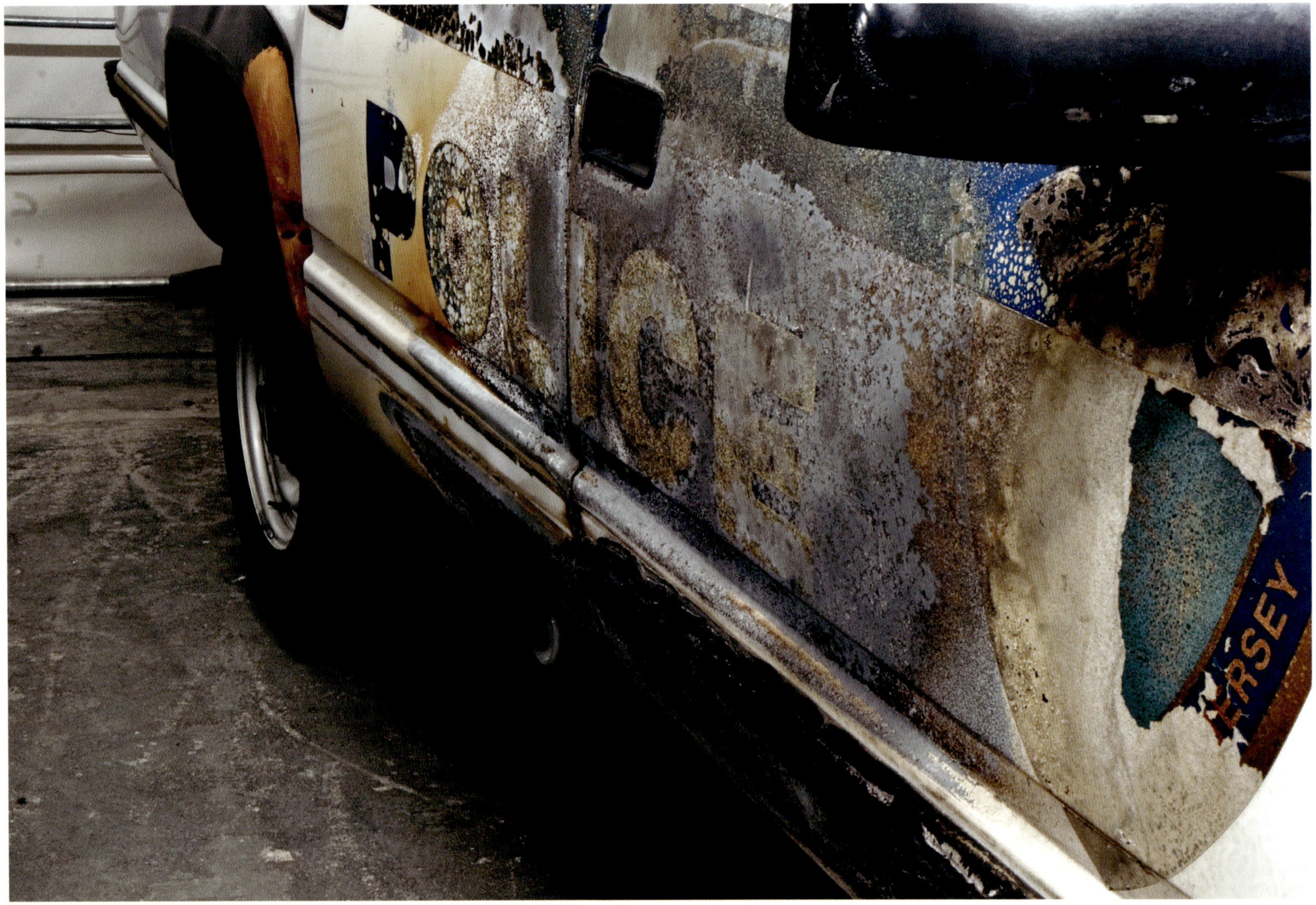

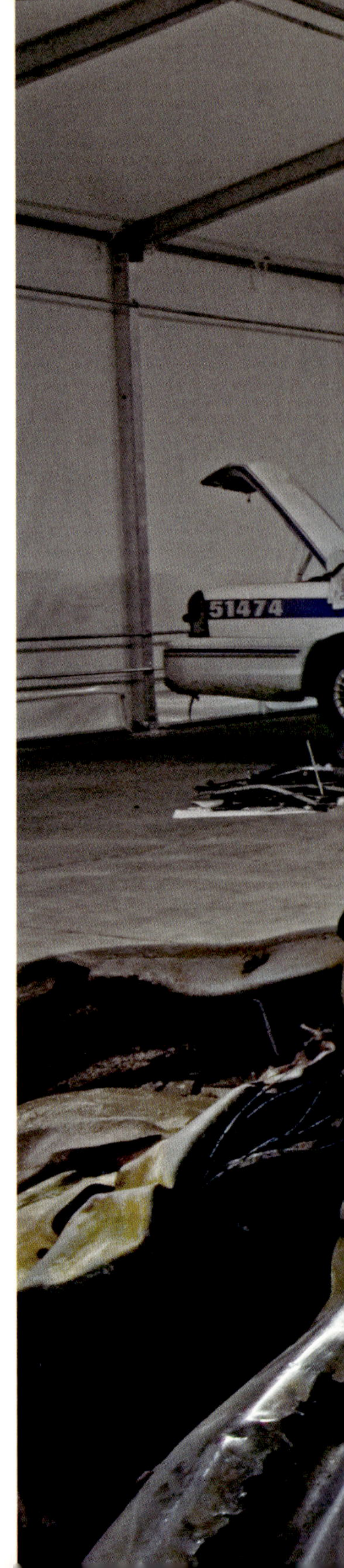
51474

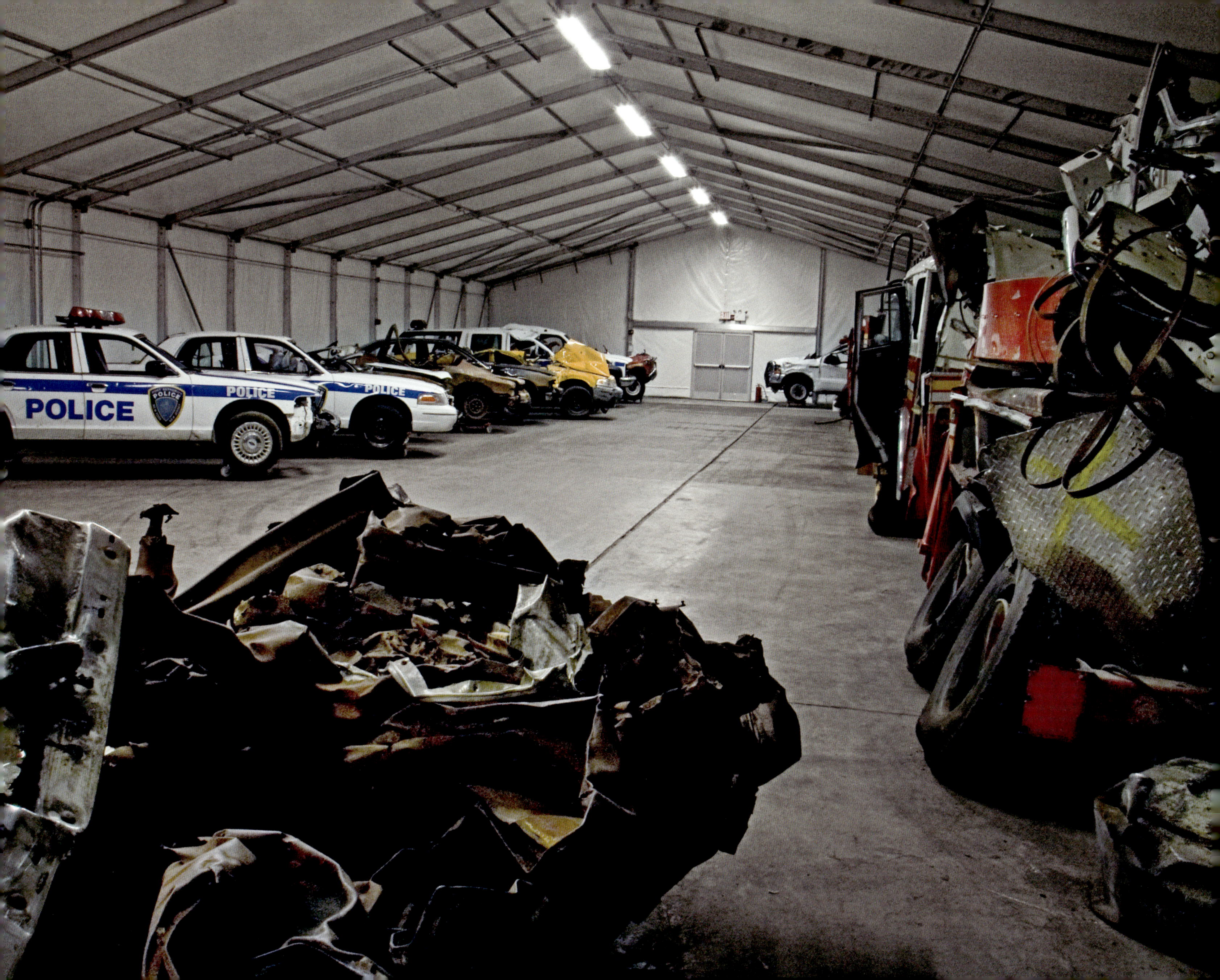
POLICE
POLICE
POLICE

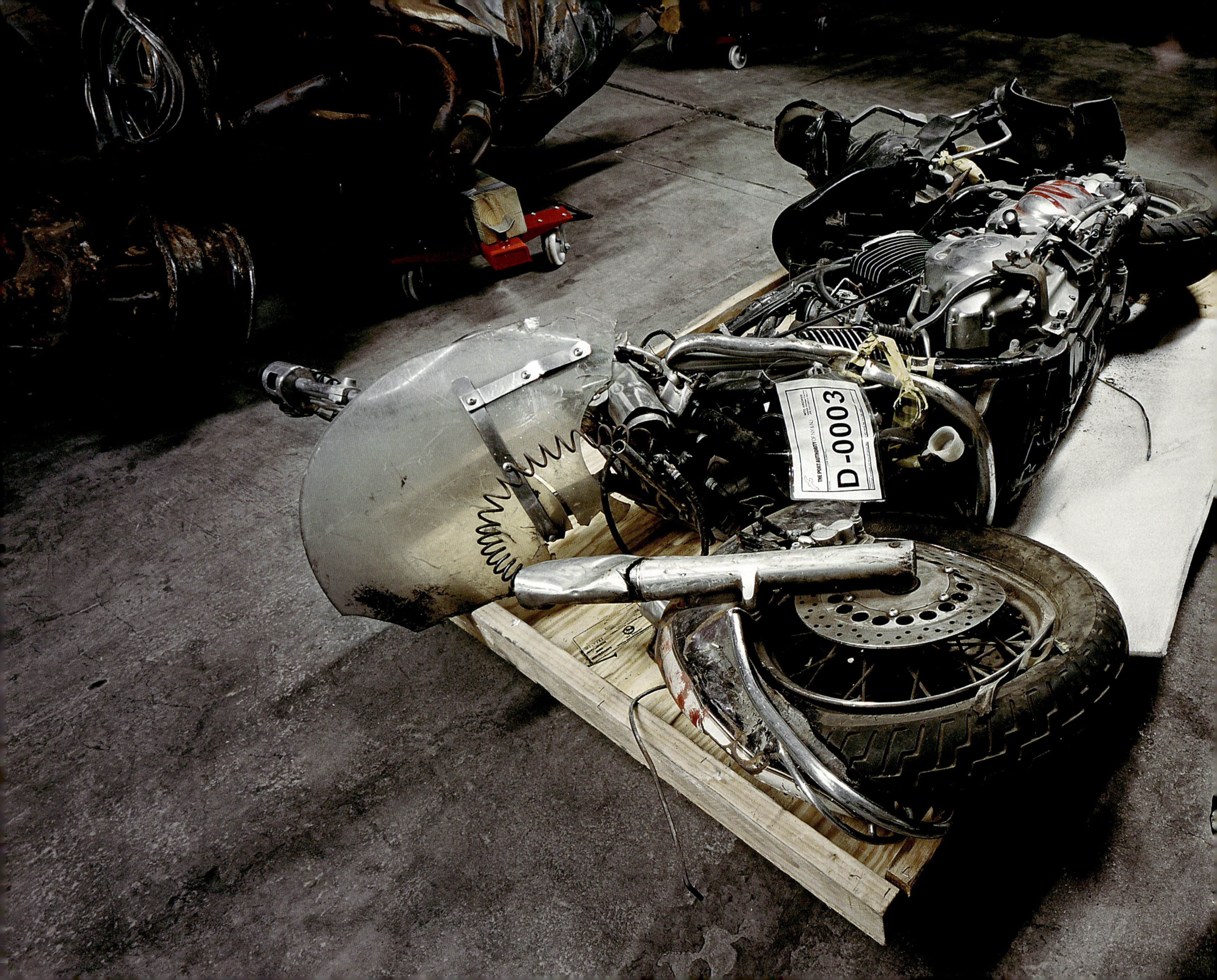
D-0003

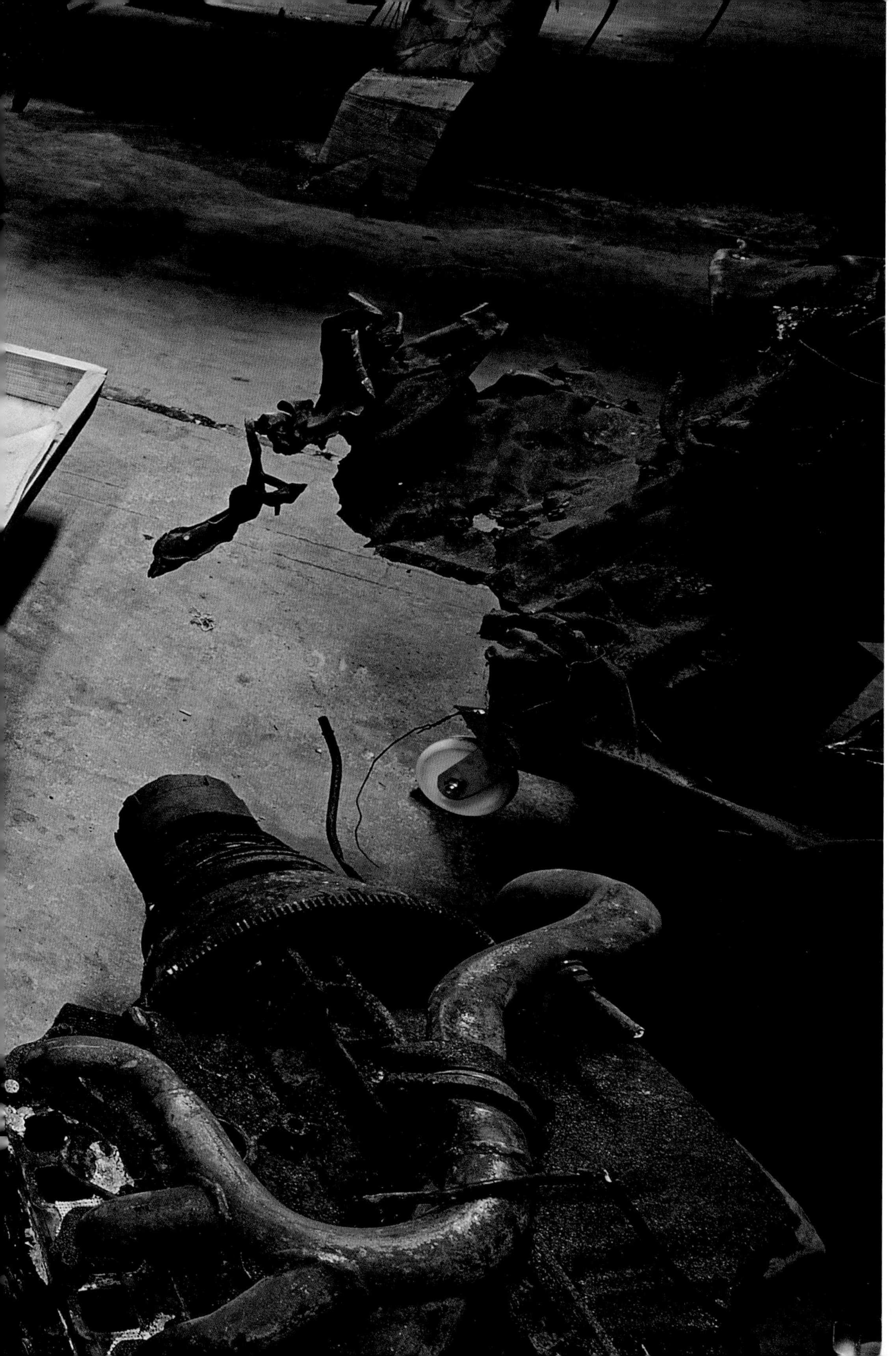

WILL IT EVER RISE?

SEPTEMBER 11 IN AMERICAN MEMORY BY DAVID W. BLIGHT

"The soil of peace is thickly sown with the seeds of war . . .
War loves to come like a thief in the night; professions of eternal amity provide the night."—**Ambrose Bierce, 1881**

The attacks on September 11, 2001, shocked, terrified, and galvanized Americans. Collectively, we did not even know the enemy who attacked us, nor at first how to properly pronounce its name, "al Qaeda." Unaware, violated, angry, from New York, Washington, D.C., and Shanksville, Pennsylvania, to the smallest towns in the Great Plains or the Pacific West, we ached to understand how this horrifying mass murder on "our own soil" could be part of our American story. We were completely unprepared for 9/11, though mass terror and genocide were already known to us as defining events of the 20th century. Our disbelief proved to be impervious to the visual record of modern history, which includes the death camps, the use of atomic weapons to end the war in the Pacific in 1945, the numberless victims of Hitler, Stalin, Pol Pot, and even Saddam Hussein. More recently, even the 1995 bombing of a federal building in Oklahoma City by a domestic terrorist, resulting in 168 innocent civilian deaths, had not prepared us for the planes hitting the World Trade Center and the Pentagon.

The sheer audacity of the attack, and the apocalyptic scale of the collapse of the two towers in lower Manhattan, the epicenter of American and world capitalism, forced us all to stumble through our grief, through the ruins themselves, and through our shattered calm and innocence. Despite its ubiquity, war always seems to surprise us. Throughout the history of the United States, it seems, Americans have been forever embracing, losing, and then regaining a sense of national innocence. This tendency to believe that America exists beyond the world's shattering tragedies and lives in a perpetually improving future is a habit of our hearts that will not die.

We have a rich historical scholarship that shows how American society descended into disunion and Civil War in 1861, after a prolonged period of apparently endless geographical expansion. The limits of America seemed bounded only by the scale of its imagination, until slavery drove armies to Bull Run Creek and the spring meadows of Shiloh.

In spite of all the suffering and destruction brought on by the Civil War, a sense of national innocence would return. The latter decades of the 19th century, the materialistic "Gilded Age," pushed America outward into the scramble for empire. America's muscular progress narrative found new voices and audiences by the turn of the 20th century in a nation teeming with immigrants demanding hope and new beginnings. And yet, the pattern would recur, with periods of intense suffering followed by—perhaps even stimulating—periods of innocence revived.

The speed and intensity of this alternation informs the writings of two commentators reflecting on the 30-year period of American history from the First to the Second World War. In 1959, Henry May wrote a remarkable book, *The End of American Innocence,* a phenomenon he traced back to the years between 1912 and 1917, and the impact of the mass deaths on the battlefields of Europe. The consequence of the First World War, he argued, was the loss of three pillars of a "dominant American credo": belief in the certainty of a Western set of universal moral values; belief in the inevitability of human progress; and faith in traditional European high culture as the model for the world.

But by the 1930s, the innocence and sense of apartness at the heart of American historical memory revived. The British historian-journalist, D. W. Brogan, arriving in 1936 in the heartland of Missouri and Illinois, marveled at an "indefinable American air of happiness and ease" and an "American natural isolationism" around him. As Europe began to revert to tyranny and destruction, Brogan thought he found the eye of the world's brewing storm in St. Louis, in the middle of the country: "the calm, dead center of a tornado whose outer boundaries were too far away for comprehension or apprehension." By 1944, when Brogan published his book, *The American Character,* he had observed "the dead and wounded from Pearl Harbor . . . being brought ashore" in San Francisco. And he had seen America rise and decisively help save "the fate of civilization" in Europe and Asia.

Yet another recurrence of innocence emerged in the Cold War consensus and prosperity of the 1950s, only to come crashing down in the civil rights revolution, unprecedented urban race riots, the Vietnam War, and the assassinations of the 1960s. Then, Ronald Reagan declared "morning again in America" in 1984, and the Cold War and Soviet hegemony in eastern Europe stunningly ended in 1989, followed by declarations of the "end of history" and an inchoate new age of "peace dividends" and *Pax Americana.* Innocence found new fruitful soil, until the invulnerable heartland of Oklahoma City exploded in terror on April 19, 1995.

If the United States is still at heart an idea, and not merely a country with economic and political divisions like any other, then this idea seems able to revive our feeling of historical innocence each time it undergoes an apparently conclusive demise. Does this mean that well into our third century as a nation, we still have not achieved a fully chastened, mature, public national memory? Is it the case that without the myth, we might never survive our reality?

And then came the planes out of the calm, sunny skies of September 11, into our workplaces, our classrooms, our homes. History had interrupted an America that had just settled down after a bitterly disputed election. In her story, "Twilight of the Superheroes" (2006), Deborah Eisenberg captured this shock for a nation, the vast majority of whom do not own a passport. "It was as if there had been a curtain," she writes, "a curtain painted with the map of the earth, its oceans and continents . . . The planes struck, tearing through the curtain of that blue September morning, exposing the dark world that lay right behind it."

The day of 9/11 has now entered into our long history of innocence lost and innocence regained. It is hard to imagine any thoughtful person fearing today, as the essayist Philip Rahv did in 1952, that American writers might live by the "illusion that our society is in its very nature immune to tragic social conflicts and collisions . . . that the more acute problems of the modern epoch are unreal so far as we are concerned." We have thought ourselves immune to tragedy before, usually right before it hits us. So often in the past, we have found ourselves gazing at an Indian massacre, the fields at Gettysburg, a lynching tree, starving children during the Great Depression, a dead Kennedy or a dead King, the abandoned or the dead in the waters of Katrina, and the ruins of ground zero, and we ask: "Is this America?" It is this question, with its inability to incorporate tragedy fully into our sense of American history, that foretells the revival of innocence.

In the wake of 9/11, we searched desperately for analogies, for moments of recognition from our past. Was it a new Pearl Harbor? A Fort Sumter? Was it John Brown's raid on Harpers Ferry in its surprise and violent shock? Where could we find markers in our historical memory to help this make sense? Was this 1861, 1914, 1941, 1968? Was this a new battle of Antietam in its scale of American deaths in one day? Within days of the attacks in New York, with families posting pictures of the missing all over the streets of Manhattan, and with the beginning of the seemingly endless procession of firefighter funerals, America and the world peered at pictures of the ruins of ground zero, at the burning, smoldering, fantastically huge pile of debris, wondering in response to the awkward musings of journalists and politicians about how this site might one day be memorialized.

As demonstrated in the Torres photographs, the ruins seemed an alternative universe of horror, an otherworldly labyrinth of physical and human destruction. Despite, or perhaps because of, their macabre nature, Torres's images demonstrate how time, life, and the world stopped on 9/11. Their shapes catch our eyes and prod our imaginations; sometimes we see only charred, twisted metal, but other times we may see the prow of a shipwreck in the mangled steel rods, fused lava in the molten rocks, or a space capsule in that fallen antenna. Above all, we feel the power of these objects fashioned by man and nature out of horror, debris, and junk, now rendered sacred because of beloved human beings who perished. The painted and inscribed Last Column is indeed a means of "remembering," as it says; memory of such loss must at some point be tangible, available to the senses, or it will float away in dust.

How would such loss be commemorated, such ruins removed and rebuilt? Indeed, some wondered why we insist on near instantaneous memorialization of major events, especially those involving great violence and sacrifice? Holocaust memorials began to appear in Europe as early as 1948, but their proliferation around the Western world required decades to take hold. The large World War II national memorial on the Washington Mall was not constructed until more than five decades after V-J Day. A Korean War monument on the great national space took more than 40 years. The various sacred grounds of American military sacrifice—Pearl Harbor, Gettysburg, Lexington and Concord, Little Big Horn, the Alamo, and others—have evolved over generations.

The truth is that we cannot know the full, or even partial, meaning of an event like September 11 in a few years, a decade, or perhaps even a generation. The extended meanings of all great turning points in history depend entirely on the developing character of their aftermath. But in the wake of the most violent century on record, and living well into the second century of the *psychological* age of human self-understanding—in which we demand recognition of *individuals* sacrificed in mass violence—we seem possessed by the urge to repair and commemorate. We have no patience for historical time and insist on immediate answers to the inherent politics of memorialization. All of these impulses are very human and, however vexing for professional historians and curators, they demand humane responses.

Any contemplation of 9/11 begins with its sense of loss; the trouble begins as we try to think in historical time. But mass death is not new to Americans. Nor are ruins. Our great death poet, Walt Whitman, seemed never to cease reflecting on his experiences nursing to Civil War casualties in hospitals between 1862 and 1865. The dead and dying overwhelmed him emotionally as they also inspired his writing.

To Whitman, those soldiers' bodies and souls were themselves a form of ruins. In *Specimen Days,* he recollected endless "hell-scenes," the "horribly mutilated . . . moaning or groaning." Whitman did not sanitize the results of war. He portrayed the suffering soldiers as a recurring national nightmare, lit by "every lurid passion, the wolf's, the lion's lapping thirst for blood—the passionate, boiling volcanoes of human revenge for comrades, brothers slain—with the light of burning farms, and heaps of smutting, smouldering black embers—and in the human heart everywhere black, worse embers." The "dead, the dead, the dead—our dead—or South or North, ours all," he wailed, unable to remove their images, or the feel of their cold hands, from his mind.

And so it was with September 11 in New York. Don DeLillo captured a similar haunting sensation in his novel *Falling Man.* Keith, a character who has miraculously survived the collapse of the towers that morning with injuries to his limbs and psyche, returns to ground zero some days later to gaze at the site. "He stood at the National Rent-A-Fence barrier," writes DeLillo, "and looked into the haze, seeing the strands of bent filigree that were the last standing things, a skeletal remnant of the tower where he'd worked for ten years. The dead were everywhere, in the air, in the rubble, on rooftops nearby, in the breezes that carried from the river. They were settled in ash and drizzled on windows all along the streets, in his hair, and on his clothes." Mysteriously, beyond science and outside of previously comprehended reality, those massive ruins had consumed the dead. And yet the dead, in a way, were and still are there.

In the Civil War, the ruins of farmsteads, rural battlefield landscapes, bleak prison compounds, and nearly whole cities seemed to consume the 620,000 dead, demanding they not be forgotten. Ruins have a way of speaking to us on divergent frequencies, depending on their age, their political meaning, and whether time has rendered them somehow into either weathered beauty or politicized images of horror.

In 1865, due to the devastation of the Civil War, America was truly a land with ruins. The country's natural landscapes, especially in the West, had inspired imagery of ruins. Unlike the haunting, destroyed abbeys of the English Civil War of the 17th century or Rome's ancient, majestic city of ruins, America's destruction in the wake of Appomattox was brand new, but also, and instantaneously, *historic,* and at many battlefields and burial grounds, sacred. The American nation, reeling with loss and despair on an unprecedented scale, was not yet old; its ruins were not those made hoary by years or beautified through decay. But it was a country that had torn itself asunder—physically, politically, and spiritually. It was now a modern society forever burdened with a deeply divisive historical memory, riven with blood sacrifice that had to be explained and memorialized. America's historic landscapes became more *interesting* because of the ruins of the Civil War.

No one understood this more than defeated white Southerners, who experienced the most devastation to their lives and property. Their ruins inspired different reactions, depending on perspective. In October 1865, just after his release from a five-month imprisonment, former Confederate vice president Alexander H. Stephens rode a slow train southward. In northern Virginia, he found "the desolation of the country . . . was horrible to behold." When Stephens reached northern Georgia, his native state, he was shocked: "War has left a terrible impression on the whole country to Atlanta. The desolation is heart-sickening. Fences gone, fields all a-waste, houses burnt."

Later, Father Abram Ryan, known as the "Poet Priest of the Lost Cause" of the Confederacy, found spiritual renewal in the South's ruins. "A land without ruins is a land without memories," said the preacher in 1878, "a land that wears a laurel crown may be fair to see; but twine a few sad cypress leaves around the brow of any land, and, be that land barren, beautiless, and bleak, it becomes lovely in its consecrated cornet of sorrow, and it wins the sympathy of the heart and of history." From such airy melancholia and real desolation, the defeated South would find an exotic and romantic niche in the American imagination.

Out of these ruins, Americans would have to imagine just how they would regenerate their country. In the wake of the war, thousands of Northern readers learned about the conditions and ruins of the South from traveling journalists. The novelist and poet John Trowbridge wrote the most lyrical of the many travel accounts published in the postwar years. As one of the first battlefield tourists, Trowbridge began his tour at Gettysburg in August 1865. Upon his arrival in the town square, he asked the route to the battlefield of the "world-famous fight." A hotel keeper informed him, "you are on it now," and directed him to a nearby house with a "rebel shell embedded in the brick wall."

Similar rituals, similar searching, occur every day in New York today; tourists ask at their hotels or at the information desk at Grand Central Station, "Which way to ground zero?" Guided around the Gettysburg battlefield by a local citizen, Trowbridge found the "stillness" of the summer day broken only by the "perpetual click-click" sound of stonecutters preparing headstones in the cemetery where Lincoln had delivered his famous address. He was especially bothered by almost countless labels of "unknown" on many of the stones. "So many killed," he remarked, "with that brief sentence we glide over the unimaginably fearful fact, and pass on to other details."

At ground zero a century and a half later, more than 40 percent of the victims left behind not a single identifiable human trace. At this site in New York, people have felt a terrible stillness in viewing the ruins slowly transformed into a beautiful memorial, accompanied by the constant sounds of construction, and under the illumination of perpetual floodlights. And they have had to face similarly unimaginable, fearful facts. As Trowbridge looked into the long rows of trenches still open and freshly dug for all the dead at Gettysburg two years after the battle, he "saw the ends of coffins protruding," and pondered warily the "awful uncertainty" of the nation's rebirth. "Will it ever rise?" he asked, without knowing an answer. How many Americans, or visitors from abroad, have stood over the ruins of ground zero, imagined the site as a graveyard, and pondered the uncertain character of the nation and the world emerging from 9/11?

Will it rise? Memorials are always about the past, but they are almost always also about the moment in which they are erected. In the case of the National September 11 Memorial & Museum, both the past it represents and the present in which it lives will be of very long duration.

In the Old Testament story of the "Valley of the Dry Bones," the prophet Ezekiel found himself in a terrible, bleak landscape; the masses of horrifying bones were "very dry." God confronts Ezekiel with a question: "Son of man, can these bones live?" An awed Ezekiel cannot know. God puts his hand on the prophet, breathes into the bones on the parched earth, and they begin to grow flesh and skin; they begin "shaking" and moving about as God pronounces: "Come from the four winds, O breath, and breathe upon these slain, that they may live." Humbled, Ezekiel, "prophesied" as he "was commanded"; and behold, the bones become flesh "stood up upon their feet." The story of 9/11 is very old, as it also seems so very new.

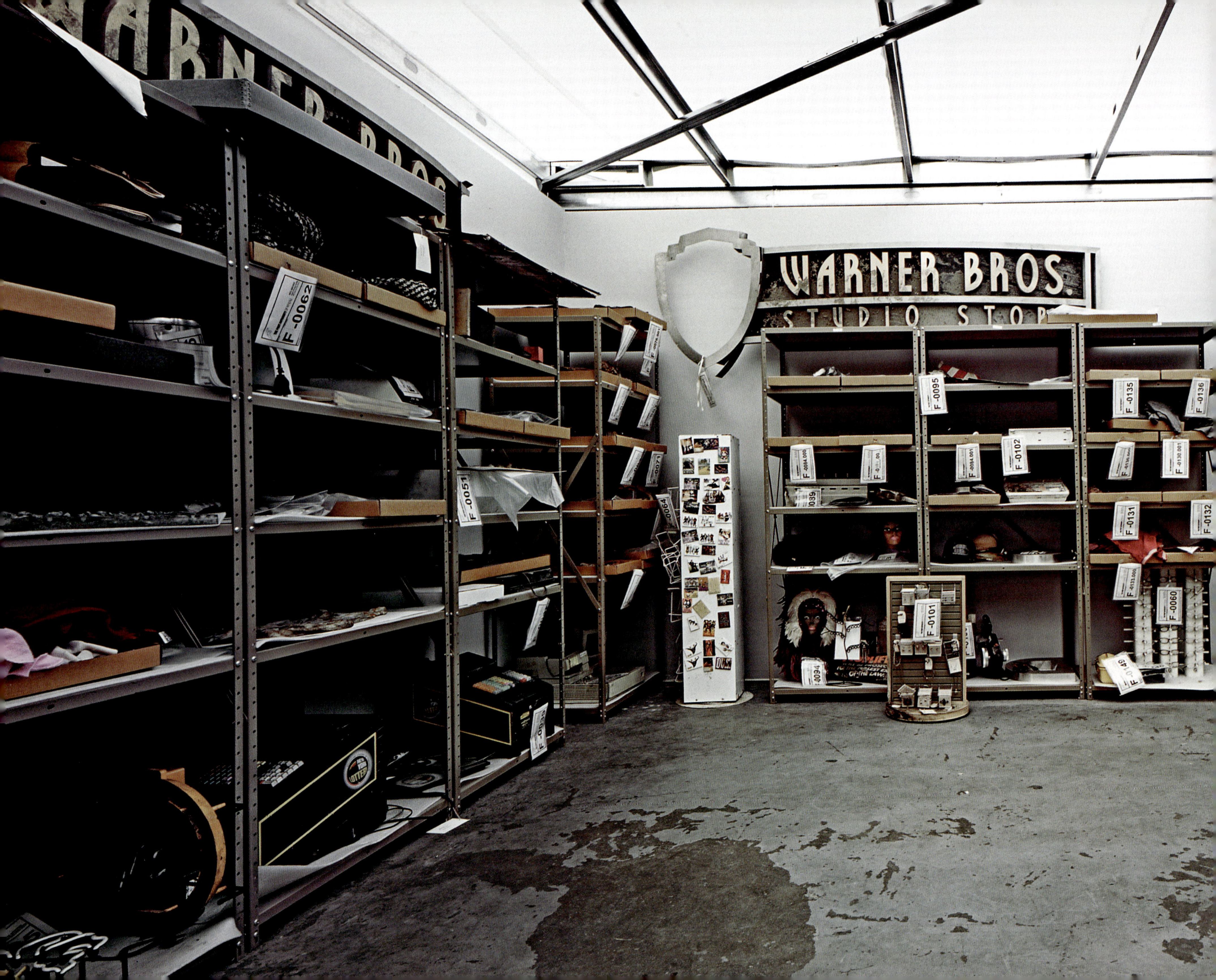
WARNER BROS.
STUDIO STORE

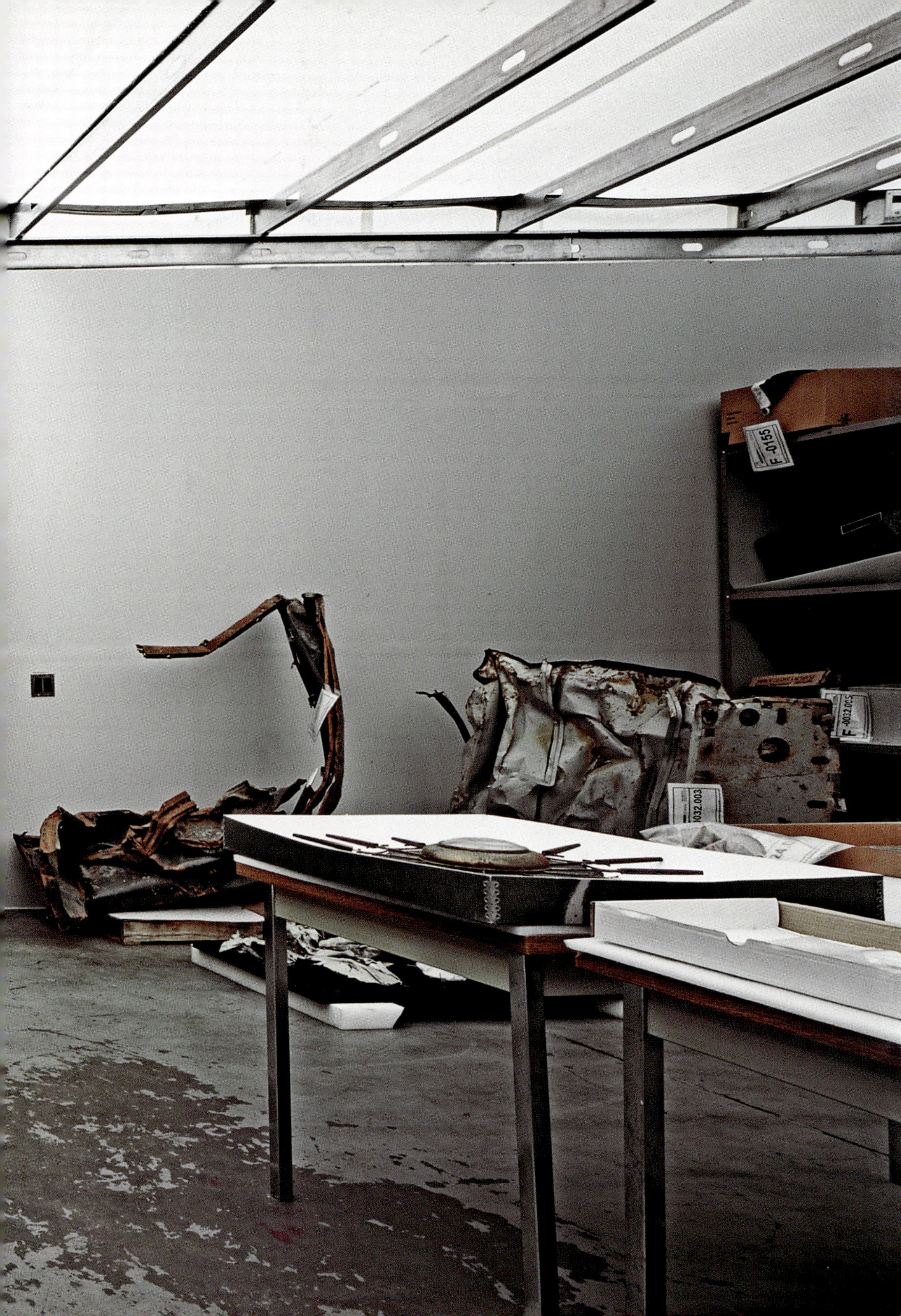

CONCOURSE SHOPS

The Warner Bros. Studio Store was one of more than 60 shops at the Mall at the World Trade Center. Located on a concourse one story below street level, the mall held 427,000 square feet of retail space and was the third largest-grossing shopping center in the United States.

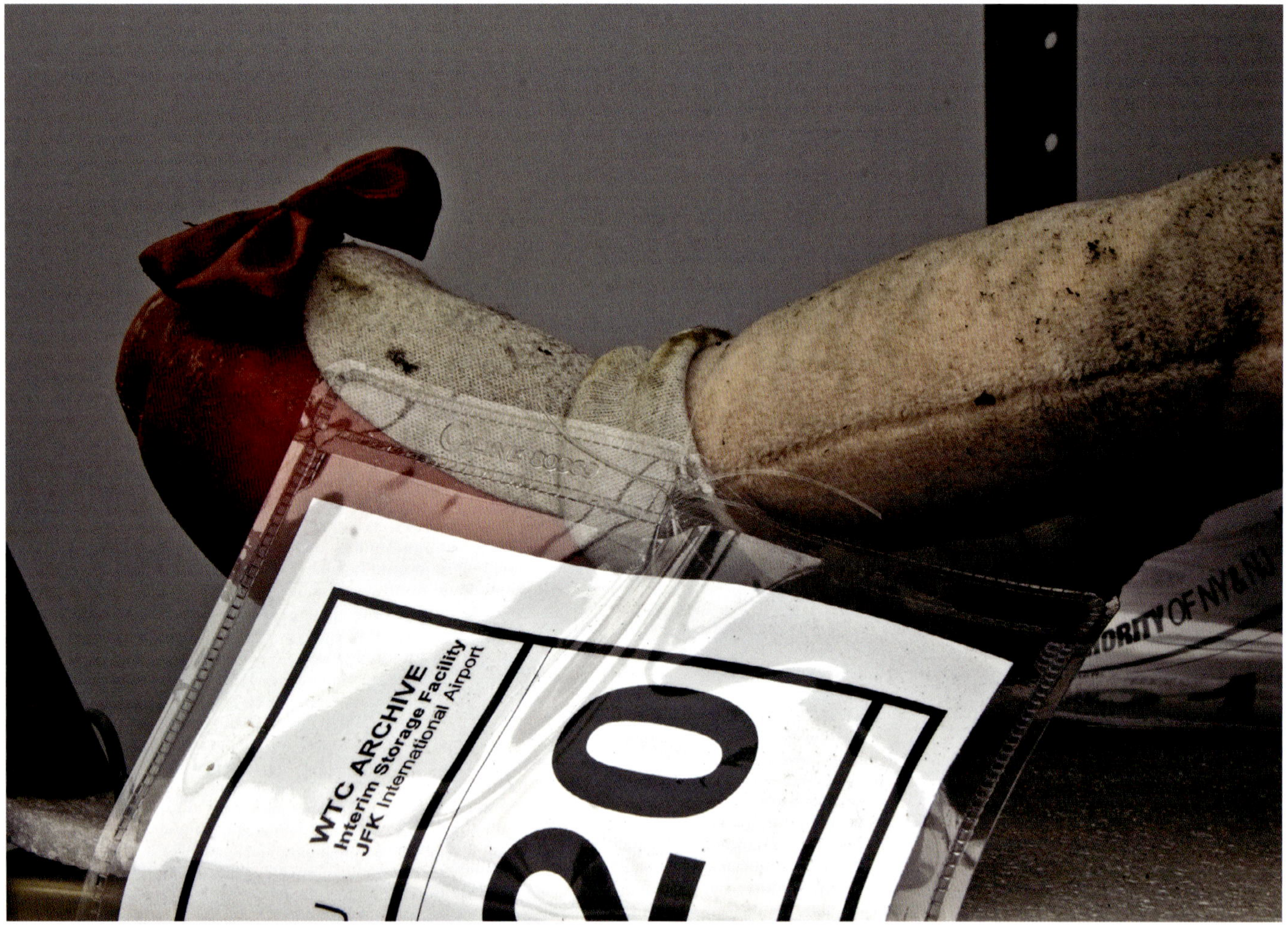

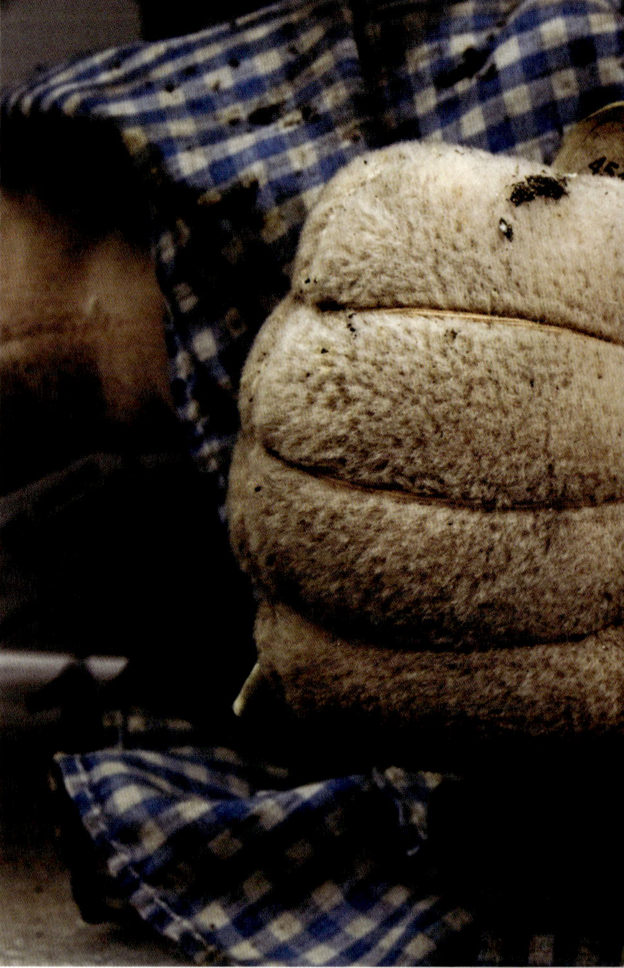

This "Dorothy" doll, based on the lead character of the film *The Wizard of Oz*, was available for sale at the Warner Bros. Studio Store.

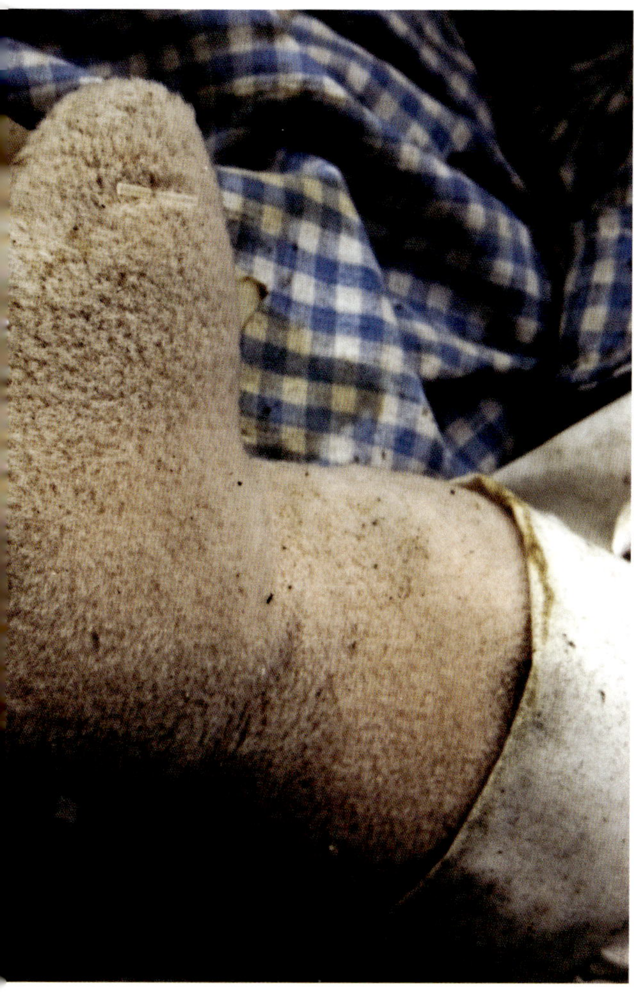

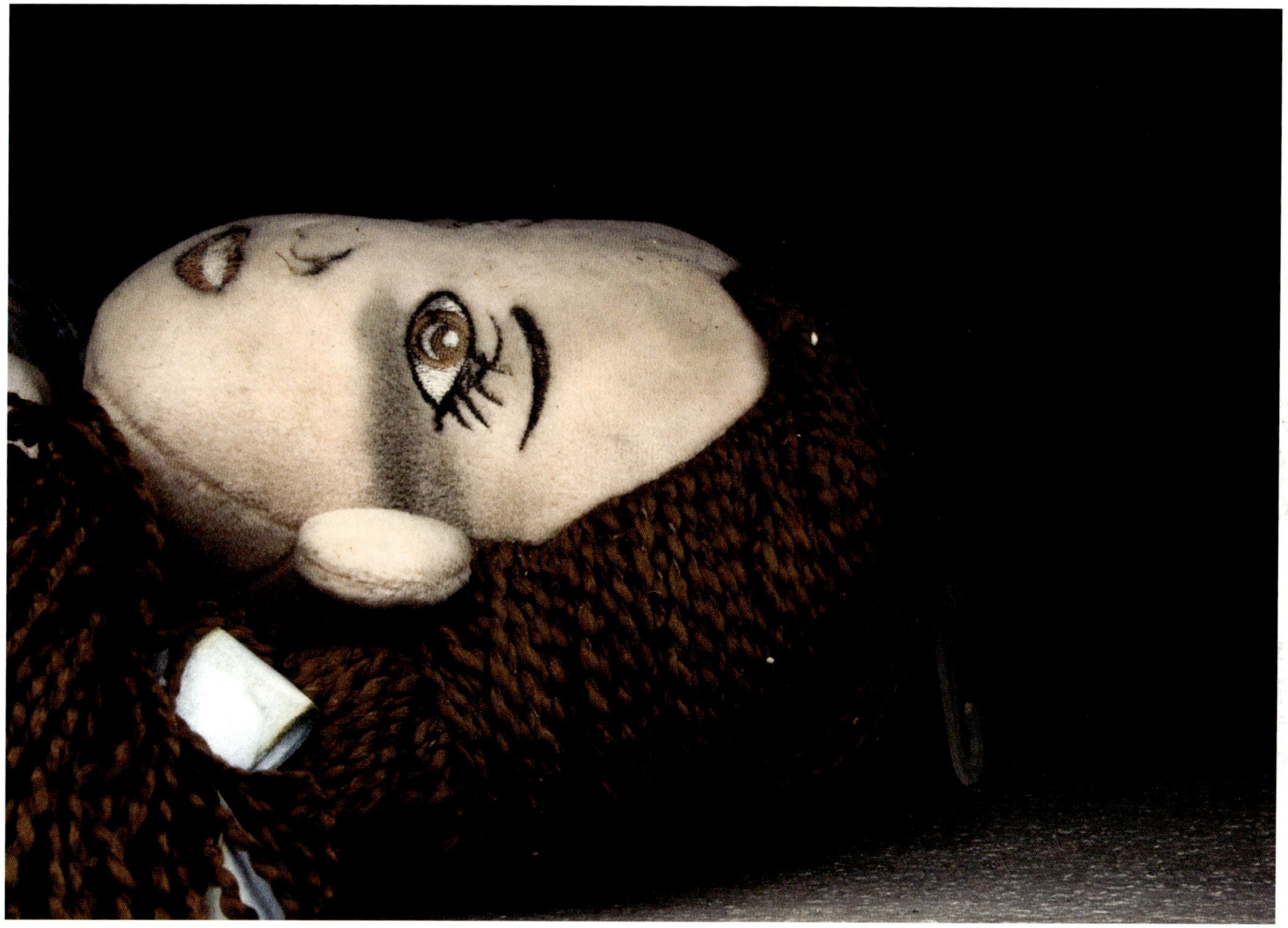

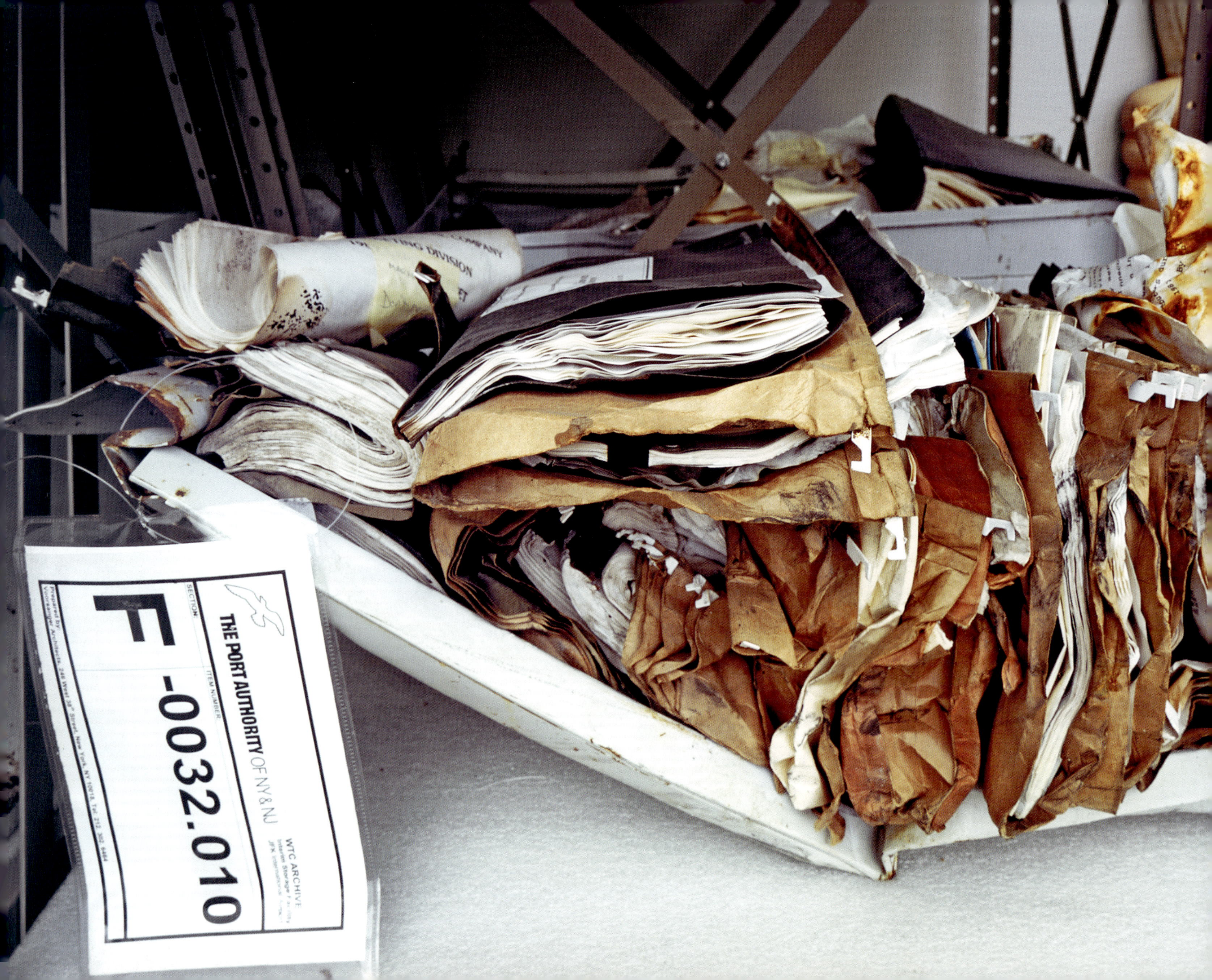
THE PORT AUTHORITY OF NY&NJ
WTC ARCHIVE
SECTION:
ITEM NUMBER
F
-0032.010

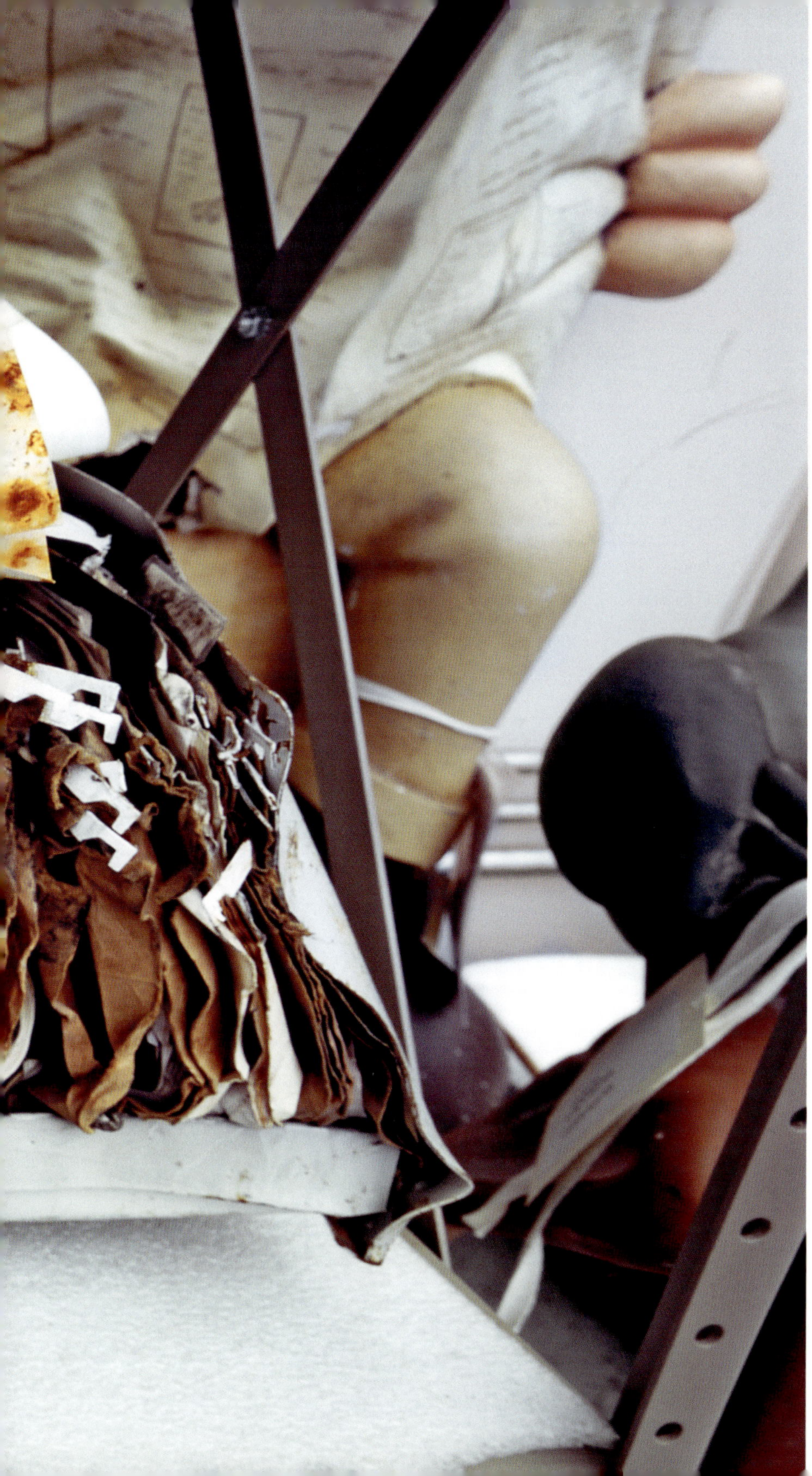

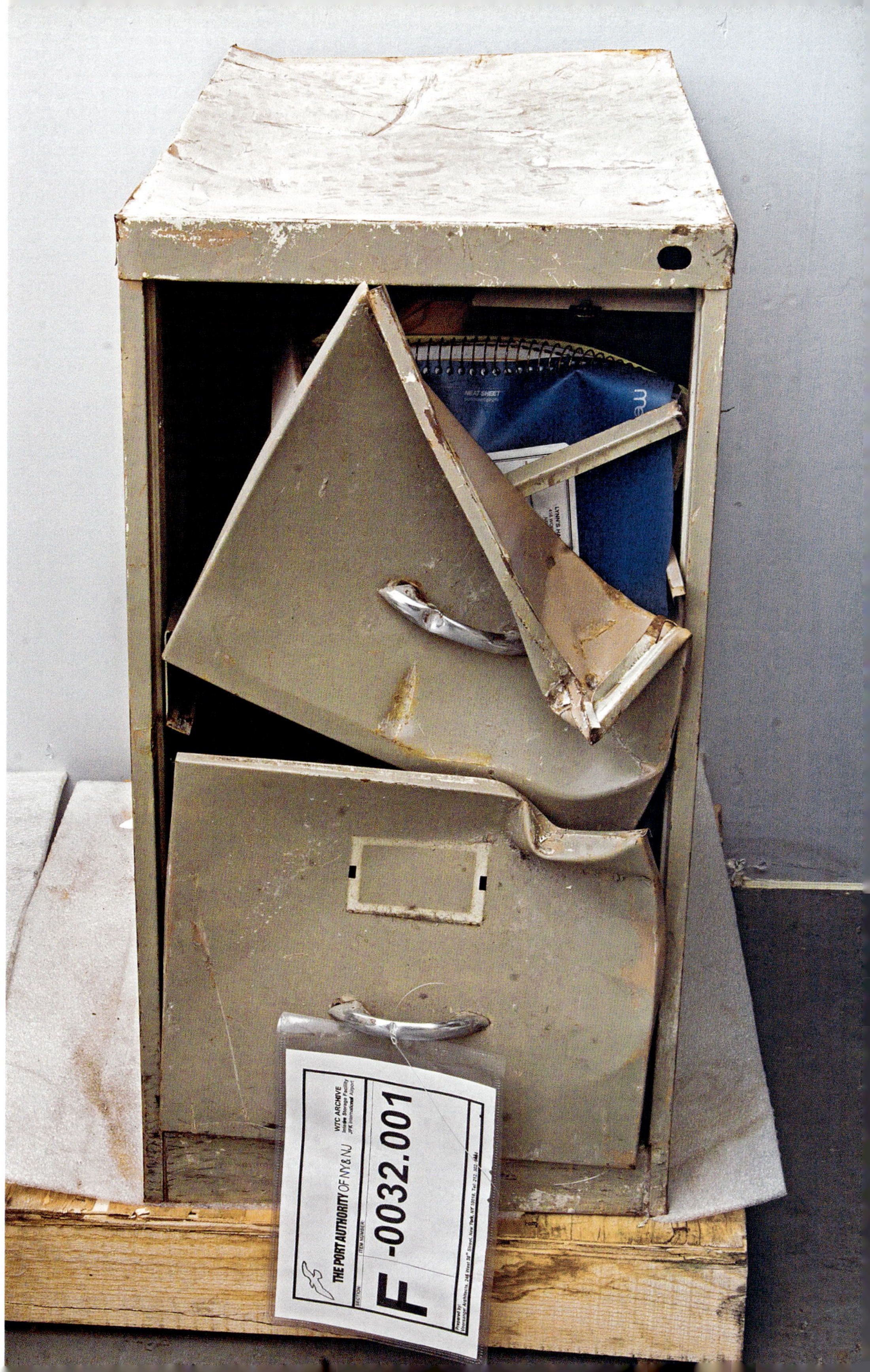

THE PORT AUTHORITY OF NY&NJ
WTC ARCHIVE
JFK International Airport
SECTION:
ITEM NUMBER:
F -0032.001

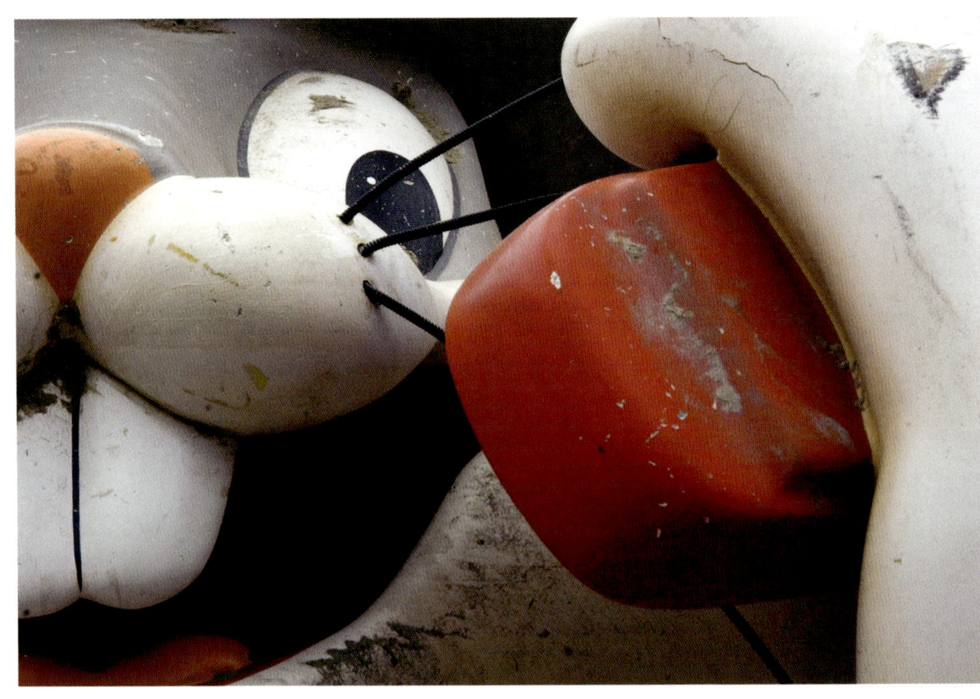
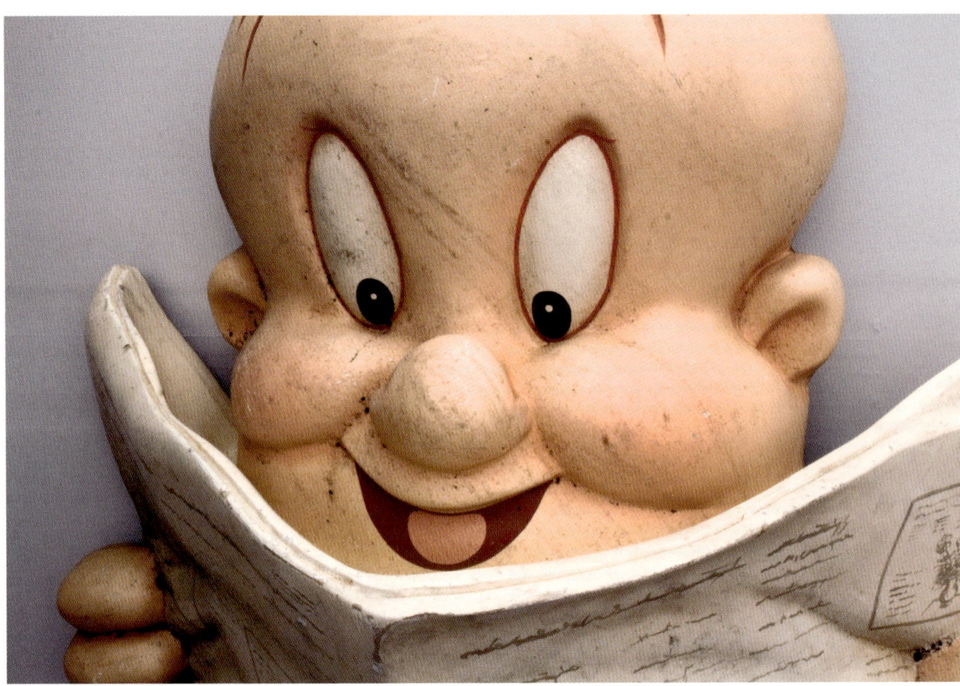
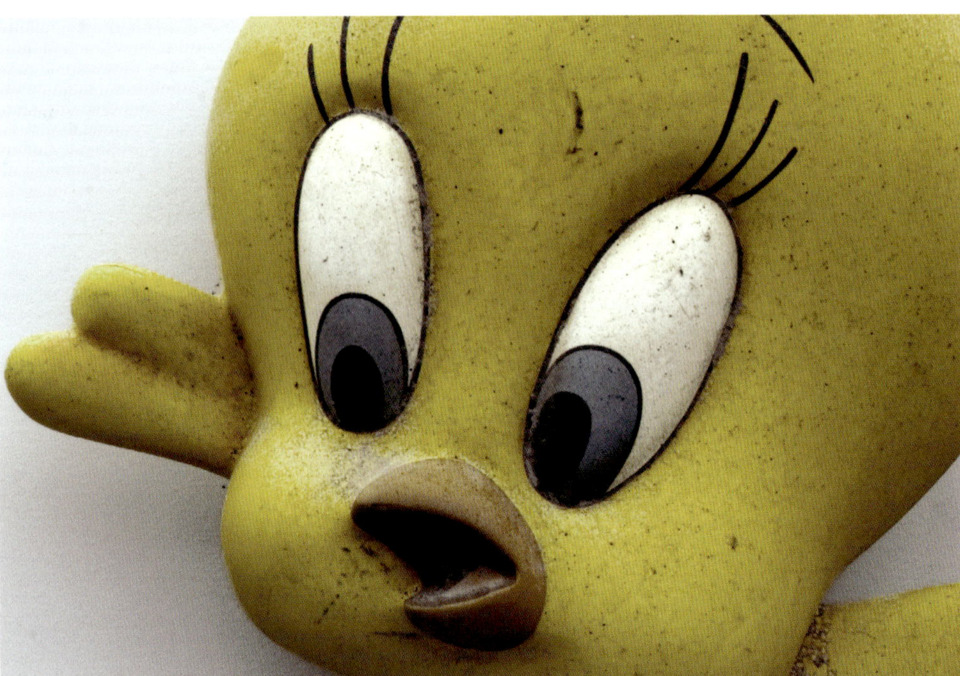
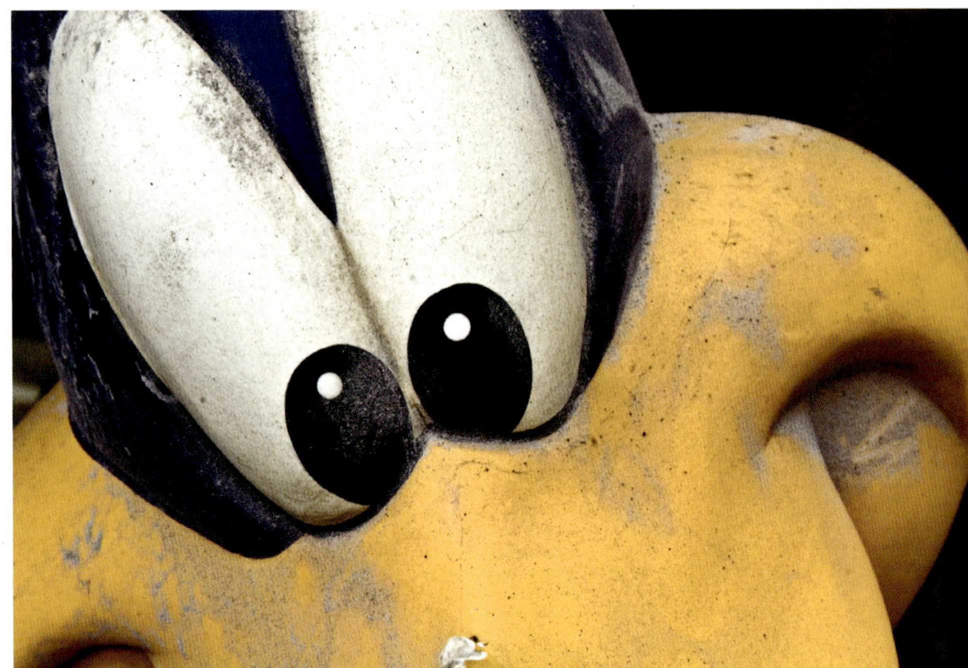

Large-scale cartoon characters salvaged from the Warner Bros. Studio Store.

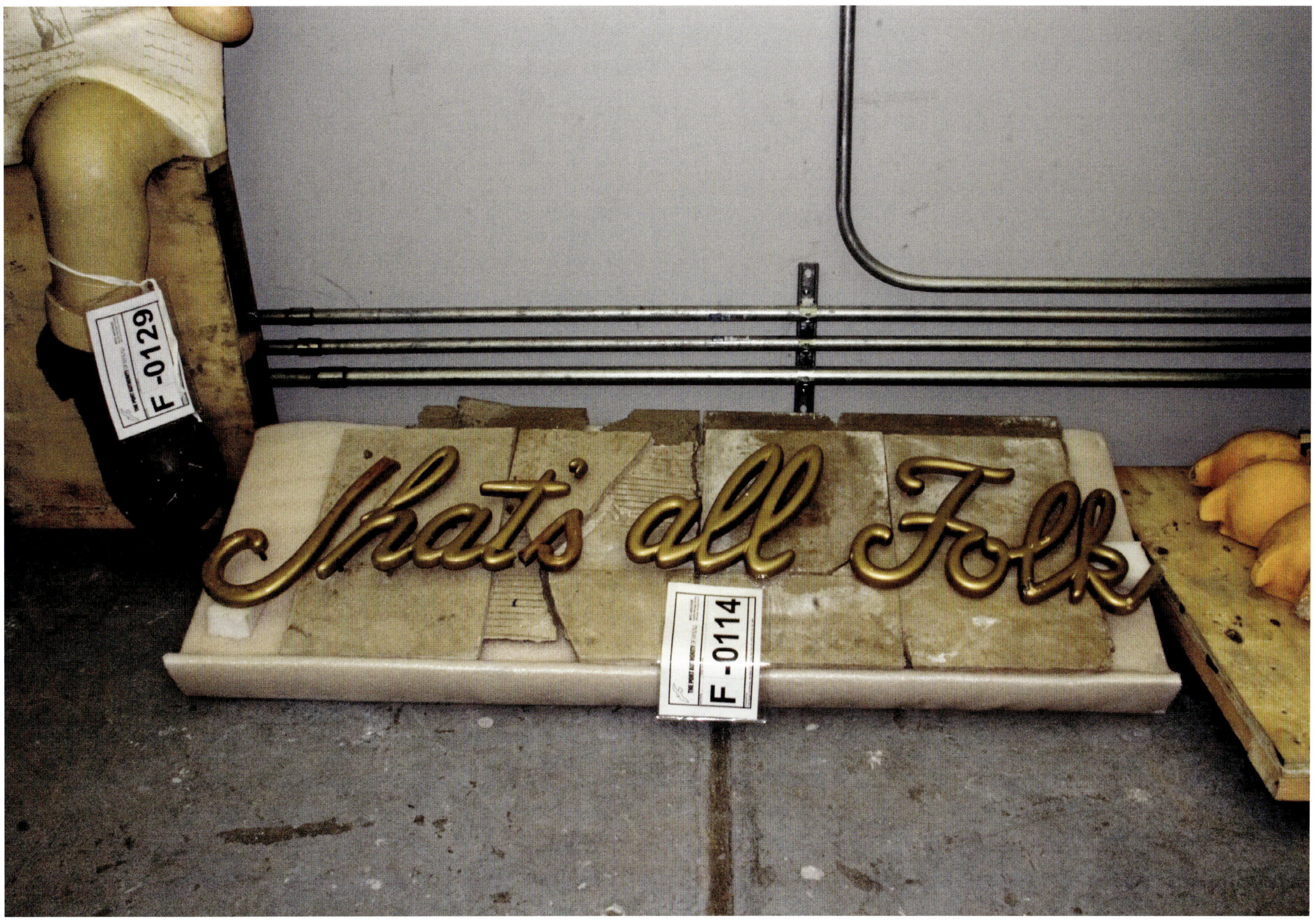
F -0129
That's all Folk
F -0114

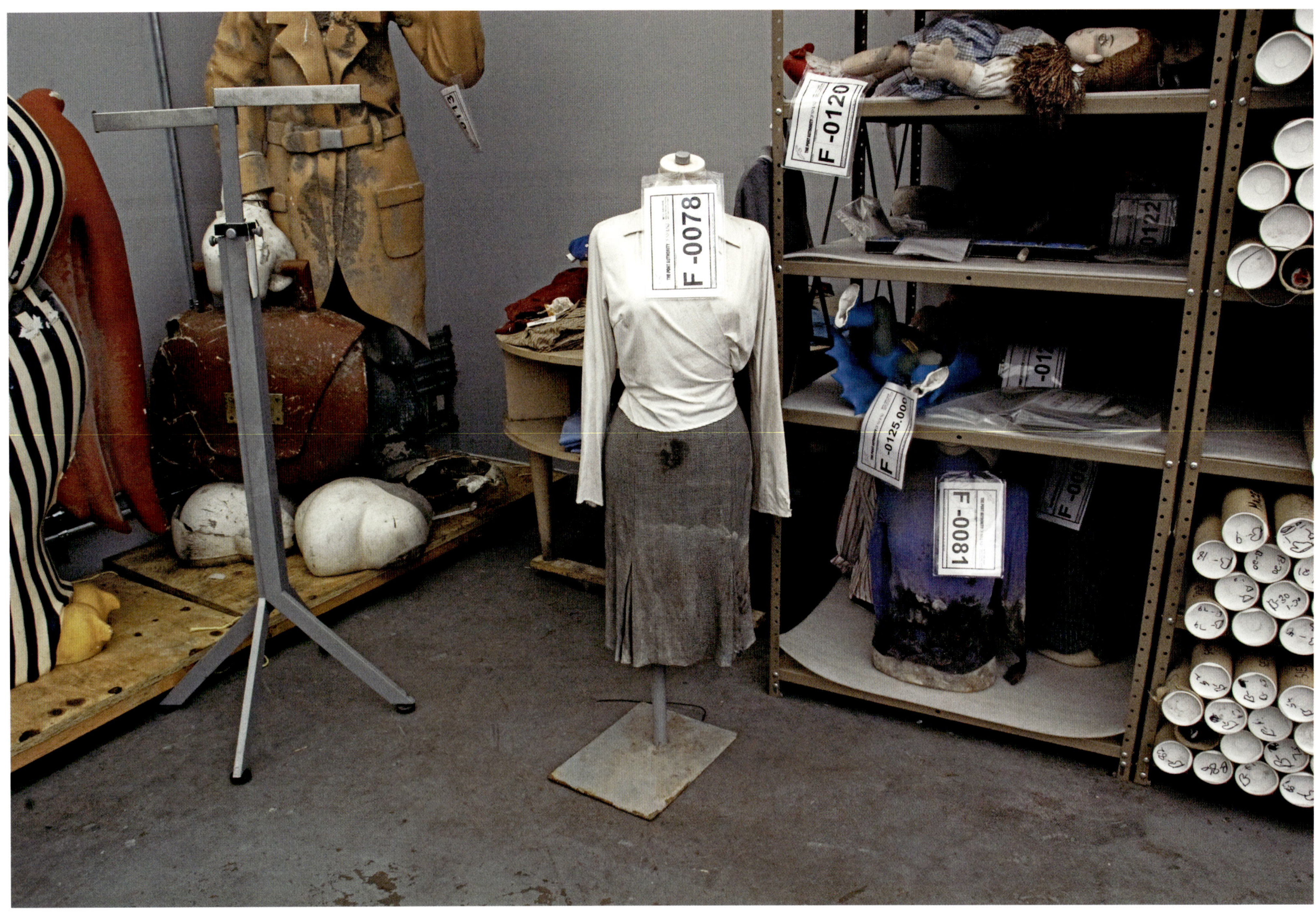

A water-stained skirt on a mannequin from one of the World Trade Center concourse shops. In some underground areas, large amounts of water pooled, coming perhaps from sprinkler systems, broken pipes, or fire control efforts that continued after the buildings collapsed.

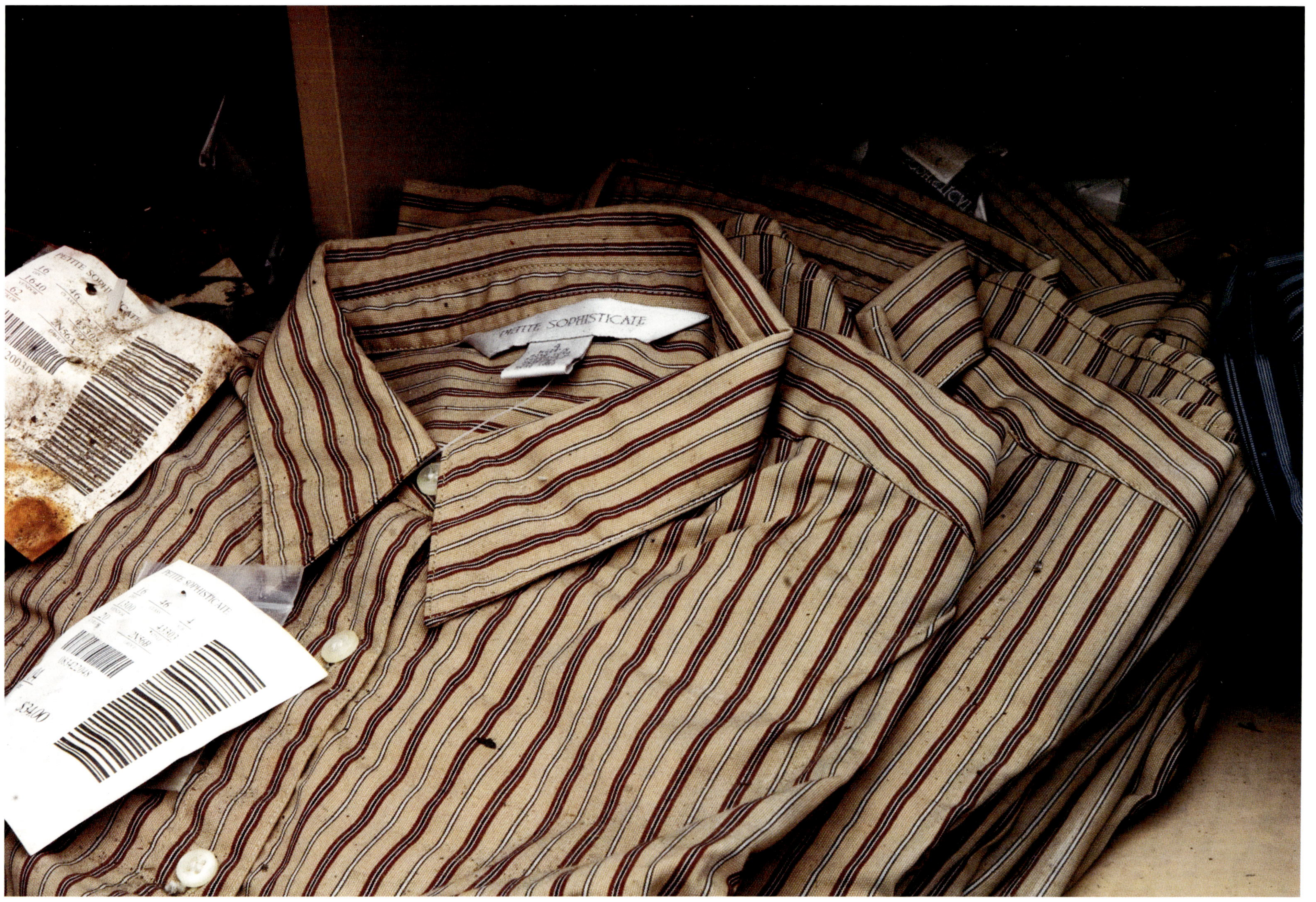
PETITE SOPHISTICATE

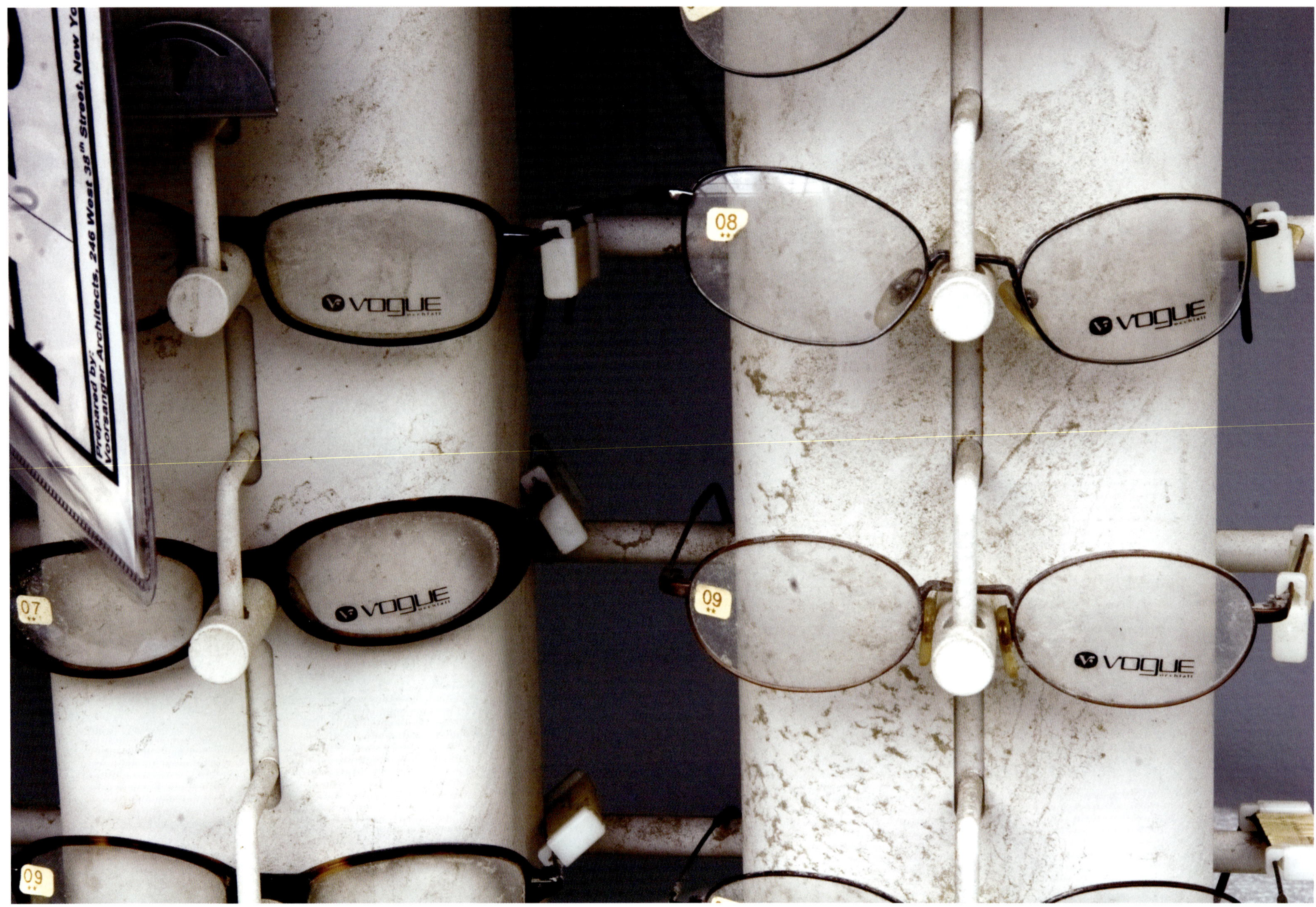
Prepared by:
Voorsanger Architects, 246 West 38th Street, New
VOGUE
08
VOGUE
07
VOGUE
09
VOGUE
09

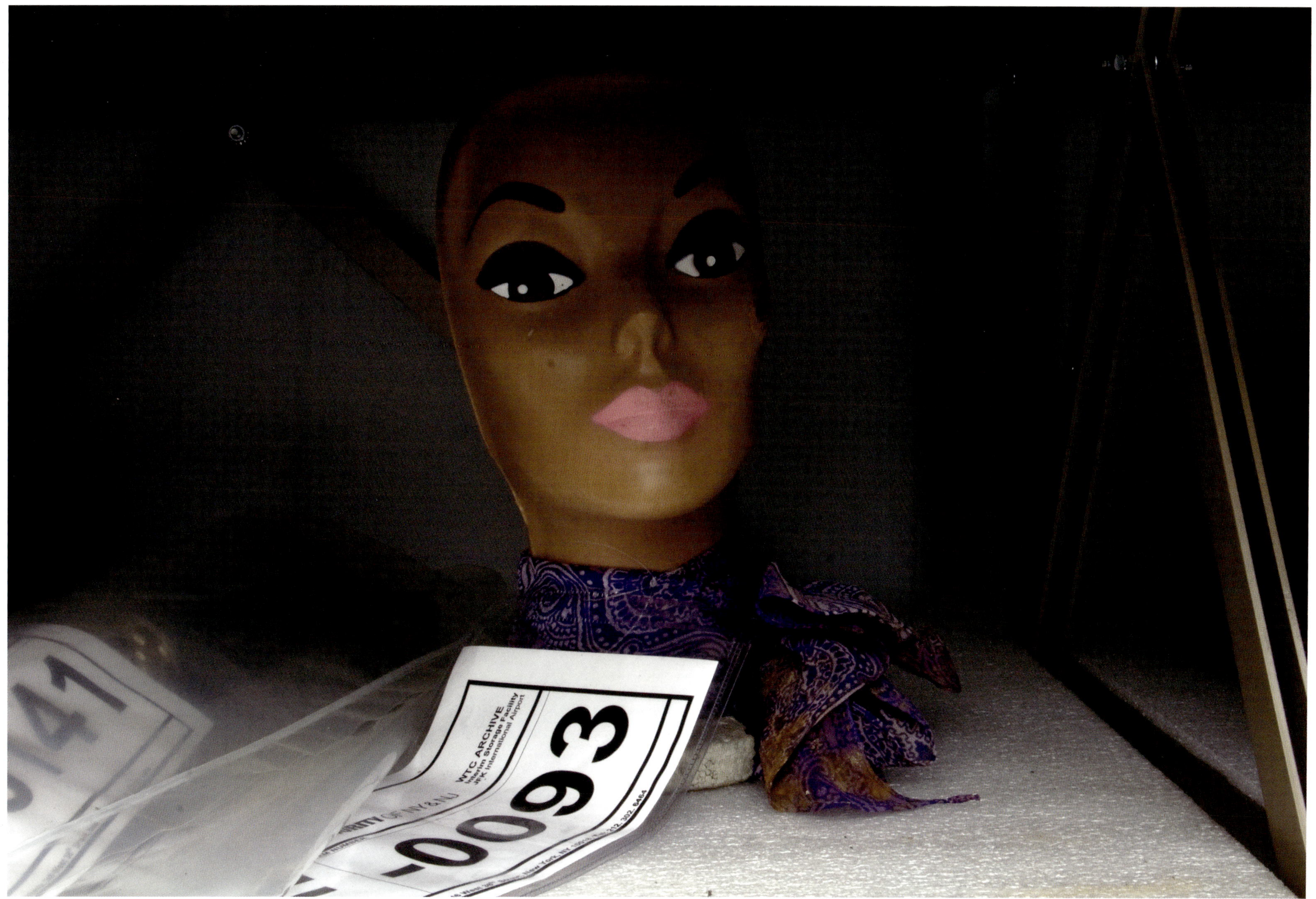
141
WTC ARCHIVE
Interim Storage Facility
JFK International Airport
-0093

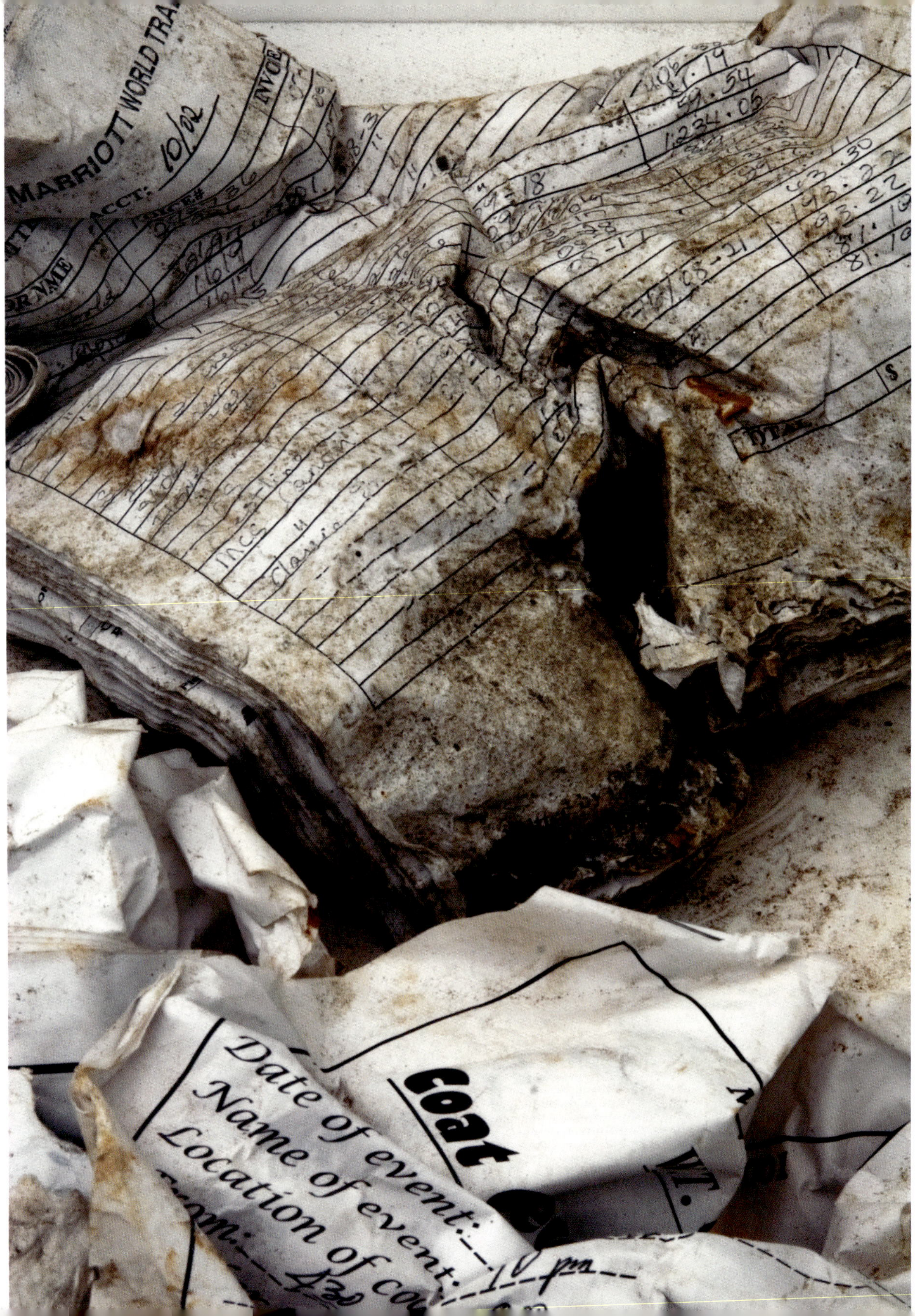

PERSONAL EFFECTS

The business card of Paul Acquaviva was found in the rubble. A vice president of eSpeed, a division of the global services firm Cantor Fitzgerald, Mr. Acquaviva, 29 years old, was on the 103rd floor in the north tower when he last spoke to his wife, following the impact of the hijacked American Airlines Flight 11 into the building. Like nearly everyone above the impact zones in each of the towers, Mr. Acquaviva did not survive. In all, 658 Cantor Fitzgerald employees died on 9/11.

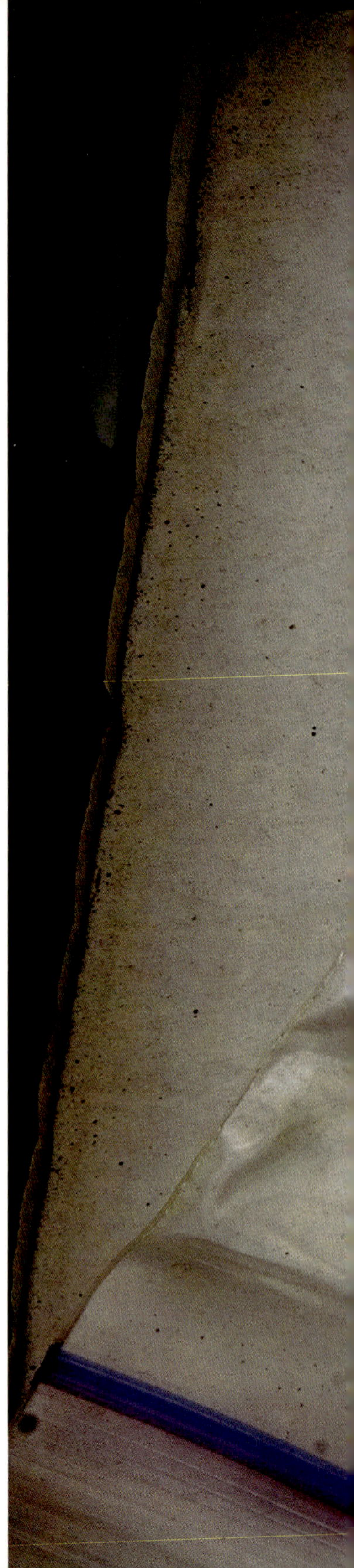

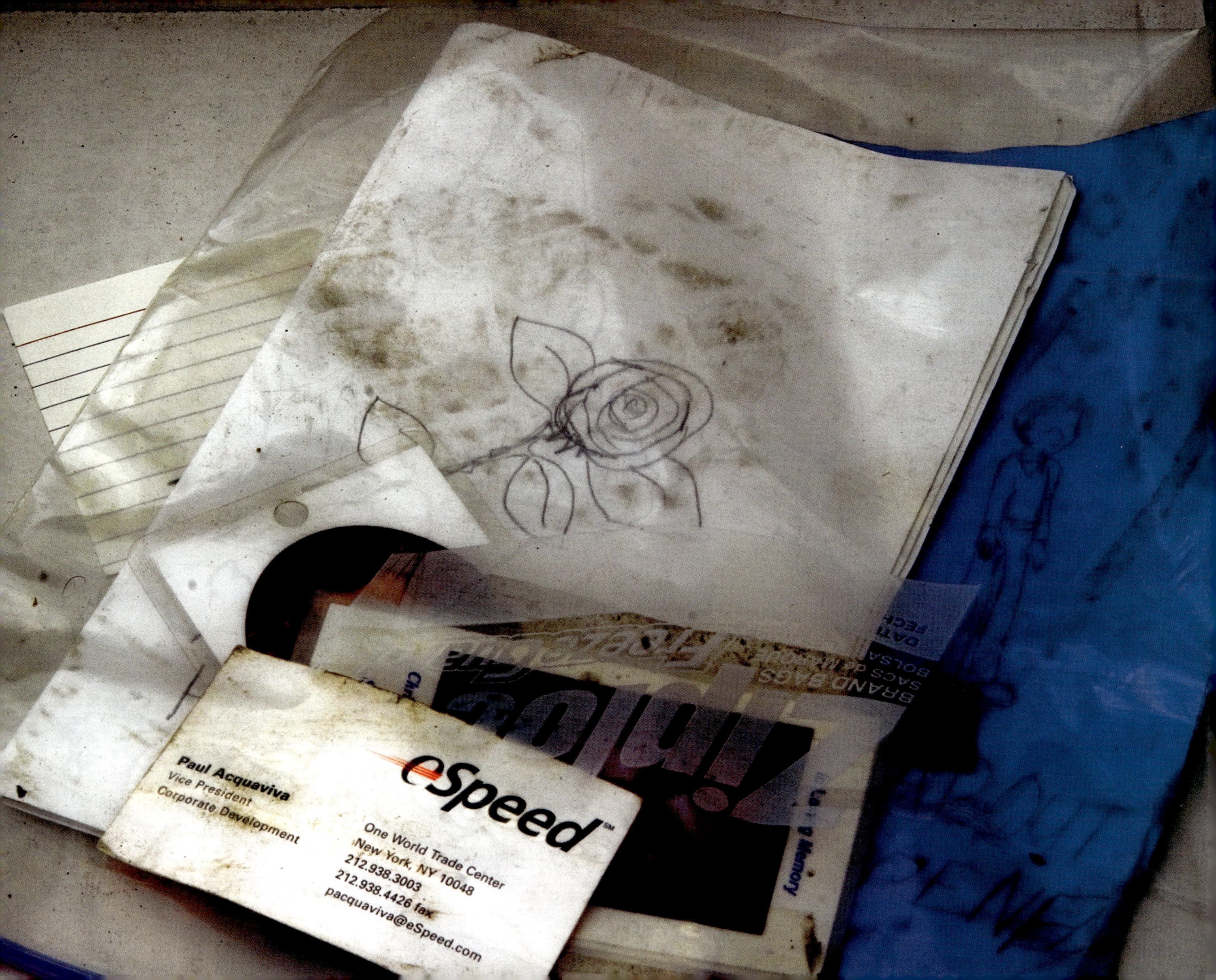
Paul Acquaviva
Vice President
Corporate Development
eSpeed
One World Trade Center
New York, NY 10048
212.938.3003
212.938.4426 fax
pacquaviva@eSpeed.com

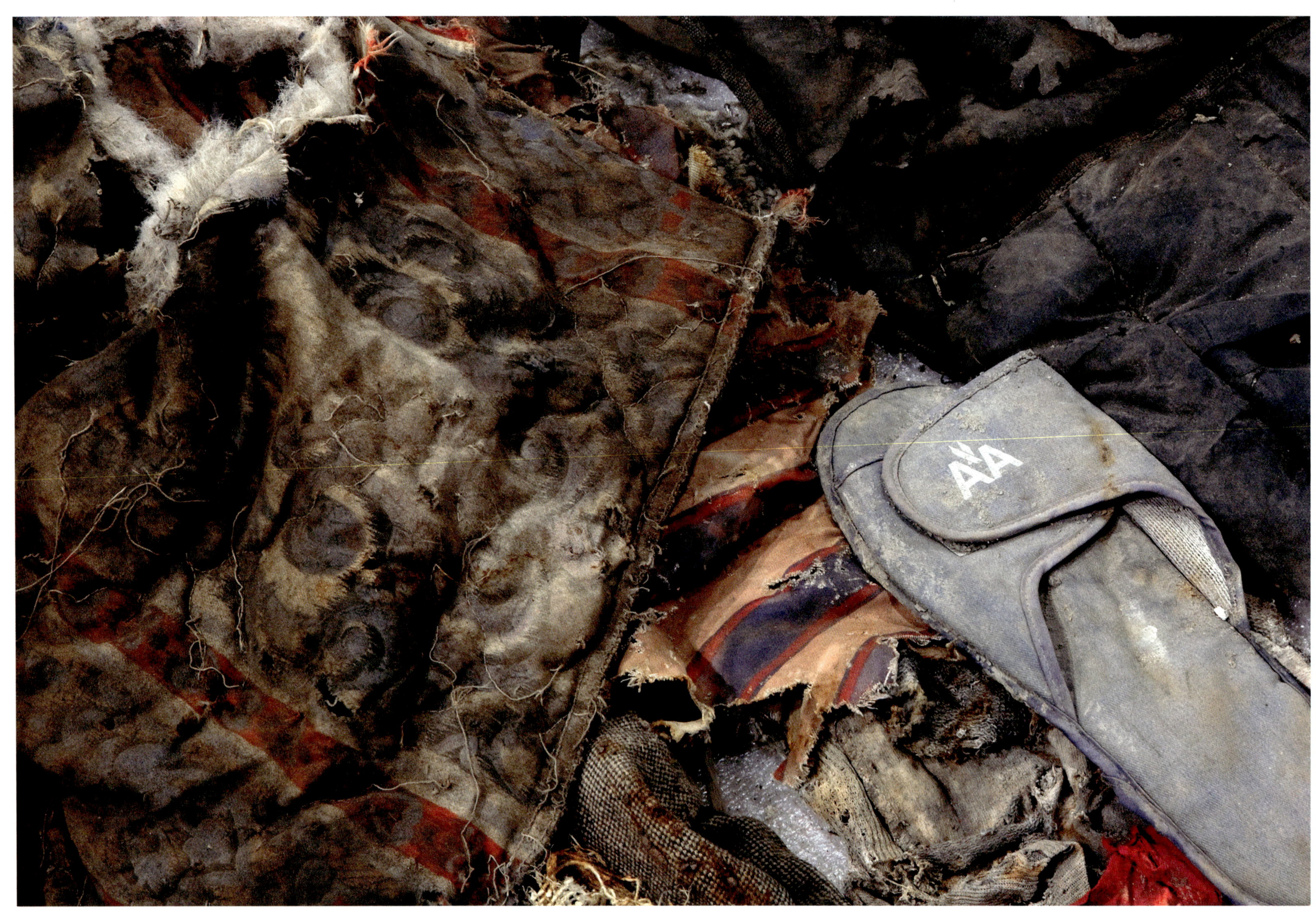

Though the hijacked American Airlines Flight 11 was intentionally crashed into the north tower, there is no certainty about the origins of this slipper, which was found in the rubble. Because this type of courtesy slipper was only distributed on international flights, perhaps one of the flight crew had been carrying it. Alternatively, it may have been one of a pair kept in a World Trade Center office.

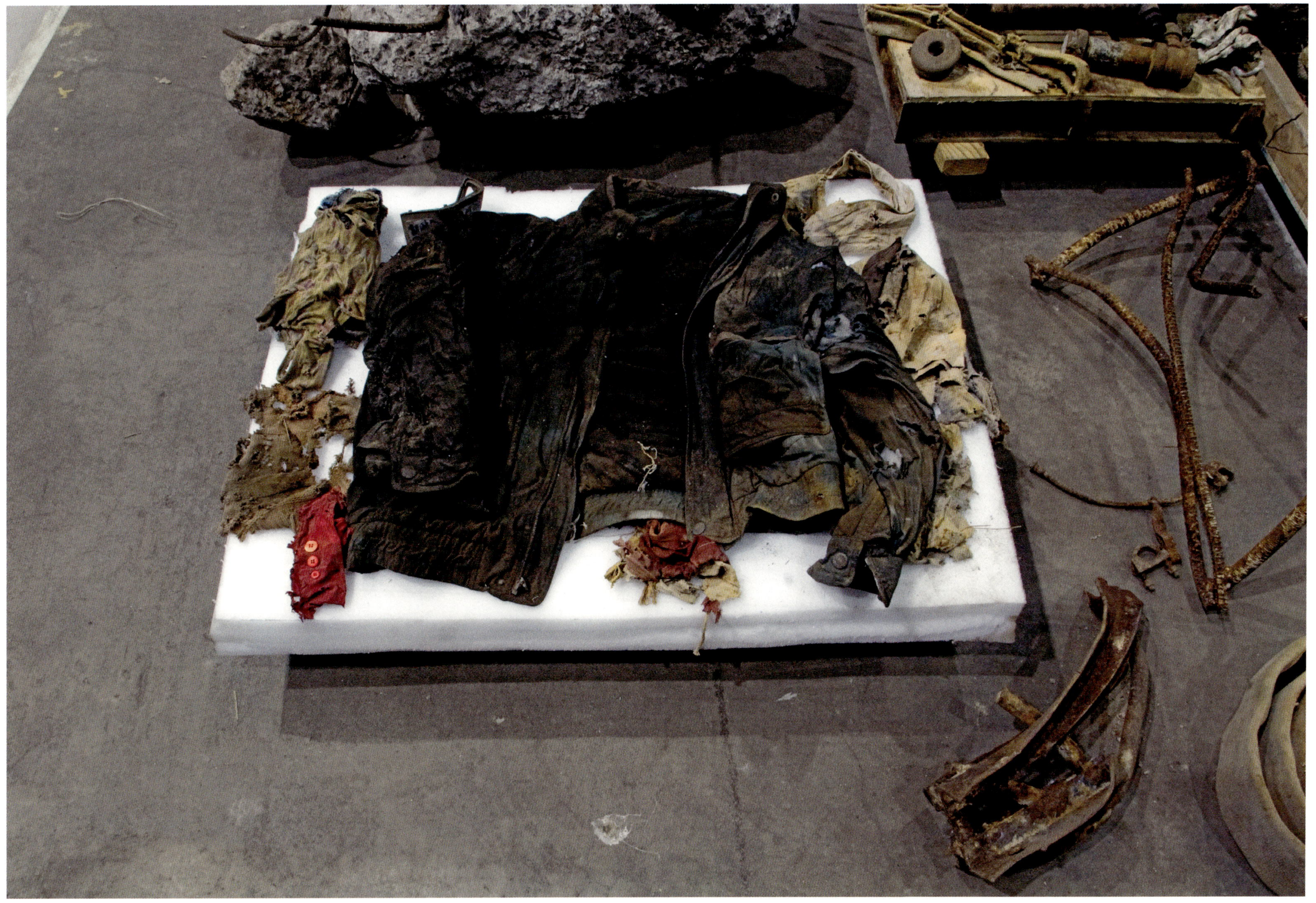

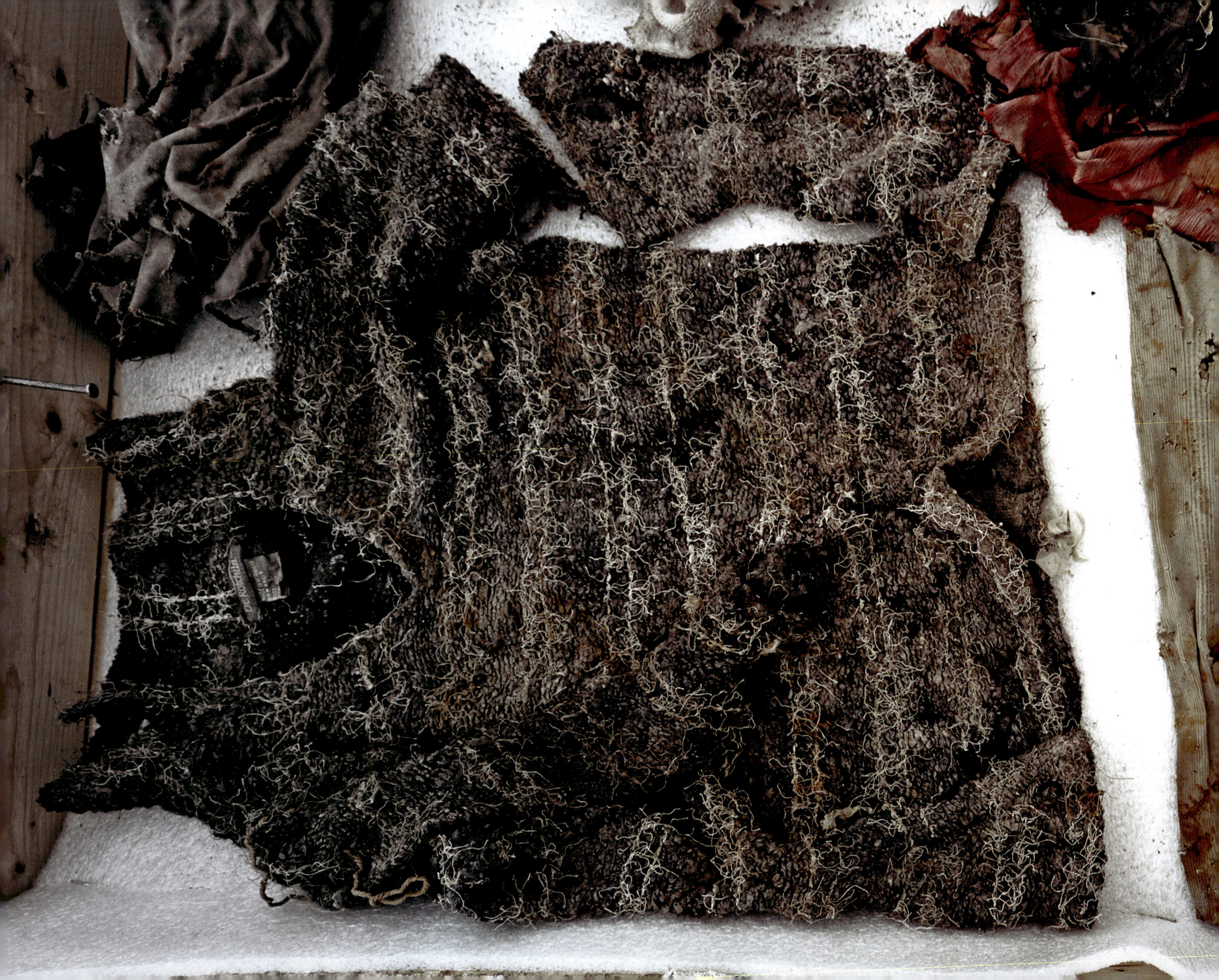

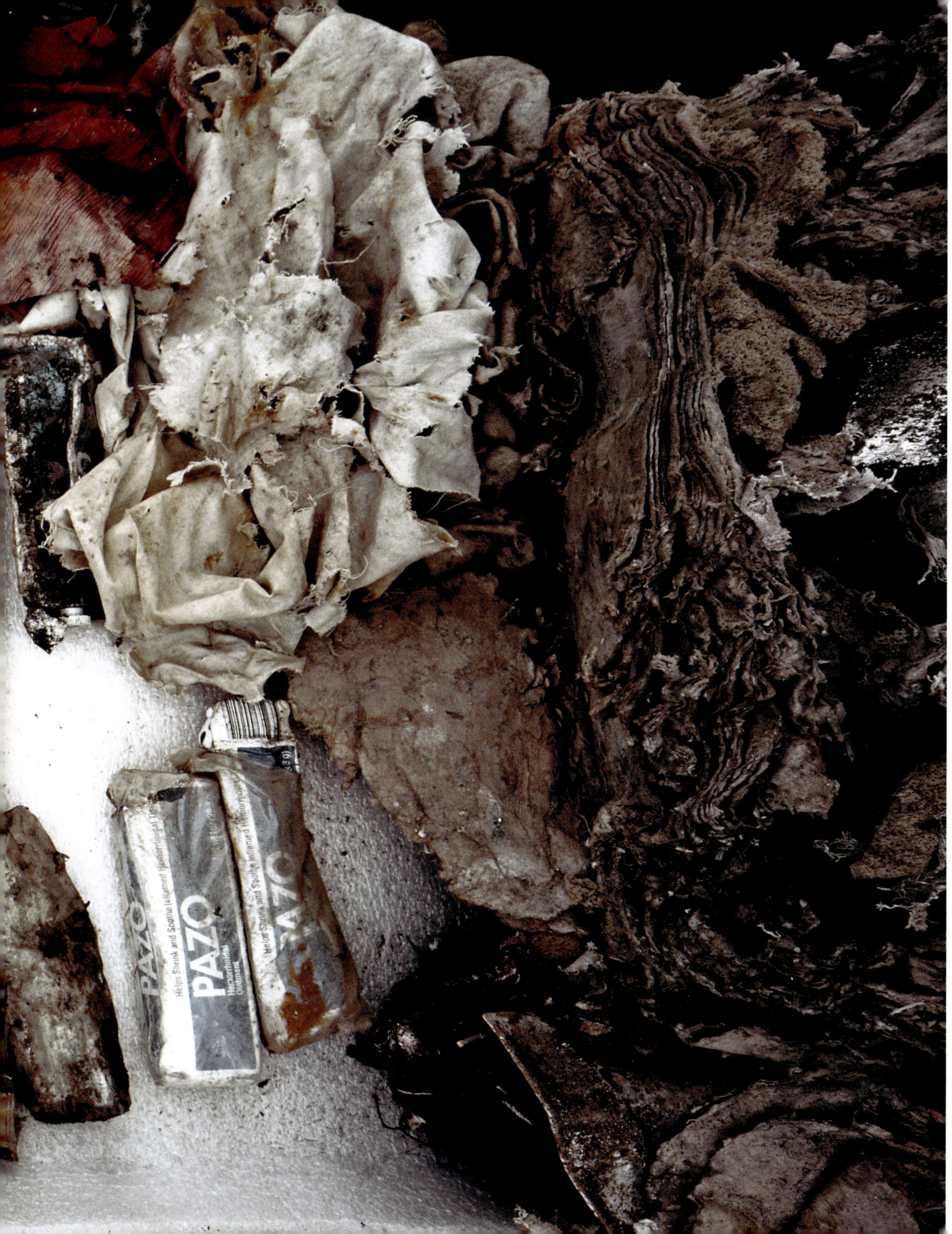

The articles of clothing shown in these photographs were taken out of a Dumpster that had been filled with construction rubble and brought to Hangar 17. As the Dumpster was slowly emptied, conservators found tattered clothing mixed in with rebar and concrete. No owners have been identified for any of these pieces.

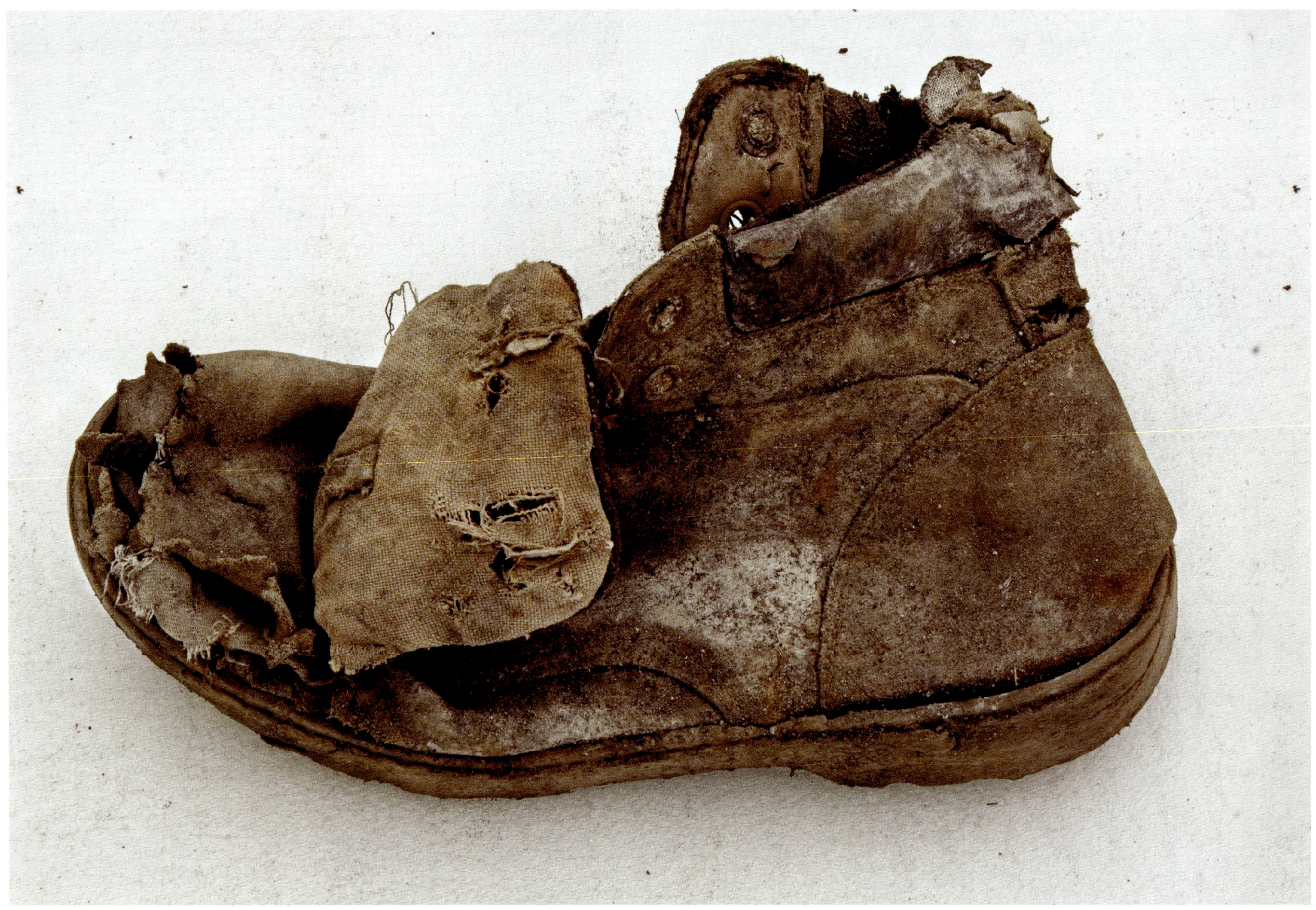

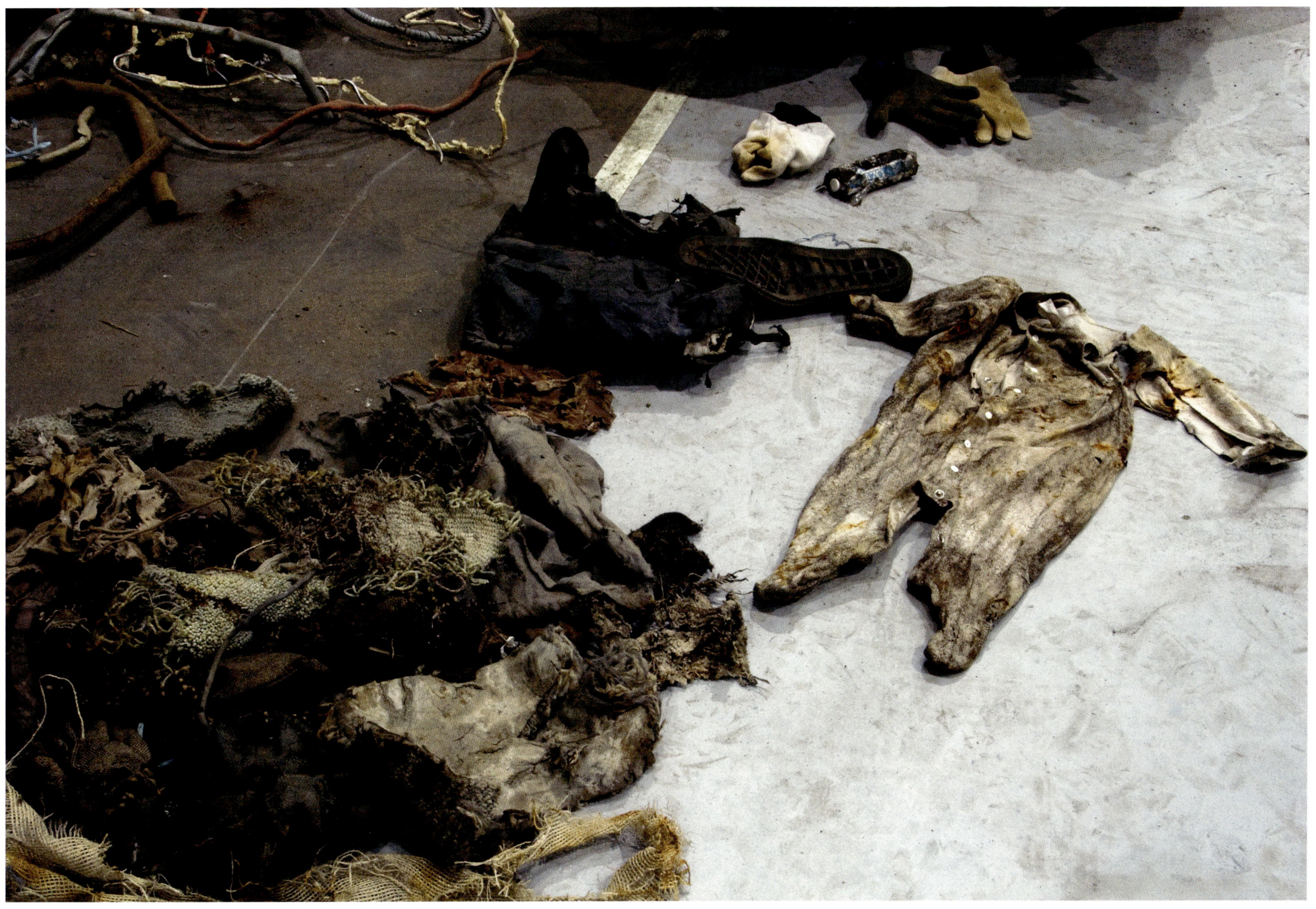

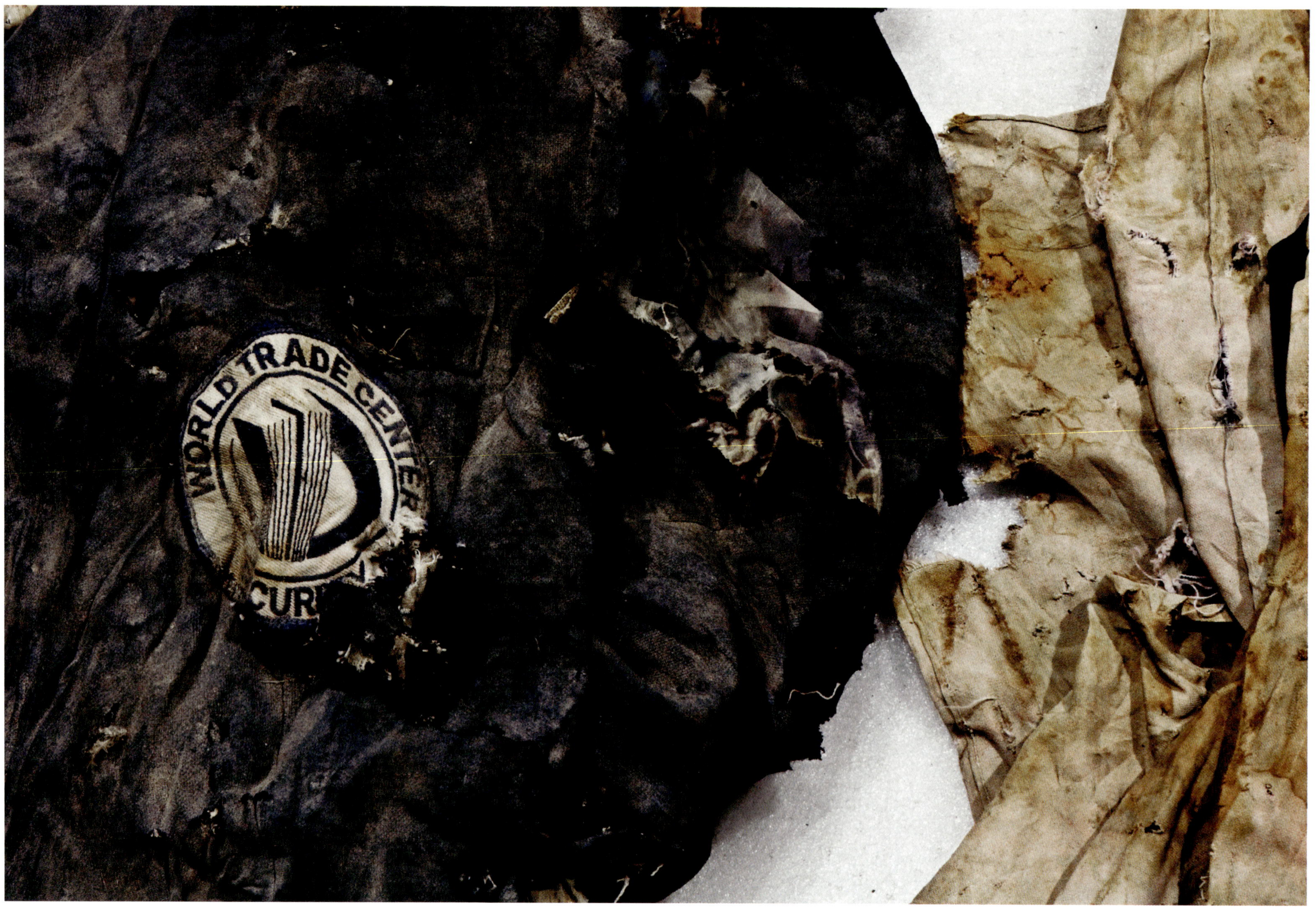
WORLD TRADE CENTER
CURI

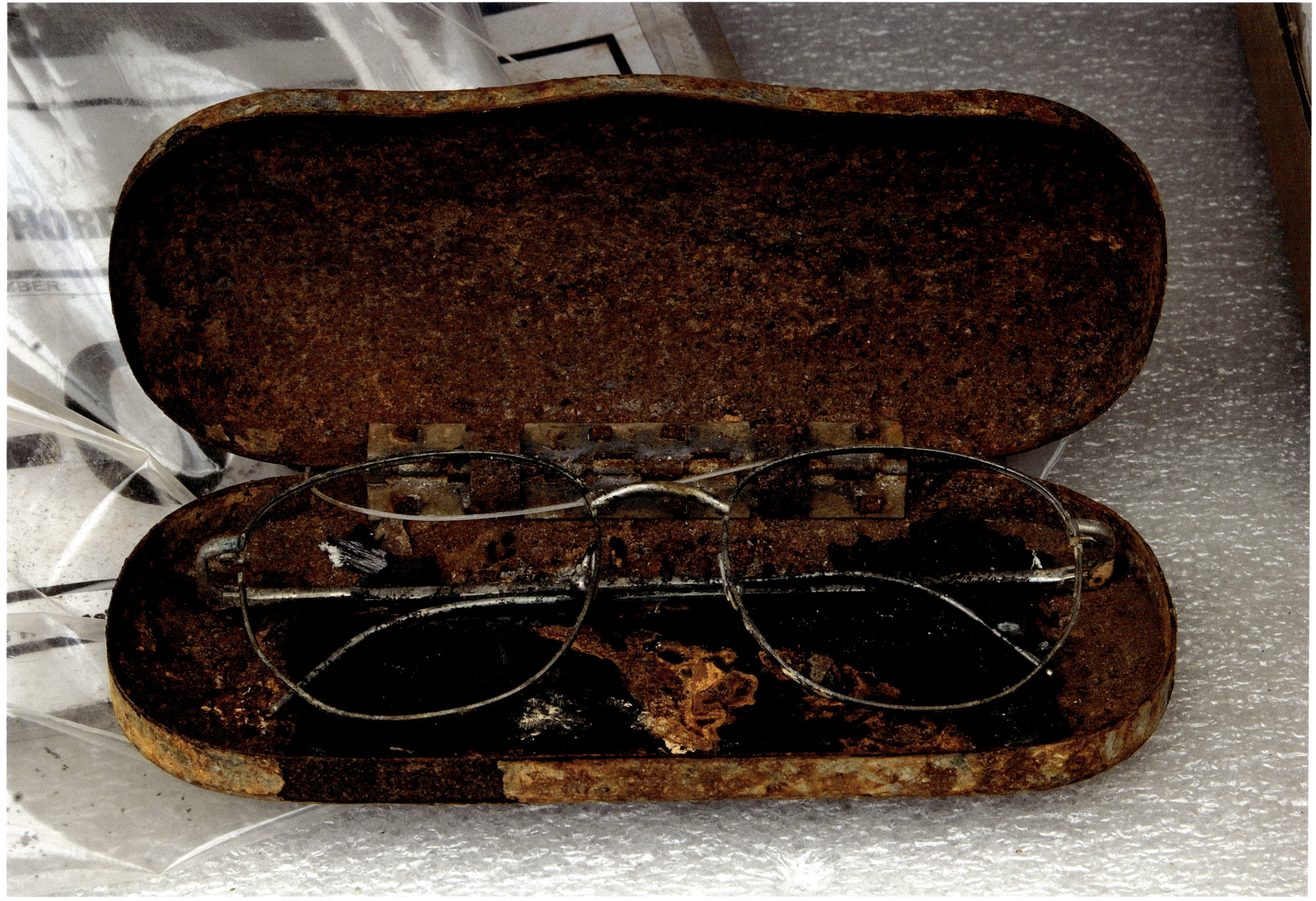

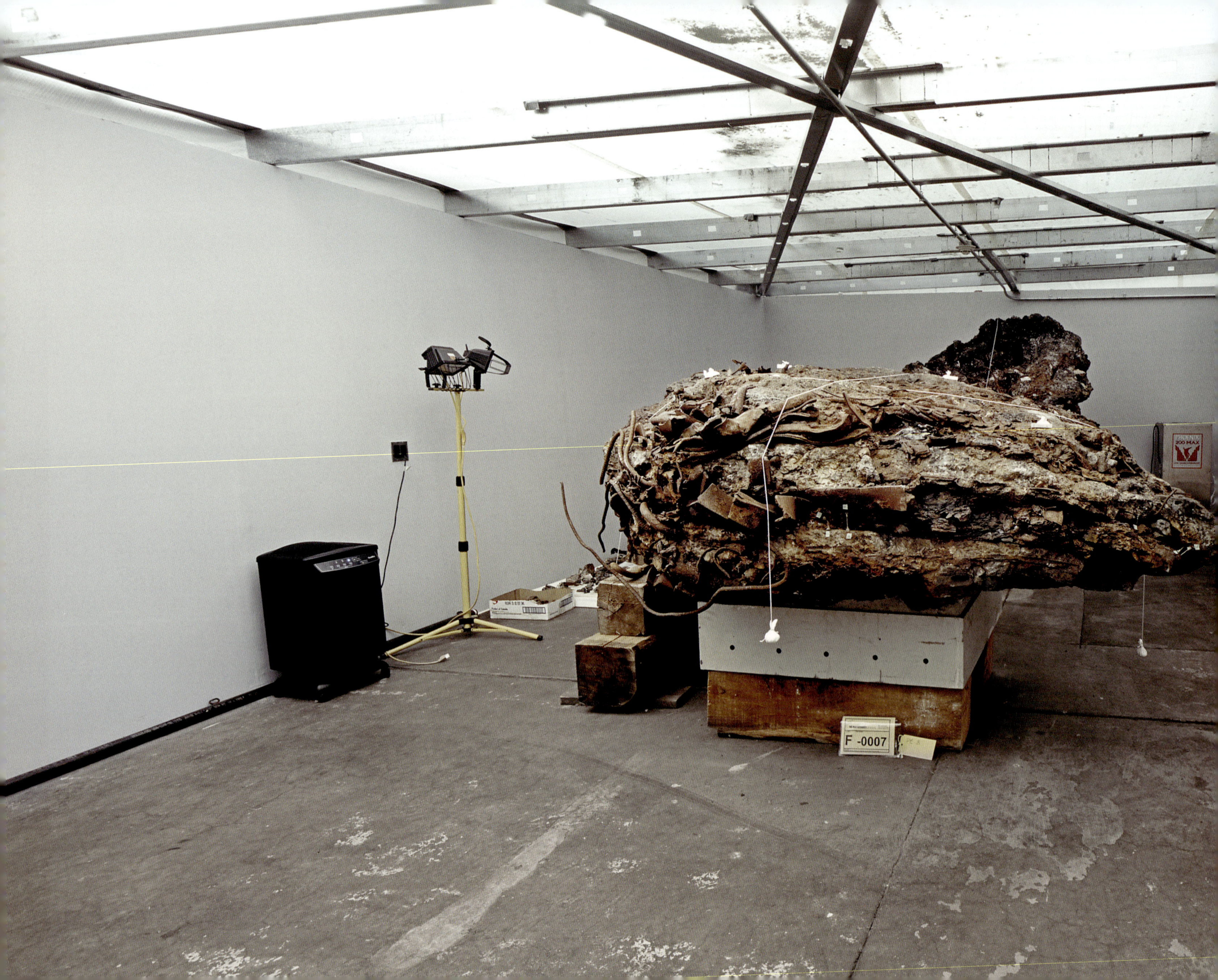
F -0007

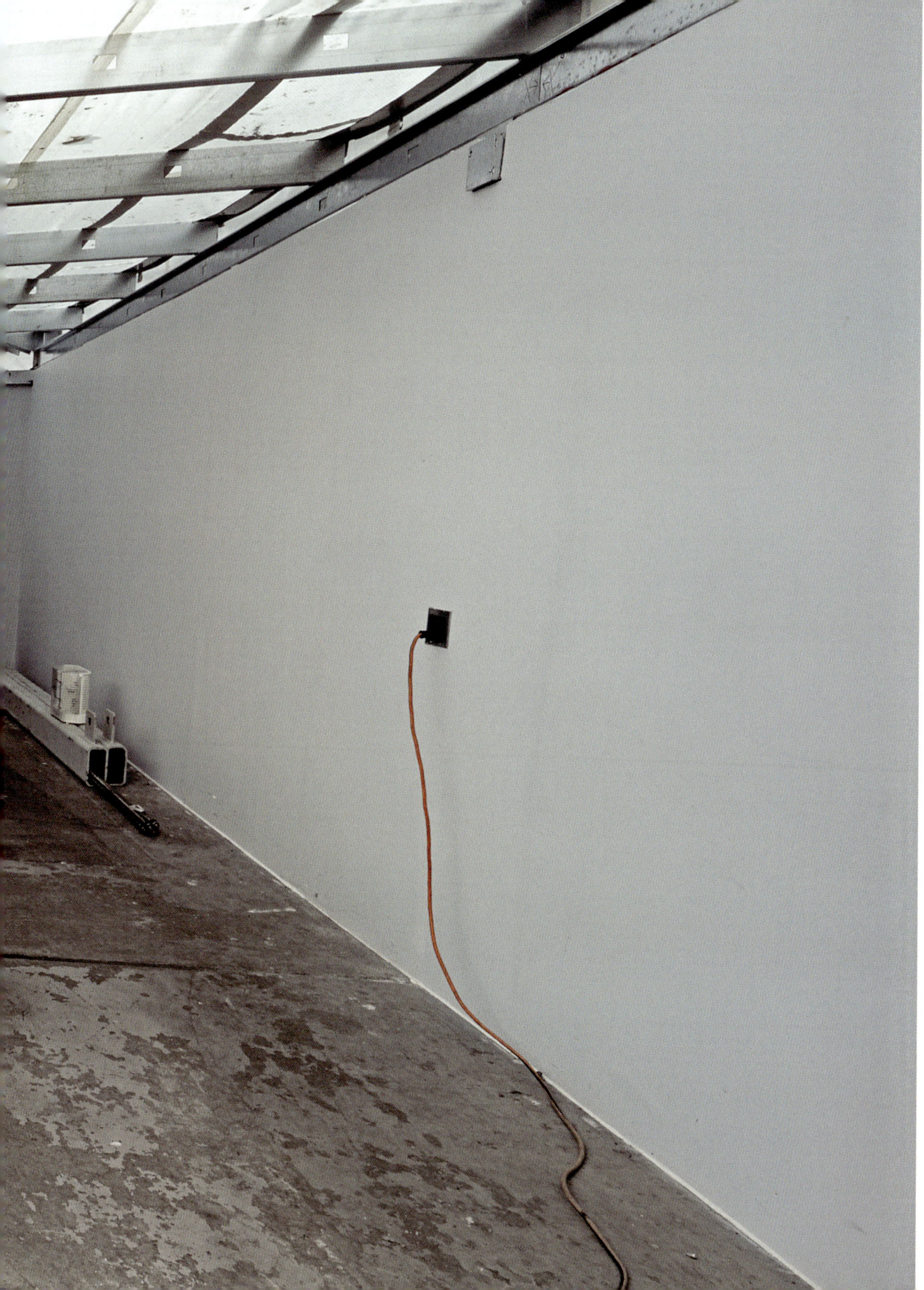

COMPOSITES

Formed during the collapse of the towers, and then months of exposure to high-heat fires, this object has come to be known as the composite. Weighing between 12 and 15 tons, it holds the compressed remnants of four stories of one of the towers, though which one is unlikely ever to be known. It is just over four feet high.

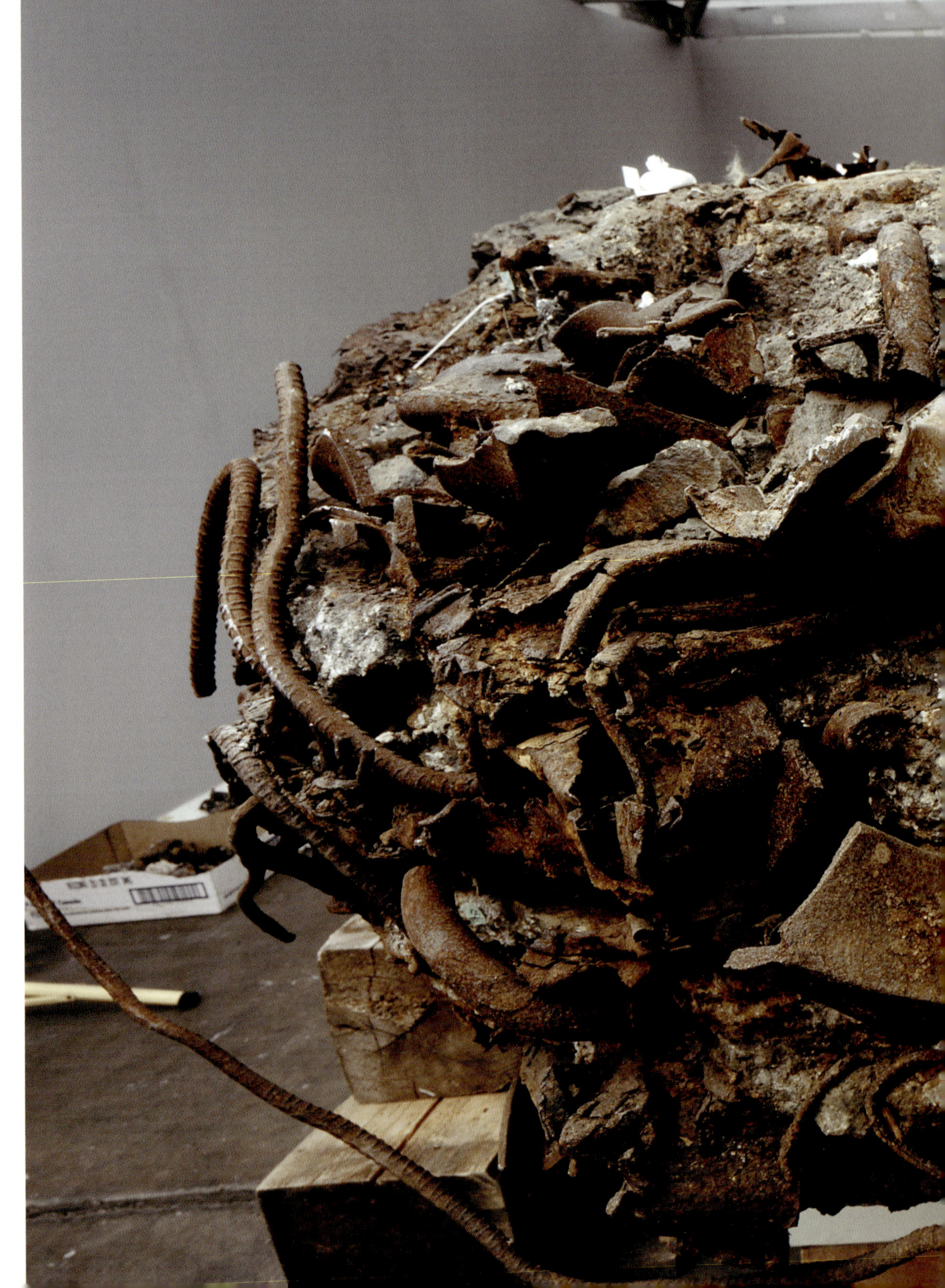

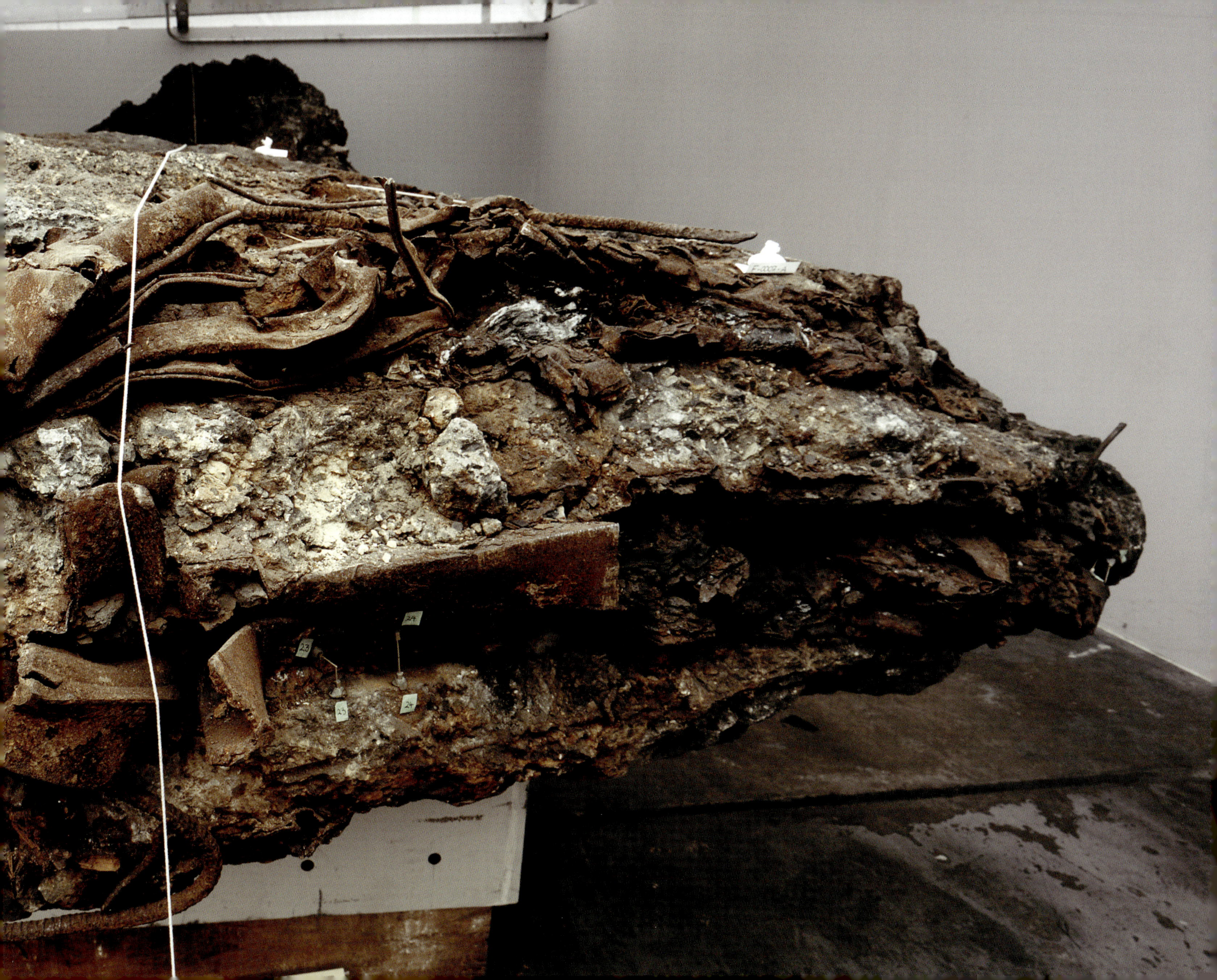

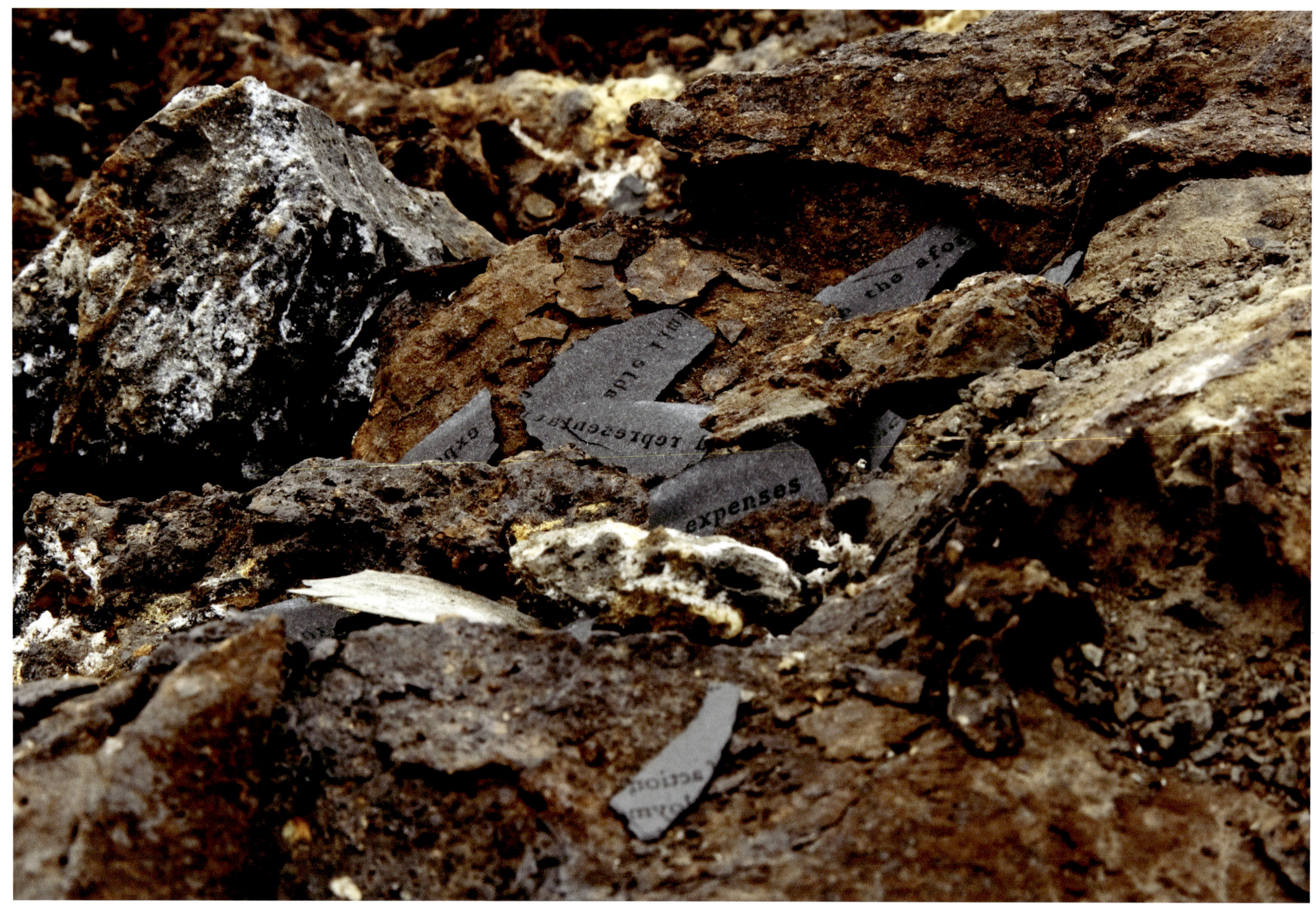

In spite of the extreme heat that forged this composite and its outdoor exposure at the World Trade Center site, bits of carbonized paper remain on its surface. In effect, these are ashes of the original paper, which remain intact, though they would disintegrate at a touch.

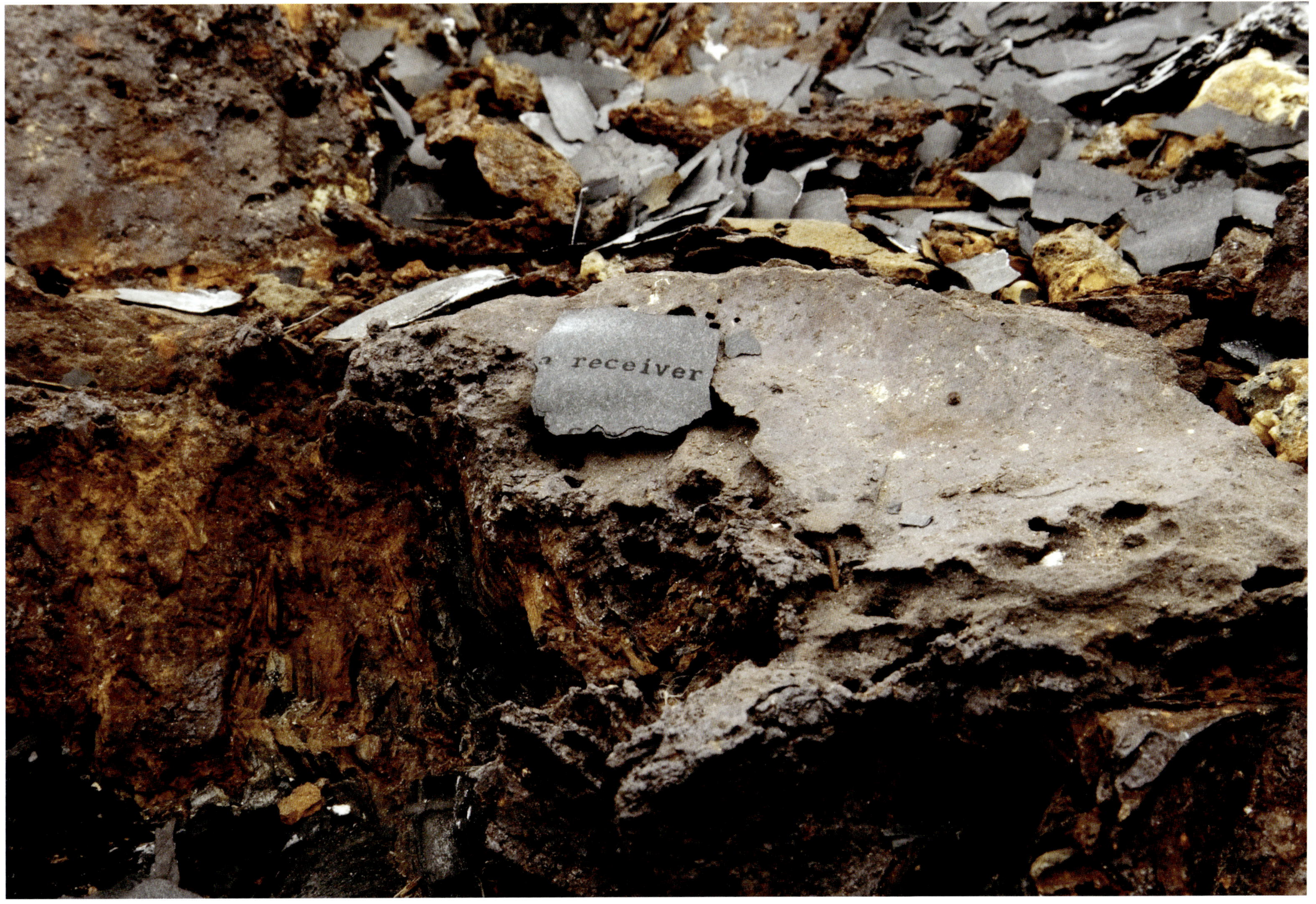
receiver

A second composite varies greatly in appearance from the first. The differences are due to their varying contents and the likelihood that, although they were both exposed to extreme heat, they were not subject to heat for the same amounts of time. Additionally, the melting points of their constituent parts differ, meaning that, in each case, the fusion of materials was unique.

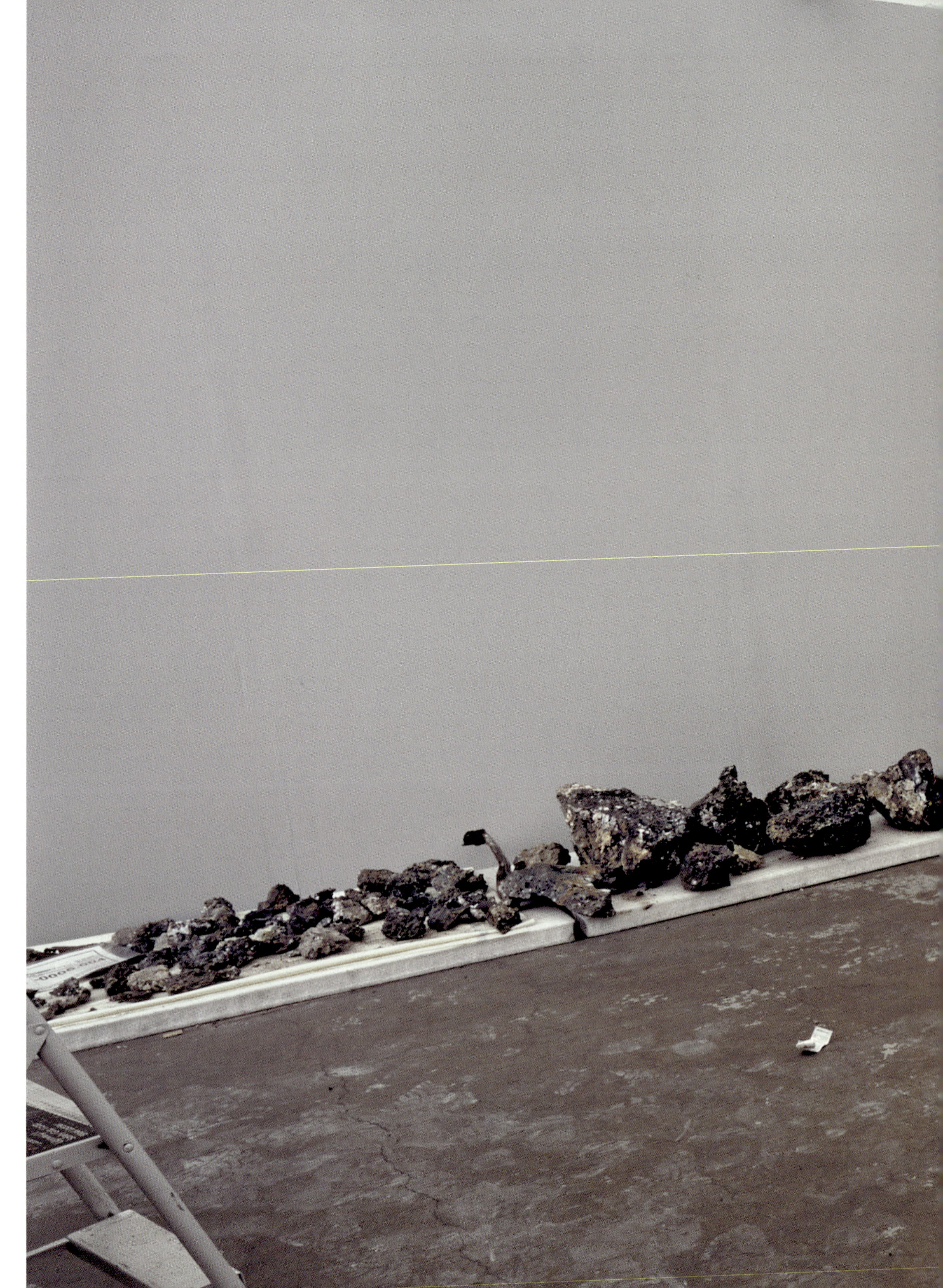

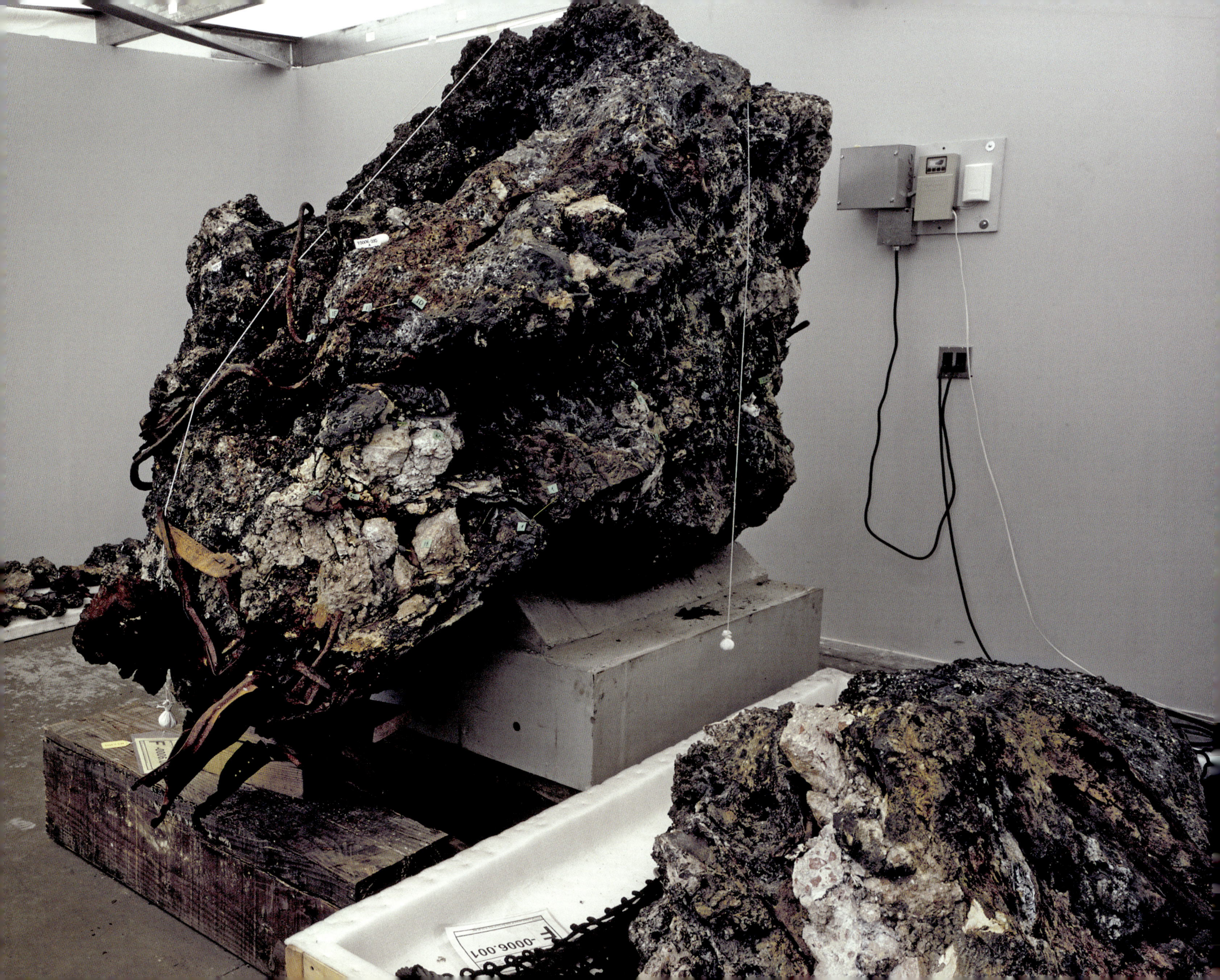

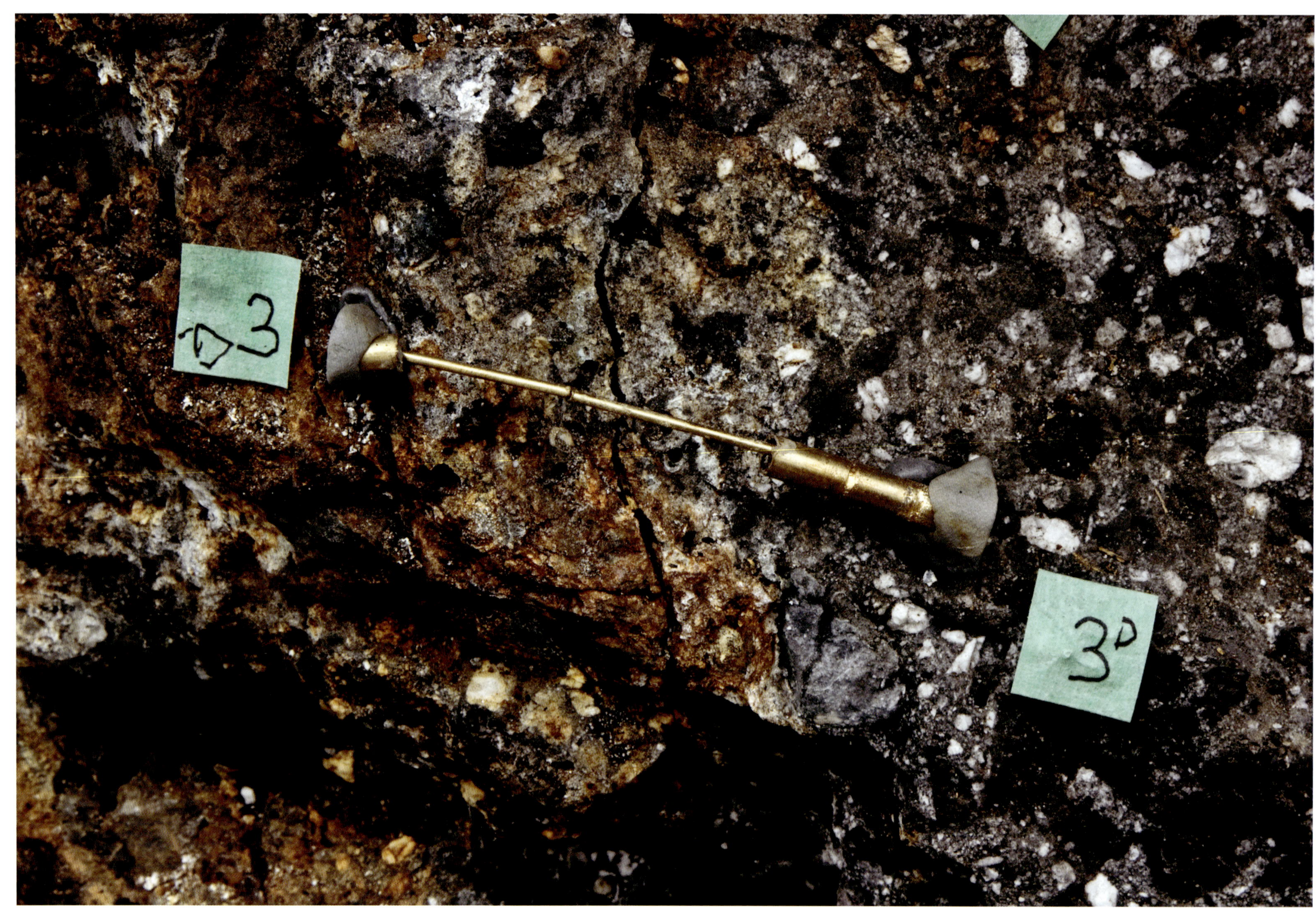

Though the composites are extremely heavy and dense, they are also fragile. To measure their stability, pins were placed along fissures and checked regularly to determine whether they were separating. Over time, some pieces have fallen off.

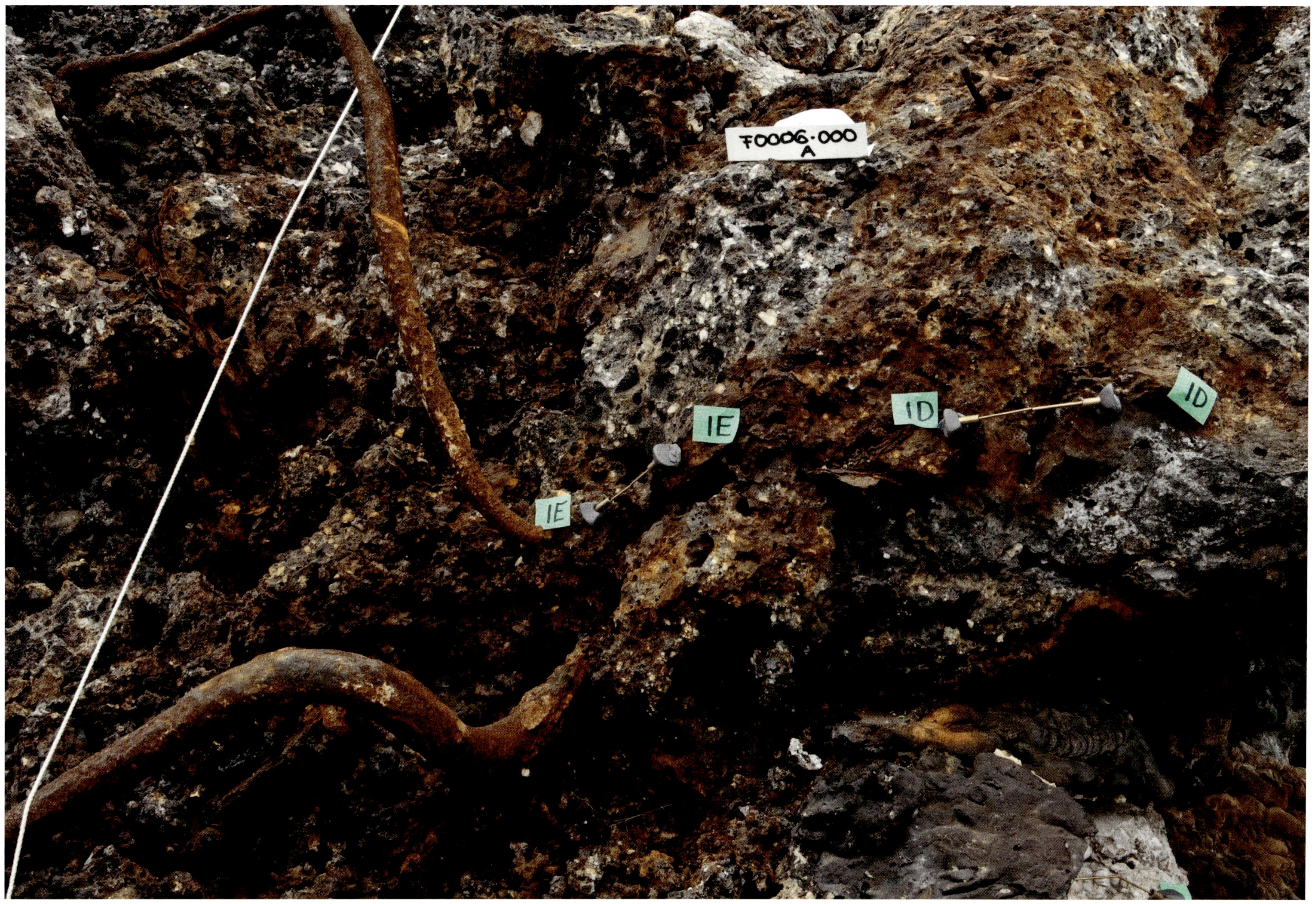
F0006.000
A
IE
IE
ID
ID

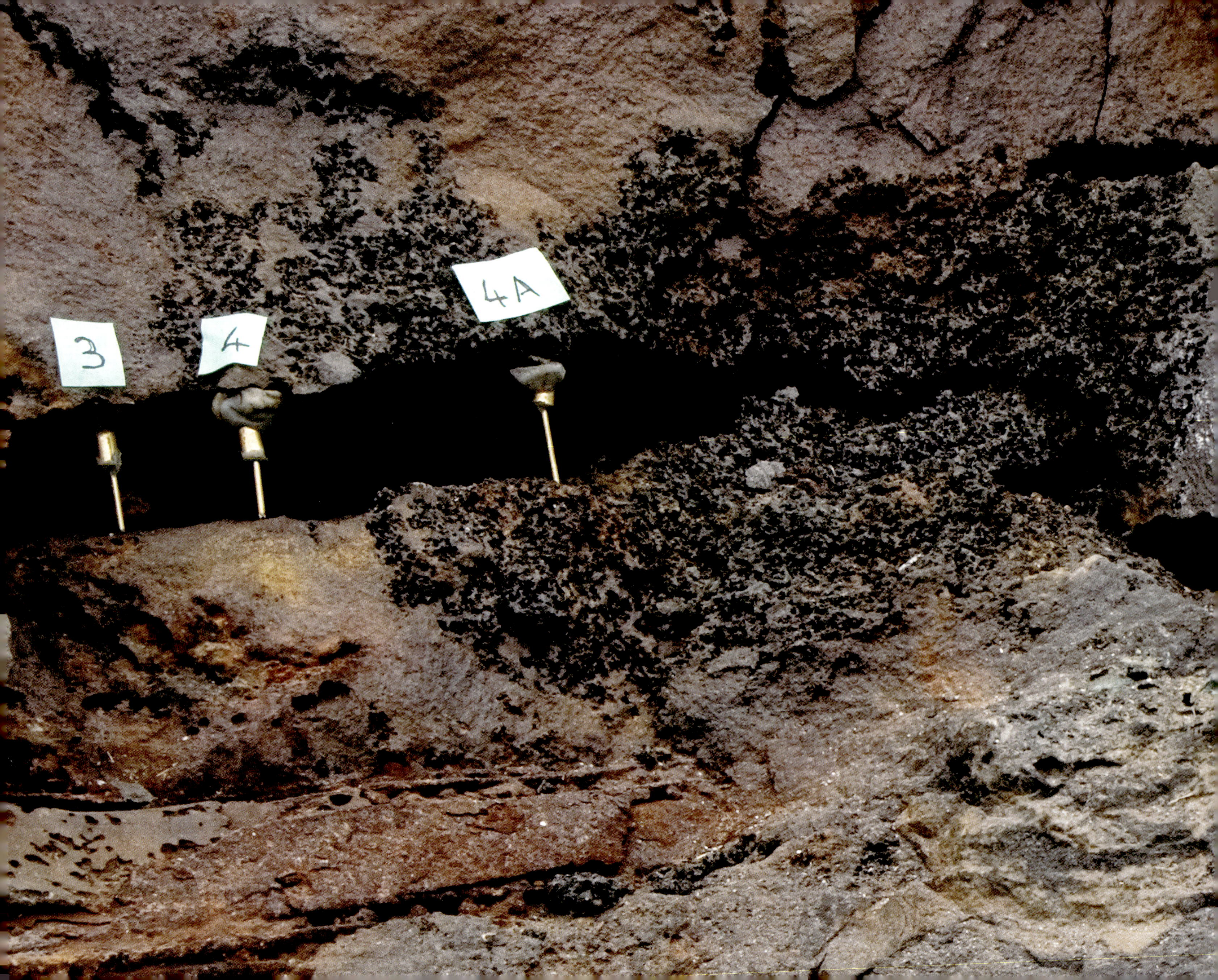
3
4
4A

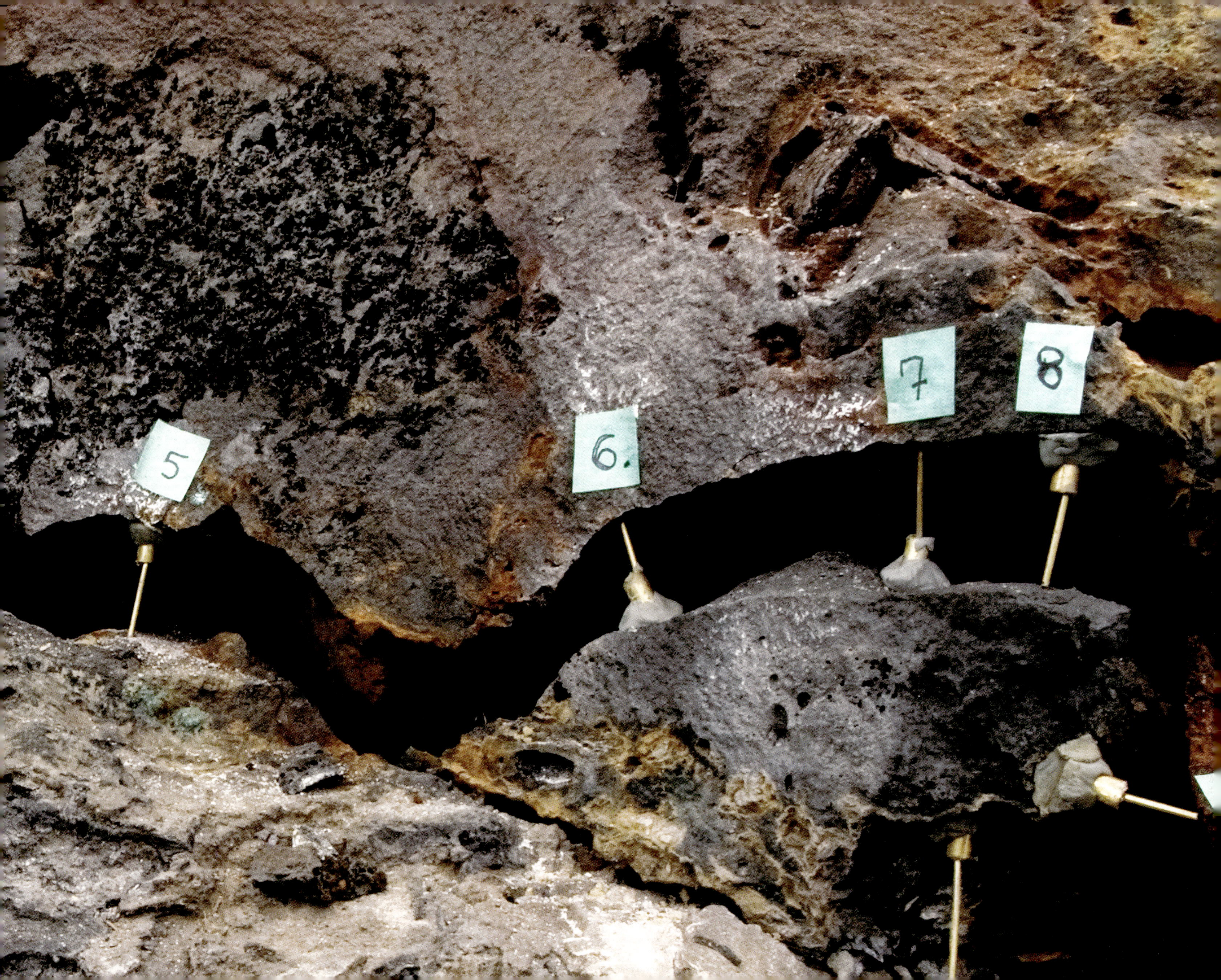
5
6.
7
8

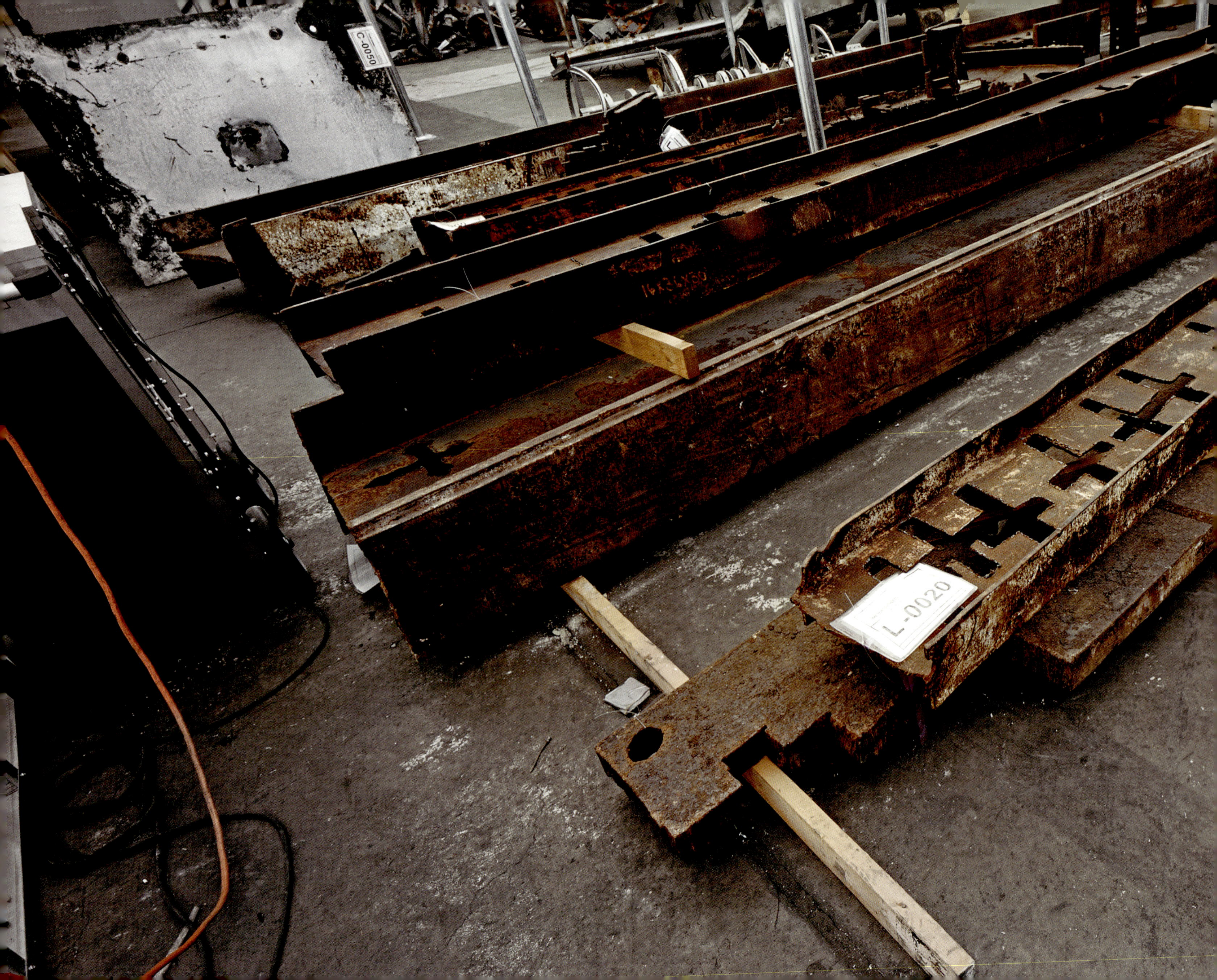
C-0050
L-0020

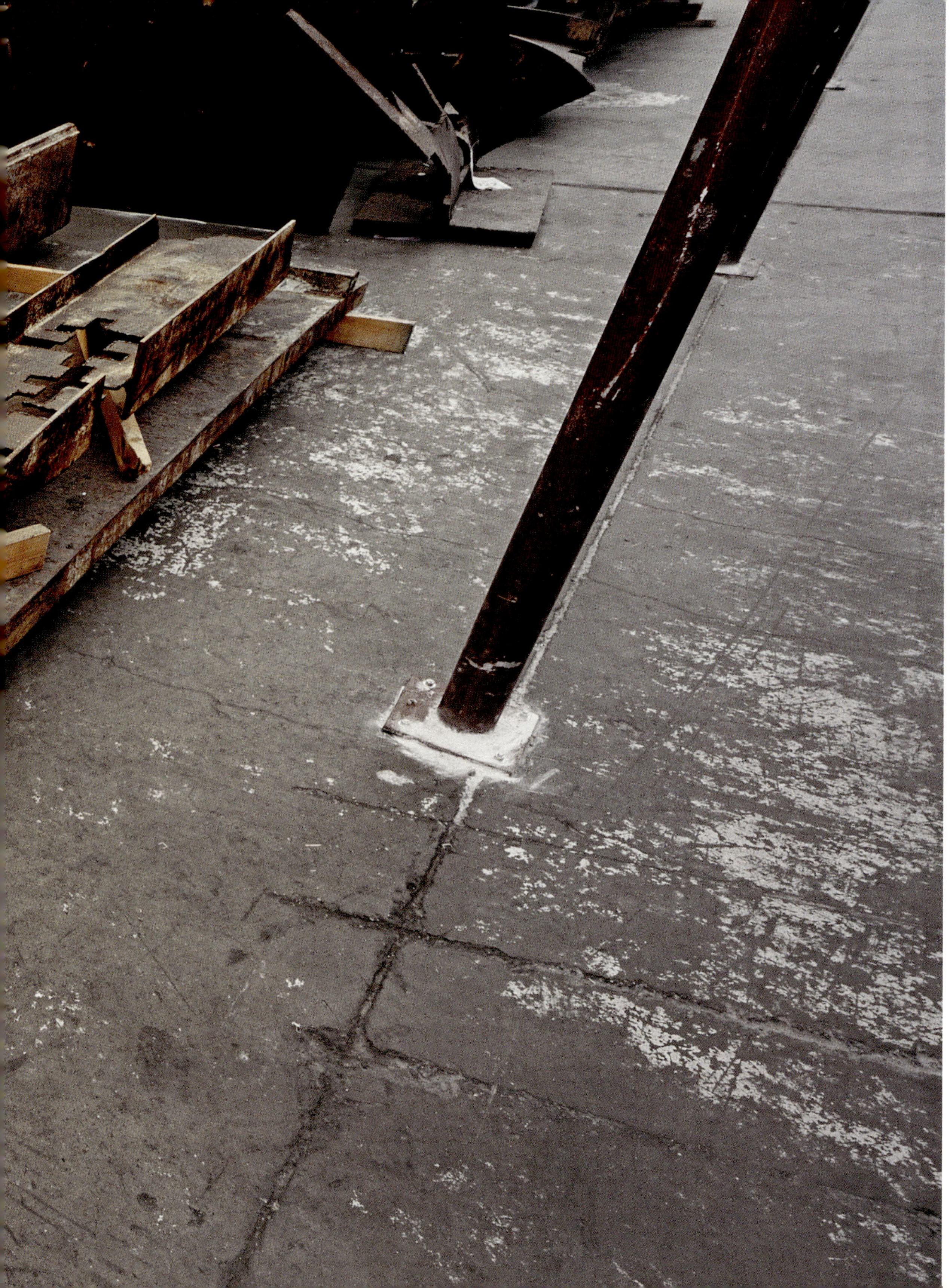

FROM GROUND ZERO

During the recovery at the site, some ironworkers would cut religious or other symbols out of pieces of steel from the World Trade Center and give them as keepsakes to family members or other visitors.

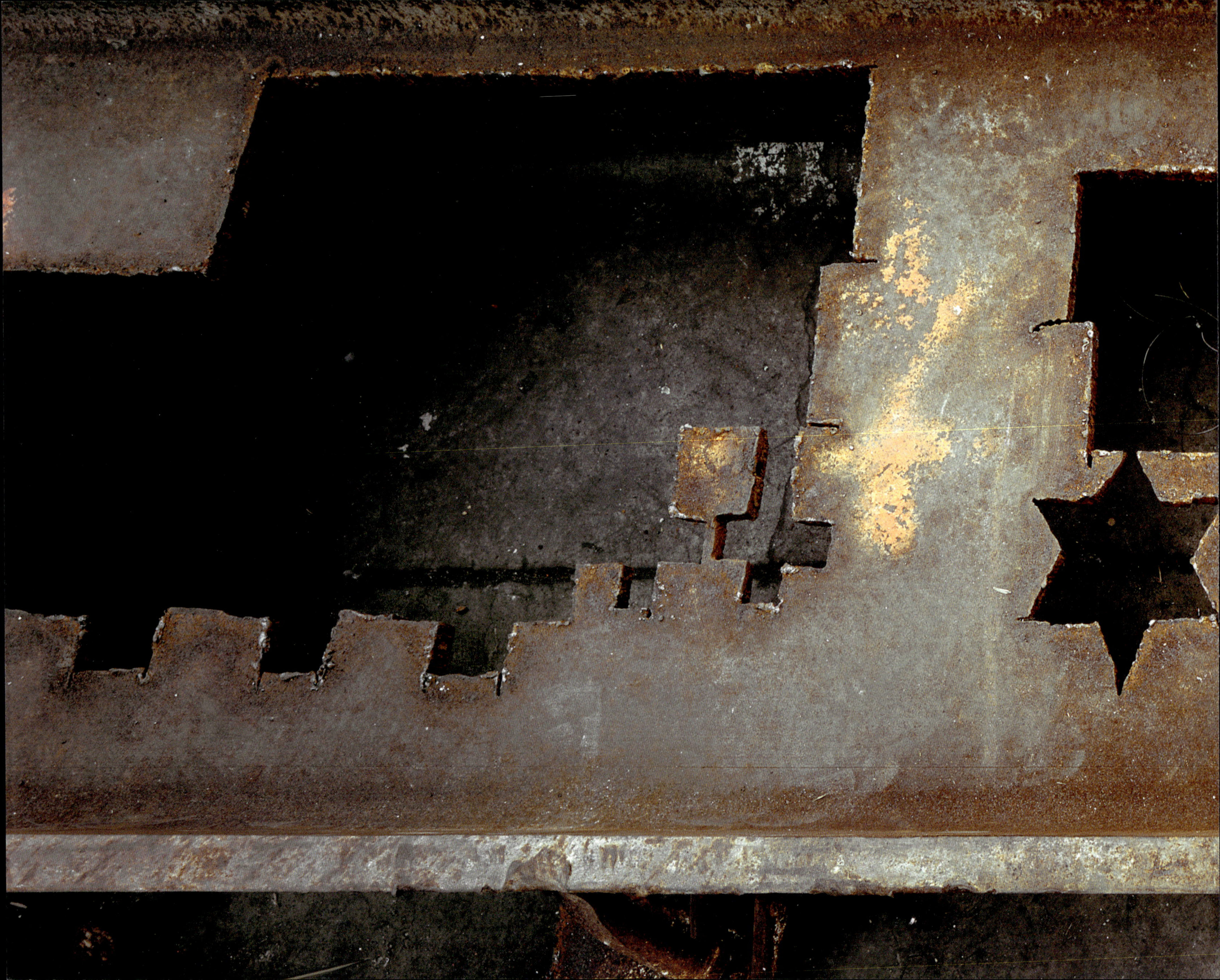

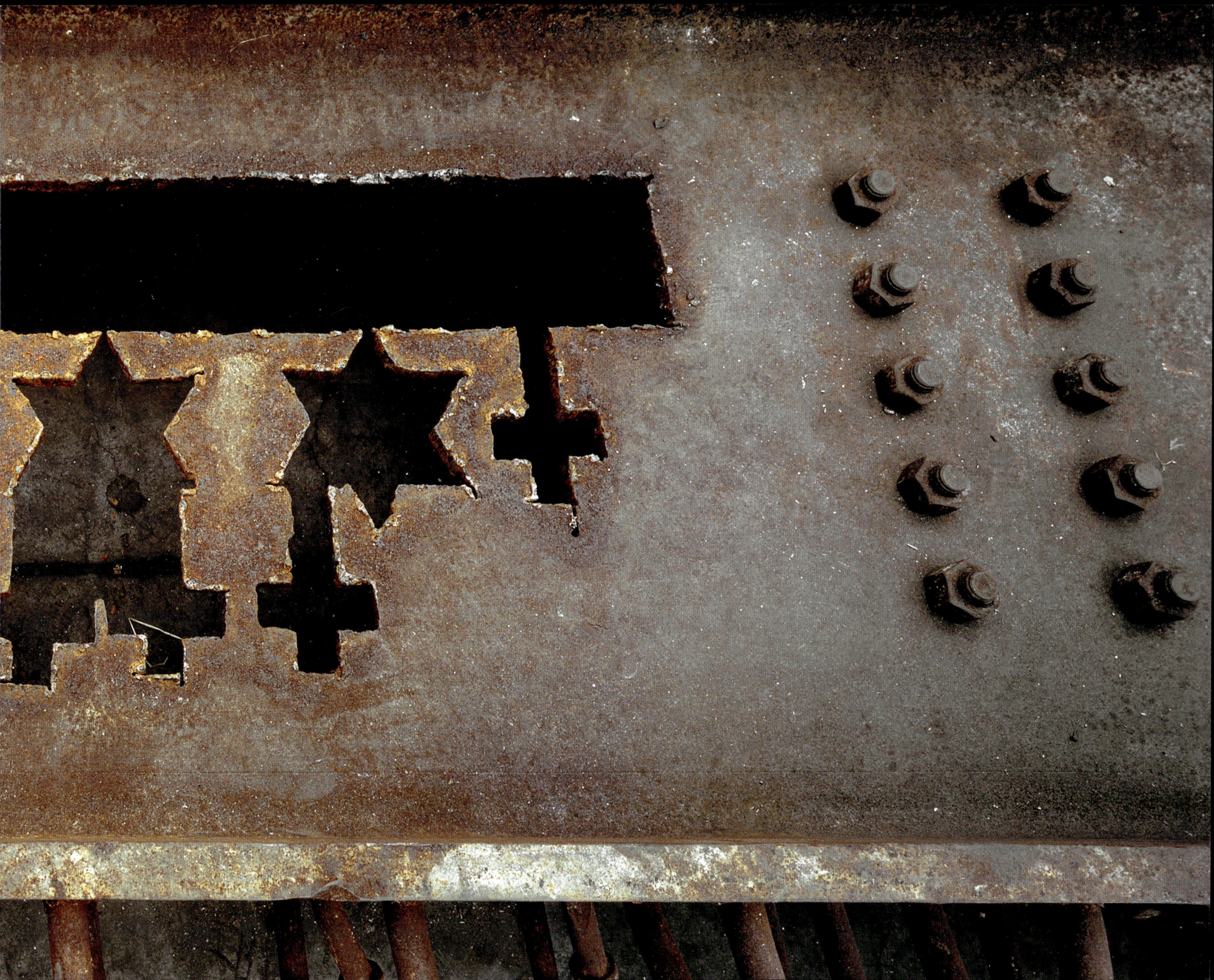

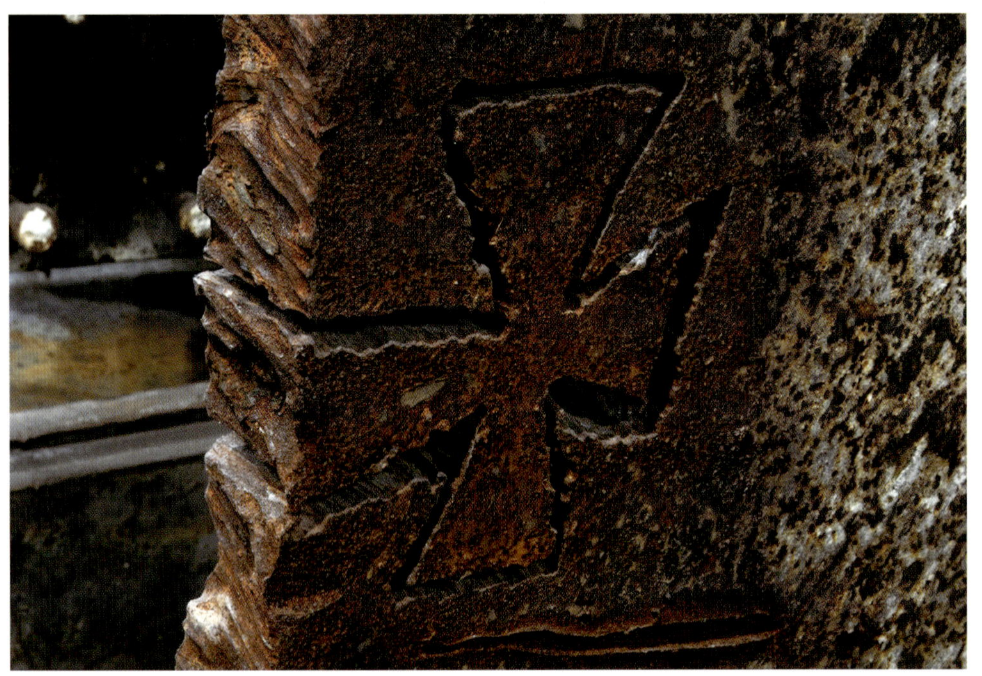

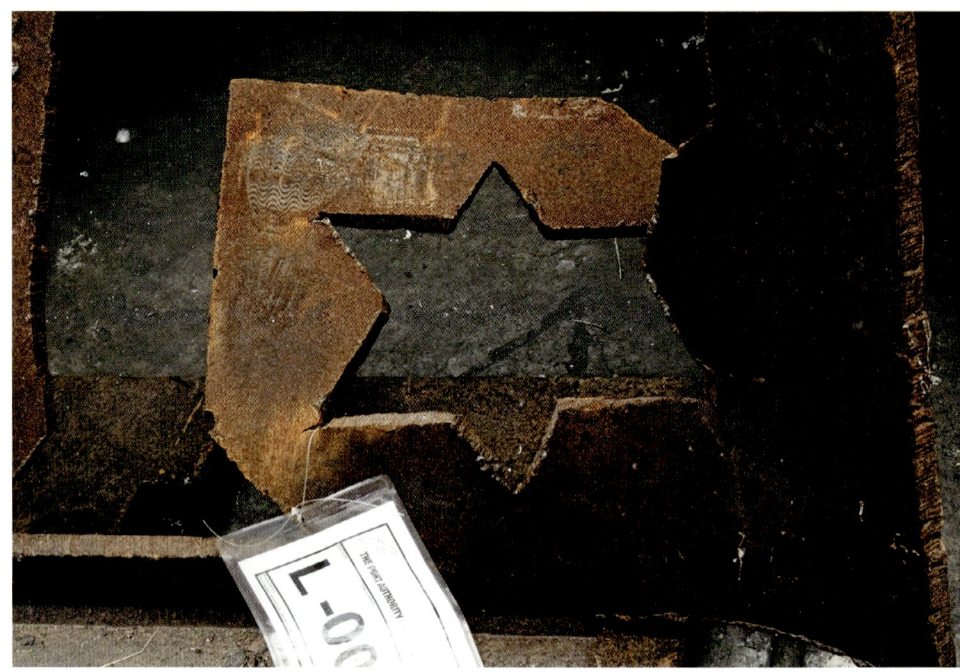

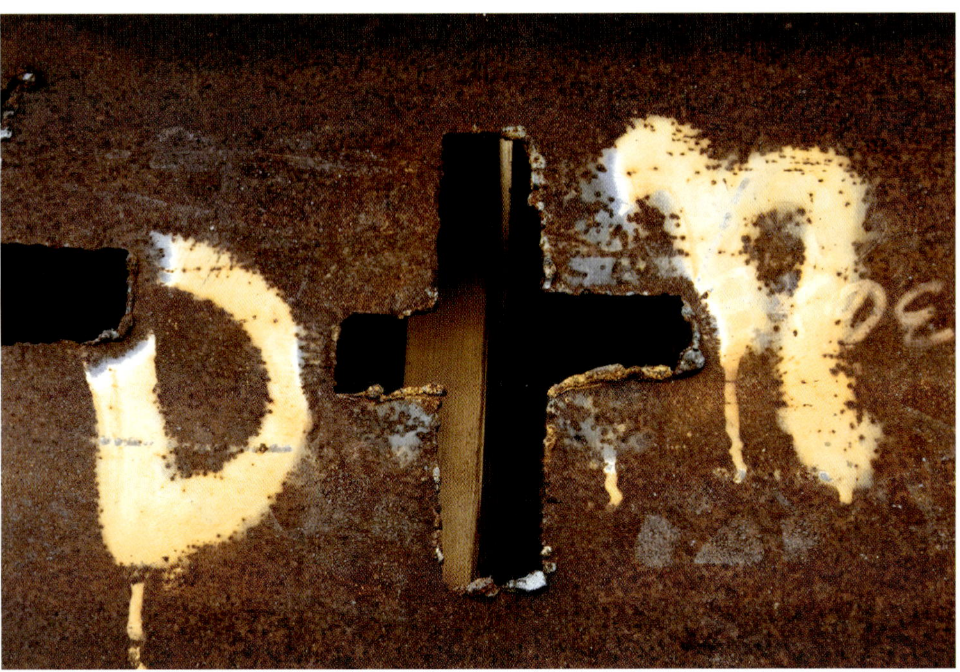

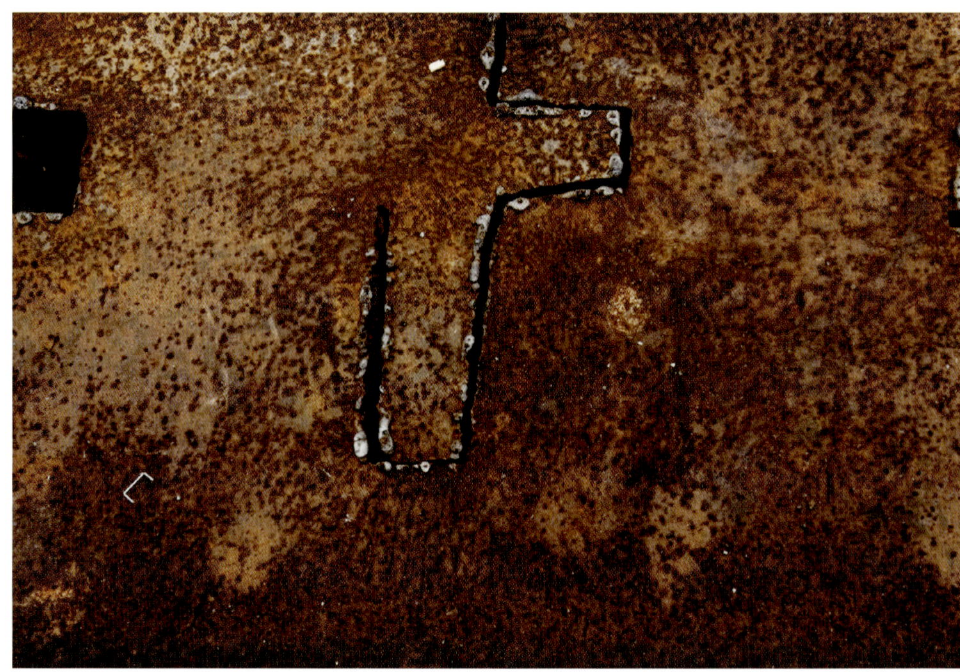

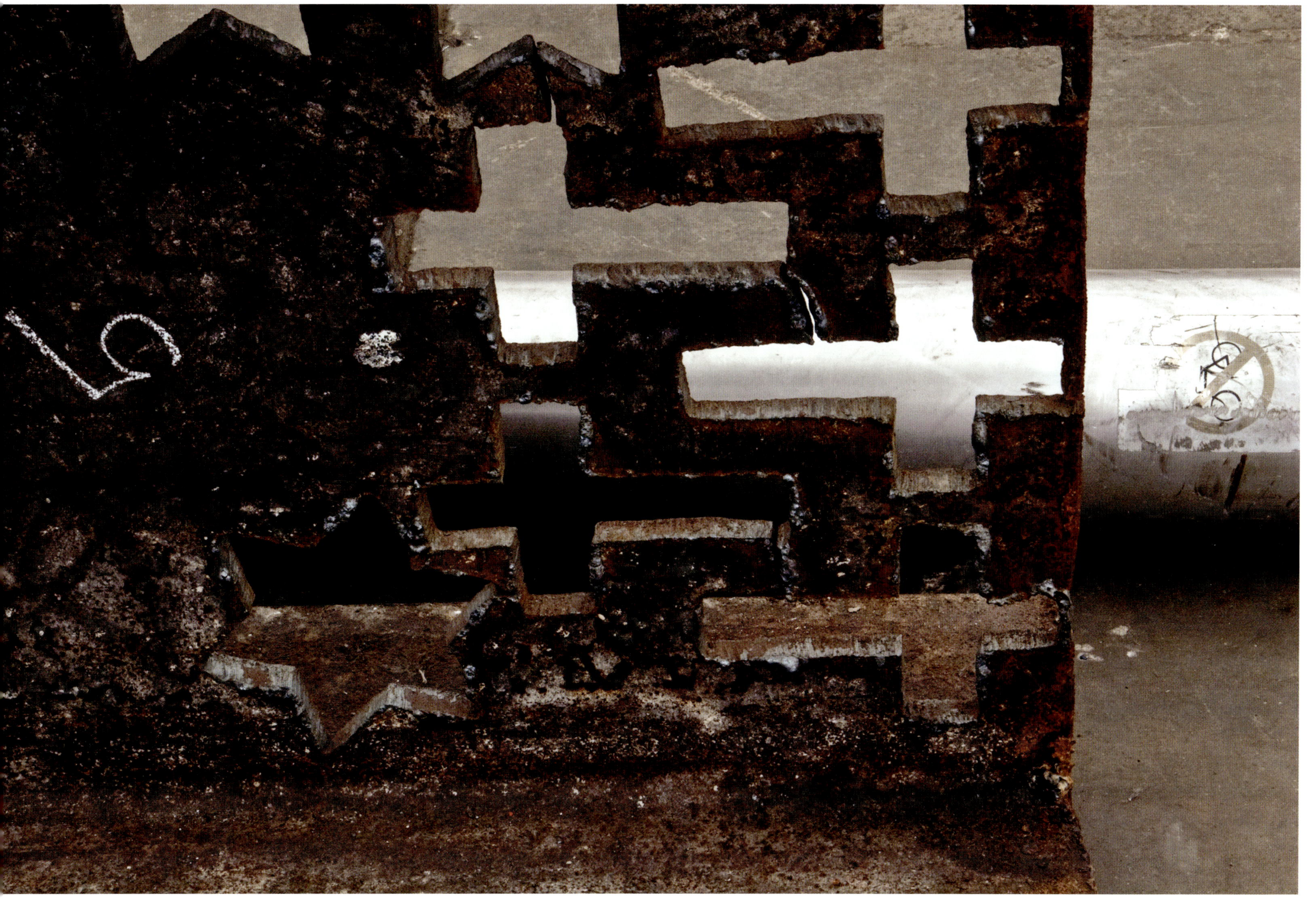

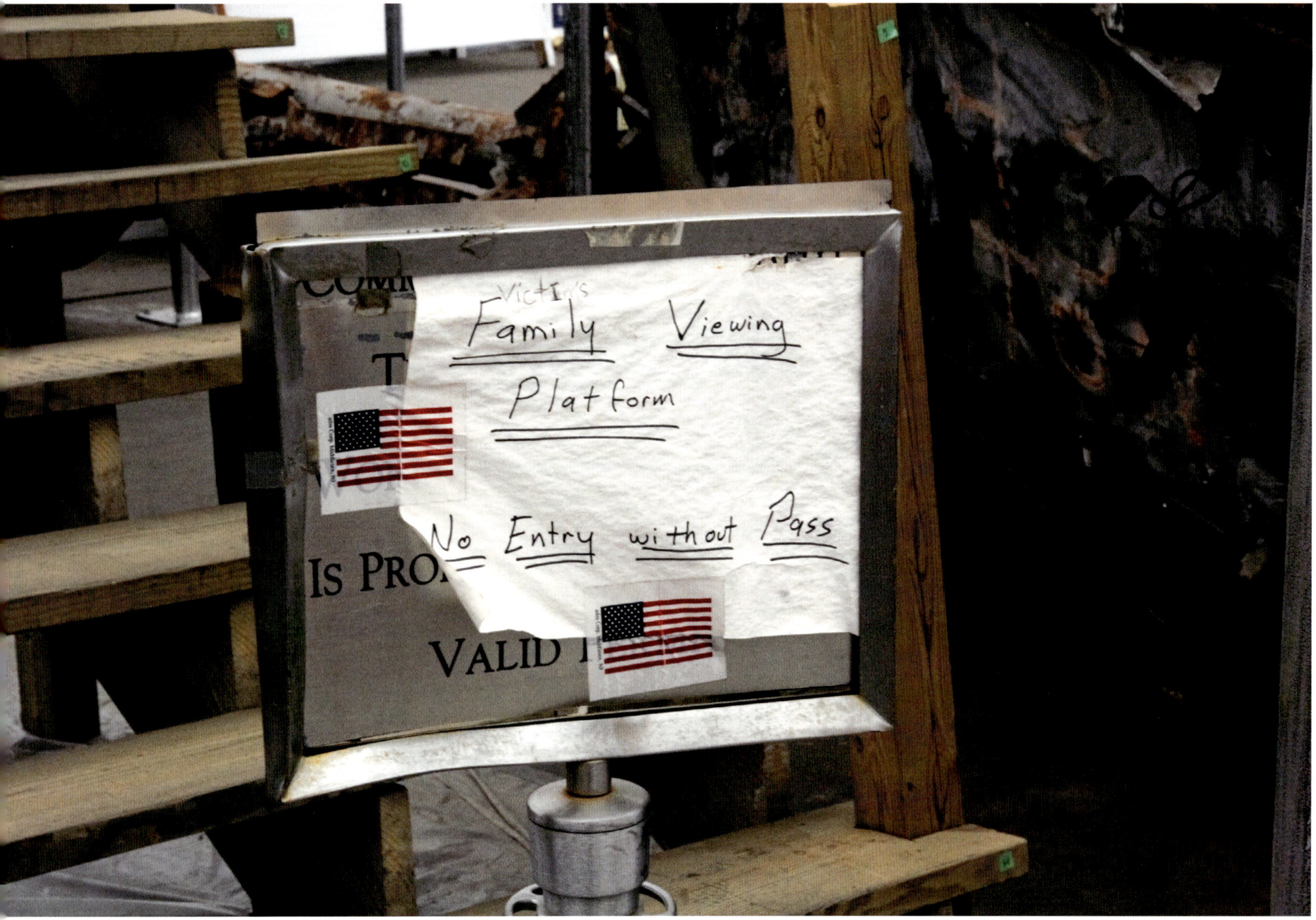

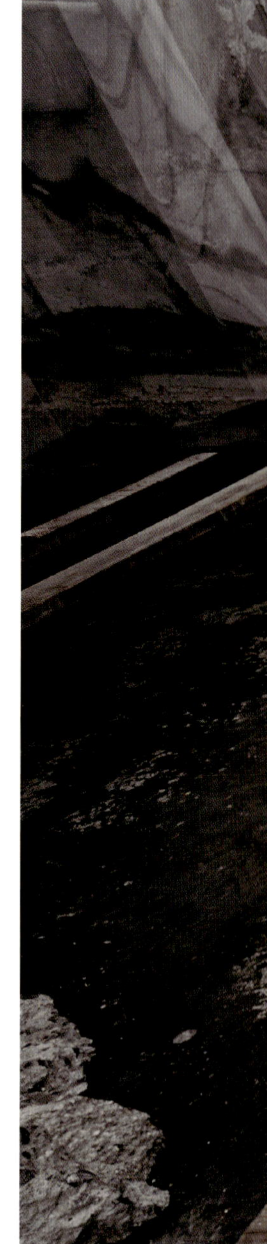

At left, a sign from the entrance to the family viewing platform.
At right, advertising signage from the concourse at the World Trade Center.

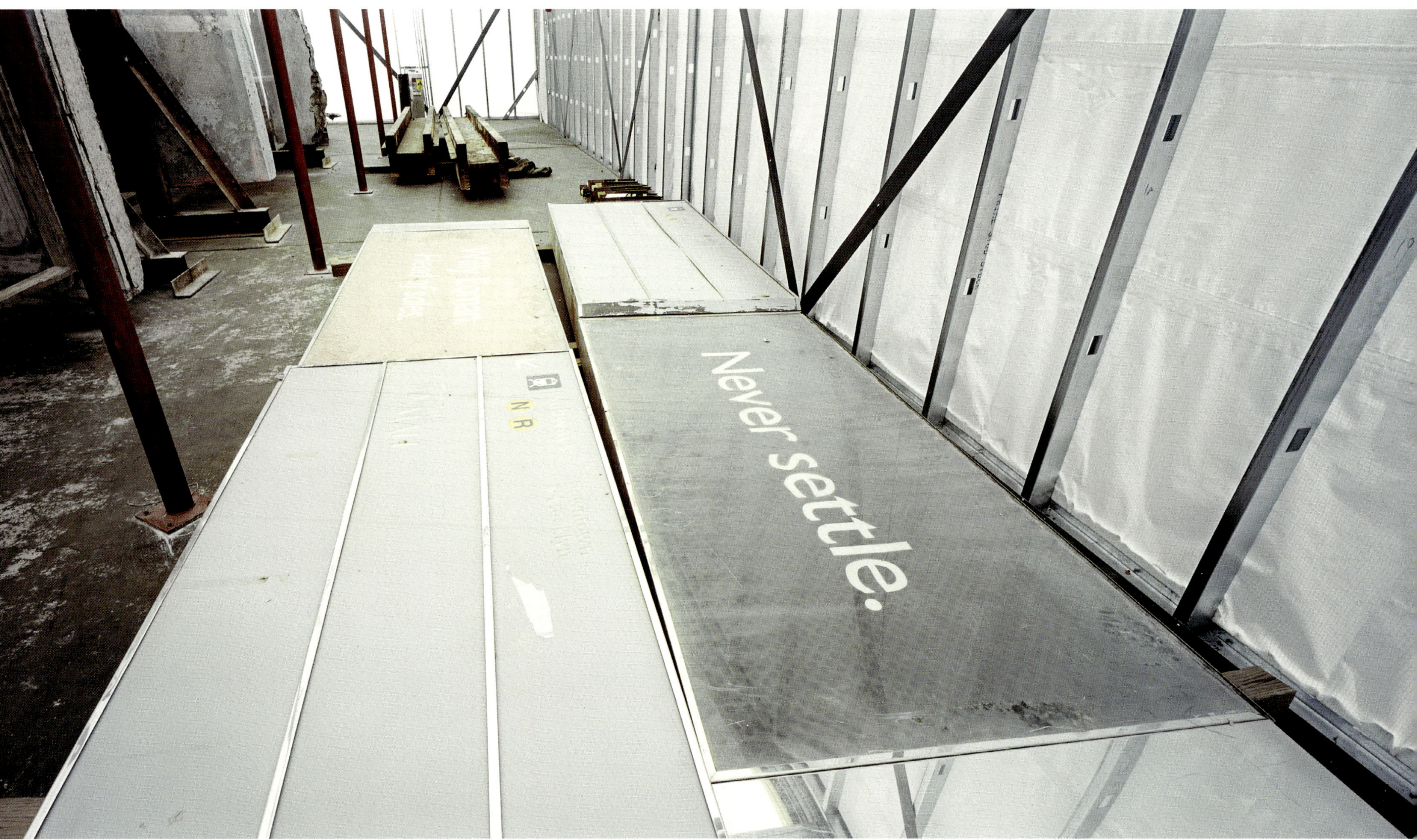
Never settle.

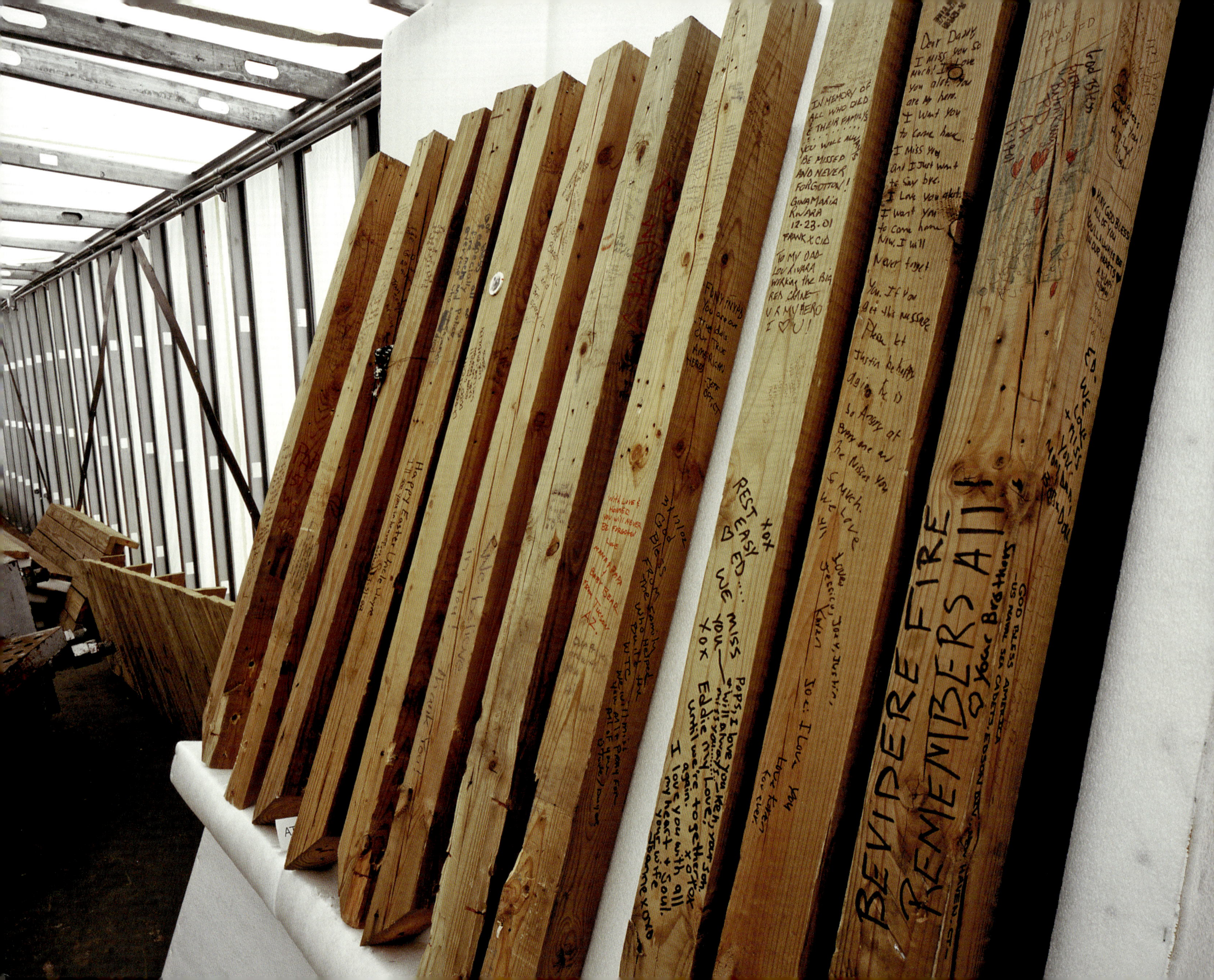

BEVIDERE FIRE
REMEMBERS All!!
Your Brothers
REST EASY ED...
WE MISS YOU
xox
IN MEMORY OF ALL WHO DIED & THEIR FAMILYS
YOU WILL ALWAYS BE MISSED AND NEVER FORGOTTEN!
GinaMaria Rivara
12-23-01
TO MY DAD - LOU RIVARA WORKING THE BIG RED CRANE
U R MY HERO
I ♥ U!
Dear Daddy, I miss you so much!

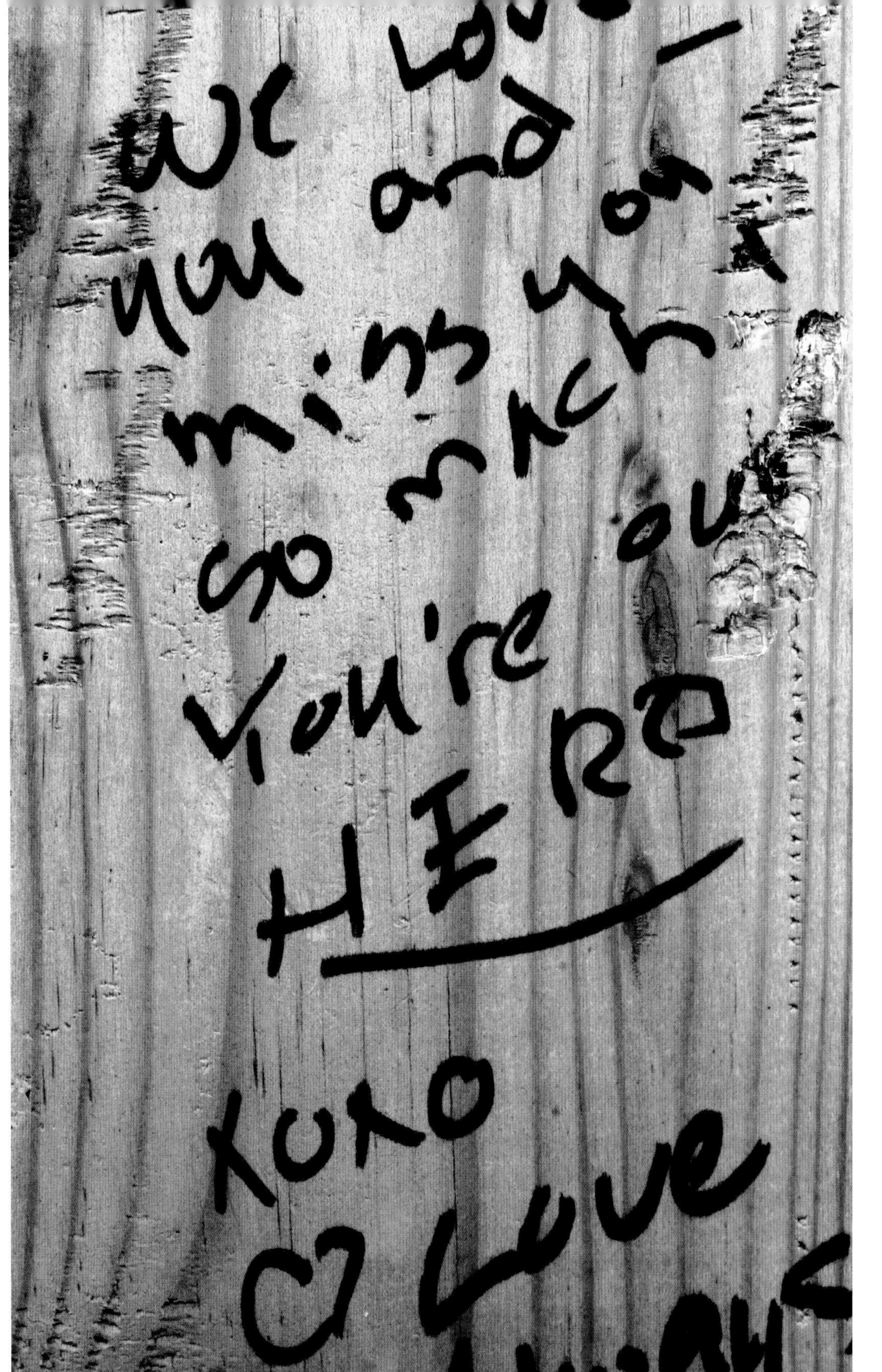

At the southwestern corner of ground zero, a platform was built to provide family members with a private place for observing the recovery effort. Family members inscribed messages to their loved ones on the wooden slats of the platform.

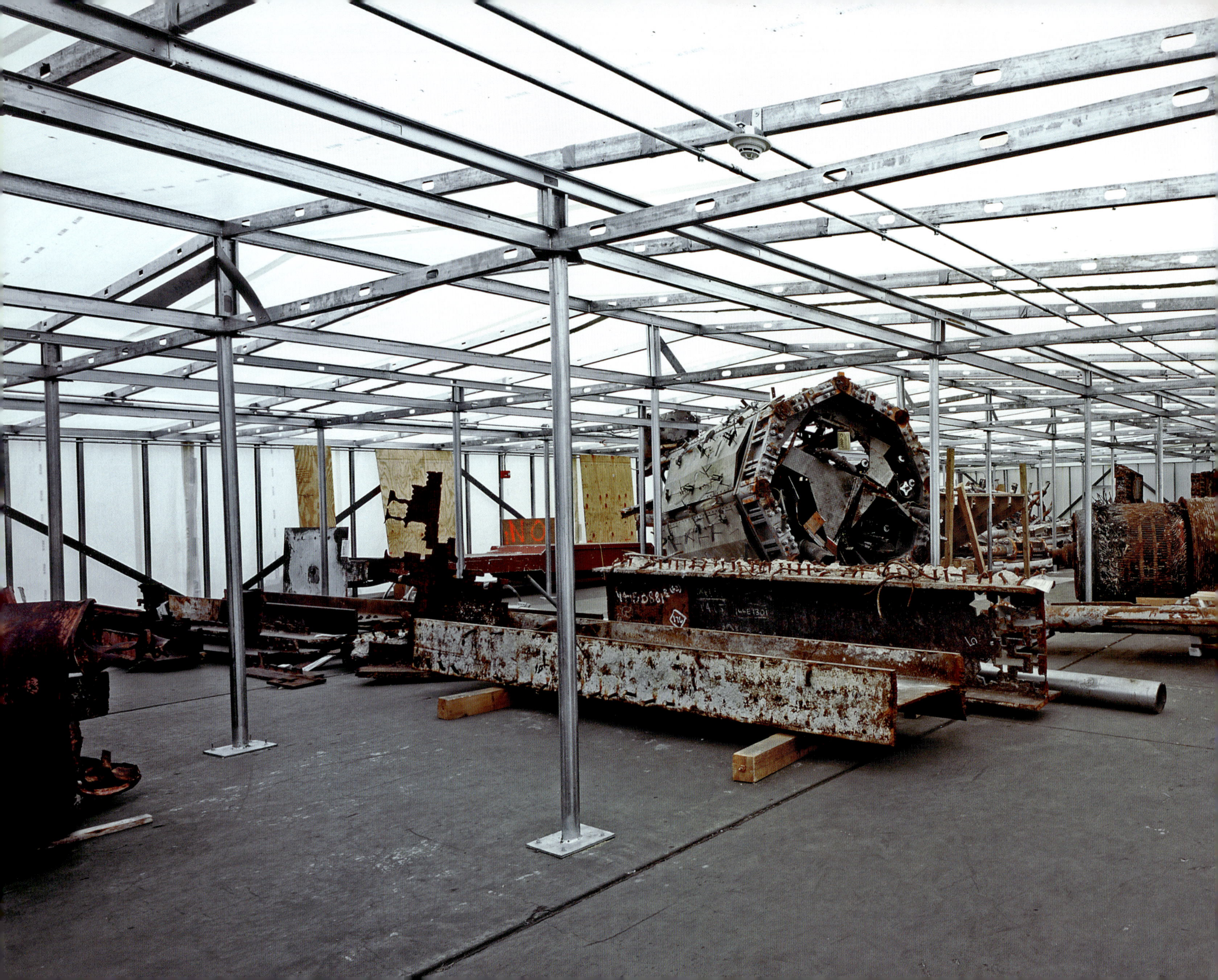
NO

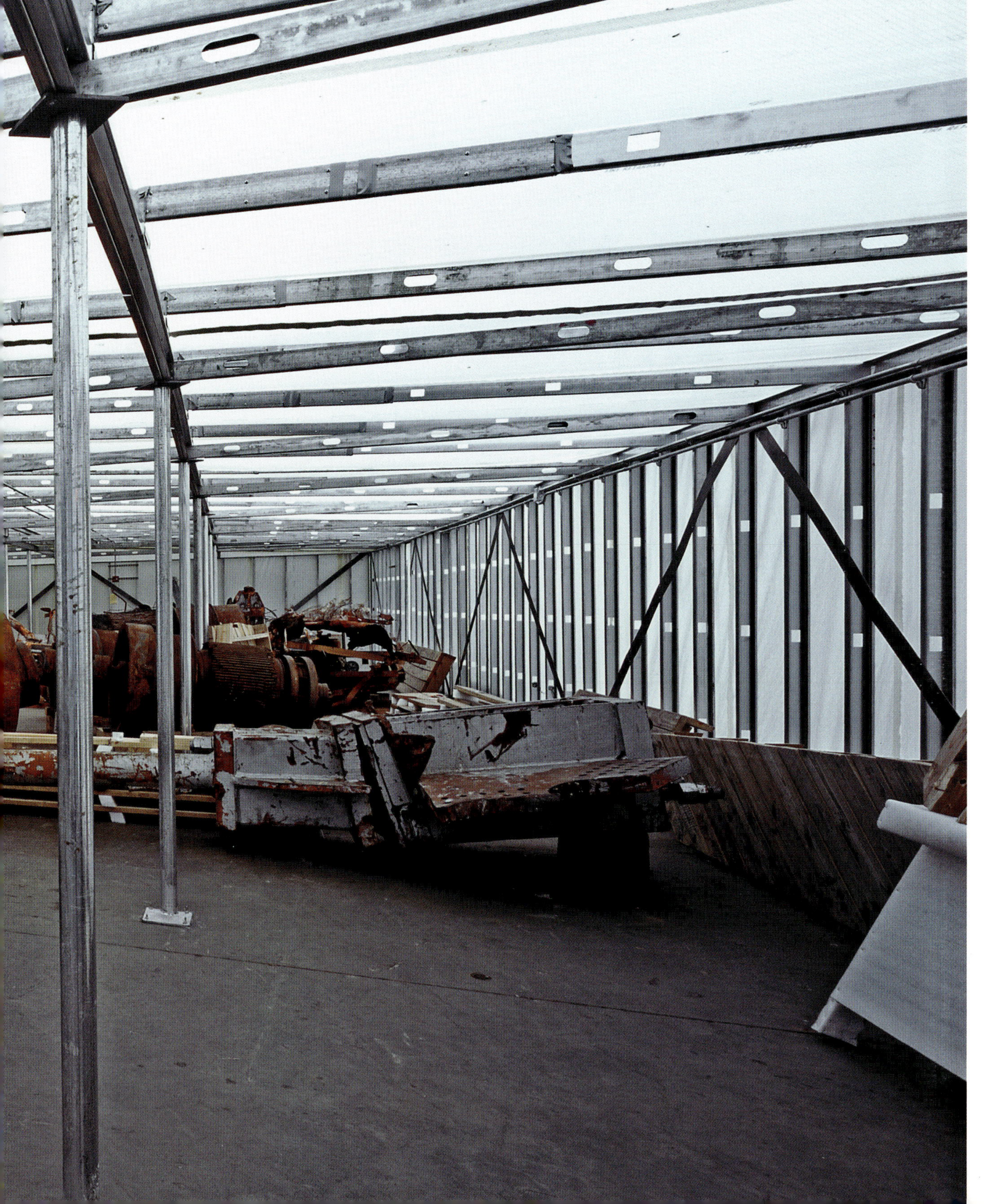

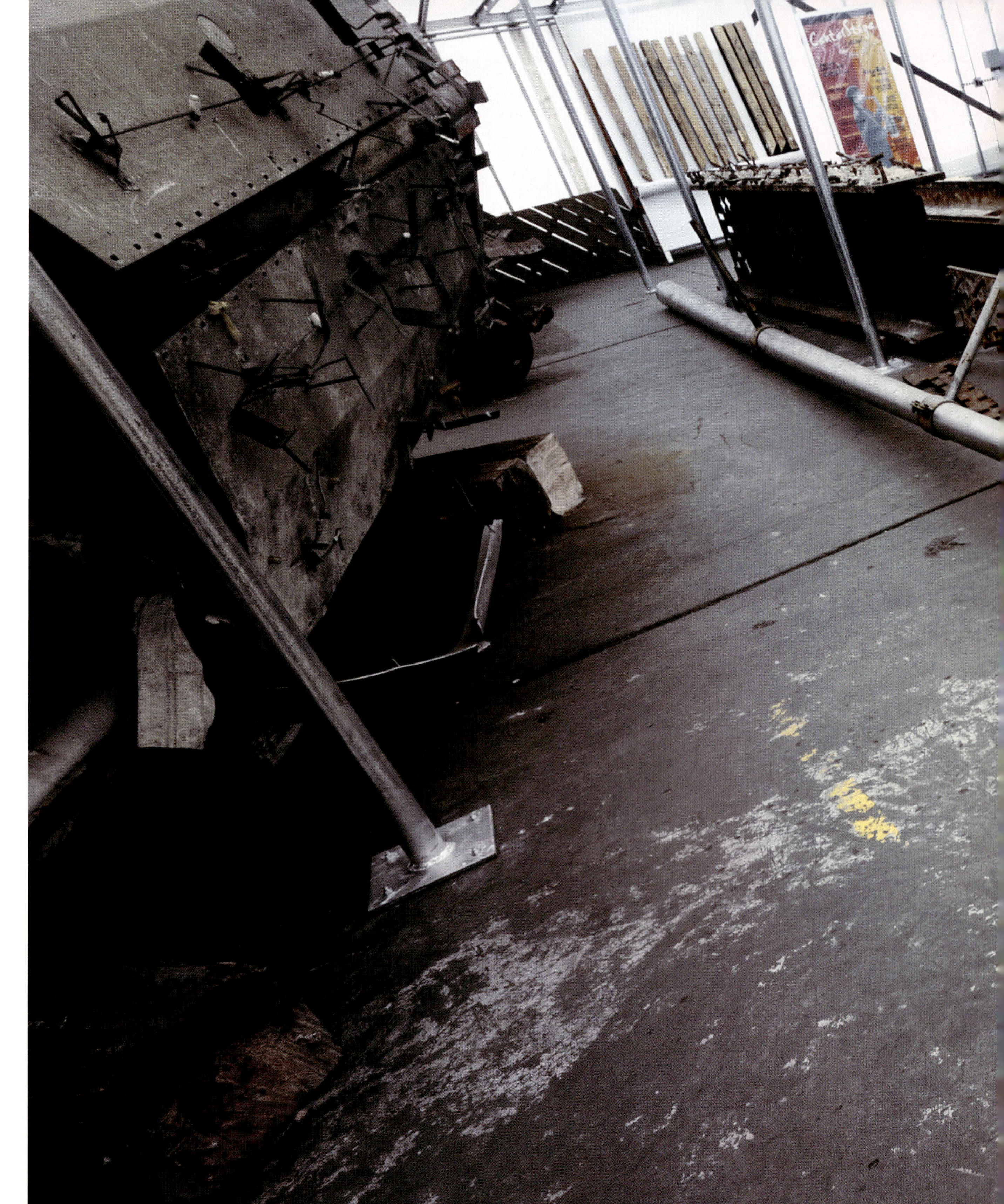

A light pole from the main plaza of
the World Trade Center.

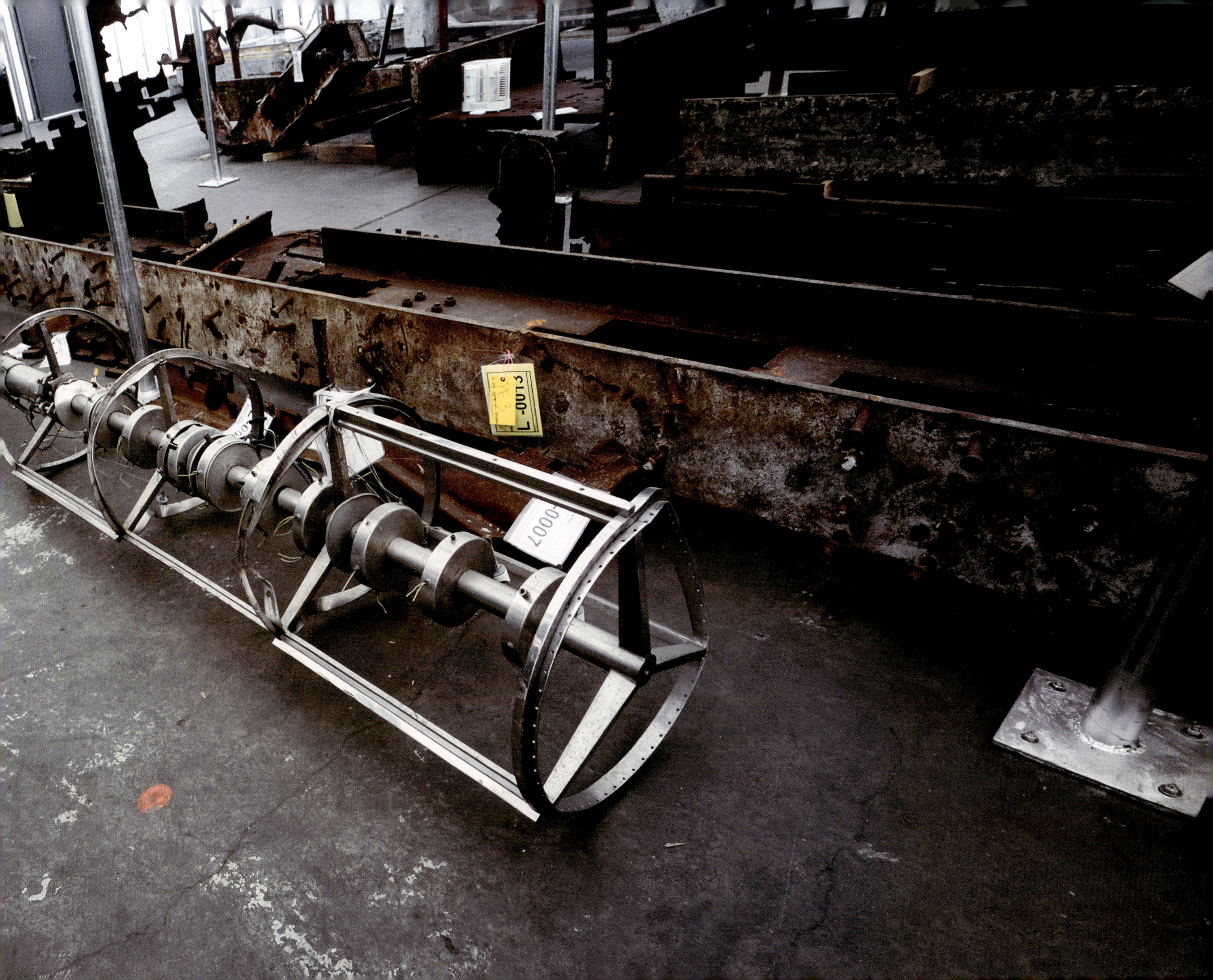

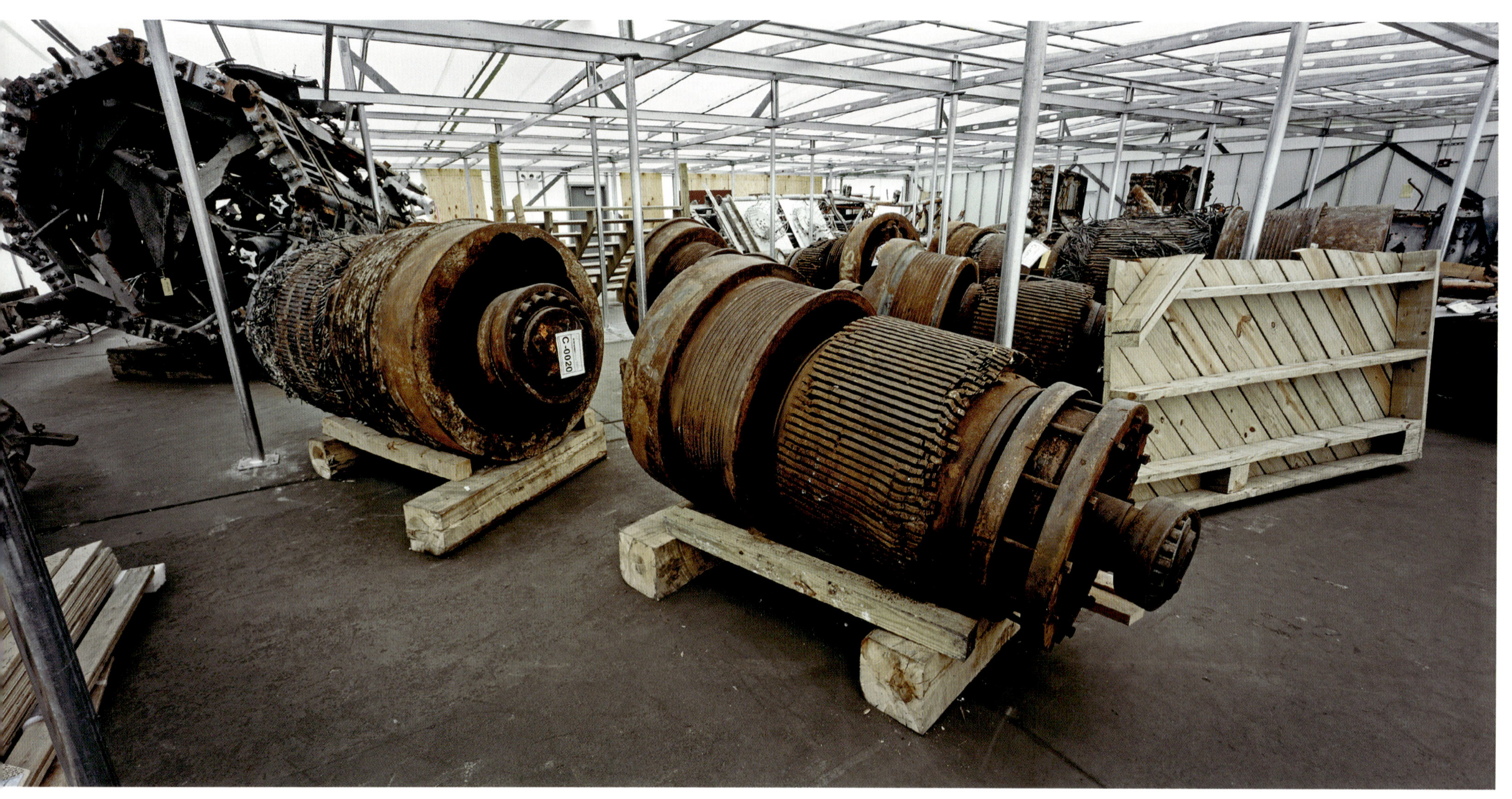

Some of the motors that powered the 99 elevators in each of the twin towers. Passengers for the upper areas of the buildings passed through sky lobbies on the 44th and 78th floors, where they changed cars. This routing channeled office tenants and visitors to elevator banks within a specific range of floors, providing express service and minimizing their travel time.

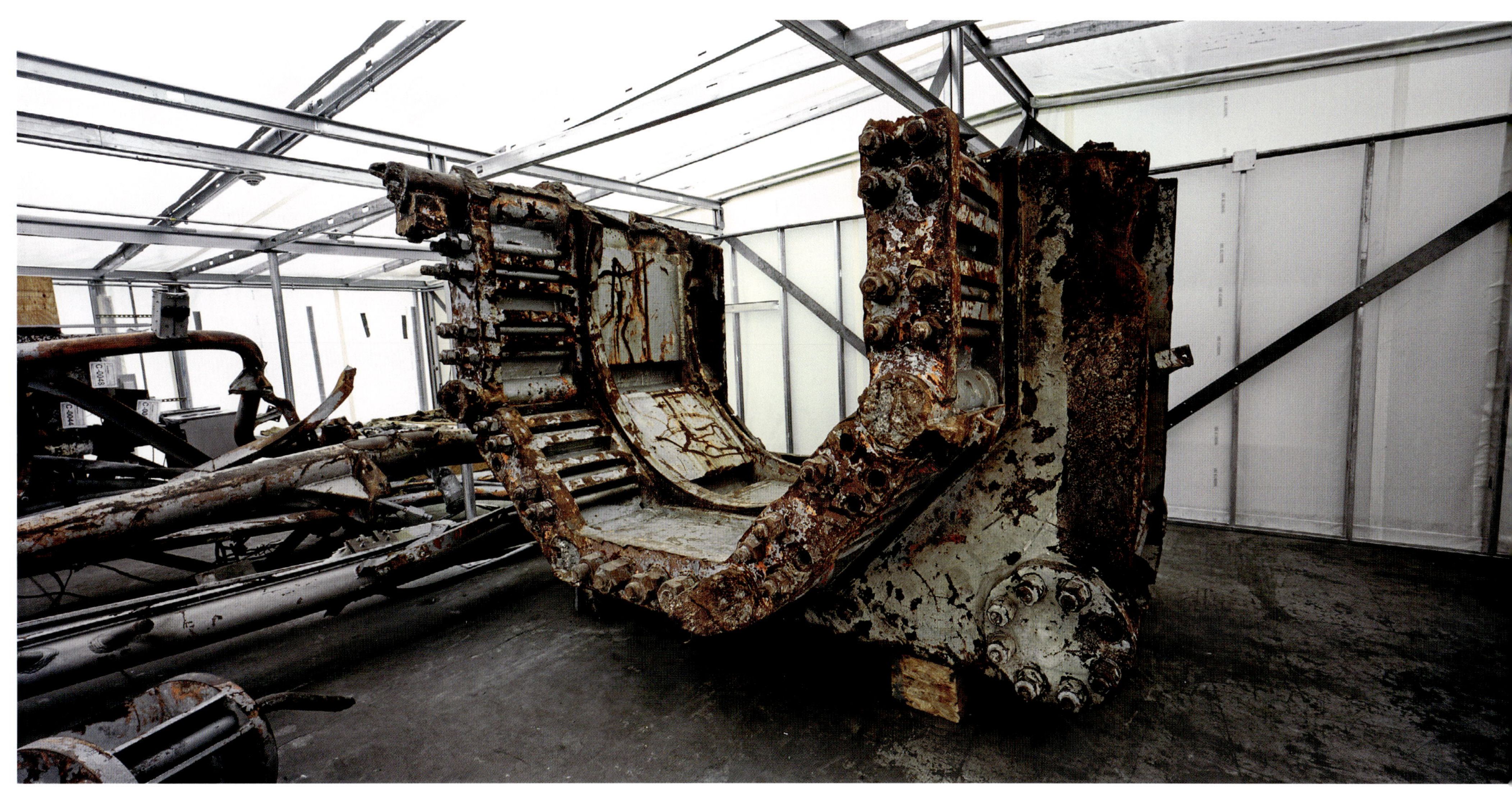

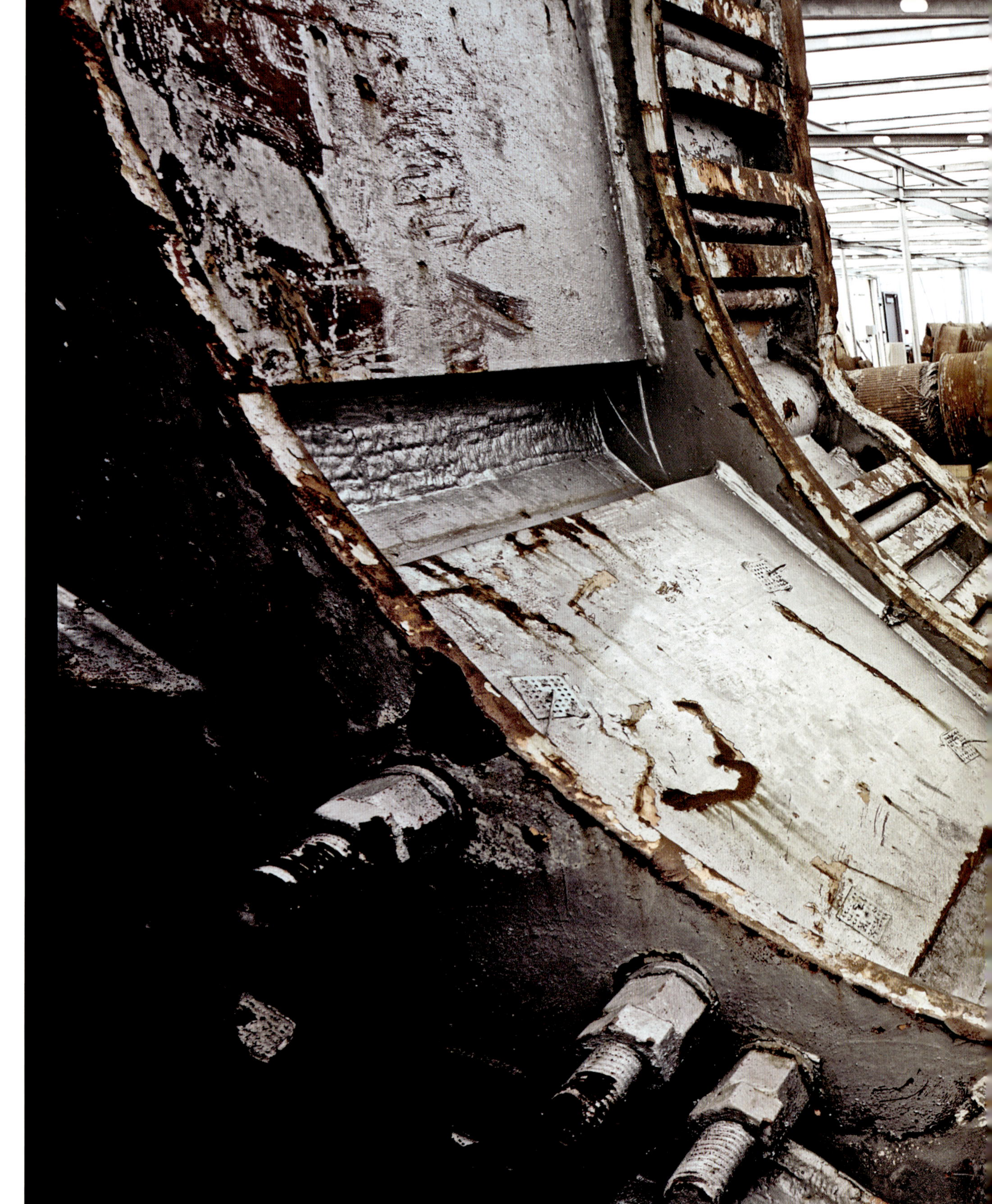

View through a portion of the broadcast antenna that fell from the top of the north tower. A number of fragments of the 360-foot antenna were kept at Hangar 17.

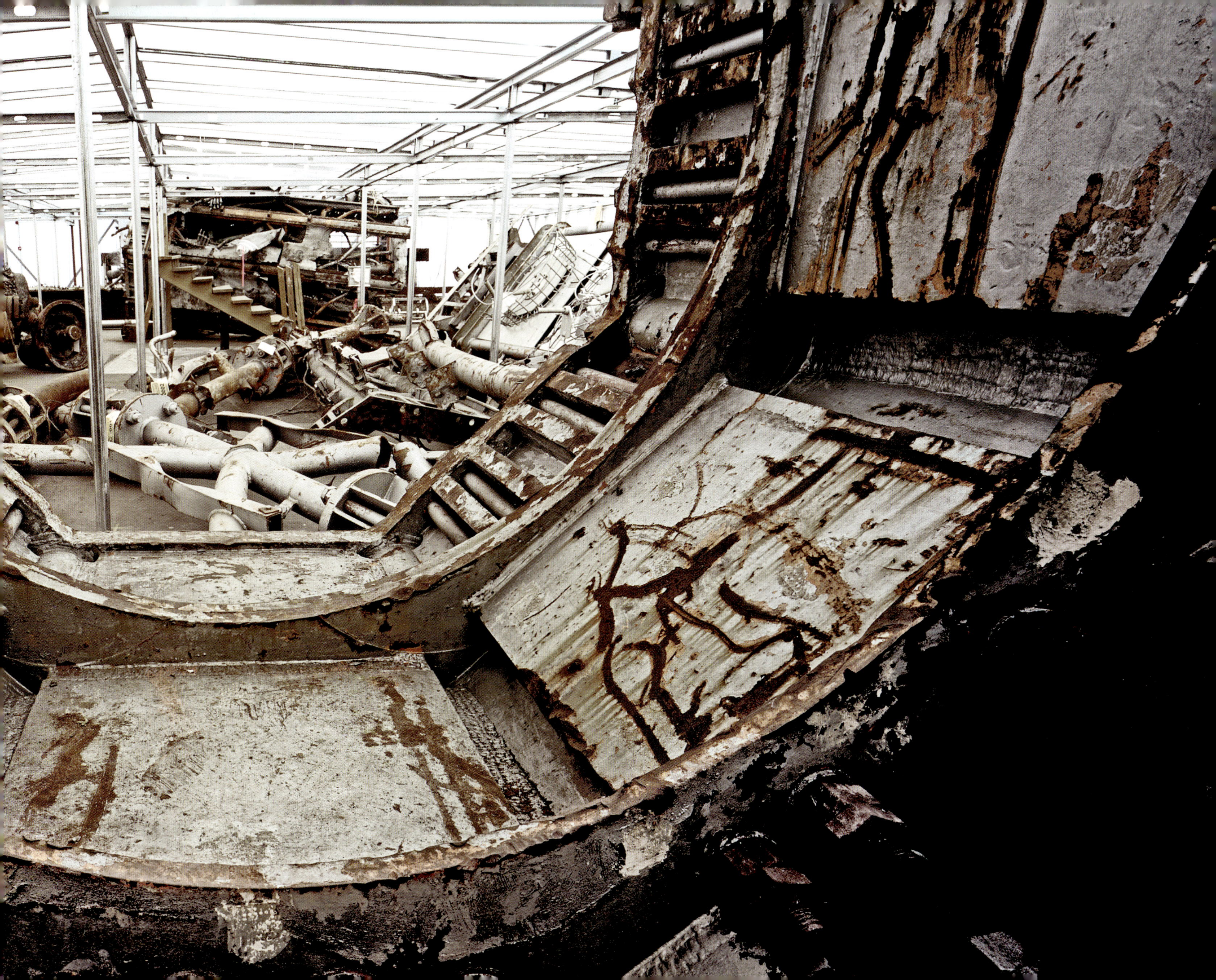

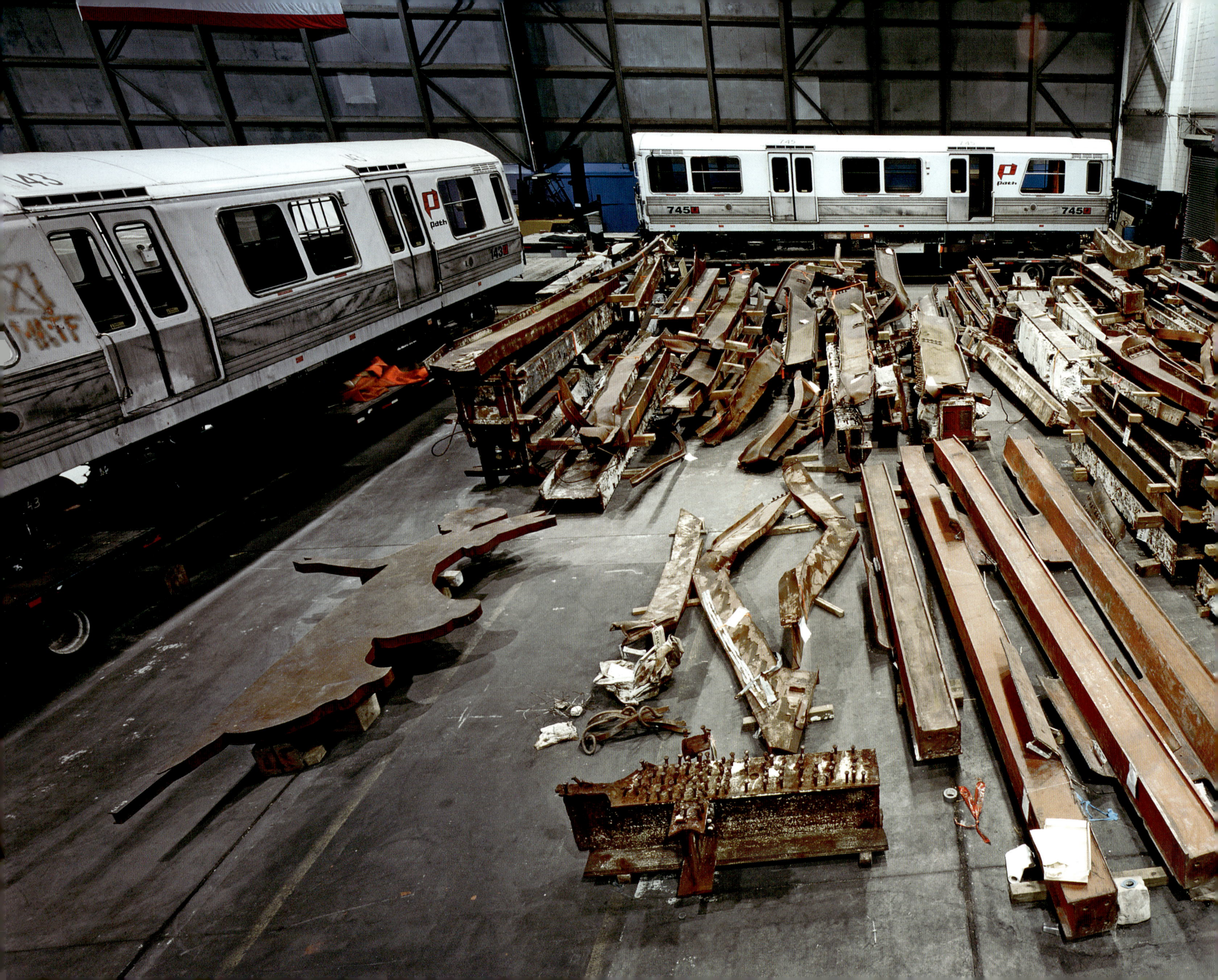
path
143
745
745
745

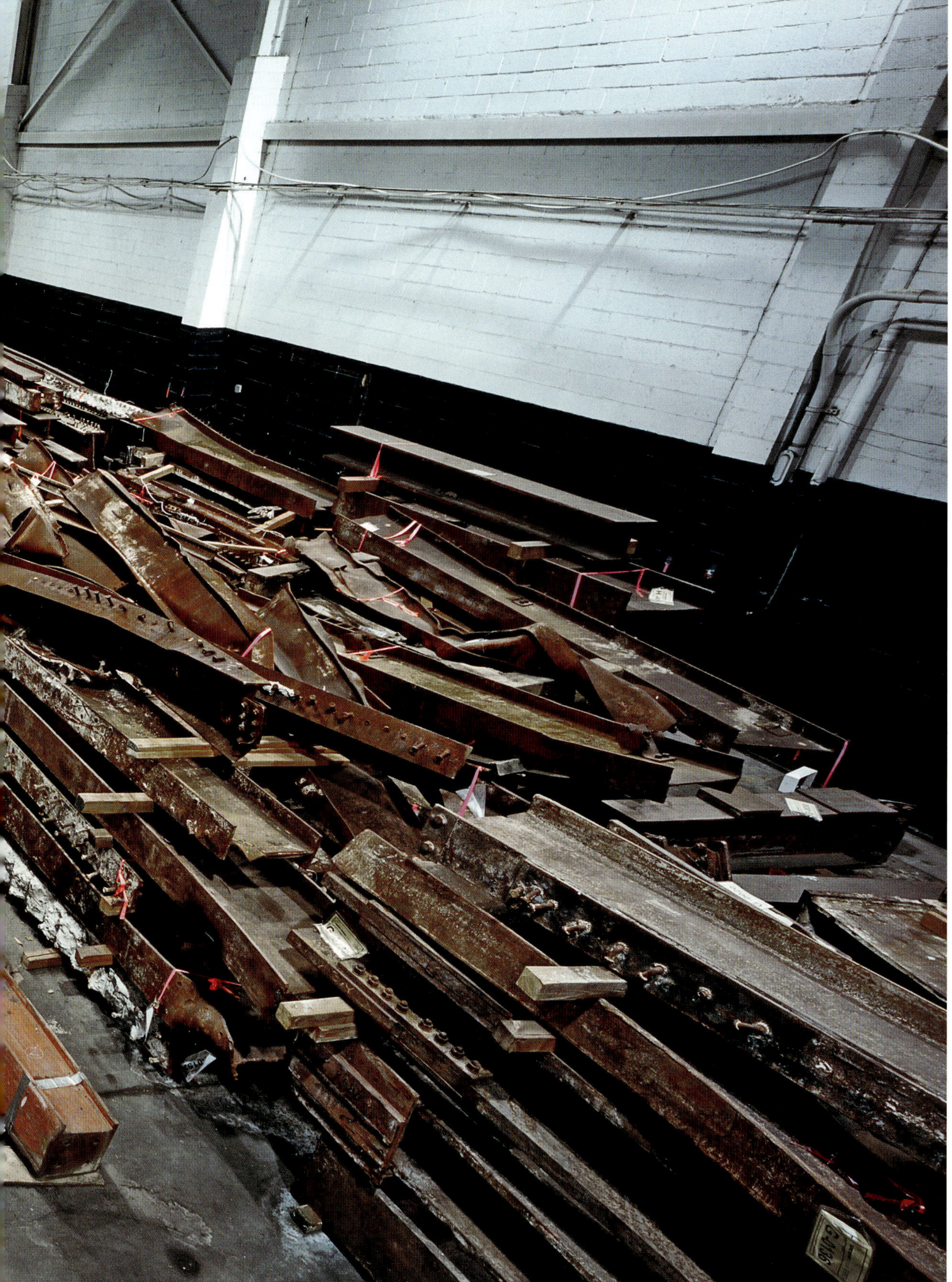

The PATH commuter rail line connects New Jersey communities with stations in Manhattan, including one that was located underneath the World Trade Center. On the morning of 9/11, Victoria Cross Kelly, PATH deputy director, was at a breakfast meeting in the north tower, when she received reports that an airplane had hit the building. Going outside to investigate, she quickly understood the risks to arriving passengers and contacted PATH headquarters to order that no further trains let commuters off at the WTC station. With trains scheduled to arrive there at two- to four-minute intervals, it is estimated that her decision spared as many as 5,000 people from the dangers of the day.

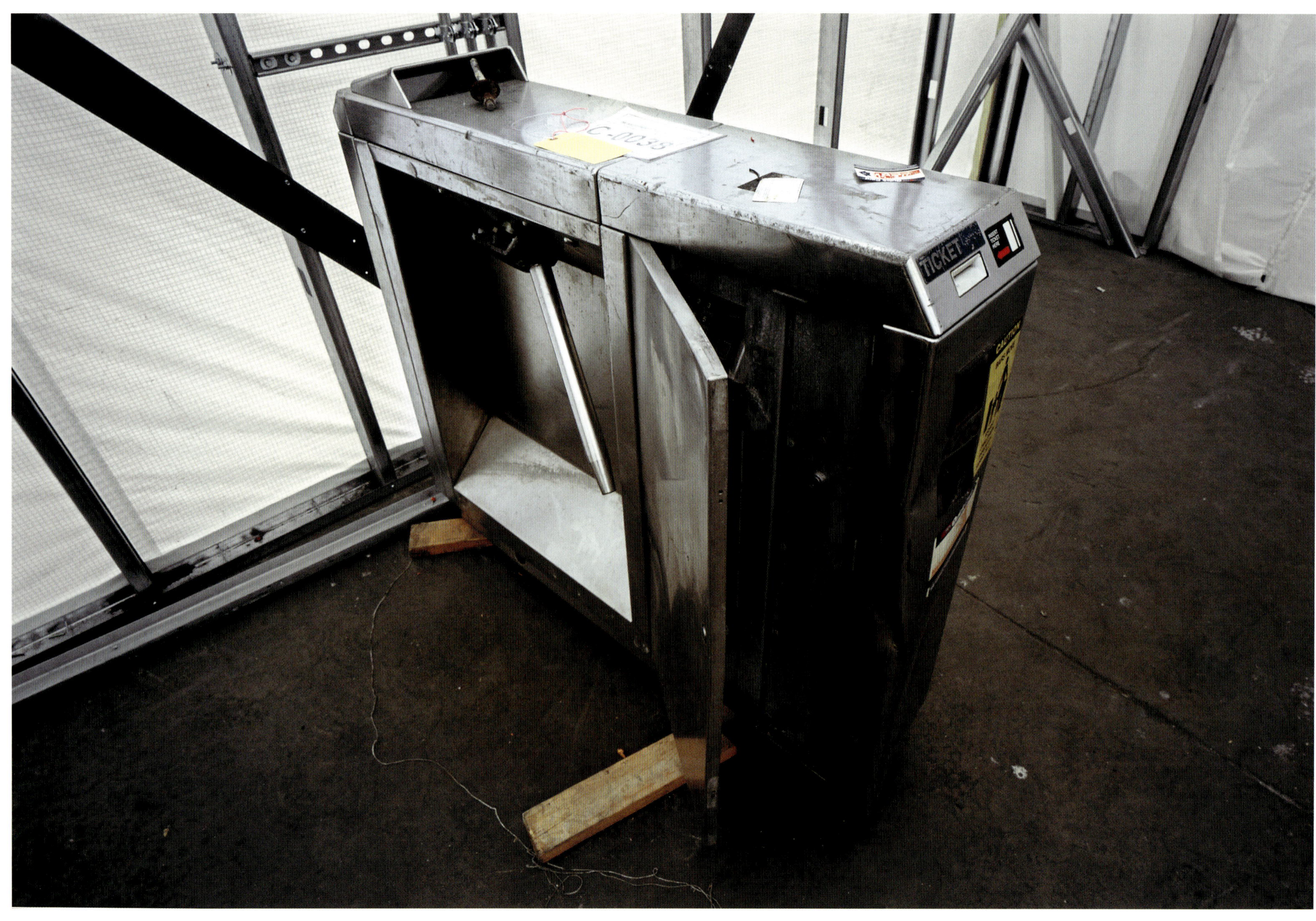

A PATH station turnstile from the World Trade Center. Tens of thousands of commuters used this station for their daily arrival in Manhattan.

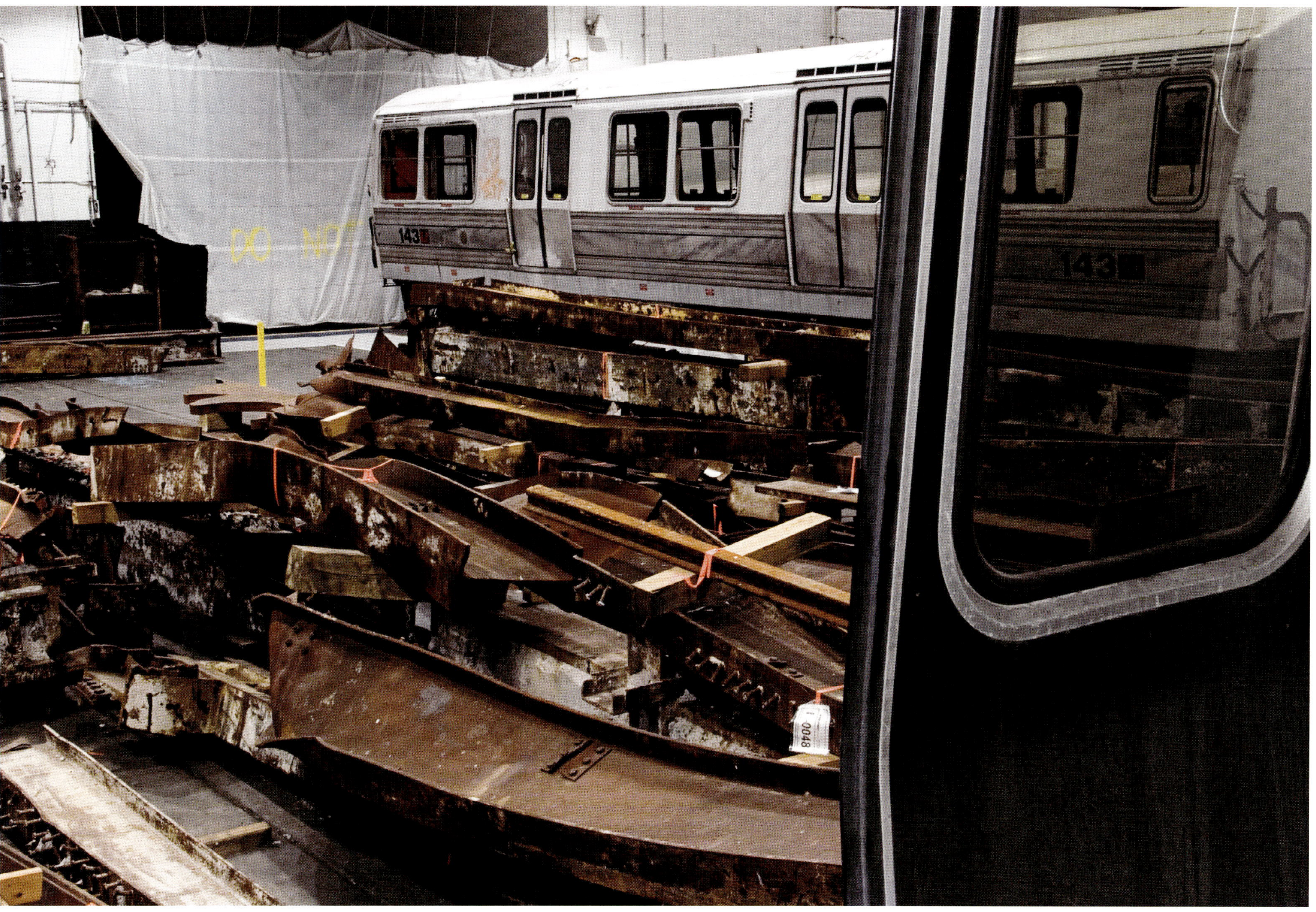
DO NOT
143
143
0048

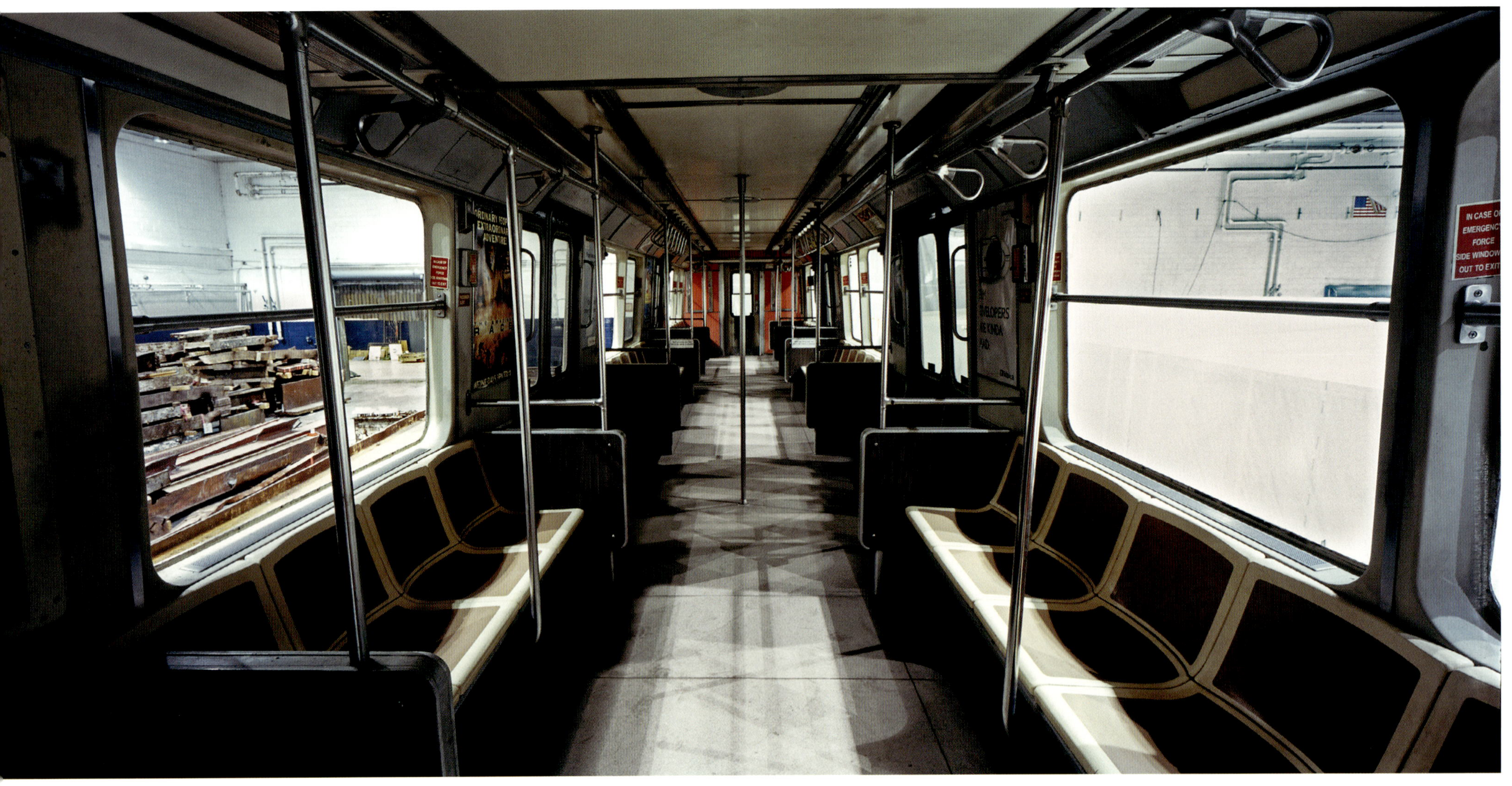
IN CASE O
EMERGENCY
FORCE
SIDE WINDOW
OUT TO EXIT

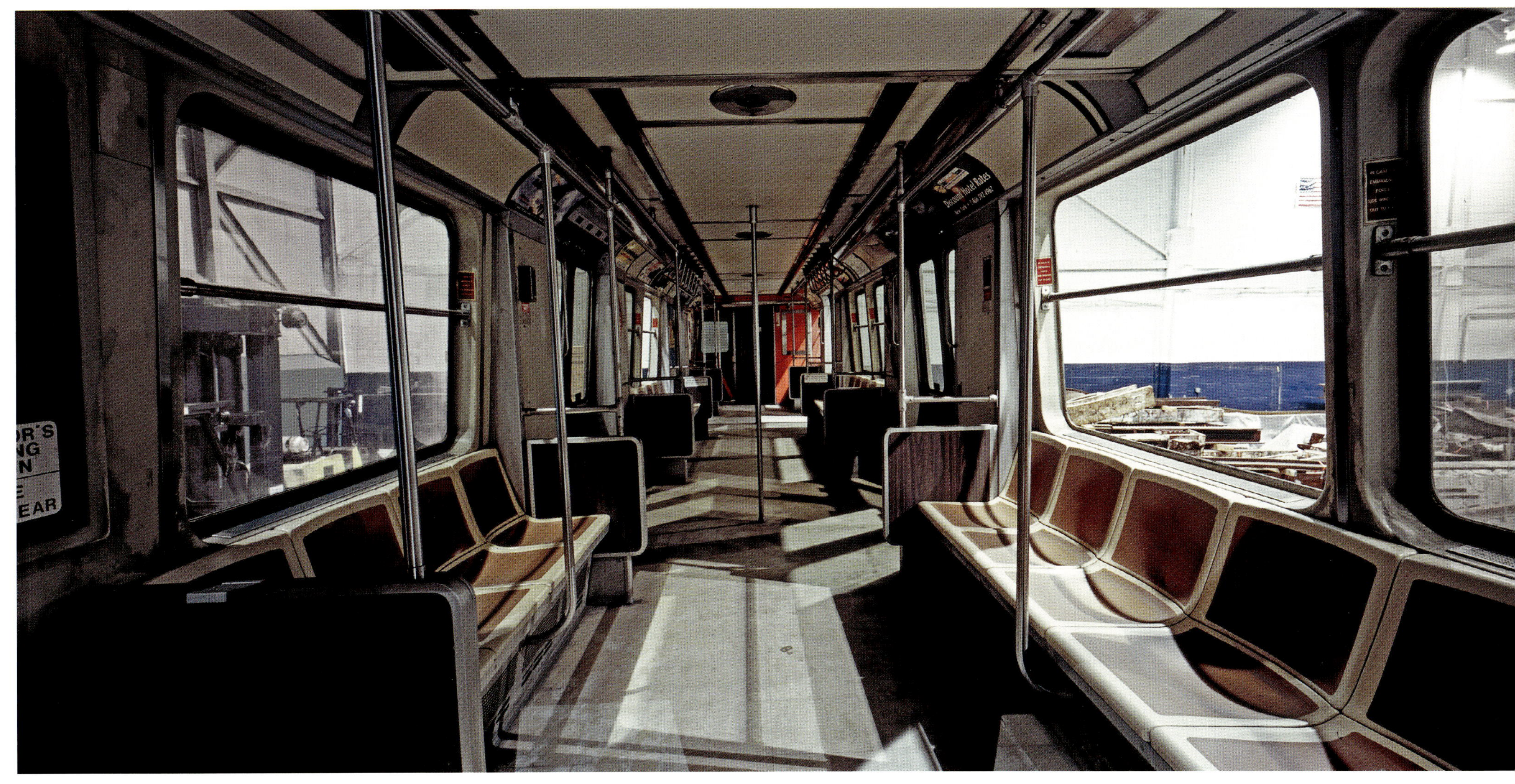
Discount Hotel Rates

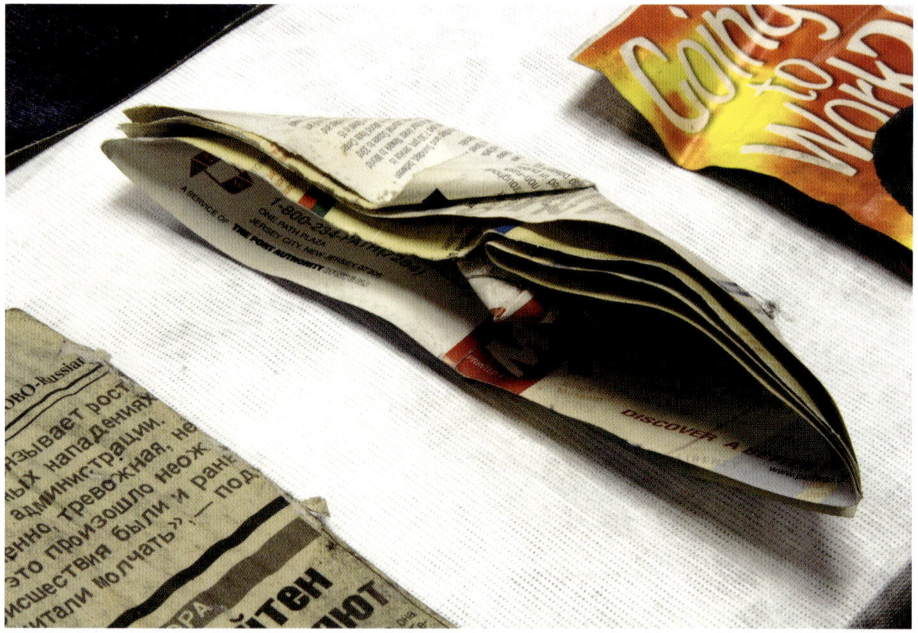

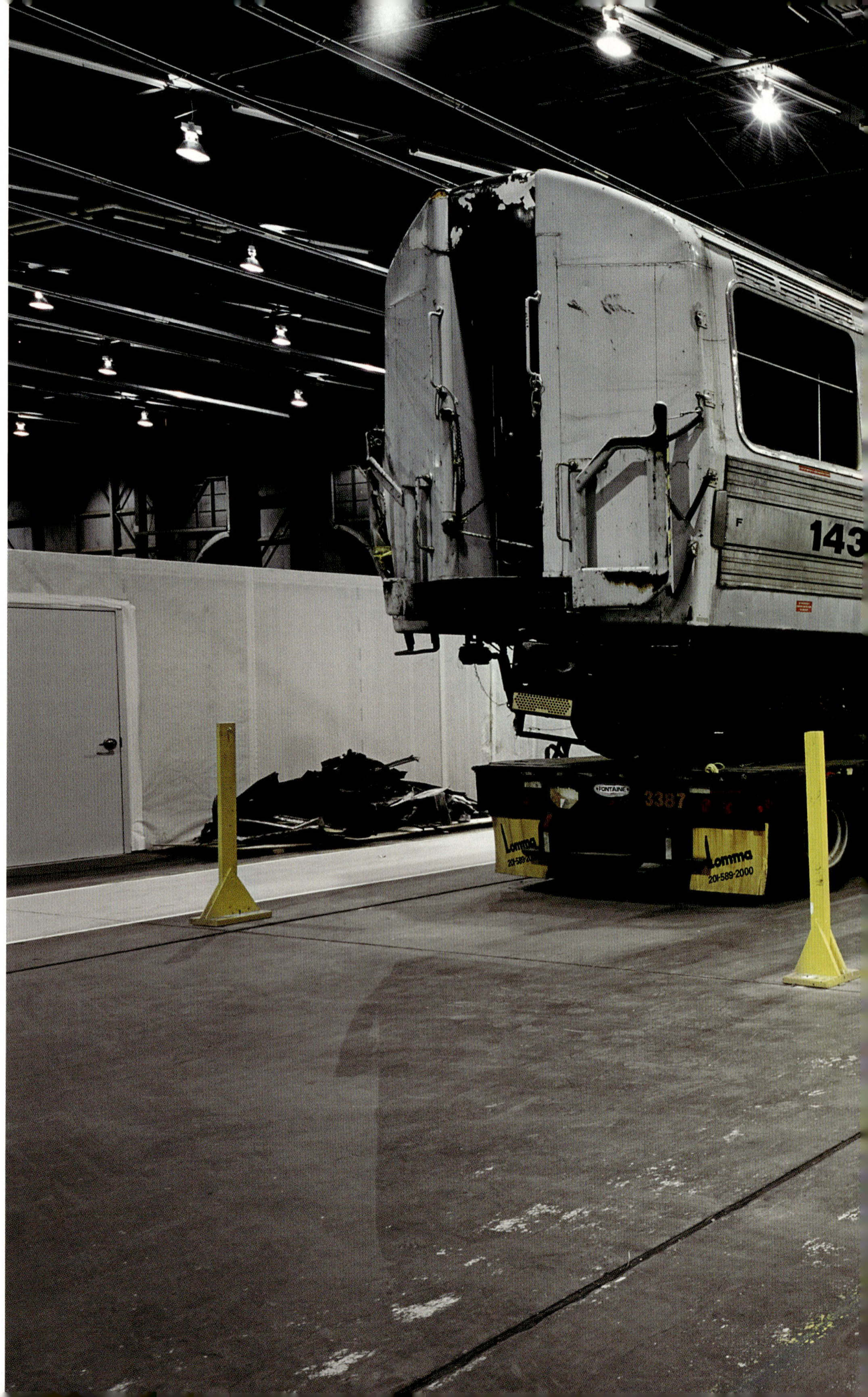
143
3387
Lomma
201-589-2000

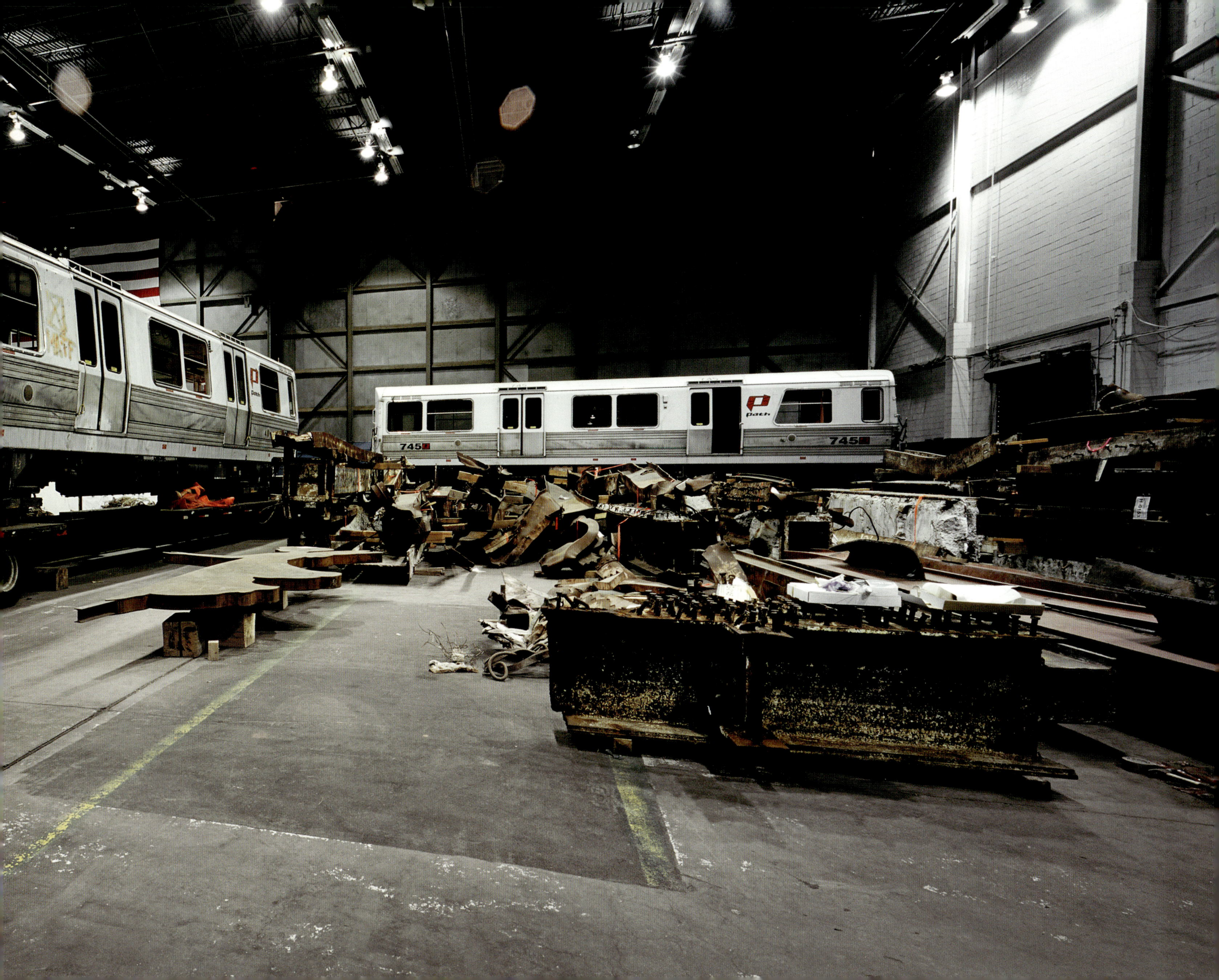
path
745
745

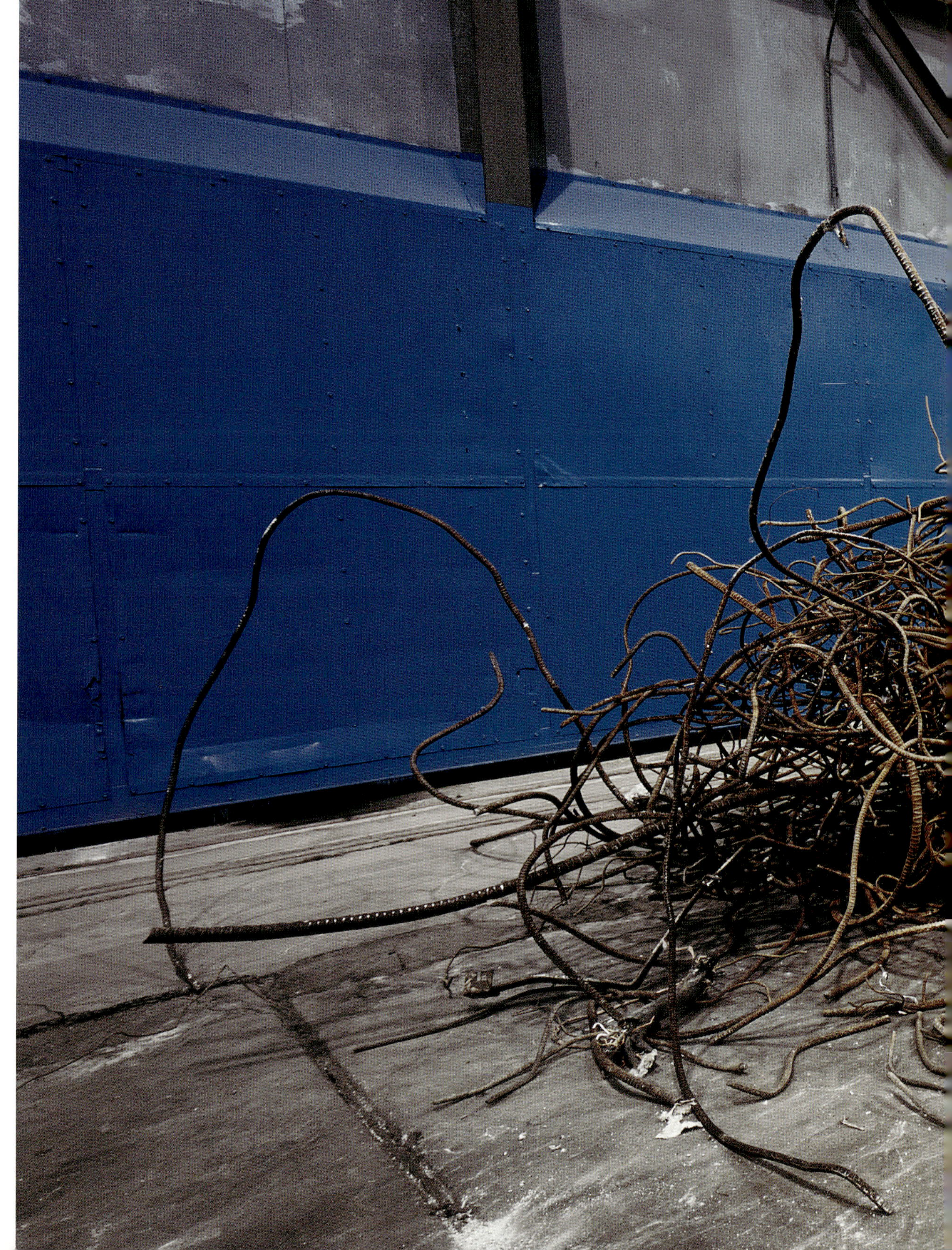

A large amount of rebar, steel bars used to reinforce concrete, was found at the site. This stack of rebar was built up in a corner at Hangar 17, the contortions of the steel providing more testimony to the physical transformation of the site.

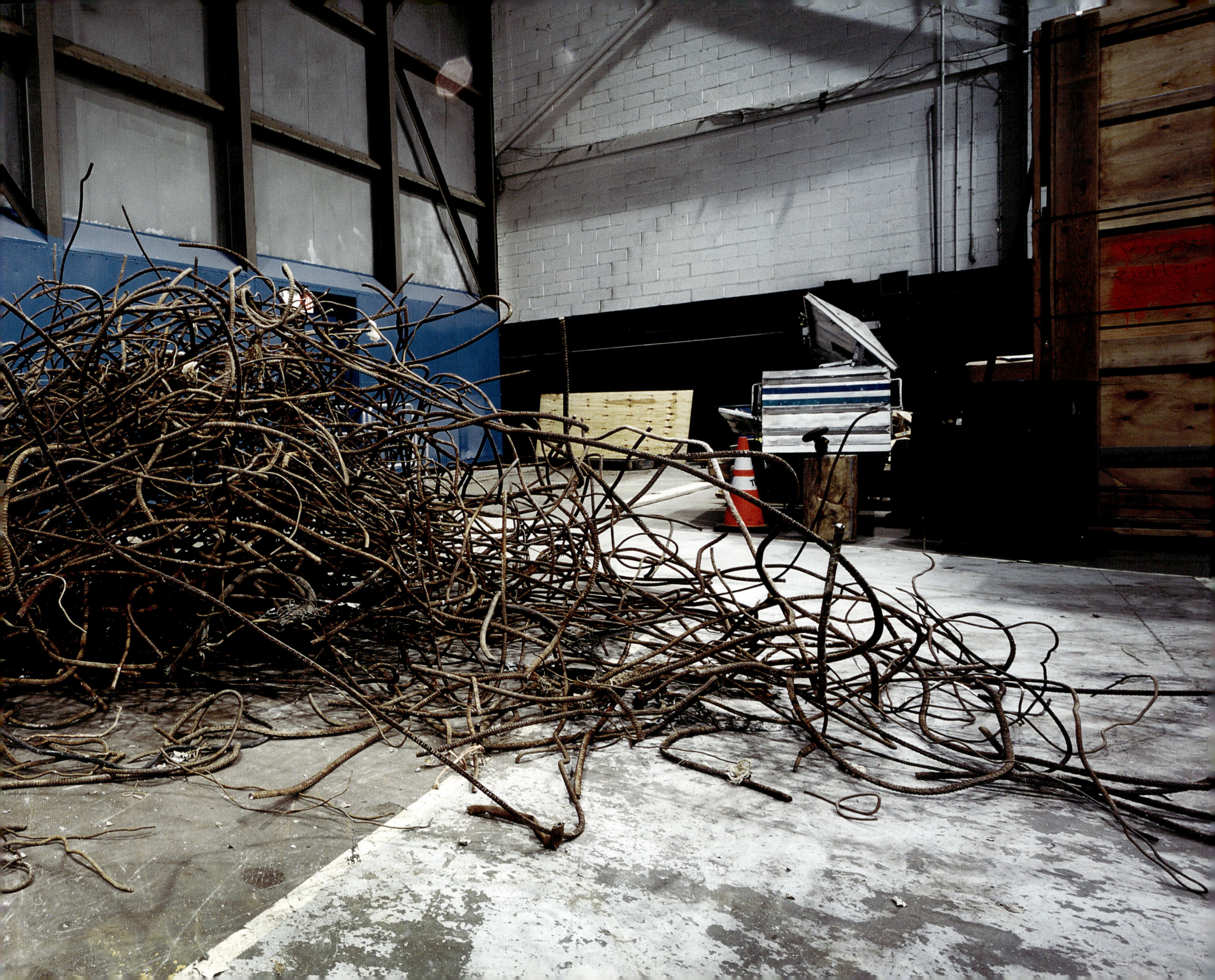

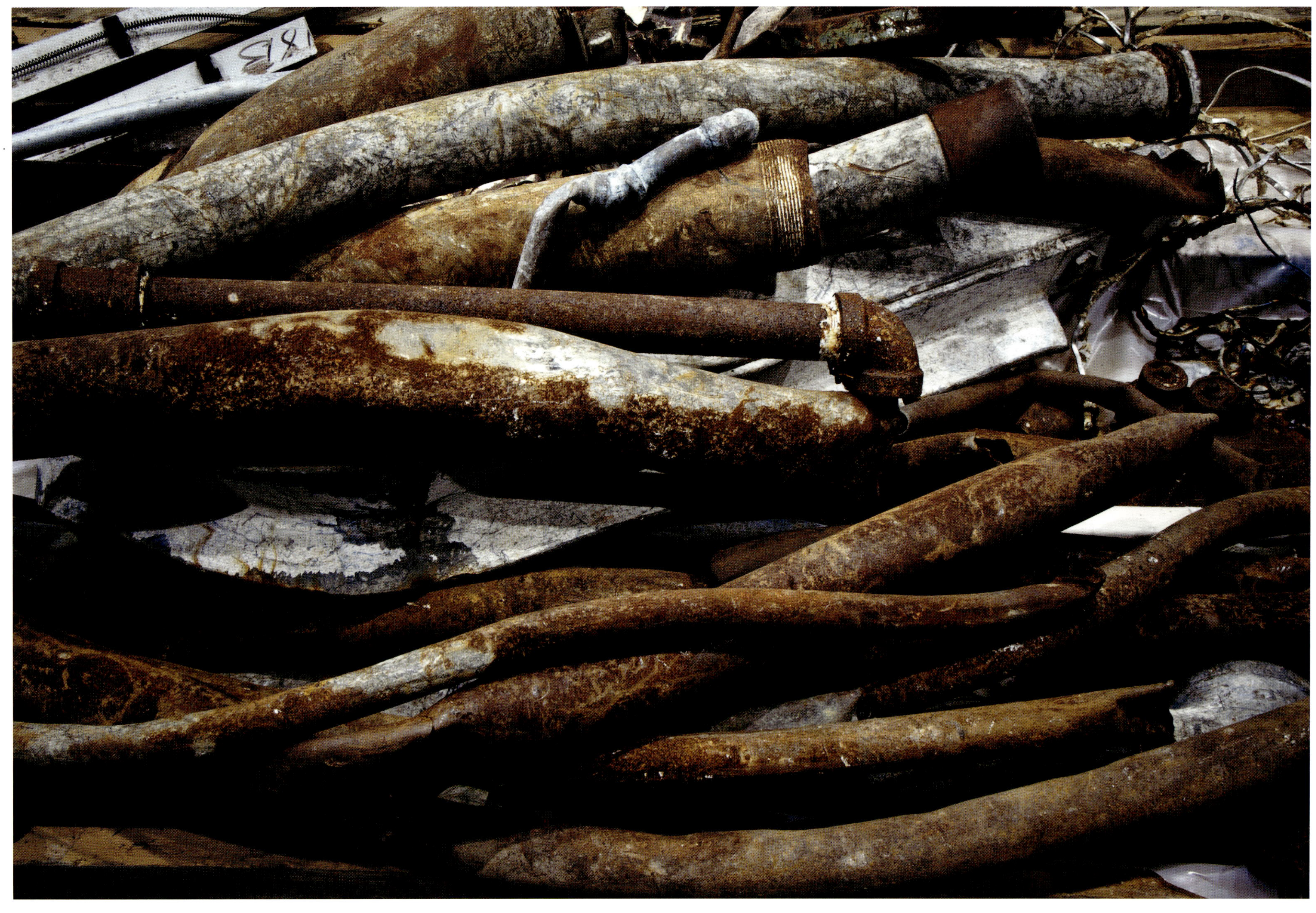

Pipes (left) and a mangled automobile seat belt (right), amid piles of rusting metal.

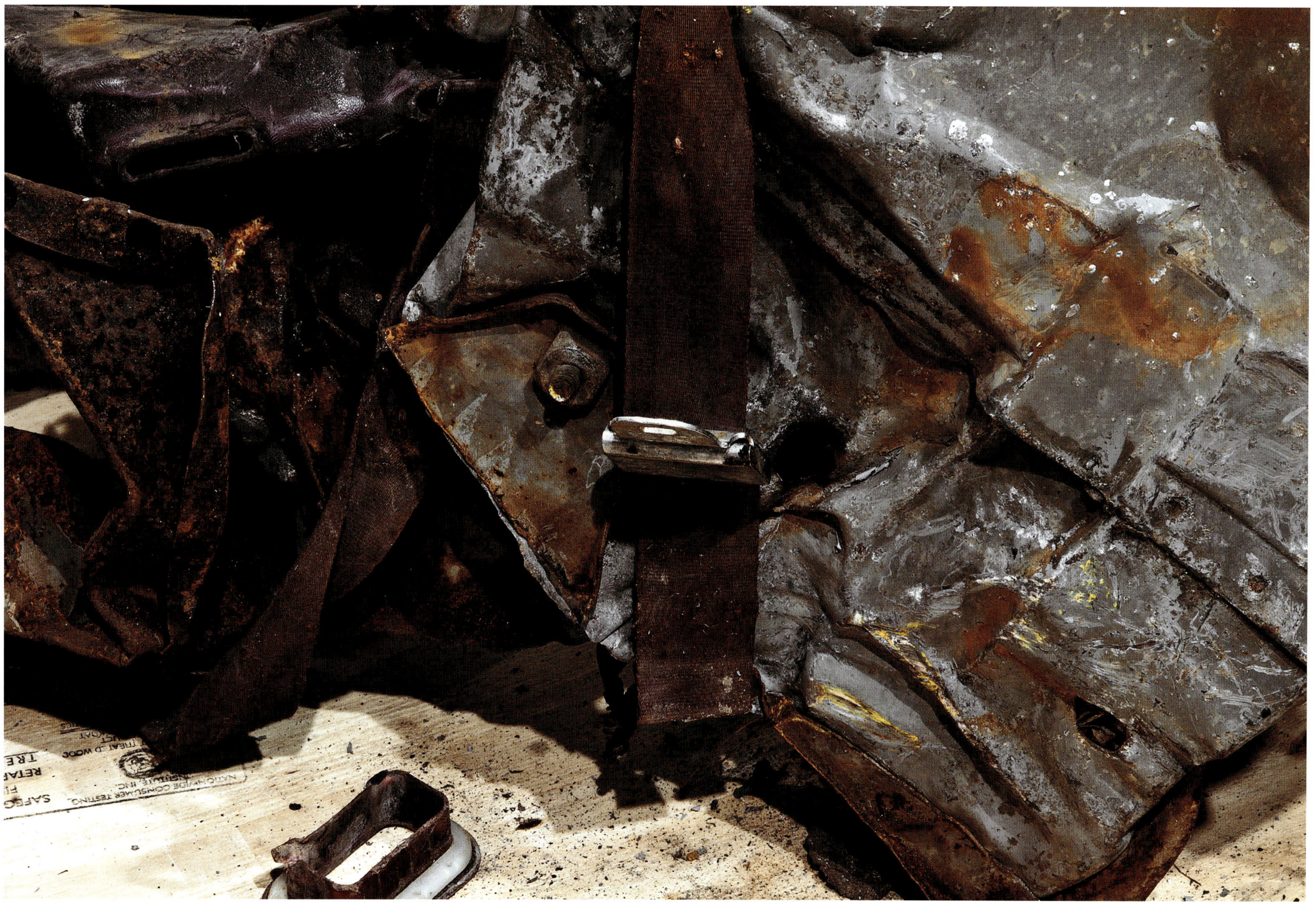

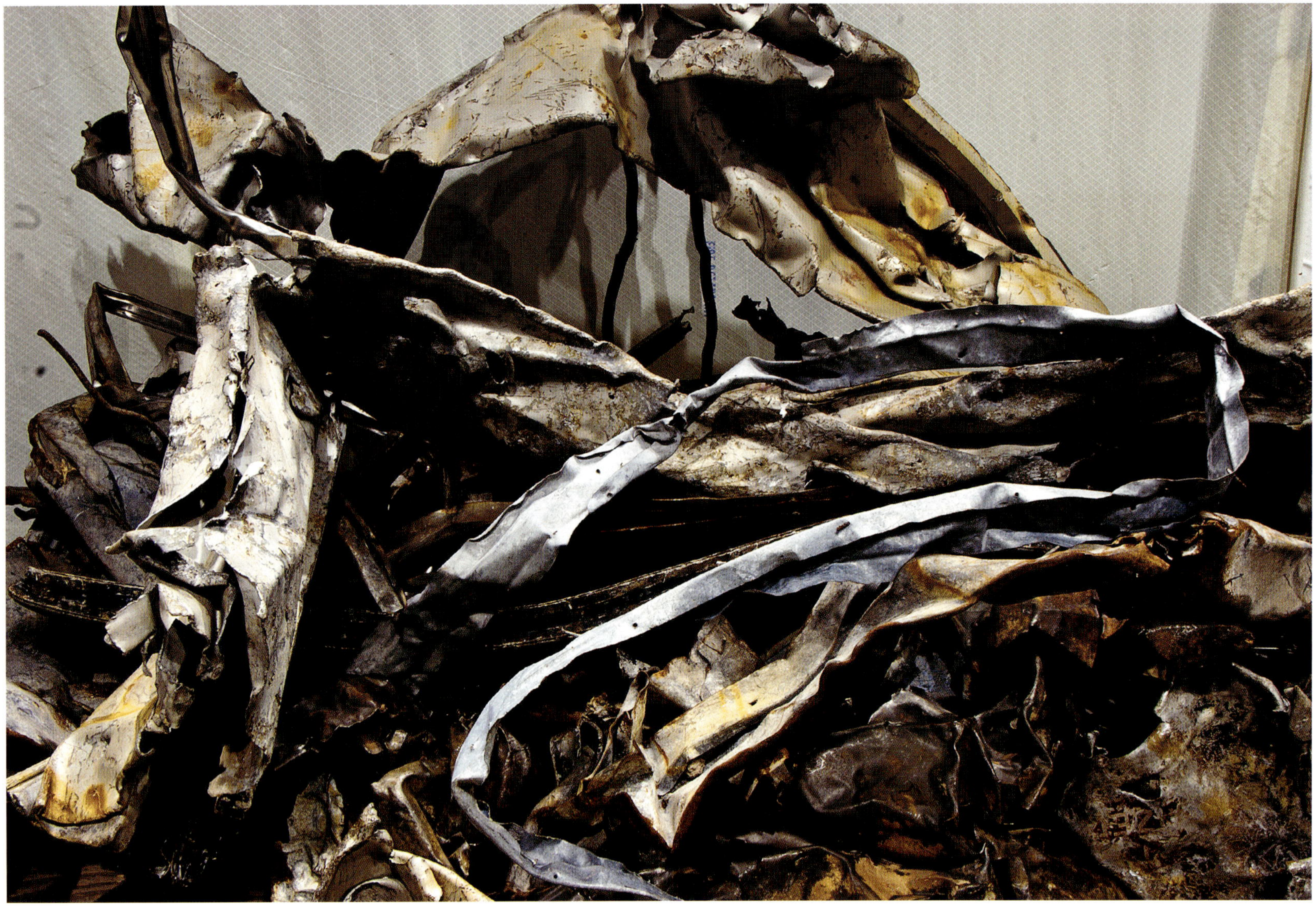

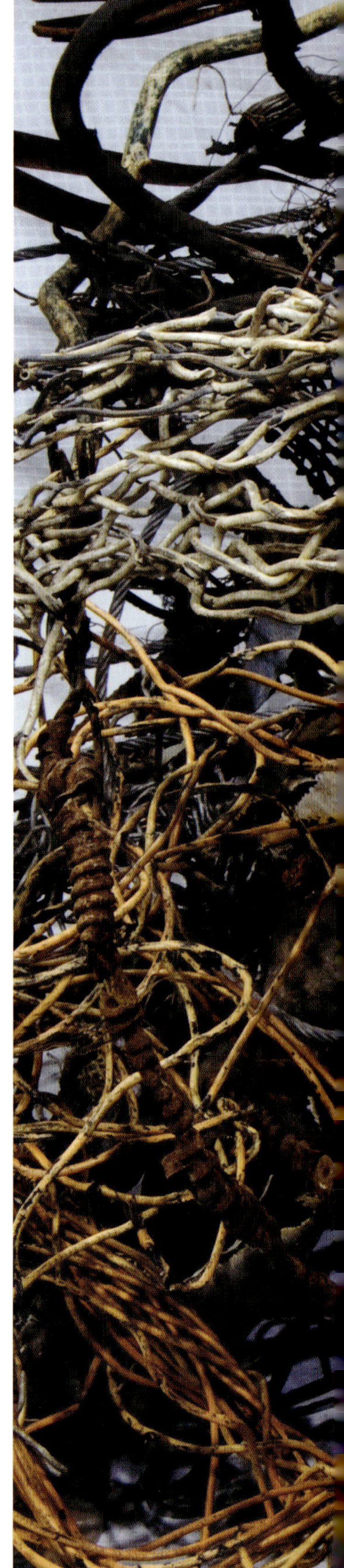

Almost none of the aluminum cladding that covered the enormous exterior surfaces of the towers survived the heat of long-burning fires. Likewise, commonplace objects like wiring were consumed in the aftermath of the collapse. Pictured here is some of what was recovered.

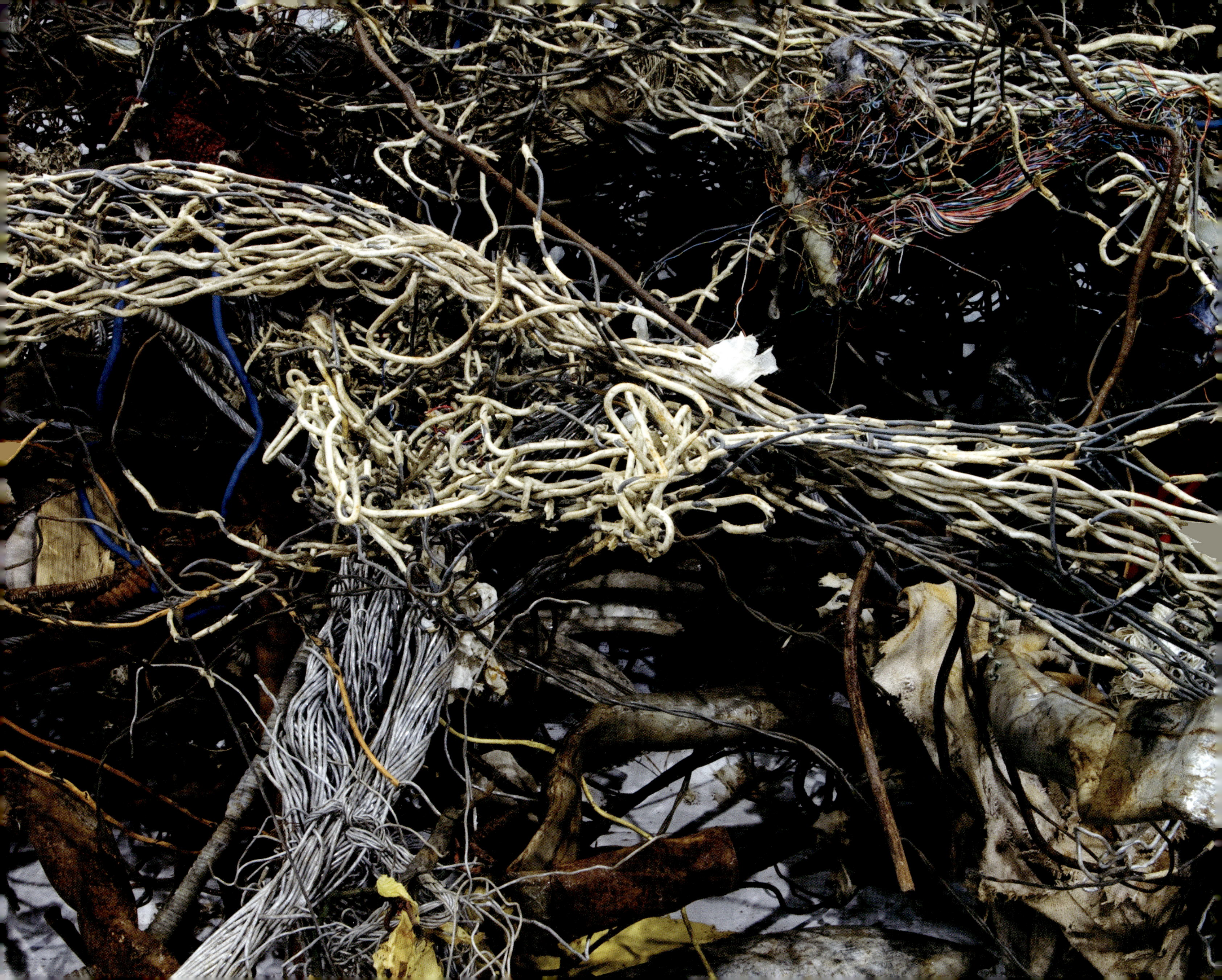

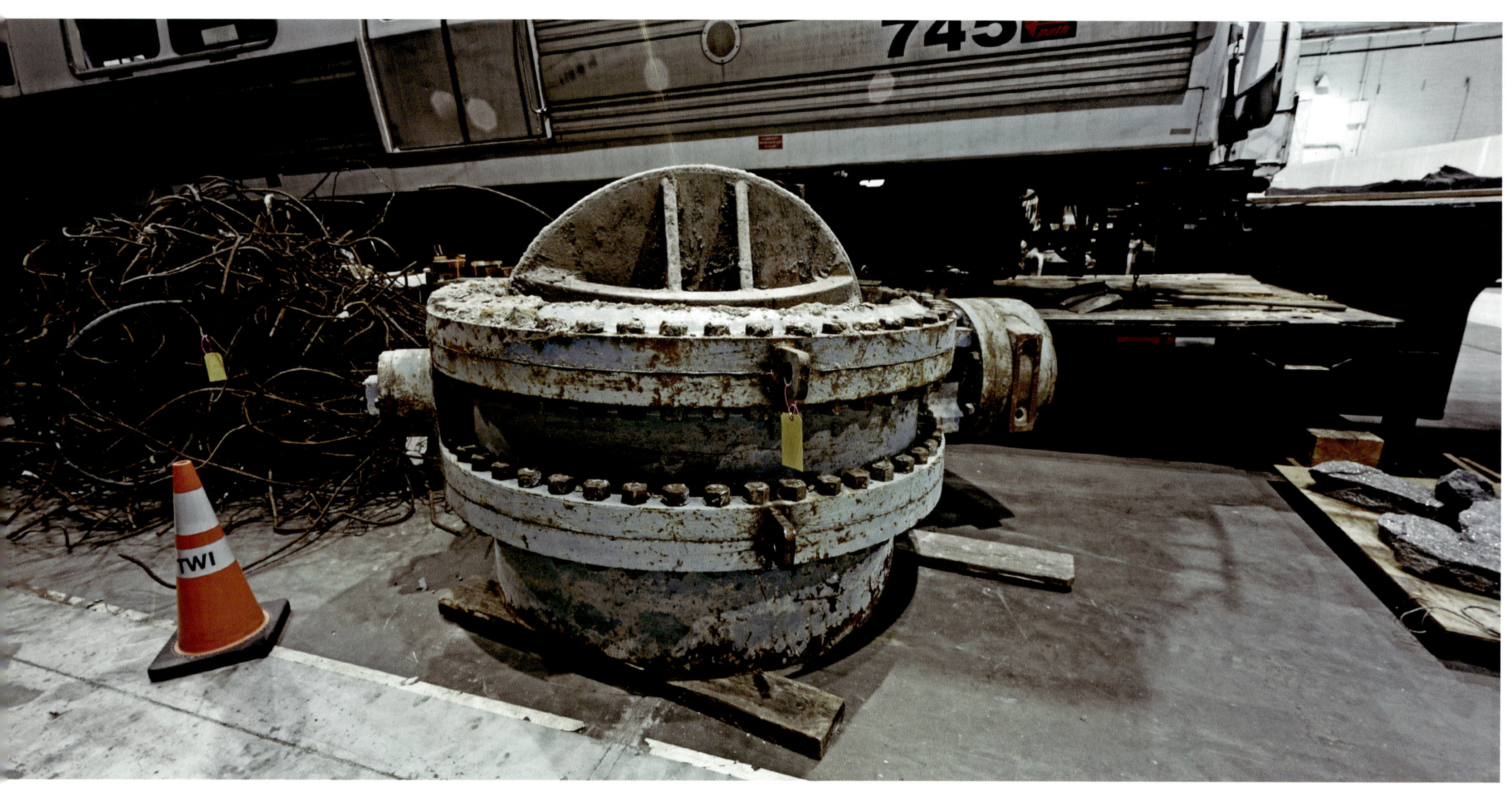

One of the valves that regulated the flow of water from the Hudson River, used in the cooling systems that served the World Trade Center. Each valve weighed some 13,000 pounds. At right are sections of the rings that lined the PATH train tunnel underneath the tower buildings.

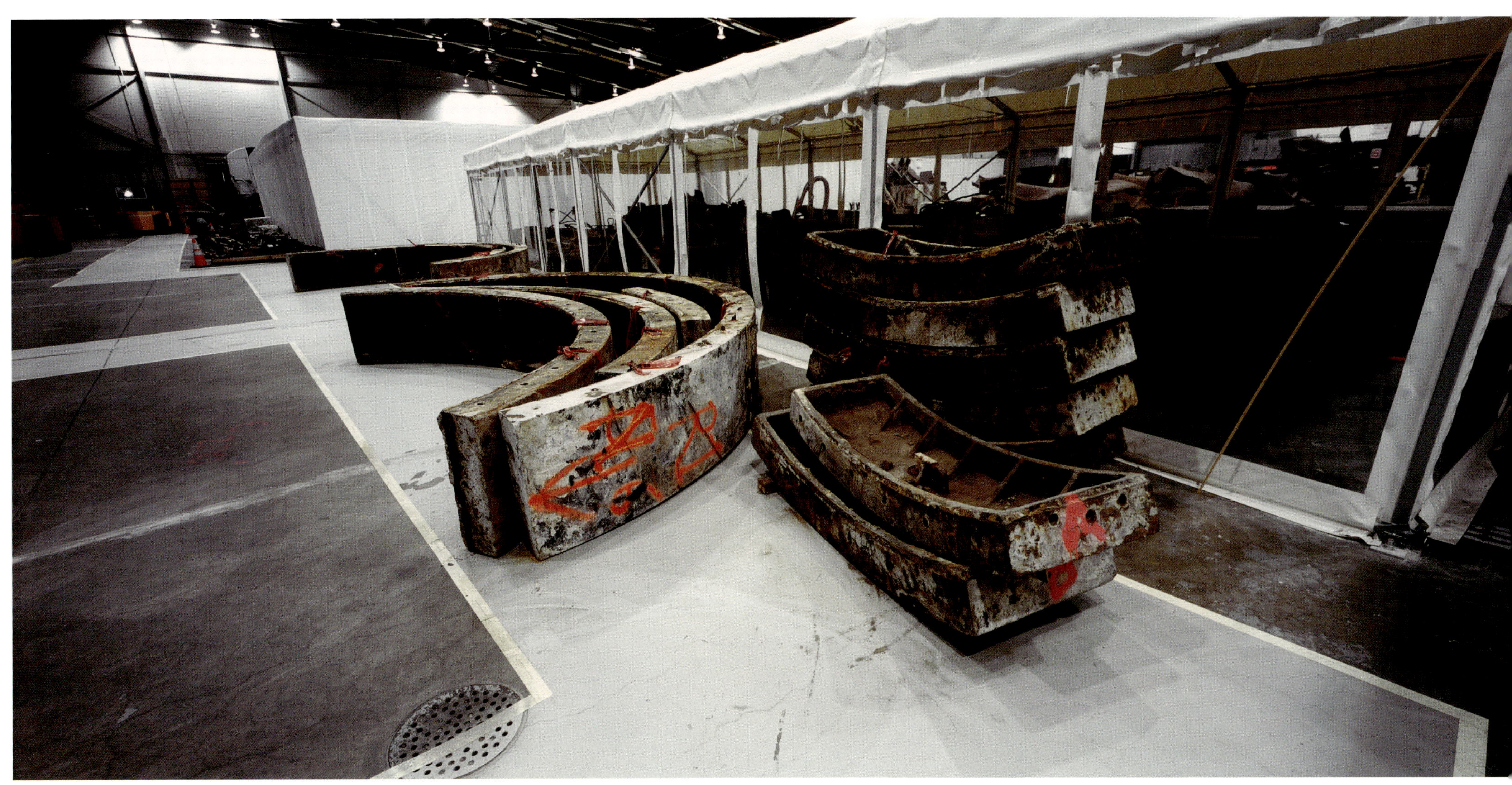

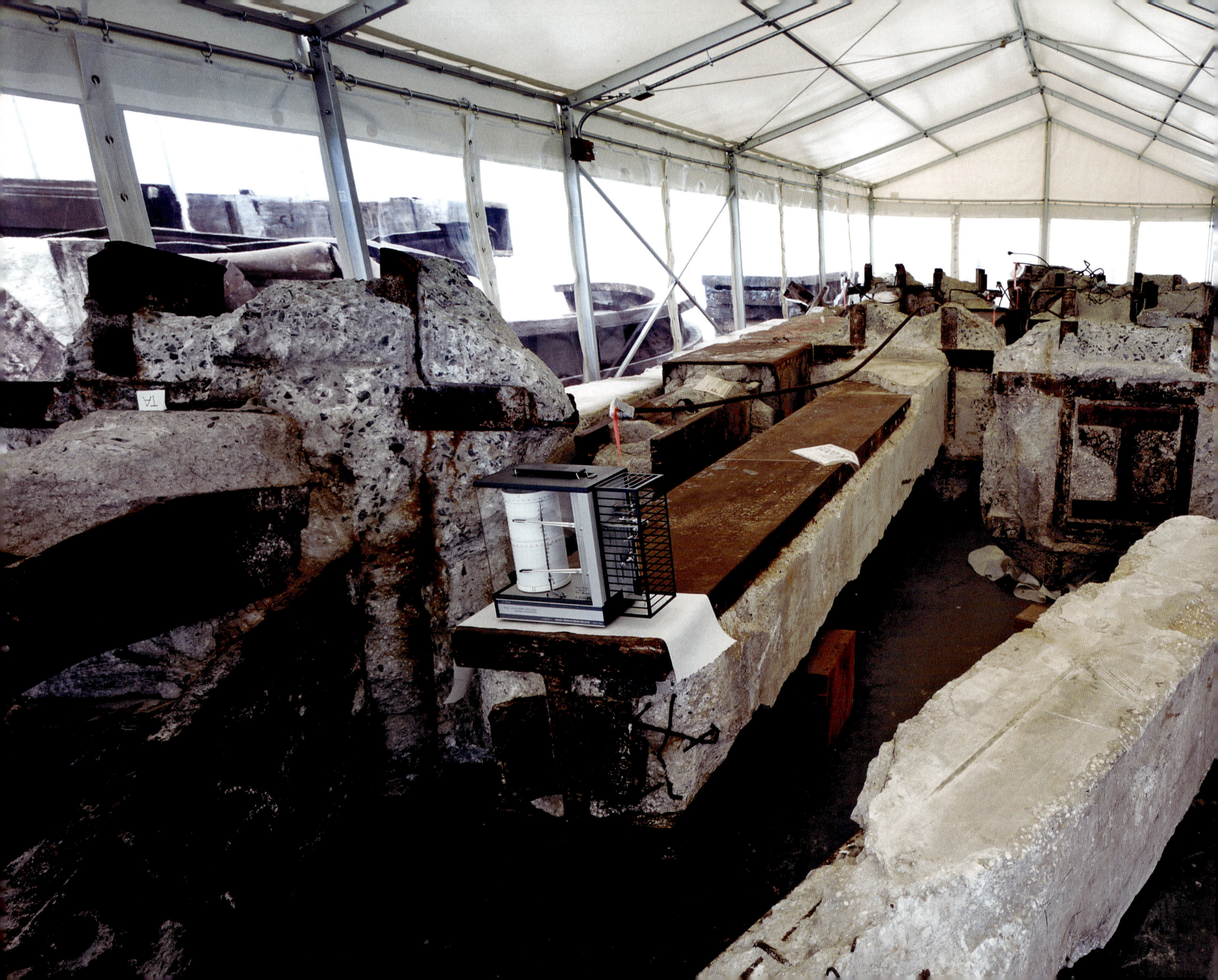

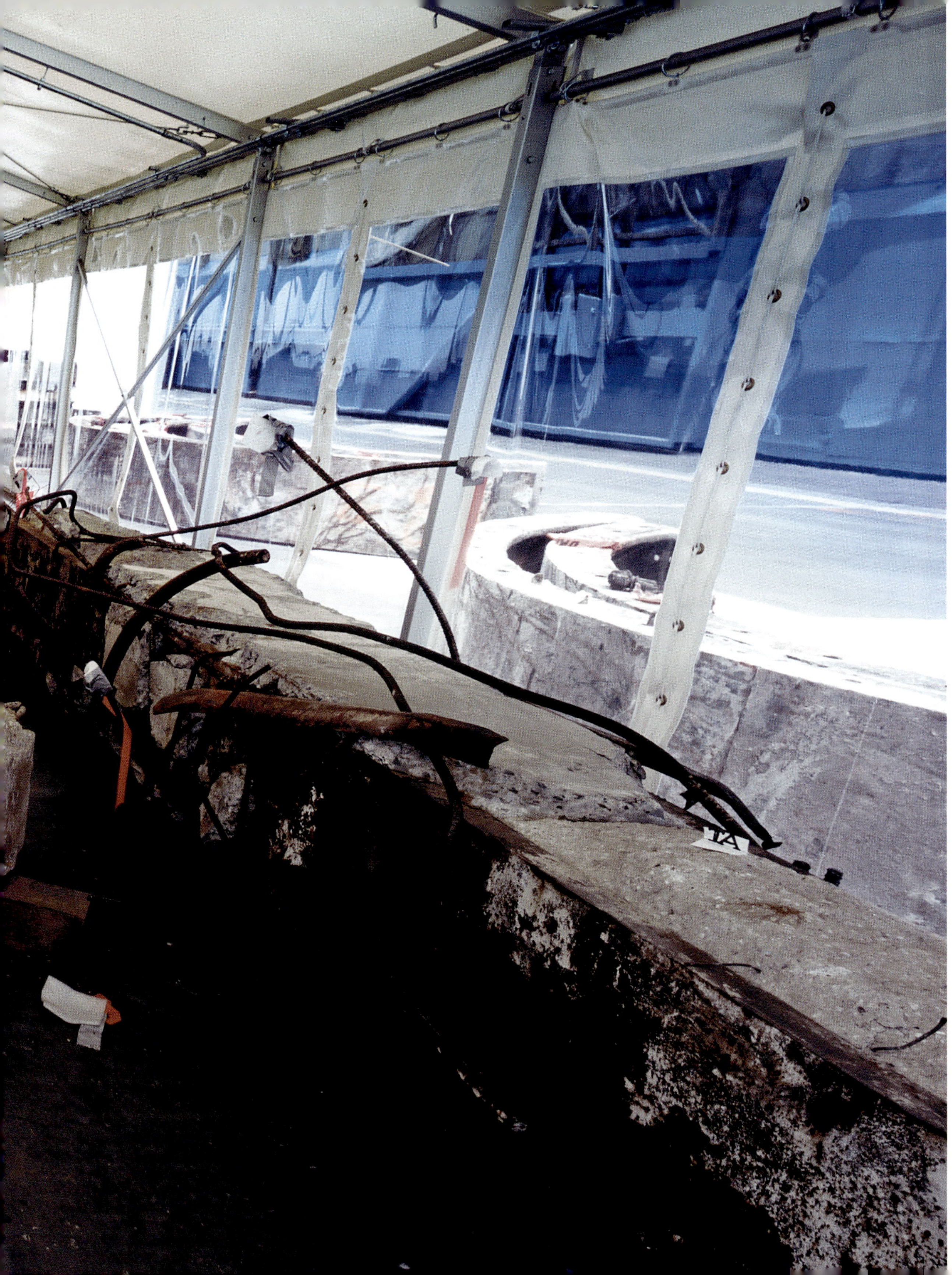

To protect steel and concrete that had not been built for exposure to the elements, conservation protocols were instituted at Hangar 17. Here, a tent enclosure has been built and a hydrothermograph measures relative humidity levels to ensure a stable environment for the artifacts.

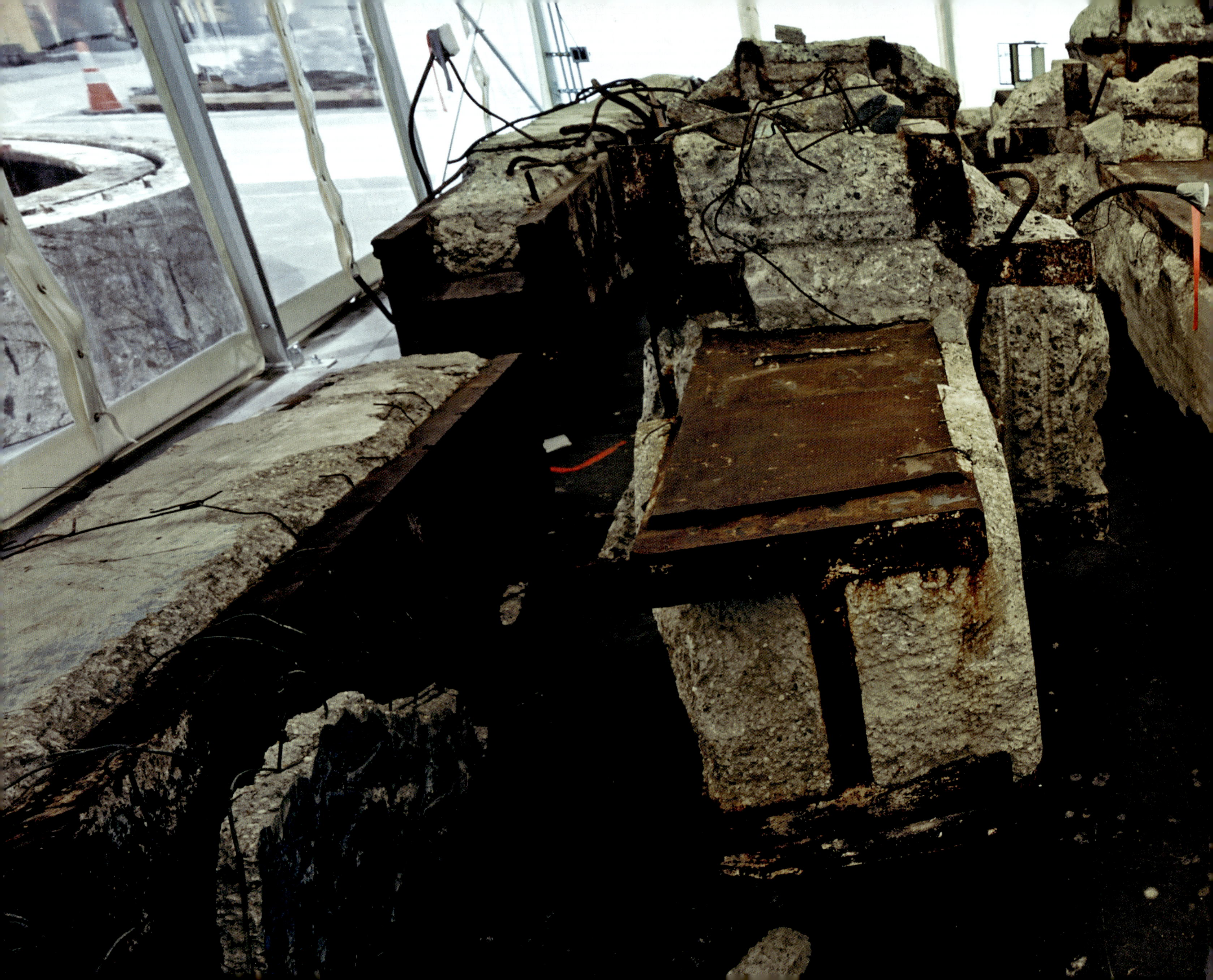

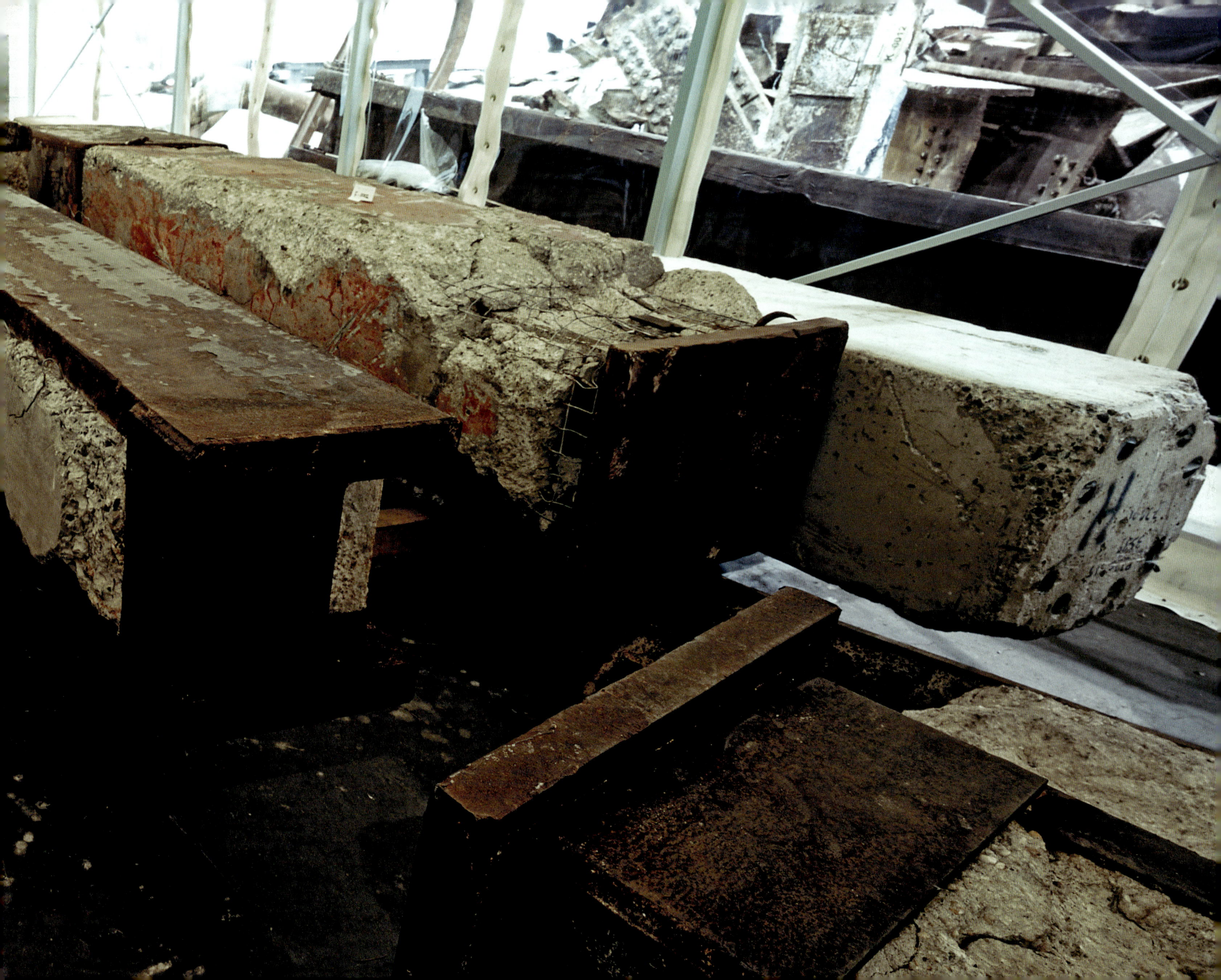

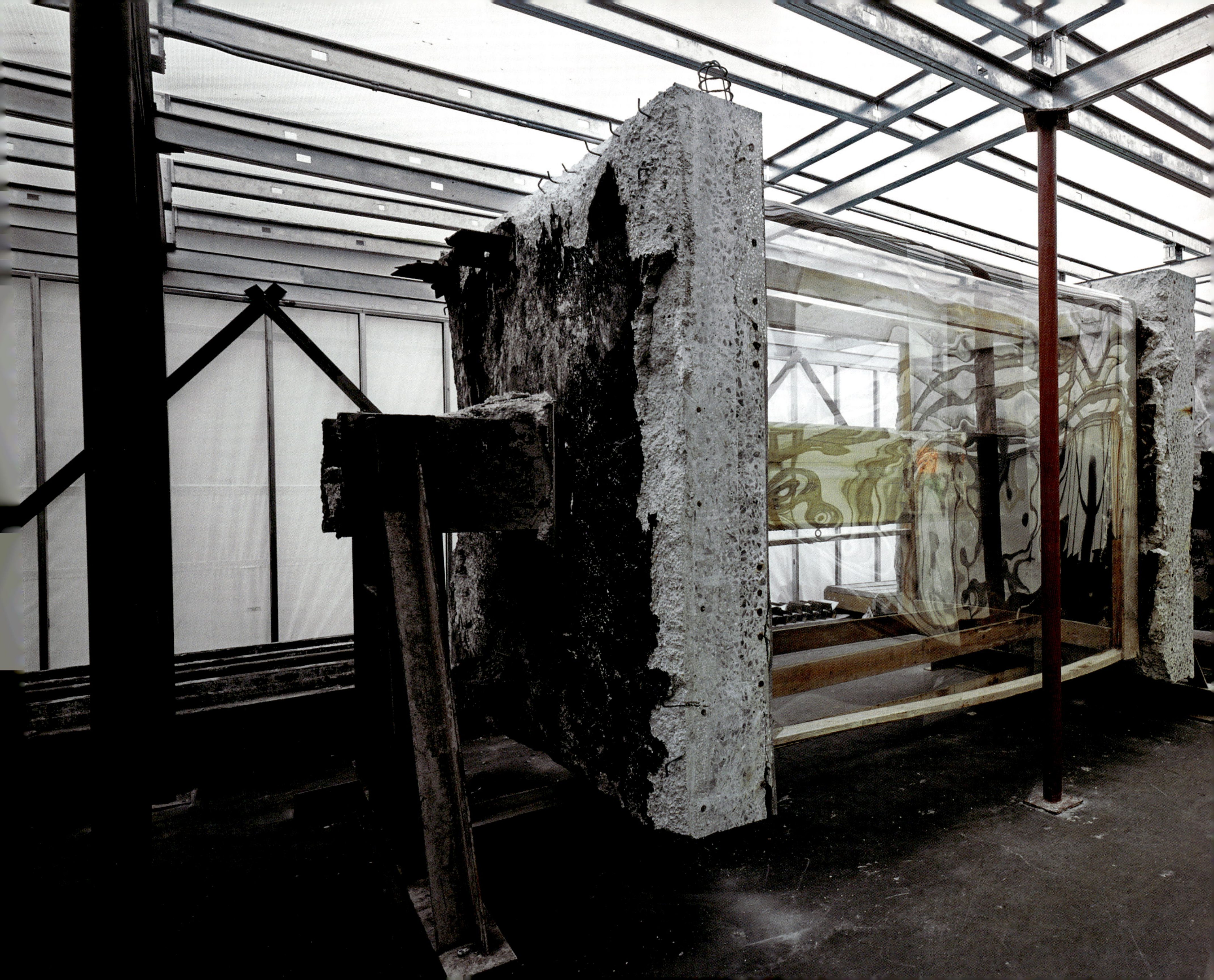

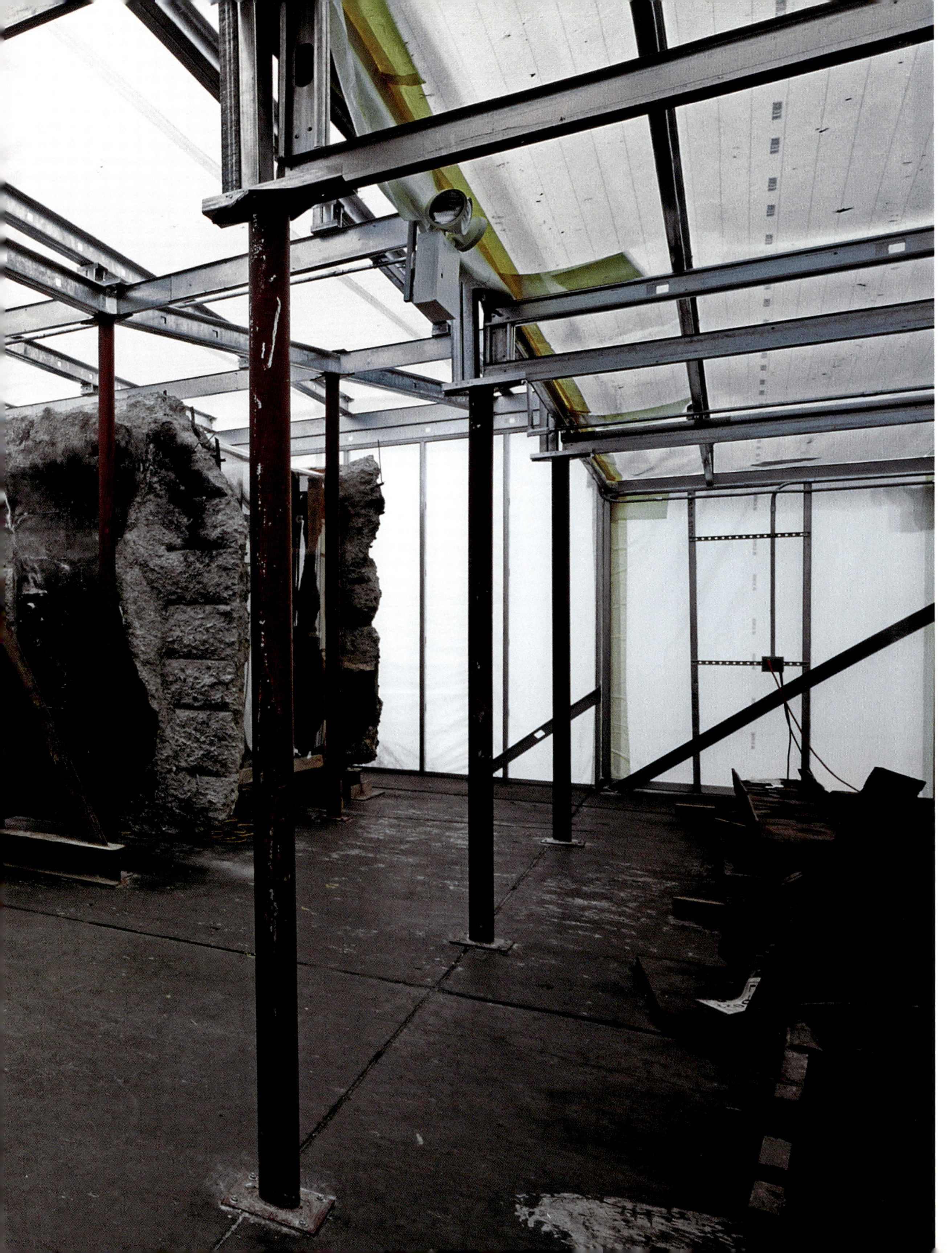

These ceiling and floor slabs were removed from the parking level of the World Trade Center to preserve the structural configurations of concrete and steel beams that were built to support the subterranean levels of the towers.

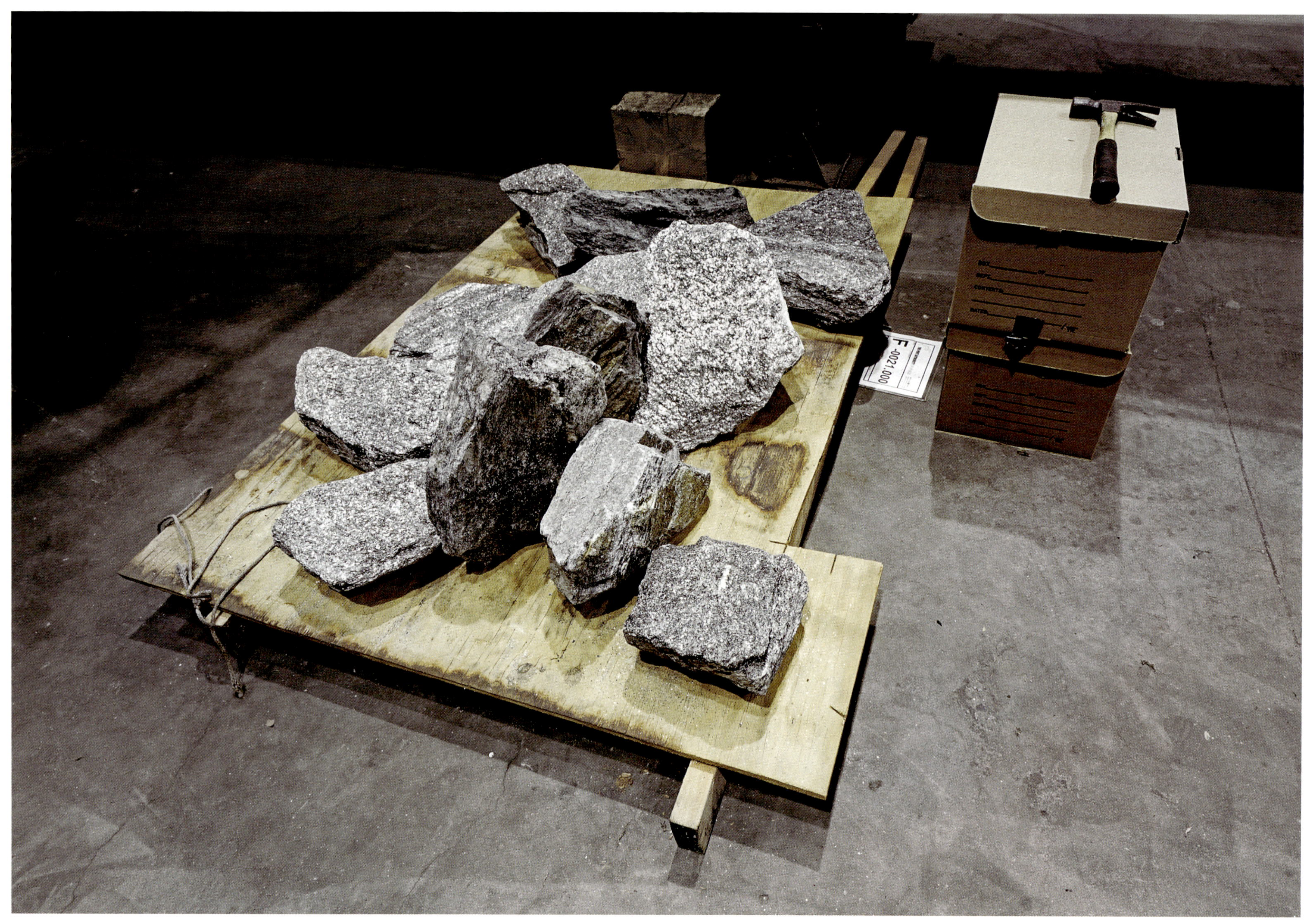

(Left) Pieces of schist from underneath the World Trade Center. Deposits of schist, an extremely durable rock, run through much of lower and midtown Manhattan, making these parts of New York City able to support the weight of skyscrapers. (Right) A planter and benches from the World Trade Center plaza.

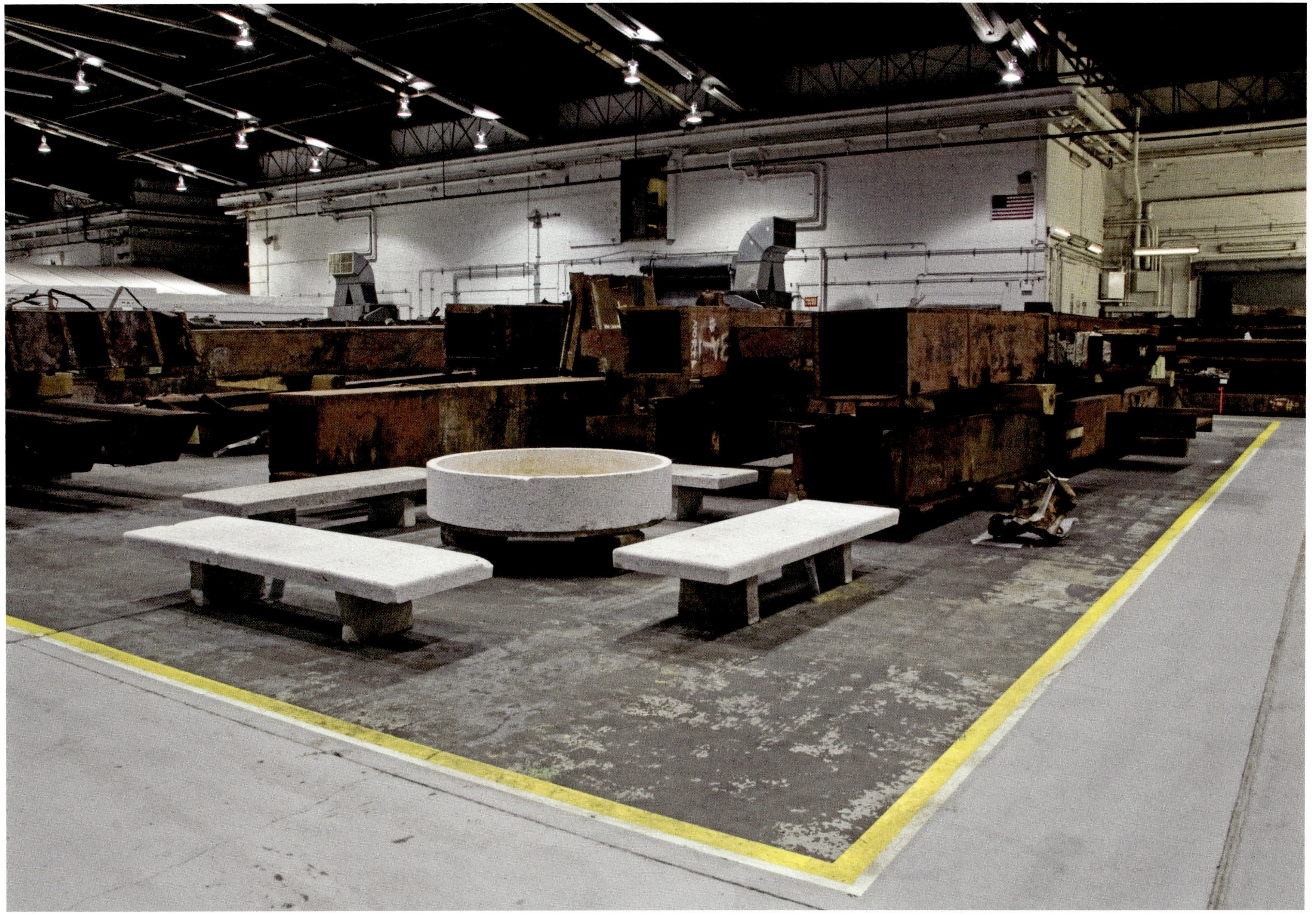

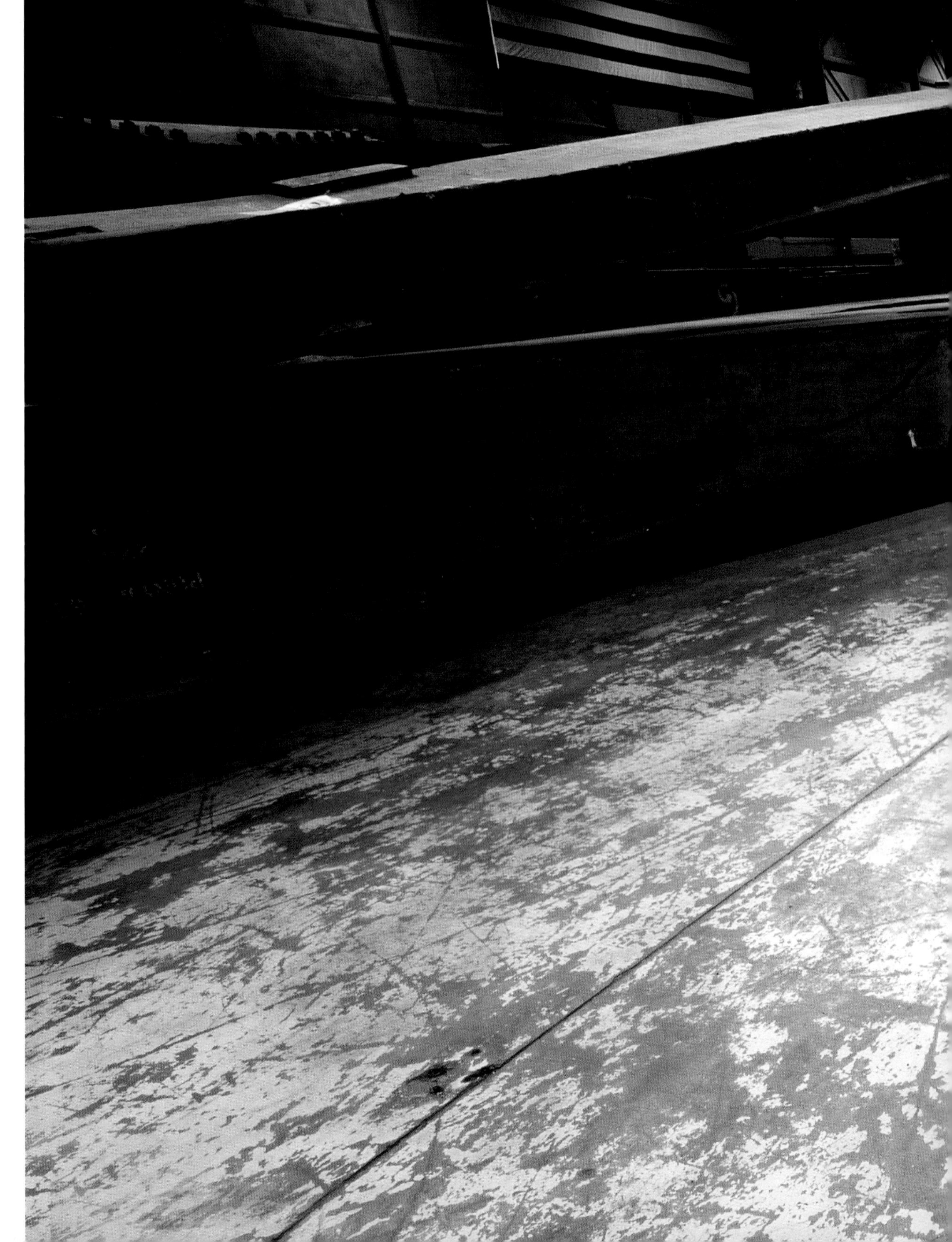

A bicycle rack from the vicinity of the World Trade Center. Some months after this rack was brought to Hangar 17, a messenger contacted the Port Authority to reclaim his bicycle. The rider came to JFK to get it, but seeing its condition, pulled a key from his pocket and took the lock, leaving the bicycle behind.

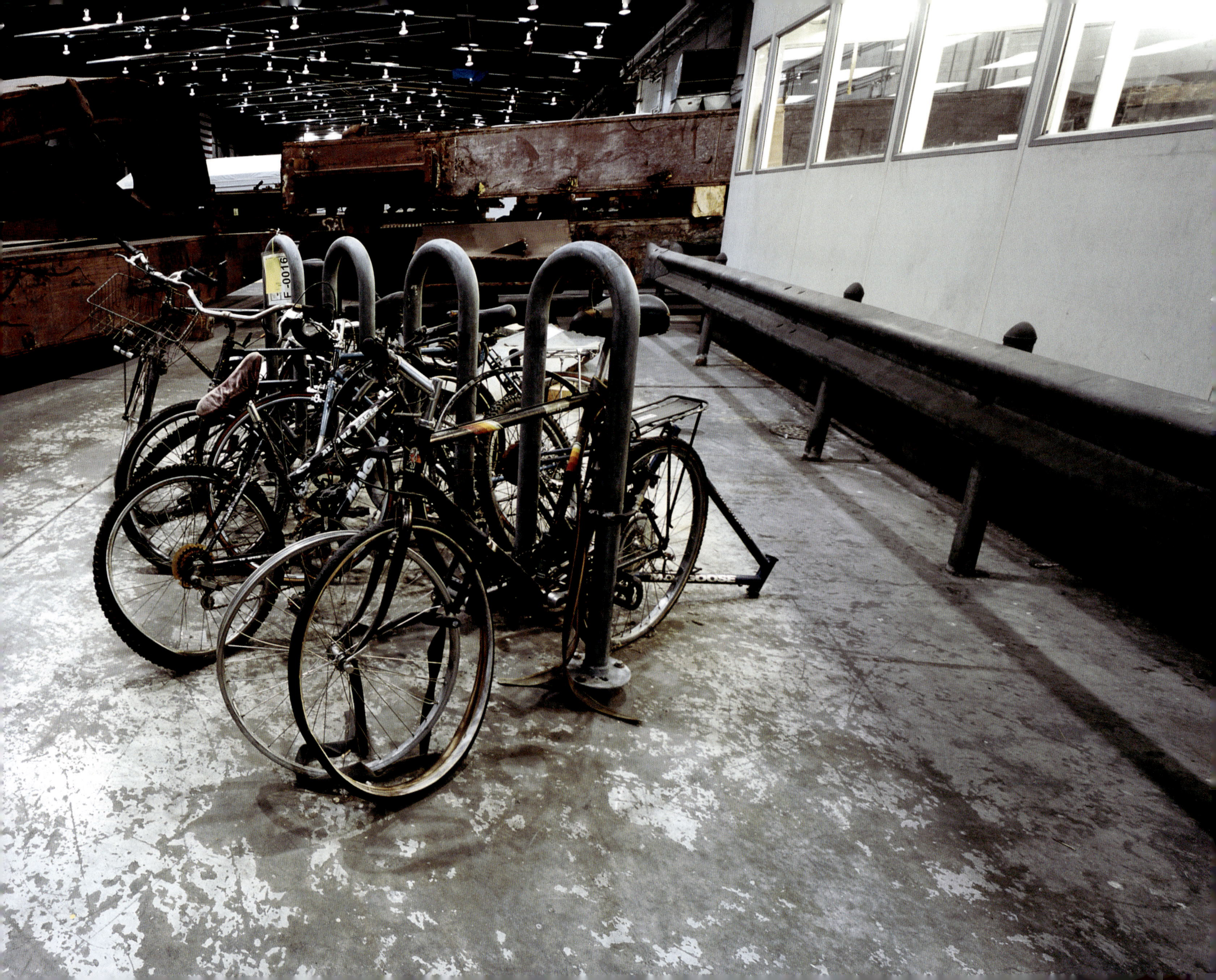
F-0016

SEEING IS BELIEVING

FRANCESC TORRES AT HANGAR 17 BY JAN SEIDLER RAMIREZ

History, like memory, is essentially iconographical. Without images there is no memory and without images neither can there be historic conscience
—Francesc Torres, from "Da Capo," 2008

The impulse to document the convulsive events of September 11, 2001, and to archive evidence of the inconceivable, has informed the creation of any number of 9/11 collections. The subject of this publication represents a unique double collection: first, an assemblage of ruins from the World Trade Center disaster that time and sentiment have transformed into objects of memory; and second, a photographic archive documenting that transformation, created on the verge of the disassembly of that collection which for nearly ten years was housed in the care of the Port Authority of New York and New Jersey at JFK's Hangar 17. Far more than reminders of the demolished landmark where that agency had been headquartered, the more than 1,500 objects sheltered at Hangar 17 evoke the grievous human loss of the attacks, which claimed 84 Port Authority employees among the nearly 3,000 dead.

From the earliest weeks that its cavernous interior began to absorb the sorrowful cargo from ground zero, Hangar 17 has served as a de facto memorial to the victims of 9/11, albeit a memorial off-limits to the public. Its sequestered location within a busy international airport complex invariably summons thoughts of where and how the 9/11 terrorist plot launched.

Commandeered in late 2001 to address the practical need for emergency storage of large items from the World Trade Center and Fresh Kills Landfill sifting sites, Hangar 17 has matured from a provisional maintenance shed to a unique space of caretaking and tribute. Climate-controlled enclosures were installed to stabilize its unorthodox collection. Conservators administered triage to the most distressed objects sent to JFK. Walkways were introduced to provide a coherent survey of the facility's contents. Stretched on an interior wall, a monumental American flag now salutes the hangar's occasional visitors.

From the outset, the Port Authority's motive in protecting these relics was to disperse them for study and commemorative purposes. Before that agenda could be implemented, however, plans for the National September 11 Memorial & Museum had to solidify. By 2008, the Memorial Museum's exhibition designs and collection policy were advanced sufficiently to have produced an extensive checklist of holdings that the new institution intended to claim from Hangar 17.

With the tenth anniversary of 9/11 in mind, the Port Authority launched an initiative to distribute pieces of World Trade Center steel to communities for their own memorials. Anticipating alterations to the habitat of Hangar 17 once the dispersal of its historic inventory was underway, the Memorial Museum approached the Port Authority for clearance to document the facility before it transitioned back to a working airport property.

The purpose of this commission was not to certify Hangar 17's content. The aspiration was to convey the evanescence of Hangar 17 as a time capsule; to immortalize, through still photographs, its peculiar dignity as a refuge for dislocated artifacts infused with hallowed pain.

The assignment went to Francesc Torres, an internationally established conceptual artist who was born in Barcelona in 1948. For Torres, photography was initially a support component of his installation pieces and experimental multimedia collages. But by 2001, photography had emerged as an independent element of his work. When Torres experienced the events of 9/11 at uncomfortably close range, his camera provided a ready option for his engagement with the catastrophe. A resident of lower Manhattan at the time, he was at home, finalizing his relocation to Barcelona after 29 years in the United States, when he heard the first plane ram into the north tower. Racing outside with his camera, Torres stayed on the streets taking pictures until his film was spent. With police urging bystanders to evacuate the area, he fled ten blocks north to the roof of his work loft. There, he witnessed people plummeting to their deaths from the burning buildings as well as the vertical collapse of both towers—a spectacle he likened in an essay in 2008, to "old images of ships sinking with their bow facing skyward after having received the fatal torpedo blow."

As a naturalized citizen of the United States, Torres had long valued America's optimism and traffic in "the infinite present." Overnight he felt the burden of a new, horrible past. Documenting Hangar 17 for the Memorial Museum seven years later posed an opportunity to reflect back on 9/11 through a camera lens.

Through much of his career, Torres has explored questions of collective memory and the property rights to history: what and who are remembered officially, and what gets silenced, suppressed, manipulated, or forgotten. In a published conversation with Torres in 2000, critic Hugh Davies reflected that although his art might appear avant-garde, Torres's thematic preferences were essentially very traditional: life, death, history; war and violence; and the struggle between rationality and irrationality.

All these ideas commingled in the wreckage preserved at Hangar 17. It is not surprising that Torres often focused his camera on the word "save," which Port Authority field agents had spray-painted onto some of these objects to spare them from disposal. Hangar 17, in his judgment, was a container of irrefutable evidence, laying bare the ferocity and brutal physics of the 9/11 attacks. Its artifacts transcended interpretive politics, forming a baseline for public memory. His task as documentarian was to respect their autonomous authority as survivors, revealing their voice without dictating their words. Consequently, no artificial illumination or restaging was employed in this assignment; objects were photographed as found. The hangar's ambient light conditions, from harsh overhead lamps to crepuscular gloom, posed challenges. Nonetheless, Torres's patience was rewarded with moments of compositional éclat when a rare shaft of daylight pierced into the facility or workers adjusted a portable floodlight, catching certain artifacts by surprise and accentuating their otherworldly essence.

Hangar 17 was not a wholly alien working environment for Torres. A number of his previous projects had been installed in quasi-industrial exhibition spaces and were conceived around commentaries probing dark episodes in our common past. Clearly, the disposition of relics inside the hangar was not an aesthetic fabrication. However, their calculated placement intrigued Torres. Forgoing his own agency as creator, Torres could admire the installation work of unknown others within its cavernous interior—as if rationalizing the arrangement of objects could rectify a degree of the mayhem unleashed on 9/11. Occasionally he detected levity's rare intrusion, photographing a vignette of phantom sociability: four deserted benches from the outdoor plaza of the Trade Center, grouped conversationally around an empty concrete planter.

Despite repeated trips to Hangar 17 during the weeks of his shoot for the museum, Torres felt jolted every time he encountered the remains of the towers spread around him. The physicality of the salvaged objects continually pulled at him. Like others, he was awed by the jagged tears and undulations animating some of this misshapen steel. Behind the camera lens, however, he worked to expose the deceit of that awful beauty, recording these pieces not as sculptures but as distorted specimens of a fearsome kinetic force. Fragments of Alexander Calder's "Bent Propeller," which had enlivened the outdoor plaza of the World Trade Center until its devastation on 9/11, appear as shards drained of the color, wit, and balance of their maker's intention.

The collection's quality of historicity also engaged Torres. By-products of a very young event in the 21st century, the World Trade Center objects appear prematurely aged if not yet venerable. Many images detail their patina of distress. His portraits of damaged emergency vehicles, for example, reveal a brew of afflictions—gashes, heat blisters, scorch marks, and scars of dismemberment—evoking the extreme conditions that claimed so many lives. Through a hollowed piece of the north tower's antenna, Torres takes a panoramic view of what could be seen as miscellaneous architectural flotsam washed onto a tented shore. The antenna segment framing the perspective resembles the hull of a decrepit ship sunk in storm and then heaved, long ago, back onto land to blanch and decay.

An impartial concentration, not to be confused with detachment, accompanied Torres to Hangar 17. All categories of artifacts deposited there received their documentary due, from the tridents that formed the signature base of Yamasaki's towers to the cartoon figure of Bugs Bunny that greeted customers browsing the Warner Bros. Studio Store in the belowground shopping mall of the Trade Center.

This is especially true of his studies of impaired vehicles rescued for the archive, perhaps attributable to the artist's affinity for cars and motorcycles (which appear in his other installations and writings) as metaphors for speed, freedom, machismo, and modernism. Within a segregated space serving as an environmentally controlled parking lot, Torres took dozens of shots of the 25 or so vehicles hauled to the hangar after an interim stay at the Fresh Kills Landfill, many still bearing the insignia of city and state agencies and each displaying unique disfigurement. Wheeled dollies had been placed beneath many of the vehicles, which were positioned to face an orderly central corridor. With his camera, Torres sweeps the interior, teasing out the conversational possibilities of those placements. Suddenly, we are looking at invalid veterans occupying opposite beds in a hospital ward, swapping war stories.

Torres memorialized specific patients in a series of haunting vehicle-centered portraits. A close-up of a yellow taxicab assumes the persona of a battered prizefighter, its facial structure savaged by a superior opponent. In another, more reminiscent of a coroner's postmortem photograph, he peers into the stabbed and charred torso of a fire department ambulance. Point blank, his camera confronts a motorcycle, mangled and immobilized on a low-lying platform, fitted with a pointless triage tag. (In fact, the label identifies it as an artifact chosen for retention in the Port Authority's Hangar 17 repository.)

Torres's use of photography at Hangar 17 often shifts from a tool of visual reporting to a technique of sensory stimulation. The absolute concentration of his camera arouses ideas of scent, sound, tactility—even acrid taste—lingering in the hangar, reminding viewers that the clues here under consideration are linked to a recent crime. The victims have barely departed the scene; the evidence may look timeworn but the fingerprints of terror seem perpetually fresh.

This sensory temperament is pronounced in prior projects of the artist's, memorably so in "The Repository of Absent Flesh," a 1998 exhibition installation for Massachusetts Institute of Technology's List Visual Arts Center. There, visitors wandered past a series of found objects (a knife, a pair of shoes, and a scorched bedstead, among others), each individually illuminated and paired with a voice recording narrating its significance. Exploring themes of war, memory, history, and politics, Torres cedes storytelling authority in the exhibition to the artifacts, which were selected to stimulate various intellectual and visceral responses from their viewers. He wrote the companion stories, most structured as intimate confessions unlocked by the objects or their sensory associations. In one, "The Glass of Memory," the protagonist, Michael/Miguel, who has spent his adulthood in America resisting any sentiments that might recall his upbringing outside Madrid just after the

Spanish Civil War, is shocked by the power of unrelated smells to suddenly trigger the aroma of his dead mother's clothes. In "Four-Legged Absences," Torres channels the "unbearable anguish" of Hannah, a woman troubled by the sight of empty chairs, which she reads as "perpetrators of silence," and records of absences "sometimes permanent and always absolute."

At Hangar 17, Torres found moments to summon comparable tensions between presence and absence, as well as the potency of memory to compensate for what is physically irrecoverable. Torres's photograph of a bicycle rack removed from the World Trade Center site, to cite only one example, achieves that eloquent interplay between what is literally there—an ordinary metal stand propping up seven bicycles with bent wheels and bruised frames—and what should be there to resolve the story's ambiguity: the spectral riders who never returned to reclaim them.

Perhaps most relevant to Torres's 2009 assignment at Hangar 17 was his recently completed "Dark Is The Room Where We Sleep," a multiyear undertaking rooted in a buried atrocity of the Spanish Civil War perpetrated by troops under General Francisco Franco. In 2004, Torres allied himself with a group of Spanish scholars and forensic anthropologists known as the Association for the Recovery of Historical Memory, who had recently begun excavating an unmarked mass grave near the town of Burgos. Torres committed to recording the exhumation, resulting in a body of searing black-and-white photographs depicting the site, those working on the disinterment, the skeletons and recovered personal effects of dozens of villagers assassinated 70 years earlier, and their contemporary descendants. By chronicling these activities and grisly findings, Torres liberated this traumatic episode from obscurity by redelivering it to public conscience, also creating a legacy for the dead and their living relatives.

Political indignation deepened Torres's investment in the Spanish Civil War excavations. But ideology never diverted him from his primary labor: commemorating, with empathy and veracity, 46 individuals massacred in September 1936. The pictures, like many captured later at Hangar 17, range from panoramic, even clinical, establishing shots (archaeological trenches, sifting grids, a medical examiner assessing a skeleton) to tightly focused details. In an essay for the exhibition catalog, Torres admitted how quickly his professional focus became undone whenever the association's team unearthed not bullet shells but beer bottle caps, pocket watches, and similar accessories of quotidian civilian life: "The feet of the victims with their shoes still on is what got to me."

Within the immensity of wreckage stored at Hangar 17, Torres's archaeological sensibilities converged on similarly arresting fragments. Hints of office life and building paraphernalia trapped within the multiton composites—amalgamations of fused and collapsed floor decking, drywall, carpeting, electronics cabling, and carbonized scraps of business paper—received his methodical attention. With equal care, he solemnized the intangibles of a solitary gray slipper extracted from a debris container. Marked with the logo of American Airlines, its context is horrifying to imagine even if its origins remain unknown. Throughout his stay, dozens of other mundane artifacts achieved surprising emotional resonance when subjected to Torres's camera. An unbuckled seatbelt dangling from a car mutilated beyond recognition, for instance, becomes a meditation on the futility of rational safety devices against the chaos of terrorism.

As an artist and a concerned global citizen, Francesc Torres believes it is our collective duty to recognize the fallibility of memory, particularly when reconstructing the cause and effect of violence, aggression, coercion, and persecution. In his view, evidentiary materials originating from such traumatic events—exemplified in the eyewitness relics preserved at Hangar 17—are resources for shared knowledge and for mooring public memory in certain tangible historical truths. Without the efforts of future-thinking collectors and committed keepers of that evidence, however, the choice between forgetfulness and remembrance becomes conjectural or a matter of indifference. The Hangar 17 collection, as documented by Torres, perpetuates the realities of September 11, 2001, reminding us that human-engineered violence of this magnitude has happened before and thus could happen again.

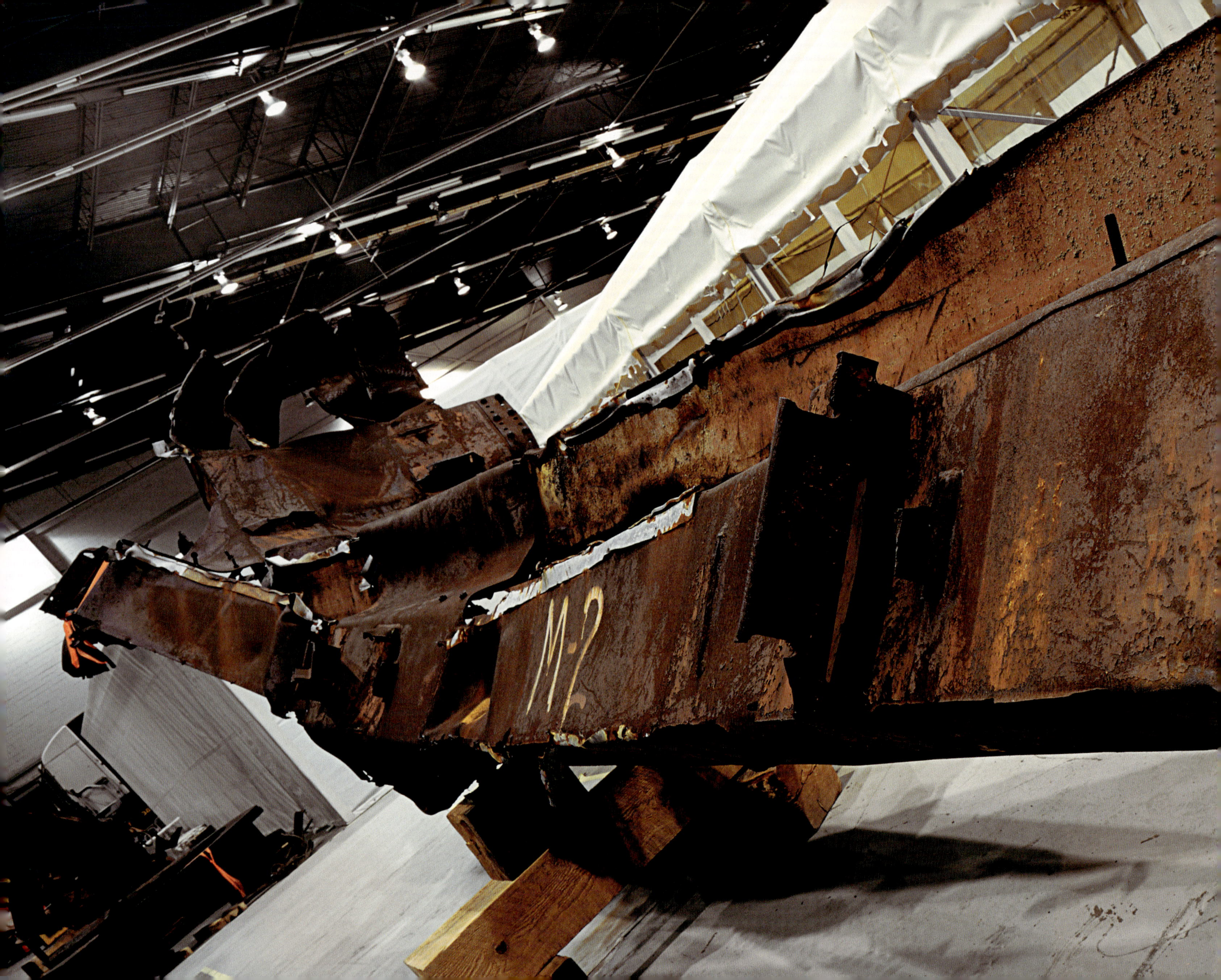
M-2

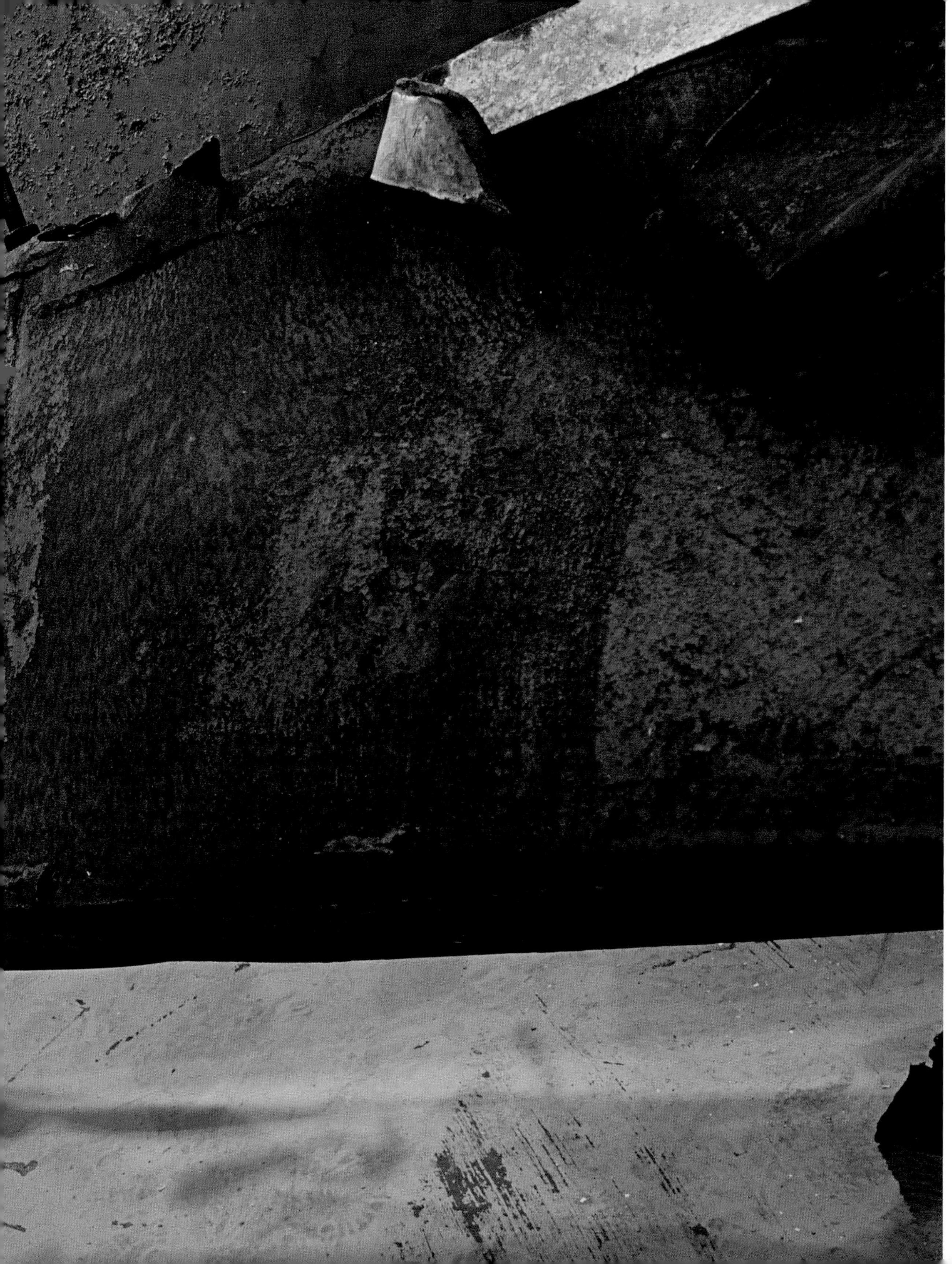

IMPACT STEEL

This steel beam, designated M-2, spanned the 96th to the 99th floors of the northern face of the north tower—the location where hijacked Flight 11 pierced the building. After the collapse, World Trade Center steel was sent to four different holding areas, where pieces were assigned identification numbers. Steel brought to Metal Management in Newark, New Jersey, was tagged with the letter "M."

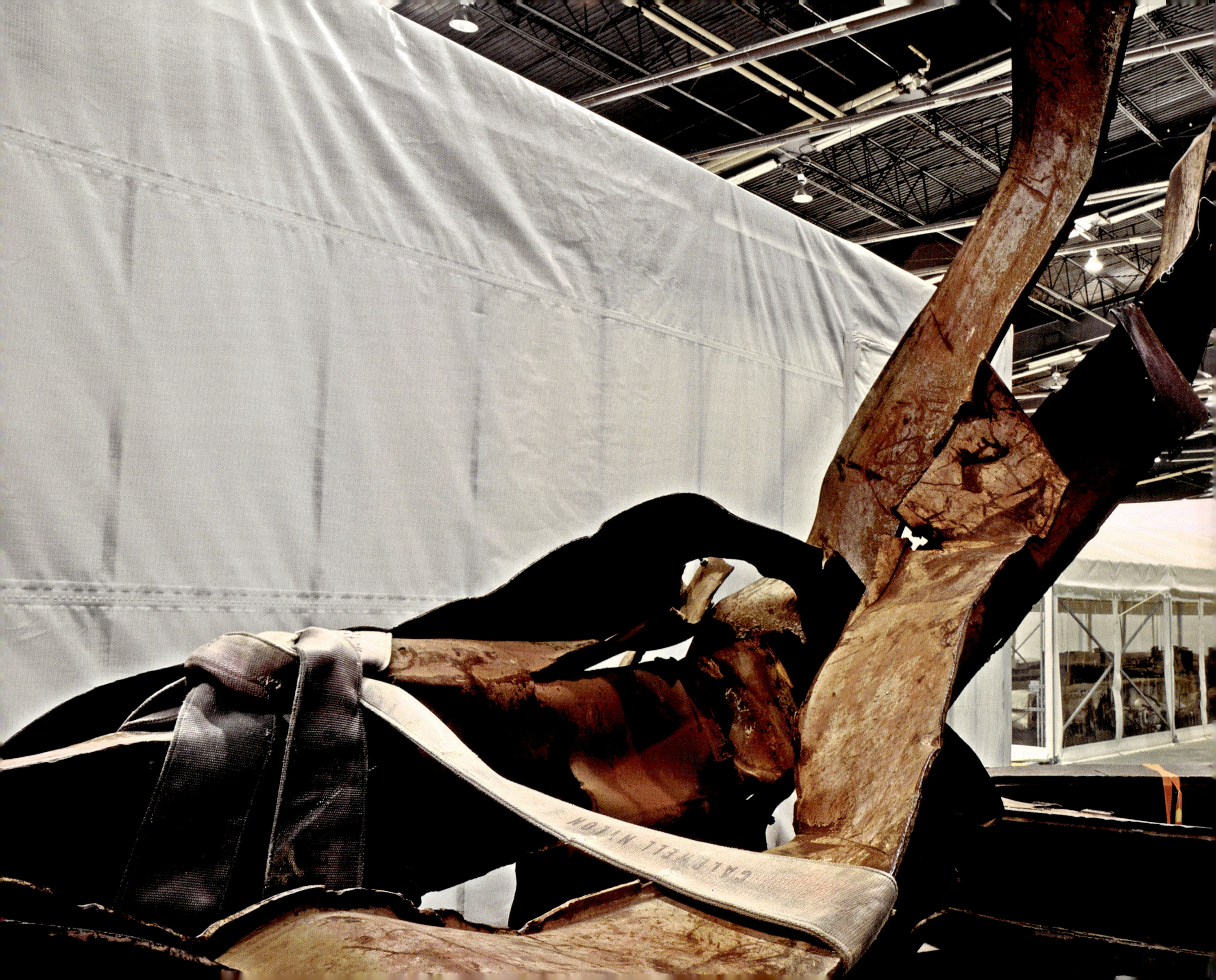
CALDWELL NYLON

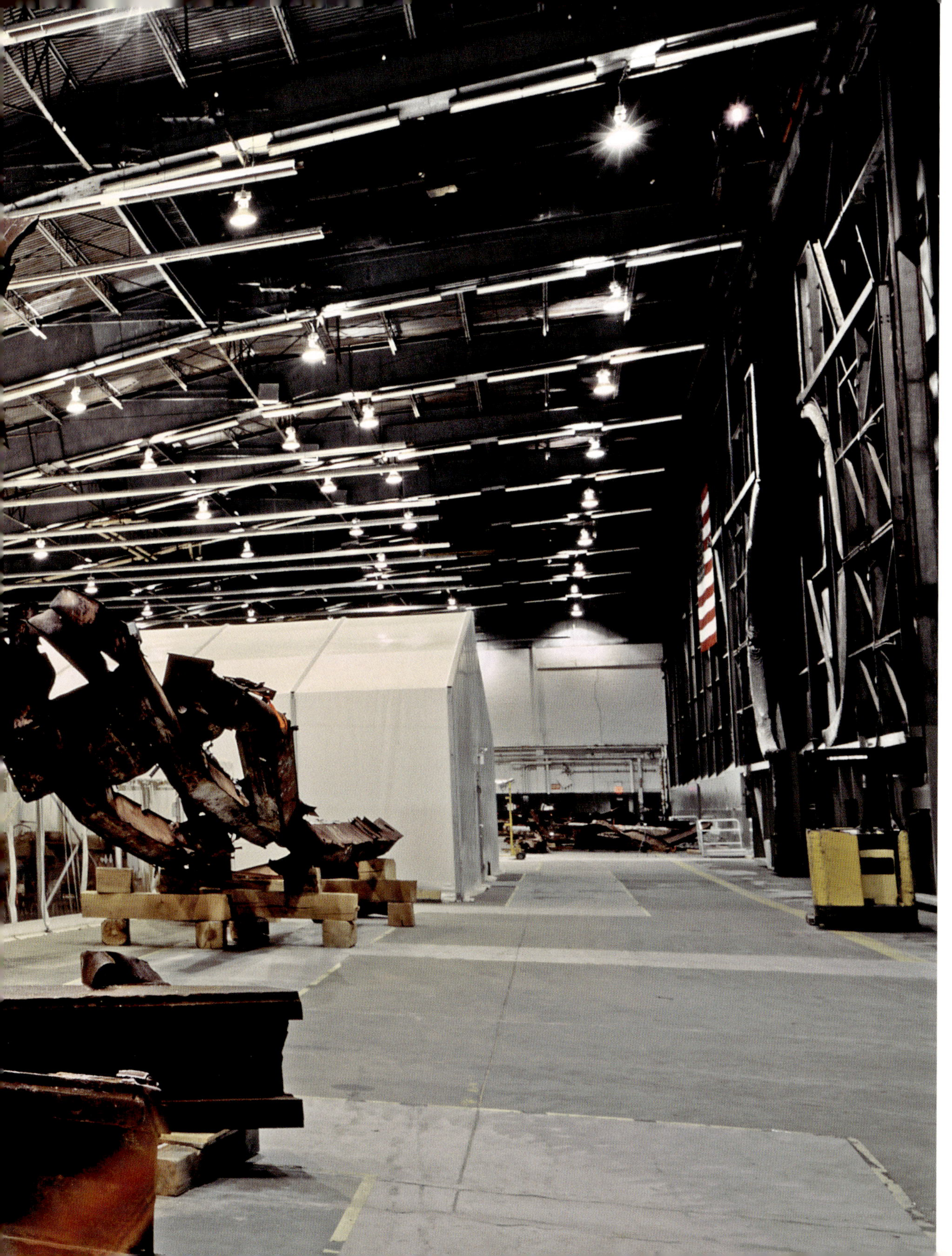

In the foreground is M-27, the companion piece to M-2, which is visible in the background. Also located on the northern face of the north tower, this beam spanned the 93rd to the 96th floors, and so marked the underside of hijacked Flight 11's strike into the building. In this image is the evidence—from above and below—of the force of the plane's collision with the building. In many cases, WTC columns were identifiable because their original markings (either stamped or stenciled onto them) survived the collapse. Investigators consulted the towers' original construction drawings, which noted the location of each beam by number, and were able to determine which beams bore the brunt of the plane's impact.

Along with other steel beams and building remnants, M-2 was taken to suburban Maryland for close study by scientists and engineers at the National Institute of Standards and Technology (NIST) to determine the causes of the collapse of the twin towers. NIST found that fires on the impact floors weakened the trusses that attached each floor to the building's exterior. As the support steel failed, whole floors gave way, leading to the pancake collapse of the towers.

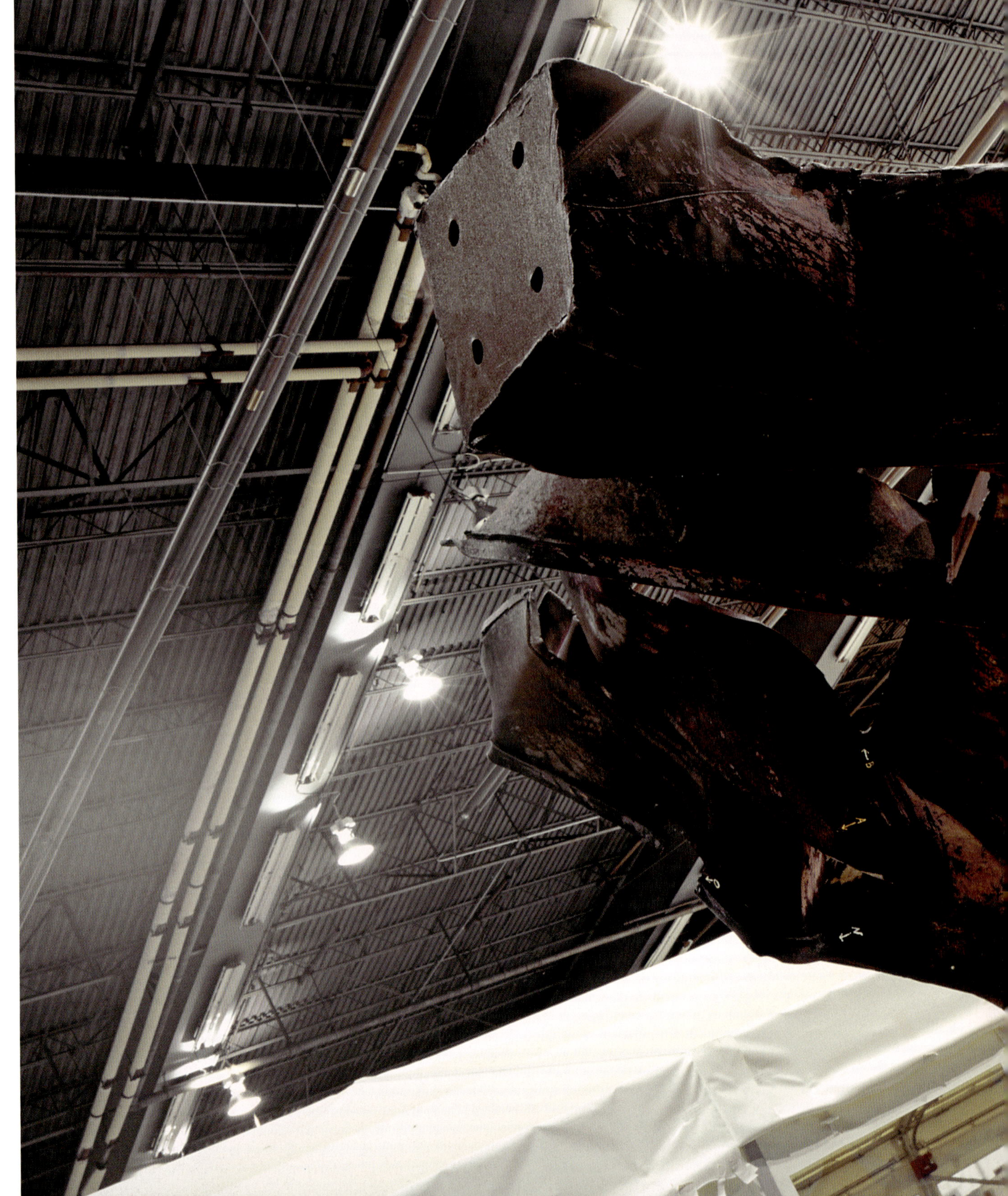

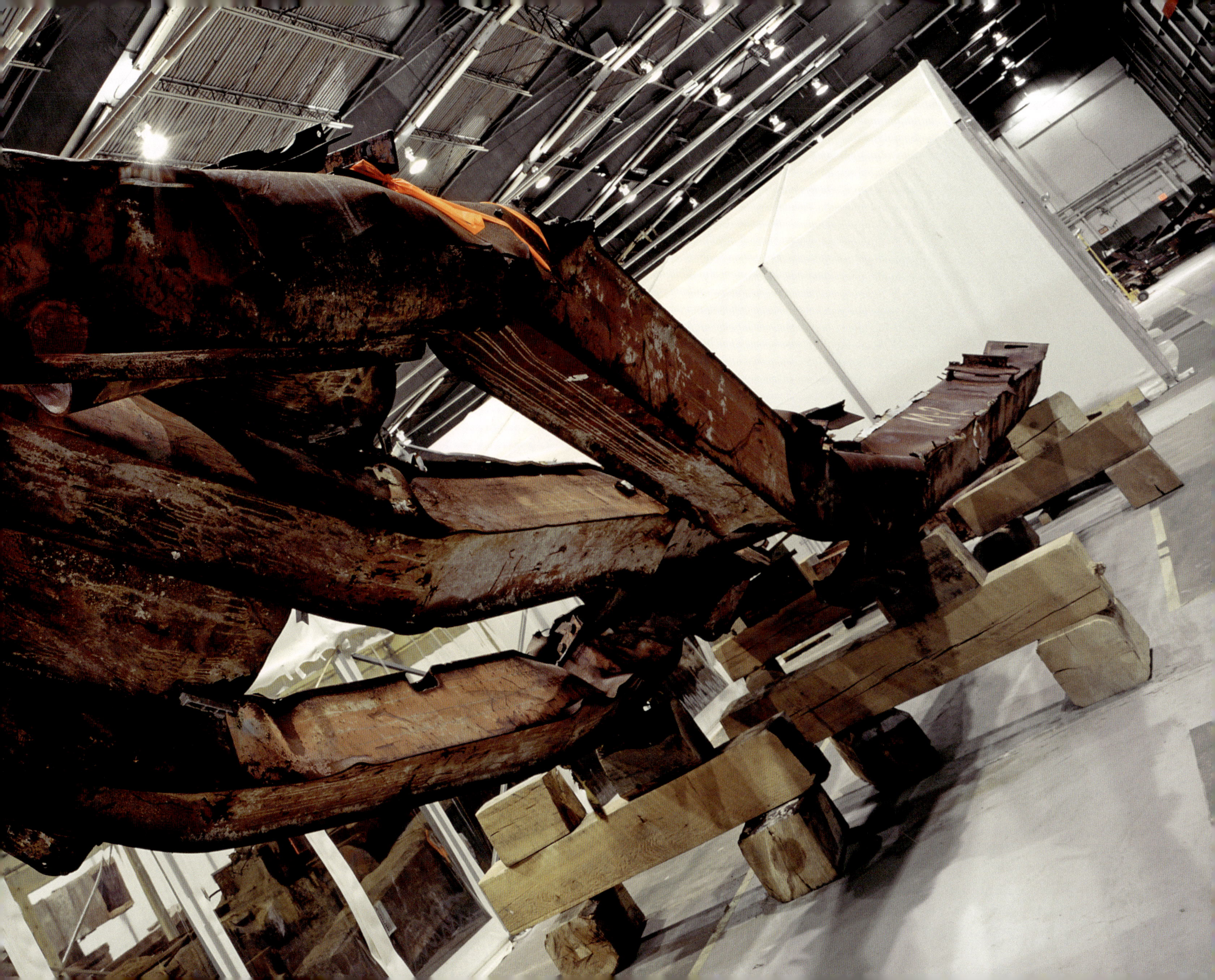

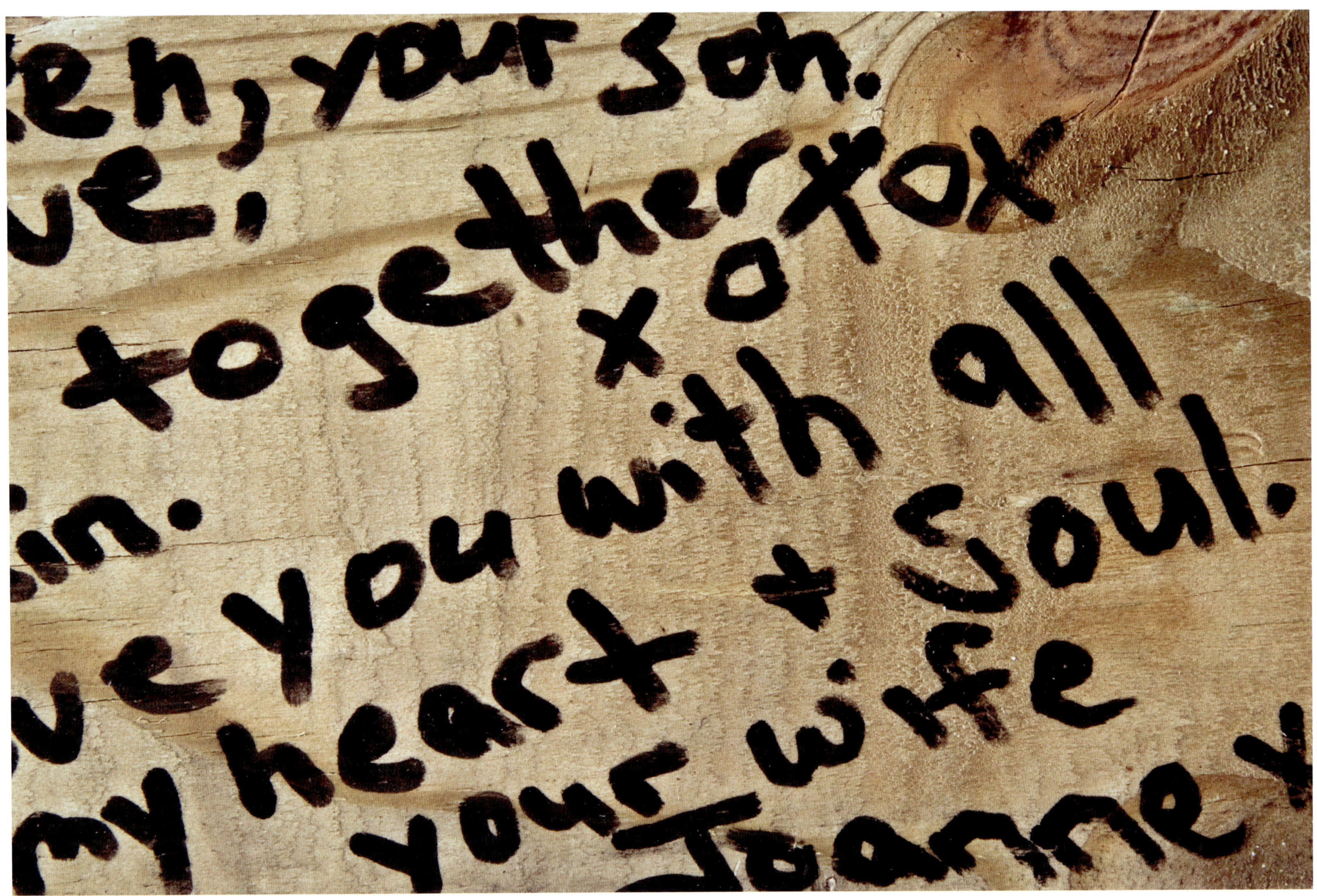
en, your son.
ve.
together x o x
in.
ve you with all
my heart + soul.
your wife
Joanne x

THE MOMENT THE FUTURE CHANGED

MEMORY IN 9/11 ARTIFACTS BY CLIFFORD CHANIN

When Hangar 17 was at full capacity, a visit there left two distinct impressions.

Most immediately, the hangar collection conveyed a definitive summary of the violence of the attack and the brutality of its consequences: the explosion of civilian aircraft into buildings, the heat and smoke that enveloped the victims, the force of the collapse of the towers. Yet the reality of what was on view at the hangar was unreal. Steel beams do not twist; fire trucks do not crumple; cement walls do not disintegrate at random. The chosen method of the attackers, the hangar made clear, concentrated heat and pressure in a way that would mutilate these seemingly indestructible objects and thereby destroy everything—and everyone—within the reach of their ruin.

The objects at the hangar were still recognizable, but their disfigurement challenged the fundamental alignment of intention and purpose that had originally guided their construction and use. That they should be deformed in these ways, and exiled in that place, was a breach that felt insurmountable.

But this was the logic of what had happened, and these objects, in their altered state, incarnated it. There is no normal trajectory that would take them from what they had been to what they had become, but it had happened anyway. The visitor was left to uncover what other trajectory there could be. From this effort would emerge the great discovery of the hangar, the thematic unity at the heart of the collection.

The objects—so deeply disarrayed, so far from normality—illuminated the unnatural trajectory of 9/11 but in reverse, from effect back to cause. They made the substance of the event clear: Disfigurement on this scale could only result from a crime of equally monumental malignancy. Here was the radical essence of 9/11, preserved, even years after the attack, inside Hangar 17. Throughout the building, physical and moral transgression lay in perfect balance.

We seldom encounter abnormality in a form so raw and unrelenting. The mind rebels against such a clear break from its normal patterns of understanding. And yet, again, the evidence of this unreal outcome was undeniable. From this came the second impression of a hangar visit.

The scene within the hangar recalled not only the attack itself, but also the ordeal of the aftermath. First, the search for survivors, followed by the recognition that there would be so few survivors. Then, the painstaking effort to recover human remains and the realization that many of those murdered had vaporized, that scant traces of these disembodied victims had mingled with the surrounding dust, with the air that we breathed. Finally, the seemingly impossible challenge of removing the mountains of debris—eventually counted at 1.8 million tons—from a pile at least seven stories deep and 16 acres around.

Individual objects spoke to these phases of the aftermath. But taken together, the hangar collection was encompassed by the sense of desolation that dated back to the first scenes at ground zero, the place where these objects had been transformed. The contents of the hangar included the emotional, as well as the physical, remnants of the attack. Though well ordered, the objects still seemed caught in the throes of the day's violence. September 11 had been marked by a sense of compression, of collapse, and this had now attached itself to the hangar collection. Nothing was upright or intact; the destruction, it was clear, had been so relentless that it reached as far as the molecular structure of some of the objects.

As a result, this cavernous space felt at odds with its contents. What had happened on 9/11 was so extreme that it reached from the global to the microscopic—from geopolitics to DNA identification. As large as it was, the hangar contained neither the massive volumes of the buildings, nor the soaring velocity of the airplanes, nor the minute complexities of the victims. A sense of missing-ness overwhelmed the building. As large as it was, the hangar held only what little remained: these objects, with their mutilated embodiment of all that would never be there.

One did not have to go to the hangar to find the realities of 9/11. Absence is the predominant theme of the event's aftermath, and there are many ways to encounter it. But the hangar concentrated this feeling to a degree that could not be felt anywhere else, including the site itself, which was under active reconstruction. In the solitude of a space so large—and yet not nearly large enough—one could approach the unsettling symmetry of the collection.

But only if one could master an unflinching calm.

Francesc Torres did.

As a result, we have a record of time and feeling stilled, set in a moment that is neither 9/11, nor apart from 9/11. It is a moment defined by the objects and by the space that contained them. Within this boundary, Torres tells a story that is always focused, but never conclusive. Repeatedly, he brings us face-to-face with an object stripped of its familiarity. We may know what this thing was, but we do not know what it has become. This uncertainty attracts us: We are drawn to define the new identity of each object. We want to engage; we want to restore the familiar.

We know, with Torres, that we cannot. But he knows something we do not. Each photograph captures more than an object; it frames our need for the familiar. We look at these pictures and strain for coherence. Torres does not tell us how to find it, or whether our need to make sense of what we are seeing will be met. Instead, he demonstrates that the need persists. In the face of mutilation and malevolence, we do not turn away.

The brilliance of Torres's work, however, goes further. He could have left us alone to face this destruction, to the search within ourselves for meaning. He does not. Instead, his images transpose the solitude of the hangar and the private agony of its objects into a collective encounter. Though he does not define coherence for us, Torres establishes that the need to find coherence is a quality that we share. Although we may not find the same meanings in the various objects we see, his work encourages us to make the effort to search for meaning in the presence of one another.

From the beginning of this project, Torres believed that he could document the full extent of the hangar—the objects and the emotions—without betraying the integrity of either the collection or the viewer. The end products of his belief are a book and an exhibition, but the animating spirit of Torres's work is a conviction that personal and collective meaning are made together. In this, he brings to the hangar an element of 9/11 that the collection never contained: the solidarity of response.

Having been downtown during the attack, Torres understands that the experience of witness remains as galvanizing today as it was then. This was the bond that was forged on 9/11, and his photographs of the hangar collection evoke it without a shred of sentimentality. This shared response, in all its shadings, was as much an artifact of the day as the objects in the hangar. Torres's grasp of this artifact is no less sure than his treatment of the hangar. Indeed, it seems to have guided the making of these pictures. Shot under the hangar's industrial lights and against its drab walls, they are meticulous, direct, and unadorned. Like that initial reaction to the events at ground zero, they seem timeless, the only possible response to what we have seen.

It is worth looking more closely at the creative strategy that brought about this result. If the pictures do indeed evoke a timeless response to 9/11, how does that response emerge? More generally, how do we engage with the extended horizon of a future that has been altered by catastrophe?

Torres's 9/11 photographs are a distinguished addition to an extensive catalog of artworks that have been produced in the aftermath of mass killing. *Guernica* is likely the best known of this group, to the point that, for many, the word "Guernica" is more likely to be associated with Picasso's painting than with the actual air attack on that town during the Spanish Civil War. The impulse to make work that recalls mass murder is not limited to a particular culture or region. It has been documented in relation to the entire litany of 20th- (and now 21st-) century atrocities.

Originating in different places and drawn out of different events, these works do not coalesce around a single history. Instead, they take disparate, agonizing histories as a common point of departure for an inquiry into what comes next. What has the world become, they ask, once the killing is over? In these artworks, history is the cause and memory is the effect. The remarkable point they establish is that different causes—that is, different histories—can lead us to the same effect. And this effect revolves around an awareness of living on the far side of rupture, in a time of afterward.

In the case of 9/11, "afterward" cannot be separated from the idea that the future itself was betrayed. For all who witnessed it, the attack was unimaginable, unlike anything that could have been seen or expected. And yet, it clearly reflected planning and foresight; someone had thought to do this, had planned for it, and had managed to make it happen. At the core of 9/11 was an imaginative leap that demonstrated how deeply the imagination could be betrayed. This most glorious human capacity, the ability to create or to see the world differently, had sent fully loaded passenger jets accelerating into buildings. Never again would the things that we saw on 9/11—or the thinking that produced them—be unimaginable. The future was now different.

We don't have tools to measure that difference. We don't know how to gauge the distance between the range of likely futures that we anticipated and the unimagined future in which we now live. And yet, we want to be able to express this difference and find ways of making it visible.

The artifacts at Hangar 17 were made in the combustion of a transition from one imagined future to another. Francesc Torres saw this, understood their sanctity as the last remnant of that transition, and preserved this sanctity so it would not disappear—like so much and so many at ground zero—without a trace. The challenge, he understood, was bringing the isolation and silence of the hangar into the open. Could the collection maintain its presence in the face of public display?

The answer to this question demands a shared response. With this publication, the Hangar 17 collection moves from a private space to the public sphere. In this movement, it recalls other transitions associated with 9/11: the physical transformation of normal objects into totems of catastrophe and the altered sense of what the future holds. In truth, 9/11 itself represents a transition still underway, and the timeless quality of the hangar photos cautions us about how long it may be before this transition is resolved.

Above all, the photographs demand a collective response because their disfigurement is still livid; it does not seem at all like something from a time that has passed. We contemplate the objects, recognize the vitality of their wounds, and face a decision that can only be answered together: Will we make meaning for these objects, or will they make meaning for us?

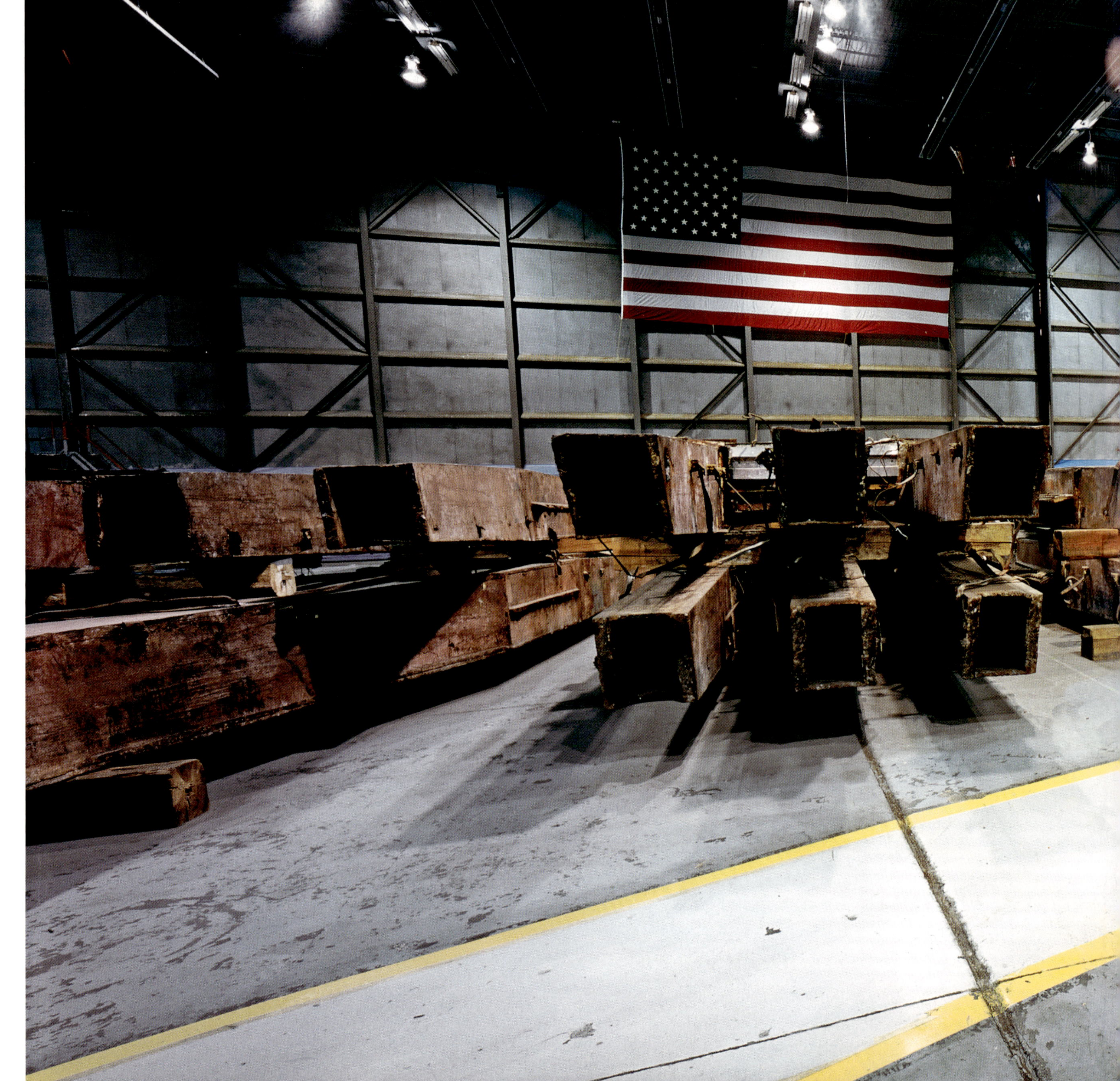

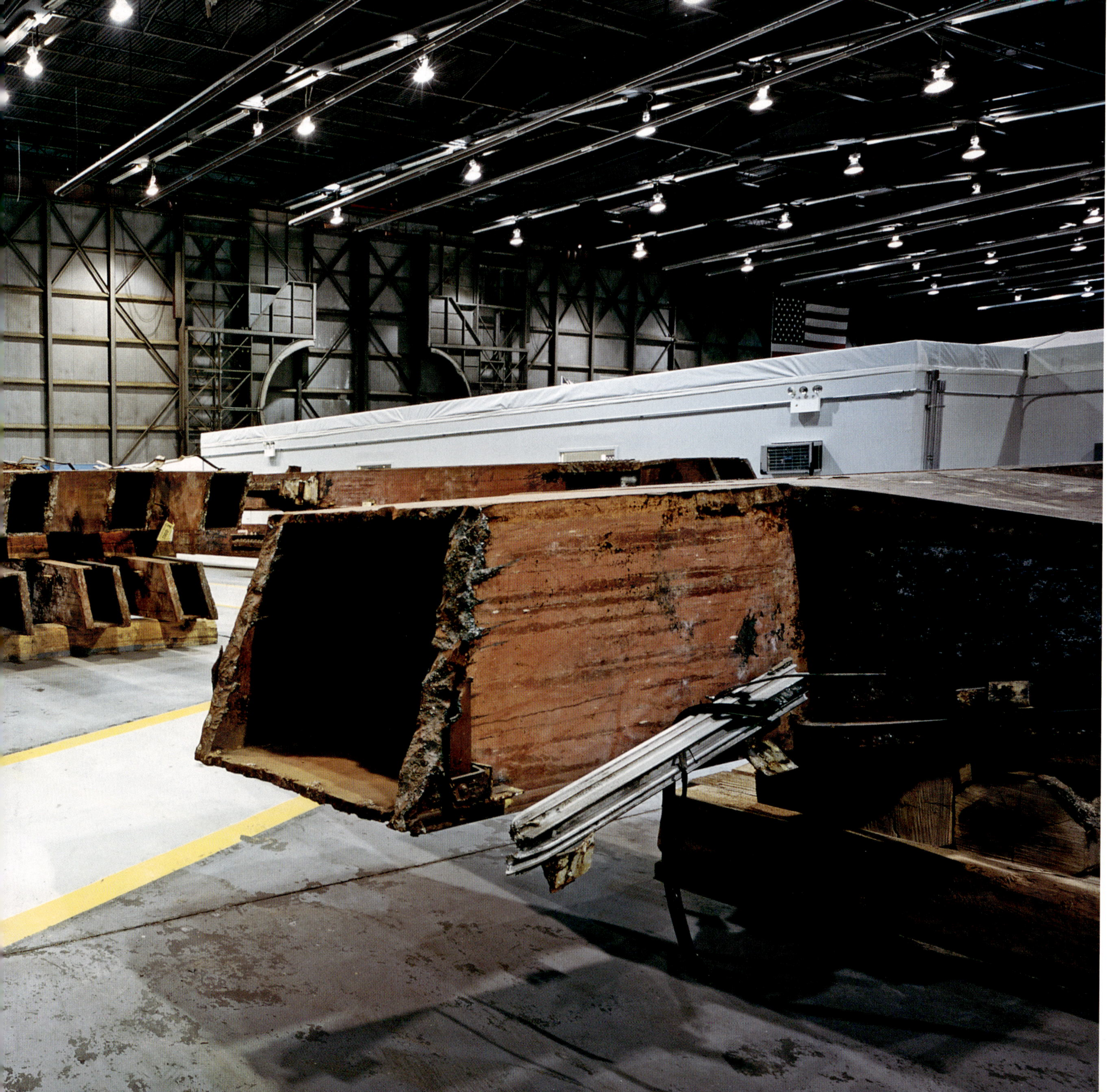

ABOUT THE AUTHORS

FRANCESC TORRES was born in 1948 in Barcelona, where he currently resides. He has also lived in Paris, New York, Chicago, and Berlin. He is represented in many international public and institutional collections. His work has been shown at the Whitney Museum of American Art (NYC); Museum of Modern Art (NYC); Los Angeles Museum of Contemporary Art; Nationalgalerie (Berlin); Stedelijk Museum (Amsterdam); Galerie Rudolfinum (Prague); State Russian Museum (St. Petersburg); Museo Nacional Centro de Arte Reina Sofia (Madrid) (retrospective); Guggenheim Museum (Bilbao); Institut Valencia d'Art Modern (IVAM); International Center of Photography (NYC); and Museu d'Art Contemporani de Barcelona (retrospective).

Torres has been awarded four Individual Artist Fellowships from the National Endowment for the Arts, a New York State Council on the Arts Fellowship (twice), the Emil Radok Prize of the University of Prague, the Picasso Foundation Prize, a Fulbright Academic Exchange Fellowship, and a National Prize for Visual Arts from the Autonomous Government of Catalonia, Spain. He was recently chair in Spanish Culture and Civilization at the King Juan Carlos I of Spain Center at New York University.

CLIFFORD CHANIN is acting director of education and senior program advisor at the National September 11 Memorial & Museum. He curated the museum's fifth anniversary exhibition, "9/11 and the American Landscape: Photographs by Jonathan Hyman," and is moderator of the museum's webcast series, *Exploring 9/11: The World Before and After*. In 2000, Chanin founded the Legacy Project, a nonprofit organization dedicated to documenting contemporary responses to historical traumas in societies around the world. Previously, Chanin was associate director of arts and humanities at the Rockefeller Foundation.

JERRY ADLER was a reporter for the *Daily News* and a writer and editor for *Newsweek* in a career in journalism that began in 1971. At *Newsweek,* he wrote about science, medicine, architecture, and many other subjects, and covered the 9/11 attacks and their aftermath. He is the author of *High Rise,* a book about building a New York City skyscraper, and co-author of *The Price of Terror,* an account of the aftermath of the bombing of Pan Am flight 103 over Lockerbie, Scotland. He wrote the 2008 PBS documentary *Medal of Honor*, chronicling the history of America's highest military award and some of those who have received it.

DAVID W. BLIGHT is professor of history at Yale University, where he is also director of the Gilder Lehrman Center for the Study of Slavery, Resistance, and Abolition. Among his many publications is *Race and Reunion: The Civil War in American Memory* (Harvard University Press, 2001), which received the Bancroft Prize, the Abraham Lincoln Prize, and the Frederick Douglass Prize as well as four awards from the Organization of American Historians. His latest book is *American Oracle: The Civil War in the Civil Rights Era* (Harvard University Press, 2011). David Blight has been a fellow at the Dorothy and Lewis B. Cullman Center for Scholars and Writers of the New York Public Library, and at the Huntington Library, in Pasadena, California.

JOE DANIELS (foreword) is president of the National September 11 Memorial & Museum. Previously, he worked at the Robin Hood Foundation; McKinsey & Company; and Cravath, Swaine & Moore.

ALICE M. GREENWALD (foreword) is executive vice president for programs and director of the Memorial Museum at the National September 11 Memorial & Museum. She previously served as associate museum director for museum programs at the United States Holocaust Memorial Museum, executive director of the National Museum of American Jewish History, and curator of the Hebrew Union College-Jewish Institute of Religion Skirball Museum.

JAN SEIDLER RAMIREZ is chief curator and director of collections at the National September 11 Memorial & Museum. Previously, she was vice president and museum director at the New-York Historical Society, deputy director for collections and chief curator at the Museum of the City of New York, and chief curator of art and history at the Hudson River Museum of Westchester, New York. She recently concluded three terms of service on the Board of Overseers of the Hood Museum of Art & Hopkins Performing Arts Center of Dartmouth College.

CHRISTOPHER O. WARD (foreword) has been the executive director of the Port Authority of New York and New Jersey since May 2008. He previously served at the Port Authority as chief of planning and external affairs, as well as director of port redevelopment from 1997 to 2002.

ACKNOWLEDGMENTS

Numerous agencies and individuals have made this project possible. We acknowledge with gratitude Paul J. Napoli & Marc J. Bern-Napoli Bern LLP, the National Endowment for the Arts, the Institut Ramon Llull, and the Government of Spain—Ministry of Culture, whose generous financial support has ensured that the story of Hangar 17 is recorded for posterity.

Long before the National September 11 Museum was conceived, Steven Weintraub, of Art Preservation Services, and his colleague, Peter Gat, devoted museum-quality care to the stabilization and conservation of the World Trade Center archive at Hangar 17. We commend them for their professionalism and foresight.

We extend deep appreciation to our exhibition partners, Willis E. (Buzz) Hartshorn, Brian Wallis, Kristen Lubben, and Carol Squiers, at the International Center of Photography, for their commitment to the realization of this documentary exhibition on the occasion of the tenth anniversary of the 9/11 attacks.

Finally, we honor the prescience of all those who, at a moment of national crisis, recognized the imperative of immediate documentation. Their insight and prompt actions have yielded the legacy of Hangar 17: a humbling and deeply moving encounter with the remnants of memory, eloquent in their witness to unspeakable acts of destruction and unfathomable loss.

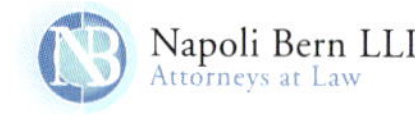

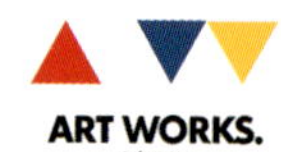

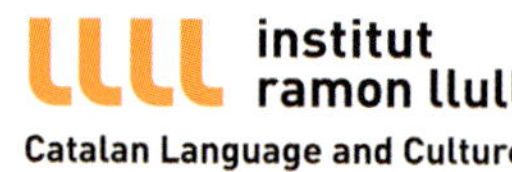

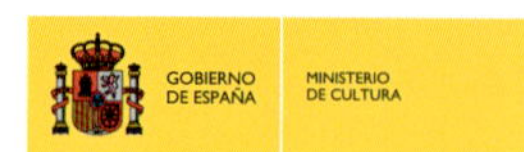

Memory Remains

Francesc Torres

Published by the National Geographic Society

John M. Fahey, Jr., *Chairman of the Board and Chief Executive Officer*

Timothy T. Kelly, *President*

Declan Moore, *Executive Vice President; President, Publishing*

Melina Gerosa Bellows, *Executive Vice President, Chief Creative Officer, Books, Kids and Family*

Prepared by the Book Division

Barbara Brownell Grogan, *Vice President and Editor in Chief*

Jonathan Halling, *Design Director, Books and Children's Publishing*

Marianne R. Koszorus, *Director of Design, Adult Books*

Susan Tyler Hitchcock, *Senior Editor*

Carl Mehler, *Director of Maps*

R. Gary Colbert, *Production Director*

Jennifer A. Thornton, *Managing Editor*

Meredith C. Wilcox, *Administrative Director, Illustrations*

Staff for This Book

Clifford Chanin, *Editor*

Yolanda Cuomo, *Art Director*

Kristi Norgaard, *Designer*

Judith Klein, *Production Editor*

Mike Horenstein, *Production Manager*

Manufacturing and Quality Management

Christopher A. Liedel, *Chief Financial Officer*

Phillip L. Schlosser, *Senior Vice President*

Chris Brown, *Technical Director*

Nicole Elliott, *Manager*

Rachel Faulise, *Manager*

Robert L. Barr, *Manager*

All photographs in this book are by Francesc Torres except for the image on page 10, which was made by Maria Iturrioz de Torres. The map of Hangar 17 on page 17 is courtesy of the Port Authority of New York and New Jersey.

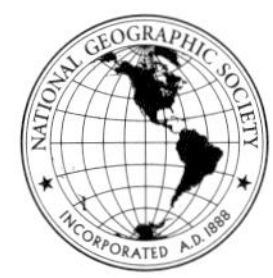

The National Geographic Society is one of the world's largest nonprofit scientific and educational organizations. Founded in 1888 to "increase and diffuse geographic knowledge," the Society works to inspire people to care about the planet. National Geographic reflects the world through its magazines, television programs, films, music and radio, books, DVDs, maps, exhibitions, live events, school publishing programs, interactive media and merchandise. *National Geographic* magazine, the Society's official journal, published in English and 32 local—language editions, is read by more than 35 million people each month. The National Geographic Channel reaches 320 million households in 34 languages in 166 countries. National Geographic Digital Media receives more than 13 million visitors a month. National Geographic has funded more than 9,200 scientific research, conservation and exploration projects and supports an education program promoting geography literacy. For more information, visit nationalgeographic.com.

For more information, please call 1-800-NGS LINE
(647-5463) or write to the following address:

National Geographic Society
1145 17th Street N.W.
Washington, D.C. 20036-4688 U.S.A.

For information about special discounts for bulk purchases, please contact
National Geographic Books Special Sales: ngspecsales@ngs.org

For rights or permissions inquiries, please contact National Geographic Books
Subsidiary Rights: ngbookrights@ngs.org

Library of Congress Cataloging-in-Publication Data
Torres, Francesc, 1948-
Memory remains : 9/11 artifacts at Hangar 17 / Francesc Torres ; edited by Clifford Chanin.
p. cm.
ISBN 978-1-4262-0833-1
1. September 11 Terrorist Attacks, 2001. 2. World Trade Center (New York, N.Y.) 3. New York (N.Y.)--Antiquities--Pictorial works. 4. Relics--New York (State)--New York--Pictorial works. 5. Rubble--New York (State)--New York--Pictorial works. 6. Hangars--New York (State)--New York--Pictorial works. 7. September 11 Terrorist Attacks, 2001--Social aspects. 8. September 11 Terrorist Attacks, 2001--Psychological aspects. 9. Collective memory--New York (State)--New York. 10. Collective memory --United States. I. Chanin, Clifford. II. Title.
HV6432.7.T68 2011
974.7'1044--dc23
ISBN: 978-1-4262-0833-1
Printed in the United States of America
11/WOR/1